American General Education Series

EDITED BY

MALCOLM S. MacLEAN

*Director of the General College
University of Minnesota*

American General Education Series

Under the Editorship of

Malcolm S. MacLean

University of Minnesota

IN 1936
ALVIN C. EURICH and ELMO C. WILSON

IN 1937
ALVIN C. EURICH and ELMO C. WILSON

STUDENTS AND OCCUPATIONS
E. G. WILLIAMSON

WRITE WHAT YOU MEAN
F. S. APPEL

HUMAN DEVELOPMENT AND ADJUST-
MENT
JOHN ANDERSON

THE PHYSICAL SCIENCES AND TECH-
NOLOGY
FREDERICK L. HOVDE

ELEMENTS OF FUNCTIONAL GOVERN-
MENT
A. N. CHRISTENSEN

STUDENT GUIDANCE
JOHN G. DARLEY and KATHLEEN B. MC CONNON

ONE HUNDRED MINNESOTA YOUNG-
STERS
JOHN G. DARLEY and KATHLEEN B. MC CONNON

ART TODAY AND IN THE PAST
RAY FAULKNER

THE THEORY OF THE GENERAL COL-
LEGE
M. S. MAC LEAN

A MANUAL FOR VISUAL EDUCATION
DEPARTMENTS
ROBERT A. KISSACK, JR.

THE MOTION PICTURE
ROBERT A. KISSACK, JR.

WHAT ABOUT SURVEY COURSES?
Edited by B. LAMAR JOHNSON

MUSIC TODAY AND IN THE PAST
GERALD A. HILL

INCOME AND CONSUMPTION
ROLAND S. VAILE and HELEN G. CANOYER

PUBLIC RELIEF: 1929-1939
JOSEPHINE CHAPIN BROWN

PUBLIC RELIEF
1929-1939

by

JOSEPHINE CHAPIN BROWN

1971

OCTAGON BOOKS
New York

Reprinted 1971
by special arrangement with Holt, Rinehart and Winston, Inc.

OCTAGON BOOKS
A DIVISION OF FARRAR, STRAUS & GIROUX, INC.
19 Union Square West
New York, N. Y. 10003

LIBRARY OF CONGRESS CATALOG CARD NUMBER: 77-173841

ISBN 0-374-91022-7

Printed in U.S.A. by
NOBLE OFFSET PRINTERS, INC.
NEW YORK 3, N. Y.

DEDICATED TO
THE REGIONAL SOCIAL WORKERS
OF THE
FEDERAL EMERGENCY RELIEF ADMINISTRATION
AND THE
WORKS PROGRESS ADMINISTRATION
IN RECOGNITION OF
THEIR DISTINGUISHED CONTRIBUTION TO
PUBLIC WELFARE
IN THE UNITED STATES

Introduction

∾∾∾∾∾∾∾∾∾∾∾∾∾∾∾∾∾∾∾∾∾∾∾∾∾∾∾∾∾∾∾

The decade of the 1930's might well have been known as the decade of destitution but for the humane leadership provided by the Roosevelt administration. With local governments harassed by debt because of relief expenditures or completely ignoring their responsibility, the year 1933 was one in which courageous and prompt action was mandatory. That action had to come from no less an authority than the Federal Government because of the national scope of the problem to be met.

Miss Brown has in this volume given an intimate and graphic picture of what took place during the decade. For most of that time she was closely related to the administration of federal relief and work relief and knows well the saga she has recorded for history. Her experience in private social work and her early relationship as an assistant to the Federal Relief Administrator, Harry Hopkins, gives her unusual equipment to interpret the philosophy of the administration and discuss the action it encouraged.

During this period the social philosophy of the man on the street has undergone a marked change. The biblical quotation "Am I My Brother's Keeper?", so often the query of charity campaigns, was taken off the signpost, brought down to earth, and made the query for every man.

No longer could we look to a few to support many in the name of charity. It became a national responsibility, for who was there among us who might not be touched by loss of income or even the loss of a home and all that he had. Concepts of public welfare were moving away from the meager grants sufficient only to keep a human body alive toward a wholehearted acceptance of the responsibility for decency and health for every individual in the nation.

During these years from 1930 to 1939 much of what really happened for the care of people came from the philosophy of a few pioneers in social work. They saw beyond the narrow concept of charity organizations to a new and more humane responsibility which had the clarion ring of "all for one and one for all."

It was early in the decade that several national organizations urged upon Congress the appropriation of funds for meeting the needs of people who were victims of unemployment. When the national program was first set up, the American Public Welfare Association assisted in the establishment of state and local units, and the record which Miss Brown sets forth in her useful volume is borne out by the field reports and office memoranda of the American Public Welfare Association.

The author necessarily writes of large sums of money, of huge organizations, and of millions of families, but she never overwhelms the reader with figures. Throughout this story of relief one acquires a growing feeling for the people who wanted work but could not find it and for those who were overtaken by old age, sickness or other disaster and could not work if they wished. It also engenders in the reader a profound respect for those who had the courage to face this herculean task and do something about it.

Public officials, especially those concerned with the human services of government, will find in this volume a storehouse of useful information—a history of successes in public administration and some failures. It also presents a challenge to build further to meet the needs of people through permanent organization with sound administration, and with the conviction that there is a justice and security which all people expect and must have from their government.

FRED K. HOEHLER
Director
American Public Welfare Association

Chicago, Illinois
January, 1940

Foreword

~~~~~~

The decade which ended in 1939 saw an unprecedented increase in public relief expenditures in the United States, as well as notable changes in governmental responsibilities and administrative methods. A system of local poor relief which had remained practically unchanged for a century and a half was superseded not only by new methods but by a new philosophy of governmental responsibility for people in need. During the ten years between 1929 and 1939 more progress was made in public welfare and relief than in the three hundred years after this country was first settled.

The story of this decade of relief is told in the following chapters. It is preceded in Part I by a brief review of the history of public relief before 1929 as a background and basis of comparison in evaluating later developments.

CHART I

Public assistance and earnings of persons employed under Federal work programs in the continental United States, January, 1933-December, 1939.

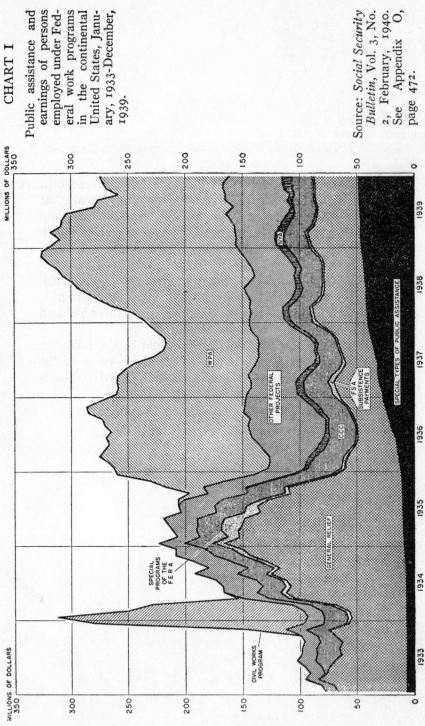

MILLIONS OF DOLLARS

SPECIAL PROGRAMS OF THE FERA

CIVIL WORKS PROGRAM

WPA

OTHER FEDERAL PROJECTS

GENERAL RELIEF

CCC

FSA SUBSISTENCE PAYMENTS

NYA

SPECIAL TYPES OF PUBLIC ASSISTANCE

Source: *Social Security Bulletin,* Vol. 3, No. 2, February, 1940. See Appendix O, page 472.

Contents

~~~~~~

xi

CONTENTS

CONTENTS xiii

CONTENTS

CONTENTS

CONTENTS

Tables

∽∽∽∽∽∽∽∽∽∽∽∽∽∽∽∽∽∽∽∽∽∽∽

Charts

~~~~~~

Abbreviations Used for Names of Programs

AB—Aid to the Blind
ADC—Aid to Dependent Children
APWA—American Public Welfare Association
CCC—Civilian Conservation Corps
CWA—Civil Works Administration
ERA—Emergency Relief Administration
FERA—Federal Emergency Relief Administration
FWAA—Family Welfare Association of America
NRA—National Recovery Act
NRS—National Reemployment Service
NYA—National Youth Administration
OAA—Old Age Assistance
RA—Resettlement Administration
SERA—State Emergency Relief Administration
SSB—Social Security Board
USPHS—United States Public Health Service
WPA— Works Progress Administration
       Works Projects Administration

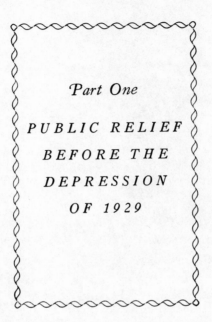

Part One

PUBLIC RELIEF

BEFORE THE

DEPRESSION

OF 1929

Chapter 1

The Relief Functions of Local, State and Federal Governments

∽∽∽∽∽∽∽∽∽∽∽∽∽∽∽∽∽∽∽∽∽∽∽∽∽

LOCAL RESPONSIBILITY

Local Poor Relief Prior to the Twentieth Century

Care of the poor has been recognized from earliest colonial days as fundamentally a function of local government. The system of local poor relief was transplanted root and branch to the Eastern seaboard from Elizabethan England in the ruthless early seventeenth century, and was later carried by pioneer settlers across the continent. This English heritage made poverty a disgrace, branded the poor man as unworthy and shiftless, and attached to relief an indelible stigma.[1]

The system has been perpetuated to a greater or less extent in the poor laws of every state in the United States. As a result large numbers of poor people—the old, the middle-aged and the young; men, women and children—have received miserable pittances of outdoor relief, that is, relief in their homes, or have been packed into almshouses during more than three centuries of American history. Far worse than the laws themselves are the vicious attitudes of scorn and superiority towards poverty and the poor which the system engendered, and which were so deep-seated and persistent, so much an integral

---

[1] See Breckinridge, Sophonisba P., *Public Welfare Administration in the United States, Select Documents.* I. The Poor Law before and after 1601. The University of Chicago Press, Chicago. 1938.

Warner, Amos G., *American Charities, A Study in Philanthropy and Economics.* Ch. VI, The Almshouse and Its Inmates, Ch. XIV, Public Charities, Thomas Y. Crowell and Co., 1894. Webb, Sidney and Beatrice, *English Poor Law Policy.* Longmans, Green and Co., London. 1910. 379 pp.

3

part of a too common type of American psychology, that despite recent changes they still constitute one of the most serious problems in public welfare today.

The responsibility of local units of government for the relief of the poor is rooted in the common law, supported by state legislation. It is also dealt with in many state constitutions.[2]

According to a fundamental common law principle, which brings out this elementary function of government in its brutal simplicity, no government worthy its name, since ancient Sparta, can allow people within its jurisdiction to die of starvation and exposure. Until modern developments of swift transportation and communication made possible the strong centralization of government, the smallest political unit was and is still largely held responsible for the relief of destitution and the prevention of starvation. This unit may be the village, the town, the city, the parish, or the county. The state, however, has always held the power to transfer the responsibility to a larger unit, for example, from the township to the county, or from the county to the state itself. In fact the state possesses, in legal theory, an unlimited and inherent power. It has, in effect, all the political power which is not specifically denied to it by the Federal Constitution. On the other hand, to the Federal Government belong only those powers which are delegated to it by the Federal Constitution.[3] In this question of Federal versus state authority lies one of the crucial phases of the problem of poor relief.

Since the first settlement of this country, colonial, territorial and state poor laws have consistently placed responsibility for relief upon local units. This happened in the Colony of Virginia as early as 1641 when the parishes, the earliest local units, were charted, and this colony "was confronted with a great problem as in England, namely, how to protect the parishes from a large number of paupers, idleness and unemployment on the one hand and on the other, how to train workers for the needs of the growing Colony. The machinery for ad-

[2] Heisterman, Carl A., "Constitutional Limitations Affecting State and Local Relief Funds," *Social Service Review*, March, 1932.

[3] See Porter, Kirk Harold, *County and Township Government in the United States*. The Macmillan Co., New York. 362 pp. 1922. p. 240.

ministering poor relief was ready at hand—the English parish system." This system was in effect until 1785 when the new State of Virginia provided for overseers of the poor in the counties which at that time superseded the parishes as local relief units.[4]

In the Colony of Pennsylvania, the first general poor law, enacted in 1705, made the township the administrative unit. It was nearly a century more before county responsibility was recognized in even two of that colony's counties and then, although the code of poor laws was subjected to a second revision of 1836, "the substance and frame work of administration of the old laws was retained." [5]

The New England colonies, soon after their settlement, placed responsibility for relief upon the towns. For example, a recent report on the Connecticut pauper laws states that in 1650 the court of magistrates was given "the power to determine all differences about lawful settling and providing for poor persons," and, in 1673, the first general poor law stated that "every town shall maintain their own poor." This report, published in February, 1937, adds: "Since the beginning of statehood, Connecticut has not changed significantly its system of poor relief." [6]

Fundamentally, the town poor relief system is fairly typical of all New England, because in that area the state is looked upon as the aggregate of the towns and cities, rather than as the basic governmental unit of which the towns and cities are subdivisions.

The principle of local responsibility was carried westward by the pioneers and formally recorded in the statutes of the Northwest Territory in 1790, and of the Missouri Territory in 1815. Upon these statutes were based the poor laws of Ohio, Michigan, Kansas, Nebraska, and the other middle western states. These gave responsibility for the support of the poor to either the township or the county more or less indis-

[4] Jernegan, Marcus Wilson, "The Development of Poor Relief in Colonial Virginia," *Social Service Review*, March, 1929.

[5] *Poor Relief Administration in Pennsylvania*. State Department of Welfare, Harrisburg, Pennsylvania, 1934.

[6] *Report of the Commission to Study Pauper Laws*, State of Connecticut, 1937. 225 pages.

criminately. "The old poor-law principles were adopted as a governmental policy on the western prairie frontier without question as to their suitability for a new American state of great agricultural resources. The old pauper-law policies and practices relating to 'local responsibility' and 'settlement' were accepted, apparently without debate, as the proper method of public care for those who were not able to support themselves." [7]

As the frontier moved still farther westward, the same imitative type of legal provision was made. The territorial government of Oregon varied the pattern a bit in 1849 and enacted a new kind of provision making the county probate courts responsible for the relief of "the lame, blind, sick and other persons, who, from age or infirmity, are unable to support himself or herself." [8]

Although on the eastern seaboard the local unit remained the town or parish, in the Middle West it became the township or county. The far western and southern states, with their still greater distances and scattered populations, largely abandoned the township unit and placed responsibility upon the counties only. In fact, very few western or southern states have had townships at all, and, where these exist, they are chiefly justice of the peace districts and are not in any other sense units of government. [9]

This principle of local responsibility apparently arose out of and fitted admirably with the Anglo-Saxon spirit of independence. It was entirely in keeping with the social and economic self-sufficiency of the "horse-and-buggy age" for local tax funds to be spent to relieve the local poor, under the control of local government, in communities where everybody knew everybody else.

But living became more complicated and the country more thickly settled; as facilities for communication and transpor-

[7] Grace A. Browning, *The Development of Poor Relief Legislation in Kansas.* University of Chicago Press. 1935. p. vii.

[8] *The Origin and Development of Family Social Work in Portland, Oregon.* Unpublished Thesis by Amelia Feary. University of Oregon, Eugene, Oregon.

[9] Porter, *op. cit.*, p. 60.

tation developed, lagging patchwork amendments to the poor laws were enacted to meet changing conditions and situations. These scraps of laws dealt not only with the question of financial responsibility, which was often put upon two, three or sometimes even four different types of local units in the same state at the same time,[10] but also with methods of administration and of care. In Kansas, for instance, 123 different legislative enactments were passed, beginning with the Territorial Acts of 1855, "Providing for the Relief of the Poor," down to the laws of 1934, which still carried the ancient label of "the Relief of the Poor." [11] In this state, as in every other, an extraordinary number of court decisions plus many and sometimes variant opinions of attorney generals have made confusion worse confounded and increased the difficulty of interpreting the laws.[12]

By the end of the eighteenth century the newly formed states had incorporated in their poor laws the following meth-

[10] An analysis of the poor laws made in 1934 showed that the states placed responsibility for poor relief upon their political subdivisions as follows:

Number of States	Political Subdivisions Responsible for Poor Relief
24	Counties
7	Counties, townships and cities
6	Counties and cities
5	Towns (all 5 in New England)
3	Counties, townships, cities and villages
2	Counties and townships
1	Towns and cities (Rhode Island)

"Poor Relief Laws: A Digest," by Lucy W. Brown. American Public Welfare Association. 1934. 25 pp.

[11] Browning, Grace A., op. cit. Especially Editorial Note by Sophonisba P. Breckinridge.

[12] After years of outdoor relief giving in Brooklyn, New York, the whole system was declared illegal and abandoned in 1879. The very fact that this could happen shows the unsubstantial nature of the foundation upon which the system of poor relief rests. See Warner, Amos, op. cit., p. 311.

When the New York State poor law was repealed in 1929 there were on the statute books 130 special laws relating to particular towns and counties, some of them enacted in 1778. Bond, Elsie M., "New York's New Public Welfare Law," Social Service Review, Sept., 1929.

ods of pauper care which had prevailed through the colonial period: [13]

1. Outdoor relief, given to "paupers" in their homes.
2. Farming out to the lowest bidder who undertook to care for a single "pauper."
3. Contract, usually with the lowest bidder, for the care of all the "paupers" of a given locality.
4. Care in an almshouse which was under the direct control of the public officials.
5. Indenture or "binding out," a form of apprenticeship.

During the nineteenth century, farming out and indenture were gradually superseded in practice by the care of paupers within the walls of almshouses: generally known as "indoor relief." "Outdoor relief," to the needy in their own homes, was found to be costly. It was furthermore assumed to encourage idleness and increase pauperism. Hence, it was reserved for emergencies and for temporary care, while the gloomy, often shacklike, almshouse became the basic form of poor relief for old and young alike.

This move towards herding more and more of the poor into the almshouse was hastened by two state reports [14] published in 1821 and 1824. These sharply emphasized the assumed evils of outdoor relief and recommended institutional care for the poor as the best means of frightening them into going to work, of discouraging applications for help and thus decreasing pauperism. The reports also recommended that workhouses be attached to the almshouses in order both to provide work for the able-bodied poor and thereby to make them self-

[13] See Folks, Homer, *The Care of Destitute, Neglected and Delinquent Children.* Macmillan, New York, 1902. Mr. Folks adds: "The farming-out and contract systems had comparatively little application so far as children were concerned. Indenture, on the other hand, although especially applicable to children, was, it is curious to note, also used as a means of caring for adults, the statutes of several States providing, at the opening of the century, that idle or vagrant persons might be indentured to respectable citizens for a period of one year." p. 3.

[14] The Josiah Quincy Report of 1821 on the Pauper Laws of Massachusetts, and a report to the New York legislature in 1824 by J. V. N. Yates, the Secretary of State, on "The Relief and Settlement of the Poor." See Breckinridge, *op. cit.*, pp. 30-54.

supporting and less costly to the community's wage earners who naturally preferred to spend their incomes on themselves. The workhouse, a well-established institution in England, had first been opened in this country in colonial Boston about 1740.[15] Compulsory labor was believed by the puritan and pioneer individualist to improve the character of the poor. This theory was a phase of their conviction that no one should eat who did not work. During the nineteenth century, workhouses multiplied over the United States, not only for these reasons, but because "the only righteous and practical check on adult pauperism, the only check at once just and efficient" was held to be "the compulsory imposition of labor on every pauper to whom God has given, in even the slightest degree, the laboring ability." [16]

The Industrial Revolution, which began in the early years of that century, brought thousands of workers pouring from the self-sufficient farming areas to the already overcrowded cities and to the uncertainties of commercial and factory jobs. Poverty increased and with it the use of both indoor and outdoor relief. The business depressions which occurred at intervals of about twenty years, beginning in 1837, added to public relief expenditures. Each depression left the relief load larger than it had been before and this load each time brought much bitter criticism upon public officials for incompetency and upon the relief system itself on the now familiar ground, confusing cause and effect, that it increased both shiftlessness and poverty. These criticisms culminated in the abolition of outdoor relief in several of the largest cities in the country during the 1880's.[17]

Fifty years later, at the beginning of the depression of 1929, almshouse care was still the basic legal method of providing

[15] Kelso, Robert W., *The History of Public Poor Relief in Massachusetts, 1620-1920.* Houghton Mifflin Co. 1922. 195 pages. "In 1735 the General Court authorized the town of Boston to erect a house in which to set the poor to work. In 1739 this institution was opened." p. 115.

[16] Quoted from an earlier source in a paper called "Experiment in Relief in Work" given by Dr. Ayres of Cincinnati, at the National Conference of Charities and Corrections, 1892. Published in the Proceedings of the Conference, University of Chicago Press.

[17] See Part I, Chapter 2.

for paupers of all ages and both sexes. The poor laws of practically every state made specific provision for poorhouses; in ten of the states the law did not mention outdoor relief at all; in about one-third, it was named as a secondary method to be used only in special, and for the most part emergency, cases; in less than half of the states outdoor relief was authorized in the law as having equal importance with the almshouse as a method of giving aid to the needy. In several states the laws still provided for the letting of contracts for the care of the poor and a few of them even yet authorized the indenture or apprenticing of children.

On the political side, as late as 1934, the Constitutions of 14 states deprived relief recipients of the right to vote and to hold office, although in four of these states the loss of franchise was limited to paupers who are inmates of poorhouses. Even the use of the term "pauper," significant in itself, remained in the titles or texts of the poor laws of 30 states.[18] Moreover the use of the so-called "pauper's oath," by which an applicant for relief swears that he is absolutely destitute, has been chiefly a matter of tradition and variable local practice, although at least nine states had some statutory provision with regard to the content or the form of the application for poor relief, or the penalties which might be imposed for obtaining relief under false pretenses.[19]

[18] Abbott, Edith, "Abolish the Pauper Laws," *Social Service Review*, March, 1934.

[19] *States in which all paupers are deprived of franchise and right to hold office*

States in which all paupers are deprived of franchise and right to hold office	*"Indoor" paupers only deprived*	*"Pauper's Oath" and/or penalties*
Delaware	Louisiana	Arizona
Maine	Missouri	Connecticut
Massachusetts	Oklahoma	Delaware
New Hampshire	Pennsylvania	Idaho
New Jersey		Illinois
Rhode Island		Kansas
South Carolina		New Jersey
Texas		New York
Virginia		Wisconsin

Delaware and New Jersey are the only states which had in 1934 statutory provisions of both types. See Heisterman and Keener, "Further Poor Law Notes," *Social Service Review*, March, 1934.

The poor laws of two-thirds of the states contained, as late as 1937, provisions which required that, before relief is given, relatives who have "sufficient ability" shall be called upon to support poor persons and if they refuse to do so they may be prosecuted.[20]

Settlement

The poor laws not only have established the principles of public and local responsibility for relief and designated the governmental units which are to support the poor, but from colonial days they have also limited local expenditures to the care of persons who belong or have "settlement" in the local unit.

The pioneer settlers in their struggles for existence looked with alarm upon the tattered stranger with the marks of illness, laziness or an empty purse about him who might become a charge upon their meager resources. The laws of settlement grew naturally out of the confusion of many different rules which each town or parish made to exclude such undesirable strangers. They were an evidence also of their unceasing struggles to shift the load of poor relief upon some other jurisdiction.[21]

The English practice of deporting criminals, public charges, and other undesirable persons to the American colonies only aggravated the antagonism of the "decent" settlers to strangers within their gates. Free use was made of the English customs of "warning out," whipping, and driving out beggars.[22]

One legal definition expresses this sense of local responsibility and its desire to keep out the unwanted stranger in these not uncertain terms:

[20] "If the poor laws are to be written in the light of modern social welfare theories, any attempt to enforce by legal machinery the responsibility of relatives, one of the surviving provisions of the sixteenth-century poor law system, should be completely abolished." Edith Abbott, "Poor Law Provision for Family Responsibility," *Social Service Review*, December, 1938. See also "Abolish the Pauper Laws," by the same author, *Social Service Review*, March, 1934.

[21] Robert W. Kelso, *op. cit.*, Chapter III, p. 36.

[22] See *Monthly Report FERA*, August 1-31, 1935. pp. 25-40, "Legal Settlement in the United States," by E. A. Williams, for a summary of the problem of legal settlement, with analysis of state legislation.

The fundamental basis of the duty to furnish support to a poor person in his settlement, the general rule being that a poor district is bound to furnish support only to persons having their settlement therein. Conversely, the place of a person's settlement might be defined as the place where he has a right to support as a pauper.[23]

Each state has enacted and often revised its own settlement laws with complicated and varied provisions which have grown out of conditions and events peculiar to its local communities. These laws deal with such matters as the length of time which a recipient must have lived within the state and in the local unit in order to acquire settlement and the right to relief; the circumstances under which settlement can or cannot be gained, and, when gained, may be lost; responsibility for the expense of support and return of a poor person who has been temporarily absent from the place of his settlement; provisions regarding the removal of poor persons who have no settlement and regulations against bringing unsettled persons into the state. They include further provisions regarding the effect of marriage, divorce and desertion on the settlement of women, and regulations governing the status of minors.[24]

The intricacies, inconsistencies and lack of uniformity in these laws have forced great and bitter hardship upon many thousands of helpless and destitute people in the United States, who have been denied relief and shifted back and forth between towns, counties and states. The requirements of the laws have been so complicated, and the various localities have been so desirous of transferring the costs of relief to other units, that protracted and expensive litigation has often resulted.[25] Peculiar hardships result from the fact that in most of the states it is stipulated that during the period required to gain settlement a person must receive no public relief, and in some states no private relief either. Discrepancies in the

[23] From "Poor and Poor Laws," 21 R.C.L. 716, Art. 1, sec. 19. Cited by Charlotte C. Donnell, "Laws Regarding Settlement in Connection with the Problem of Interstate Relationship under a Federal System," *Social Service Review*, Sept., 1930.

[24] Hirsch, Harry, *Compilation of Settlement Laws of All States in the U. S.* Introduction by David C. Adie. Revised as of January, 1938. New York State Department of Social Welfare.

[25] *Our Settlement Laws, Their Origin; Their Lack of Uniformity; Pro-*

periods necessary to gain or lose settlement in the same state and differences in the periods set by different states cause both confusion and distress, since settlement can be and often is lost in one state before it is gained in another.

Periods required to gain state settlement ranged, in 1930, from six months or less in 11 states to ten years in 4 states; and settlement could be lost in periods of absence ranging from less than thirty days in the case of South Dakota to five years in the case of 4 other states, unless a new settlement was gained elsewhere.[26]

About three-fourths of the states have finally provided for the relief of the "unsettled poor" until they are removed to their place of settlement. Six of these states, New York and the New England states except New Hampshire, have used state funds for this purpose (see p. 18 below). The rest provide that the locality within which the dependent person is found shall give relief, subject to reimbursement by the governmental unit in which that person has settlement, if he belongs in the same state. If, however, he has settlement in another state or has no settlement at all, there is of course no provision for reimbursement. For this reason, the localities have generally attempted to rid themselves of the "unsettled poor" as soon as possible, by passing on the newcomers to the next town or county or state, or by sending them back to the places where they once had settlement.

Local Poor Relief in the Twentieth Century

The actual administration of poor relief in the twentieth century still shows the brutal influence of Elizabethan England and of rigorous pioneer and puritan colonial America as clearly as do the terms of the state poor laws themselves. Studies of the methods which were in use in local poor relief

posed Measures of Reform, 1933. Harry M. Hirsch, Bibliography. N. Y. State Department of Social Welfare.

Carl A. Heisterman, "Removal of Non-Resident State-Poor by State and Local Authorities," Social Service Review. June, 1934.

Carl A. Heisterman, "Statutory Provisions Relating to Legal Settlement for Purposes of Poor-Relief," Social Service Review. March, 1933.

[26] Hirsch, op. cit. See also 1939 Revision, published by The American Public Welfare Association, Chicago, and Chapter 16 below.

offices between 1911 and 1932 reveal practices and attitudes which had evidently changed but little in two or three hundred years.[27]

One fundamental fault in the haphazard methods of administering relief was the quality, character and training of the men and women who did the job. Public officials who were responsible for the administration of relief were often elected or appointed to discharge some other function and handled relief merely as a part-time or extra duty. There was little or no recognition that special qualifications were needed for those chosen to deal with dependent people. Relief might be and was administered, depending upon the terms of the state law, by county commissioners, by the county court, by grand juries, by township trustees, by justices of the peace; or overseers of the poor, or poor commissioners might be elected or appointed to serve full time.

A study made in New Hampshire, in 1931, discovered 700 different officials, most of them elected to discharge other functions, who were administering public relief in 245 separate county, city and town units. 140 of these units had populations of less than 1,000 persons, only 14 of them had over 5,000. These figures are particularly interesting in view of the fact that New Hampshire has only ten counties and an area of little more than nine thousand square miles, with a population of 465,293.[28] In 1934 Ohio, with 88 counties, had 1,535 local governmental units, townships, cities and counties, responsible for some form of public outdoor relief.[29] In Pennsylvania's

[27] Most of the material presented in this section is drawn from reports and administrative studies of poor relief practice made between 1911 and 1932 in 23 different states, representing every section of the country except the Southwest. Most of the information was secured by field workers who visited poor relief offices, interviewed the officials who were administering the relief, inspected records, talked with representative citizens in the various communities and in many cases visited the families who were receiving relief. A list of these reports and studies is given in the Bibliography, page 483.

[28] According to 1930 Census. See report of "A Survey of the Organization of the State, County and Town Governments of New Hampshire," by the Institute for Government Research of the Brookings Institution, Washington, D. C., 1932.

[29] Report of the Ohio Commission on Unemployment Insurance, Part II, "Ohio's Statutory Provisions for Poor Relief."

67 counties there were 967 persons legally charged with the administration of poor relief in 425 poor districts, 366 of which were in 15 counties,[30] before the Public Assistance Law was passed in 1937.

Among a majority of these early officials the characteristic attitude was indifference. They took paupers for granted. Their general objective appeared to be to conserve the public funds by keeping relief expenditures to the lowest possible figure. They made little attempt to secure any accurate information about the circumstances of the applicants. Relief was usually given on the basis of whatever personal knowledge the administering official happened to have, no matter how scanty. This was supplemented by hearsay and gossip. They made very few visits to the homes of the poor. They put much emphasis upon the difference between the "worthy" and the "unworthy" poor, but to both the ineradicable stigma of dependency was attached as soon as they were given even emergency or temporary relief, however small the amount might be. To be "on the town" or "on the county" was the lowest state outside prison to which a member of the community could descend. Moreover, it was necessary to be absolutely destitute in order to be eligible for relief, and in many localities a "pauper's oath" was required in the form of an affidavit or a signed statement attesting the applicant's need.[31] Once on the lists many paupers never got off, and their relief continued until they moved out of town or died. A defeatist philosophy, widely held by public officials, assumed that this must be so, and hence a *laissez-faire* policy and general indifference contributed to the creation of a class of chronic dependents.

The officials kept very few records concerning relief grants and these were usually fragmentary and unsatisfactory. They supplied but little information regarding relief expenditures or the circumstances of the recipients which justified helping them with public funds. The records often consisted of no more than the lists of names of relief recipients which were printed in annual reports of the county government or in the

[30] *Poor Relief Administration in Pennsylvania,* p. 15.
[31] See p. 10 above.

newspapers, supplemented by the financial reports of the county treasurers which gave the unitemized amounts of grocers' bills and the accounts of other tradesmen who furnished goods to the poor.

There was ample evidence in reports of the studies already mentioned that this system encouraged petty graft as well as the use of relief for political power. Merchants sometimes failed to report the death of customers who were on the relief lists and continued to collect for their private tills the pittances of the dead from the relief funds of the town or county. Legal restrictions on pauper voting were usually not enforced in the states where they existed. Hence men and women on relief built up a solid vote for officials from whom they got relief. Inability to pay the poll tax in states where one was required by law was often likely to be a practical barrier to the exercise of the franchise by paupers. A few states definitely provided against this contingency by exempting them from the payment of this tax, thereby recognizing their rights as citizens but also leaving the way open for direct purchase of votes with relief funds.

In accord with the general notion that relief cost must always be kept at the least possible minimum, eight states specified in their laws, by 1933, the maximum amounts which might be given to persons in need.[32] The actual practice in the remaining states which set no legal maximums resulted in making such small grants as to furnish conclusive evidence that administrative policy and tradition were as potent as legal restrictions in keeping expenditures on a minimum basis. The amounts given in many localities ranged from $2 to $5 a week for a family of five. In some places they were as low as a starvation $3 per month. Such grants were occasionally paid by check or in cash, but the usual method was to give relief "in kind," either orders for groceries or fuel or the articles themselves, such as packages or baskets of food, secondhand clothing, bedding, or loads of wood or of coal. The giving of

[32] L. W. Brown, op. cit. The maximum amounts ranged from $8 per month per person in Alabama to $200 per year in New Jersey, with Michigan and Minnesota limiting payments in any one year to $20 and $35 respectively. The other states with legal maximums were Idaho, Indiana, Iowa and North Dakota.

relief in kind was based on the theory that if paupers were given cash they would waste money or spend it unwisely. Many were the stories, most of them apocryphal, of women spending relief checks on cosmetics and permanent waves, men on lotteries and horserace bets. As long as they had to be supported by the town, the town claimed the right, therefore, to dictate what they should eat and wear and where they should live. Not even the morals and general behavior of paupers were exempt from this official supervision.

The conviction still prevailed generally that relief should be made so disagreeable to the recipient that he would be persuaded or forced to devise some means of self-support in order to get off the list as swiftly as possible. This deterrent policy was the only early poor relief method of rehabilitation. It was conceived also as a stern warning to those on the borderline of dependency to practice thrift and keep out of the pauper class and as a stimulus to those who were already "on the town" to struggle doubly hard to better their condition. The most common way of making relief distasteful was to make the grants smaller than the lowest wages which the recipient could possibly earn, if he really exerted himself and got a job. This was the doctrine of "less eligibility," inherited from the English poor relief system. It has probably had more to do with keeping relief standards on a low level in this country than any other one factor in three hundred years of relief history.

STATE RESPONSIBILITY

Because political structure has been moving by lagging and hesitant steps from small local units to larger ones, state responsibility for persons in need has always been secondary to that of the local unit of government. Not until local machinery and local resources had proved inadequate did the state begin to provide institutional care for handicapped paupers. State funds for the "unsettled poor" were supplied only to persons who had no local settlement and therefore no legal claim upon the relief funds of any specific locality within the state.

The amounts appropriated from state treasuries for outdoor relief have always been relatively small compared to the sums spent for unemployment relief after 1931. Only six states have regularly provided for the "unsettled poor," a few more have made emergency appropriations through the years for "disaster relief" as occasion arose. Pensions for needy soldiers and sailors, however, represent a more general charge upon state budgets, but the expenditures for this purpose have not been large. State contributions to Mothers' Pensions, aid to the aged and to the blind which were made before 1936 are but a fraction of the expenditures made by the states for these categories since the Federal social security program went into effect.

The State Unsettled Poor

The state poor relief for the "unsettled poor" or the "state poor" was probably the earliest example of the use of colonial or state funds for the care of persons in need, the first real breakover from local to state responsibility. The Connecticut records show that in 1657 the New Haven Colony court ordered the town of Southold to advance £5 for the relief of "certain persons who had arrived in said town from Long Island," and to deduct this sum from the next town tax payable to the colony. In 1750 the records set forth clearly that in case the poor and defective belonged "to no town or place in this colony," they were to be maintained "at the cost and charge of the colony." In 1795 the State of Connecticut became responsible for the expenses of "any non-inhabitant who needs relief for the duration of 3 months, after which expenses are to be paid by the town." [33]

Responsibility for the "unsettled poor" was first assumed by the Colony of Massachusetts in 1677 as a result of the suffering occasioned by King Philip's War.[34] Similar provisions

[33] Report of the Commission to Study the Pauper Laws, State of Connecticut, pp. 4 and 40.

[34] Kelso, Robert W., op. cit., p. 57.

Breckinridge, op. cit. "The State Poor in Massachusetts and their Care."

There was also a provision in Oregon for refunds from the state treasurer to counties for the care of poor persons who were not residents of any county in the state. "An Act to Amend an Act for Support of the Poor," approved October 24, 1866, Oregon Legislature, Assembly Laws, 4th Regular Session. Cited in unpublished thesis by Amelia Ann Feary, University of Oregon.

were made in other New England states where much the same conditions existed and a like philosophy and tradition prevailed.

The first "state poor" in New York were patriot refugees in the Revolution, people left homeless by the British invasion from the North and refugees evacuated from the City of New York in the face of British occupation. Under these emergency pressures the local poor relief apparatus broke down in many places and settlement laws were, for the time being, practically suspended. At least they were not invoked against the "respectable" people who fled from their homes, and who were destitute because of their loyalty to the Revolutionary cause. It is easy, therefore, to understand why in 1798 the state provided the means by which relief to unsettled persons might be supplied with some degree of permanence.[35]

Five or six states have continued since colonial days to spend state funds for the care of the "unsettled poor" or the "state poor," as a regular part of their governmental relief system up to and during the recent depression. Although the other states have made very little provision from their state treasuries for this particular category, the responsibility of state governments for certain other types of relief has been much more widely distributed.

Disaster Relief

The principle of state responsibility has always been further enhanced by sudden and violent trouble. Certain states

[35] Schneider, David M., *The History of Public Welfare in New York State, 1609-1866.* University of Chicago Press, 1938, 381 pages. pp. 95-106; 134; 208. See also Creech, Margaret D., *Three Centuries of Poor Law Administration, A Study of Legislation in Rhode Island.* University of Chicago Press, 1936. 325 pages.

"As early as 1775 there appeared a slight modification of the principle of local responsibility when the colony assumed the expense of the relief of the destitution which came as a result of the Revolutionary War, when the red-coats had committed depredations and left property sadly damaged. And cash grants as well as firewood and food were granted by the State Assembly for a period of six years. But the principle of local responsibility continued as the emergency period receded." Introductory Note by Edith Abbott.

in the Middle West during their pioneer days met emergency needs and gave disaster relief out of their state treasuries. Nebraska made appropriations at the time of the grasshopper scourge in 1875 and the drought of 1890; Kansas, for destitute settlers in 1860, 1871 and 1872; for seed loans when the crops failed in 1891 and for seed and coal in the depression of 1893. In Nebraska the funds were distributed under direct supervision of the state; in Kansas by county commissioners. Provision for emergency disaster relief, for drought, storms, floods and other "Acts of God," have been made throughout the years by states in every part of the country, but only as emergency, temporary expenditures to meet specific needs.

As late as 1930 and 1931, Arkansas, Illinois, Louisiana, Minnesota, Missouri, South Carolina, Florida, made appropriations of this nature, the sums ranging from nearly a million dollars for flood relief in Illinois to $1,500 in South Carolina for sufferers from a hailstorm. The total of the appropriations made by these seven states during the two year period was approximately $1,300,000.[36]

Veterans' Relief

On the theory that men in the armed services of governments are employees of those governments in work of a peculiarly hazardous and "seasonal" kind, needy soldiers and sailors have been for many years the beneficiaries of special state legislation. This theory is also bolstered by all the popular emotions of patriotism and by the fact that veterans in any considerable number may exert a political bloc pressure. Therefore, for whatever reasons, by 1910 all but six states had made statutory provision for relief of Civil War veterans and many states had provided relief to the veterans of the Mexican, Indian and Spanish-American wars and the Boxer Rebellion. Since 1918 relief for World War veterans has been provided by 30 states, in addition to Federal bonuses and pensions.[37]

[36] State Provisions for Emergency Disaster Relief, Drought, Storms, Floods, and similar disasters: Laws of 1930 and 1931: U. S. Children's Bureau Chart. 2 pages. Unpublished.

[37] Data on veteran relief legislation compiled by Robert C. Lowe, Division of Social Research, Works Progress Administration. Cited by Geddes

Categorical Assistance in State Institutions

Early in the nineteenth century, state governments began to assume responsibility for the institutional care of certain categories of paupers who had been hitherto local charges. The almshouses had become the dumping ground for dependents with every kind of handicap and disability, the insane, the sick and infirm, the deaf, the dumb, the crippled, the criminal; men, women and children of all ages.

The establishment of state institutions for special classes of these handicapped people was in effect the beginning of categorical relief, or relief by special classes. The states were prompted not only by humanitarian motives, but by the fact that there were usually too few inmates in any one category in a single town or even a county to justify a local institution, and also because the type of care essential to be provided for each category was ordinarily more costly than the local government was prepared to assume.[38]

The state's selection of categories for its care was made on the basis of a need or disability other than, or in addition to, poverty. Those who were merely poor and not otherwise handicapped were left to subsist on local relief.

The first categories to be drafted off from local communities to state institutions were the insane, and then defective persons of teachable age, the deaf and the dumb. Later on special state provision began to be made for juvenile delinquents, the feeble-minded and the crippled. Virginia had established a colonial institution for the insane in 1769. The State of Kentucky founded the Lexington Asylum for the Insane in 1822, and another institution for the deaf and dumb

in *Trends in Relief Expenditures, 1910-1935,* Division of Social Research, WPA. 1937, p. 3.

[38] The practice varies in regard to county payments to the state for the care of county charges in state institutions. Warner in his *American Charities,* p. 313, says: ". . . at first the cost of supporting them [the insane in state institutions] was assessed upon the county or township from which they came. The difficulty of collecting these assessments, together with the fact that the local desire to save money resulted too often in the denial of relief needed, has led to the removal of an increasing number to the support of the state at purely state expense."

in the same year.[39] New York State opened a House of Refuge for Delinquents (boys) in 1826 and Massachusetts established a School for Feeble-minded and Idiotic Youth in 1848. New York opened a state institution for the crippled in 1863 and two years later an Institution for the Blind, although the state had thirty-four years earlier begun paying for the care and instruction of blind pauper children in a privately supported institution.[40] It was not until 1894, however, that the first State Institution for Epileptics was established in Ohio.[41]

Dependent children, as distinguished from other categories, were not classified as needing special state institutions until quite late. Although private institutions, both religious and secular, were early established to receive children from the almshouses or to prevent their commitment, it was not until the middle of the nineteenth century that the states assumed any large responsibility for child care or contributed any considerable sums of money for that purpose.

Large numbers of "paupers" of various ages and disabilities were still left to the care of local communities in the almshouses,[42] in spite of the fact that the number of state institutions or of private institutions receiving state subsidies rapidly increased.

State Boards of Charities

With the state assuming responsibility for categorical aid, setting up various types of institutions supported by state funds, and with the populations in these institutions growing constantly, the need for agencies to inspect and supervise them led to the creation of State Boards of Charities. The first

[39] Breckinridge, Sophonisba, op. cit., p. 14; "The Establishment of State Institutions," pp. 68-149.
Warner, Amos, op. cit., p. 142.
[40] Schneider, op. cit., pp. 208-9, 325, 367, 371.
[41] Warner, op. cit., p. 288.
[42] In 1904, 108,387 inmates, or 78.6% of the total almshouse population, were classified as having the following disabilities: Insane, 11,807; feeble-minded, 22,914; epileptic, 2,106; blind, 4,107; deaf-mute, 1,023; paralytic, 6,556; crippled, maimed, or deformed, 20,727; old and infirm, 23,463; bedridden, 4,402; rheumatic, 11,282. *Paupers in Almshouses,* 1904. Bureau of the Census, U. S. Dept. of Commerce and Labor, Government Printing Office, Washington, 1906, pp. 36, 37, 186.

state to take this action was Massachusetts in 1863. New York followed three years later, and by the end of 1873 nine other states had done likewise.[43]

These state agencies were vested with authority variously exercised, to inspect and supervise the administration of state institutions and to inspect and advise county institutions (chiefly jails and almshouses), but they were given no specific jurisdiction over outdoor poor relief.[44]

In 1904, 40 years after the first state agency was set up, only 15 states had established Boards of Charities. By 1913, however, the Bureau of the Census reported "there is not a single state that does not, in some form, recognize its duty to secure better care for those who can not care for themselves."

Nevertheless, the tabulation of laws made by the Bureau shows that ten states had in 1913 no legally constituted central authority responsible for the "administration and supervision of care for the dependent classes." Eighteen years later the White House Conference reported that "in five states no state department concerned with general public welfare problems has been established." [45]

[43] 1867	1869	1871	1873
Ohio	Illinois	Kansas	Connecticut
	North Carolina	Michigan	Wisconsin
	Rhode Island		
	Pennsylvania		

See Stevenson, Marietta, *Public Welfare Administration,* 1938. Macmillan. pp. 8-9.

See also Breckinridge, *op. cit.,* pp. 237, 292, 557.

Summary of State Laws Relating to the Dependent Classes 1913, Bureau of the Census, U. S. Dept. of Commerce, pp. 6, 312-46.

[44] Except in six states which supervised the expenditure of state funds for "unsettled cases," as already noted. See p. 18 above. See also Potter, "Public Welfare Administration, Integration or Separation," *Social Service Review.* Dec., 1937. p. 652.

[45] White House Conference on Child Health and Protection, Section IV A. Organization and Equipment of State Departments, Jan., 1931. The five states are "Arkansas, Idaho, Mississippi, Nevada and Utah. The Dept. of Public Welfare in Idaho is primarily a health department. Arkansas had provided a State Department, but this was abolished in 1927. Utah has a juvenile-court commission and Arkansas a commission for crippled children."

In 1913, twenty-one states exercised no state supervision over any form of local relief, and the remaining twenty-seven supervised almshouses only, outdoor relief being left to the discretion of local officials.[46]

The lack of legal jurisdiction, however, did not keep officials of the State Boards of Charities from recognizing the importance of the local outdoor relief problem. In 1874, the first "Conference of Boards of Public Charities" met in New York City. Representatives of four state boards attended. This conference was later to become the National Conference of Charities and Correction, and, later still, the National Conference of Social Work. The state officials gave poor relief a prominent place on their programs, and were especially concerned about the need for statistics showing the extent of disease, insanity, crime and poverty.[47]

It was not until 20 years later, however, that the first legislation was enacted requiring reports to a central state office from all local relief officials. This was the famous Indiana Reform Law of 1895,[48] which required the local officials to keep records of all relief given and to send none too detailed reports to the State Board of Charities. A system of reporting resulted which made possible a rudimentary form of state regulation and supervision.[49] Later developments showed,

[46] Summary of State Laws Relating to the Dependent Classes, 1913. Bureau of the Census: Tabular Review, pp. 312-29. The ten states (p. 23) having no central authority are Oklahoma, Delaware, Georgia, Idaho, Mississippi, Nevada, New Mexico, South Carolina, Texas, Utah. The twenty-one states: Alabama, Arizona, Arkansas, Delaware, Florida, Georgia, Idaho, Iowa, Kansas, Kentucky, Maryland, Mississippi, Nevada, New Mexico, North Dakota, South Carolina, South Dakota, Texas, Utah, Vermont and West Virginia.

[47] See Abbott, Edith, *Some American Pioneers in Social Welfare*. University of Chicago Press, 1937. 189 pages. Appendix II, The First Public Welfare Association. pp. 176-189.

See also early *Proceedings* of National Conference of Charities and Correction.

[48] The State Board in Kansas had considered a study of poor relief in 1887 but this legal action in Indiana was the first of its kind. For the Kansas situation see "The Development of Poor Relief Legislation in Kansas" 1935. University of Chicago Press, by Grace A. Browning. pp. 45-7.

[49] Butler, Amos W., *Official Outdoor Relief and the State: Proceedings*

however, that the supervisory relationship established was more apparent than real and that the improvement in local methods was not lasting.

A number of states followed the example of Indiana and required that reports on local outdoor relief be made to the State Boards of Charities or some other arm of the state government. These reports which were published in the appropriate annual state reports were usually limited to total expenditures, although in some cases they included the number of families or individuals aided. Many of the figures were undoubtedly inadequate or incorrect since the local relief records in the large majority of rural counties and townships, the country over, were themselves inadequate, obscure, or entirely non-existent.

Legislation for County Welfare

In 1917 the first state laws were enacted providing for county units of public welfare in North Carolina and of child welfare in Minnesota, under the supervision of central state agencies. During the following decade somewhat similar programs were initiated in eight other states, either by legislation or through the activity of a state agency.[50]

Although at least three of these states, North Carolina, Missouri, Minnesota, provided that the county welfare unit should or might administer outdoor poor relief, in no case was the state agency given the right to supervise this function. It is,

of National Conference of Charities and Correction, Baltimore, 1915. pp. 441-2. Also *Indiana Bulletin Charities and Corrections,* March, 1906, p. 71.

[50] By legislation in Alabama, Kentucky, Missouri, Nebraska, South Dakota, Virginia, West Virginia, Wisconsin; by activity of a state agency in Georgia, New Mexico, Iowa; United States Department of Labor, Children's Bureau Publications: No. 169—The County as a Unit for an Organization Program of Child Caring and Protective Work, by E. O. Lundberg, 1926; No. 107—County Organization and Child Care and Protection, 1922; No. 173—Public Child Caring Work in Certain Counties of Minnesota, North Carolina, and New York, by H. I. Curry, 1927; also list of State Agencies Concerned with Child Welfare; County Welfare Agencies: Selected Laws and Illustrative Charts, Dec., 1931. Also, The County as an Administrative Unit for Social Work, by Mary Ruth Colby, U. S. Children's Bureau, 1933.

therefore, hardly surprising that the 1931 White House Conference report on state public welfare organization failed to mention outdoor relief as a concern of state departments of welfare. Also it is significant that a report of the Census Bureau on relief expenditures in 1929 and 1931 cited only funds spent by local agencies and listed no state agency or official of any description as a source of information regarding either expenditures or numbers of persons aided.

This was the situation in regard to state responsibility for local poor relief in 1931 when state agencies began to appropriate funds for unemployment relief and to supervise both state and local relief expenditures. During the following eight years the picture changed so radically that in September, 1939, the state departments of welfare, in about three-quarters of the states, supervised or directly administered general relief in their local units.[51]

Categorical Assistance Outside of Institutions

Approximately one hundred years after the states began to provide institutional care for certain categories of handicapped persons, the first state legislation was enacted for categorical assistance outside of institutions, that is, for persons in their own homes. This state assistance took the form of aid to the blind, mothers' aid and old-age pensions, which represent the most important participation of state governments before 1931 in the direct care of persons in need outside of institutions, and are particularly significant in view of recent developments under the Federal Social Security Act of 1935. The first state law for aid to the blind was passed in 1907, for dependent children in 1911, and for the aged in 1923.[52] Although 45 states had by 1931 enacted legislation for mothers' aid, and, four years later, 28 and 27 states respectively had laws providing for old-age pensions, and aid to the blind, it is important to note the relatively slight extent to which state funds

[51] See Part IV, Chapter 14. For account of Census Bureau report see pp. 73-74 below.

[52] Aid to the Blind, Wisconsin, 1907. Mothers' Aid, Illinois, 1911.

Aid to the Aged, Montana and Nevada, 1923 (an Arizona law of 1915 was declared unconstitutional).

See *Social Security in America*, Social Security Board, Washington, 1937. 592 pages.

were made available for these programs. In many cases no appropriations were made at all, or those made were very much less than the amount required if the states were to meet their share of the costs in fulfilling the purposes of the legislation. The result was that programs which might have been statewide were actually less than fifty percent operative. Depending so largely upon local funds, they reached in many counties only a fraction of those who were in need and eligible for assistance.

In 1934, the year before the Federal Social Security Act was passed by Congress, of the 24 states which then had laws providing aid to the blind, only eleven spent any state funds. In four of these same states no county funds at all were expended. The total amount spent by counties in the 24 states was $3,480,000, only about $100,000 more than the amount spent for the blind by the 11 state governments.[53]

Of the 28 states with laws for old-age assistance in 1934, state funds were spent in 16, with 6 states each carrying all the cost of their programs. State and county expenditures in 28 states totaled approximately $32,000,000.[54]

In 1934 Mothers' Aid laws were not operative at all in New Mexico, Arkansas and Mississippi. Alabama was operating under a law passed in 1932 authorizing home care of dependent children from local relief funds; Georgia and South Carolina had passed no legislation. In the 42 remaining states probably less than half the counties were actually administering benefits. This is a fair assumption since, in 1931, the Federal Children's Bureau found that aid was being given in 1,490 (55%) of the 2,723 counties in the United States, which were at that time authorized to administer such benefits. Reports received from 26 states in 1934 indicated that at least 171 counties in these states had discontinued aid.

Although in 1934, 16 states had authorized state contributions to these benefits, in 2 of them no appropriation was made and in 5 others the state fund was too small to be of real as-

[53] Round figures: p. 303. *Social Security in America.* State expenditures (11 states) $3,397,219. See Public Provision for Pensions for the Blind in 1934. U. S. Dept. of Labor, 1935. 19 pages.
[54] *Social Security in America,* pp. 155-167.

sistance. Total state expenditures for the year were approximately $5,600,000 in 14 states, while the counties in 43 states spent about six times as much.[55]

The extent of state responsibility for categorical assistance is measured not only in terms of amounts of money spent but in terms of direct state administration or authority given to the state to supervise local units. The extent of a state program also depends largely upon whether the law is mandatory upon the counties of the state or merely permissive.

The essential weakness in the mothers' aid programs undoubtedly lay in the fact that the majority of the state laws were permissive rather than mandatory. Also 37 of the 45 states entrusted the administration of aid to local units with little and in some states no specific provision for state supervision. In 14 states the responsibility for local administration was placed in the juvenile courts, ostensibly to remove the allowances to mothers from the stigma and low standards of poor relief. For the same reason special local agencies were provided in 7 states. In 14 other states, however, the administration was in the hands of the town or county commissioners, the same officials who handled the regular poor relief.[56]

Twenty-two of the 28 old-age pension laws were mandatory upon either the state or local units. One state, Delaware, was directly responsible for administration. Of the other 27 where local units administered the program, 16 states had no supervisory authority whatever and the remaining 11 exercised complete supervision over the local programs.[57]

The laws which provided pensions for the blind were mandatory in 19 states out of the total of 27. In twenty of these the administration was local with various degrees of state supervision and in the other 7 the state had direct responsibility.[58]

In general it appears that, as these categorical programs developed during the years from 1907 to 1934, the mandatory

[55] Op. cit., pp. 233-249.
[56] A Tabular Summary of State Laws Relating to Public Aid to Children in Their Own Homes in Effect January 1, 1934. United States Children's Bureau Chart No. 3, 1934.
[57] See op. cit., p. 161.
[58] Ibid., p. 306.

CHART II

Number of children in whose behalf mothers' aid and aid to dependent children payments were made in 1938 and the number in whose behalf mothers' aid payments were made in 1935, per 1,000 population under 16 years of age (see Table 1 and text, p. 32).

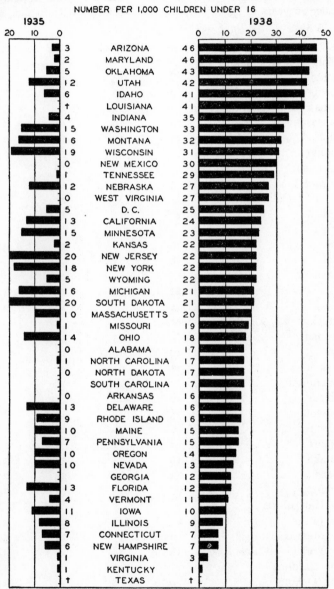

NUMBER PER 1,000 CHILDREN UNDER 16

1935			1938				
3	ARIZONA	46					
2	MARYLAND	46					
5	OKLAHOMA	43					
12	UTAH	42					
6	IDAHO	41					
†	LOUISIANA	41					
4	INDIANA	35					
15	WASHINGTON	33					
16	MONTANA	32					
19	WISCONSIN	31					
0	NEW MEXICO	30					
1	TENNESSEE	29					
12	NEBRASKA	27					
0	WEST VIRGINIA	27					
5	D. C.	25					
13	CALIFORNIA	24					
15	MINNESOTA	23					
2	KANSAS	22					
20	NEW JERSEY	22					
18	NEW YORK	22					
5	WYOMING	22					
16	MICHIGAN	21					
20	SOUTH DAKOTA	21					
10	MASSACHUSETTS	20					
1	MISSOURI	19					
14	OHIO	18					
0	ALABAMA	17					
1	NORTH CAROLINA	17					
0	NORTH DAKOTA	17					
	SOUTH CAROLINA	17					
0	ARKANSAS	16					
13	DELAWARE	16					
9	RHODE ISLAND	16					
10	MAINE	15					
7	PENNSYLVANIA	15					
10	OREGON	14					
10	NEVADA	13					
	GEORGIA	12					
13	FLORIDA	12					
4	VERMONT	11					
11	IOWA	10					
8	ILLINOIS	9					
7	CONNECTICUT	7					
6	NEW HAMPSHIRE	7					
1	VIRGINIA	3					
1	KENTUCKY	1					
†	TEXAS	†					

Source: Public Aid for the Care of Dependent Children in Their Own Homes, by Dorothy R. Bucklin, *Social Security Bulletin*, Vol. 2, No. 4, April, 1939.

TABLE 1

Number of children in whose behalf payments for mothers' aid and for aid to dependent children were made per 1,000 population under 16 years of age, by states, in a specified month in the years 1935-38 [1]

State	1935	1936	1937	1938
Median for states making payments	8 [2]	14	16	20
Alabama	0	16	15	17
Arizona	3	23	32	46
Arkansas	0	16	19	16
California	13	16 [3]	20 [3]	24 [3]
Colorado	.. [4]	20	29	34
Connecticut	7	7	8	7
Delaware	13	14	16	16
District of Columbia	5	29	29	25
Florida	13	12	12	12
Georgia	..	..	8	12
Idaho	6	27	35	41
Illinois	8	7	9	9
Indiana	4	6	27	35
Iowa	11	10	10	10
Kansas	2	1	13	22
Kentucky	1	1	1	1
Louisiana	.. [5]	23	33	41
Maine	10	14	14	15
Maryland	2	31	40	46
Massachusetts	10	12	16	20
Michigan	16	14	20	21
Minnesota	15	17	16 [3]	23 [3]
Mississippi	0	0	0	0
Missouri	1	1	1	19
Montana	16	14	25	32
Nebraska	12	18	24	27
Nevada	10	13	12	13
New Hampshire	6	7	8	7
New Jersey	20	21	22	22
New Mexico	0	15	26	30
New York	18	18	18	22
North Carolina	1	1	9	17
North Dakota	0	0	4 [3]	17 [3]

State	1935	1936	1937	1938
Ohio	14	14 [3]	16 [3]	18 [3]
Oklahoma	5	28	39	43
Oregon	10	10	10	14
Pennsylvania	7	8	15	15
Rhode Island	9	8	13	16
South Carolina	..	..	7	17
South Dakota	20	19	22	21
Tennessee	1	1	21	29
Texas	.. [5]	.. [5]	.. [5]	.. [5]
Utah	12	26	35	42
Vermont	4	7	7	11
Virginia	1	.. [5]	.. [5]	3
Washington	15	29	35	33
West Virginia	0	0	24	27
Wisconsin	19	24 [3]	27 [3]	31 [3]
Wyoming	5	21	22	22

[1] Rates based on population under 16 years of age estimated by the Social Security Board with the advice of the U. S. Bureau of the Census, as of July 1 of each year.
[2] Does not include Colorado.
[3] Includes some children aged 16 or over.
[4] Figures not available.
[5] Less than 1 child per 1,000.
Source: Public Aid for the Care of Dependent Children in Their Own Homes, by Dorothy R. Bucklin, *Social Security Bulletin,* Vol. 2, No. 4, April, 1939.

features tended to increase, and the administrative or supervisory function of the state was more clearly recognized and applied. There was also a marked increase in the amount of state money appropriated for all three categories of assistance, until 1931, when unemployment relief began to make heavy demands upon public funds. From 1931-1935 expenditures for categorical assistance remained fairly static, and constituted only a small percentage of total public relief expenditures.[59]

The values inherent in state participation were clearly stated by the White House Conference on child welfare held in 1931. The report of this conference on aid to dependent children recommended "provision of state funds, distributed to the local units according to need, with the object of equalizing resources on the same principle which operates in distribution

[59] Geddes, Anne E., *Trends in Relief Expenditures, 1910-1935.* Works Progress Administration, 1937, 117 pages.

of educational funds in many states." In 1935 the report of the Committee on Economic Security to the President of the United States was even more insistent. "Laws for aid to dependent children should be mandatory upon the local units, and state equalization funds should be made available to counties for aid purposes, in amounts sufficient to bring this aid throughout the state at least to a minimum level of adequacy, both as to number of families aided and amount of grant. If well administered, state aid will act as an effective powerful lever in raising administrative standards of investigations, budgetary practices and other procedures."

The report continues:

Federal grants-in-aid can be extended to this tax-supported and publicly administered form of child care without unusual administrative difficulties. Through Federal participation laws for aid to dependent children can be made effective in the States and in local areas which have made no provision, or have markedly inadequate provision, for this method of preserving family life for dependent children. Like the State fund in relation to the counties, a Federal fund would be an instrument for improving standards in backward States and would tend to equalize costs.[60]

This argument for Federal grants-in-aid was used with equal effect by the Committee on Economic Security in presenting the need for adequate aid to yet another category, the aged. No better evidence could have been produced than the facts and figures given in these reports which show the indifference and neglect of local governments when the leverage of state funds and state administrative pressure was lacking. The same type of evidence shows up the common failure of state governments to assume responsibility in the absence of any stimulus whatever from Washington.

FEDERAL RESPONSIBILITY

The Constitution of the United States gives to Congress the power "to lay and collect taxes, duties, imports, and excises, to pay debts, and provide for the common defense and general

[60] *Social Security in America.* pp. 246-48. See also Part III, Chapter 7 and Part IV, Chapter 14.

welfare of the United States." Upon the interpretation given to this clause of the Constitution has depended the policy of the Federal Government in regard to its responsibility for relief to people in need.

In 1854, Dorothea Dix,[61] pioneer reformer, presented to Congress a moving appeal for Federal aid in the form of millions of acres of land to be given to the states for the benefit of the insane. A bill to this effect was passed by Congress and vetoed by President Pierce.[62] In his veto message the President maintained that the welfare clause [63] in the Constitution did not give the Congress the power to provide for the indigent insane, nor for any indigent persons. He argued that if the Congress had power to make provision for indigent insane outside of the limits of the District of Columbia, it had "the same power to provide for the indigent who are not insane; and thus to transfer to the Federal Government the charge of all the poor in all the States." He further stated, applying the same notion—that help to the poor makes them more helpless

[61] Dorothea Lynde Dix, a native of New England frontier lumber country, a teacher and philanthropist, was the greatest inspiration of the humanitarian movement to improve the cruel treatment of the insane. As a result of her untiring efforts during the half century between 1830 and 1880 "thousands of demented souls were released from dungeons, caves, and prisons, and placed in hospitals where they were given care and treatment befitting the sick and unfortunate of humanity. She popularized institutional treatment for mental diseases and aroused a social conscience; and through her personal activities thirty-two hospitals were established in America and several in Europe as well. Also at least two in Japan may be traced to the inspiration which she gave Jugio Arinori Mori while he was the Japanese chargé d'affaires in Washington." Marshall, Helen E., *Dorothea Dix, Forgotten Samaritan,* University of North Carolina Press, Chapel Hill, North Carolina. 1937. 298 pages, Bibliography.

[62] See Abbott, Edith, *Some American Pioneers in Social Welfare.* Select Documents with editorial notes. University of Chicago Press, 1937. 189 pages. *Dorothea L. Dix, 1802-1887.* pp. 107-124. Reprinted from *Social Service Review.* I. 117-37. Also Breckinridge, *op. cit.*

[63] "Section 8. The Congress shall have Power to lay and collect Taxes, Duties, Imposts and Excises, to pay the Debts and provide for the common Defense and general Welfare of the United States; but all Duties, Imposts and Excises shall be uniform throughout the United States." The Constitution of the United States of America. U. S. Gov't Printing Office, Washington, D. C. 1935. page 10.

and dependent—to governmental units as had been applied to individual paupers, "that if Congress is to make provision for such objects, the fountains of charity will be dried up at home, and the several states instead of bestowing their own means on the social wants of their own people, may themselves, through the strong temptation, which appeals to states as to individuals, become humble supplicants for the bounty of the Federal Government, reversing their true relation to this Union." [64]

For more than three quarters of a century Pierce's veto controlled Federal relief policy; and it was not reversed until 1933 when the Federal Emergency Relief Act became law.[65]

At the time of President Pierce's veto, the making of land grants by the Federal Government to the states had been for years an accepted practice. In fact, the right of the Federal Government to give the states both land and money had never been questioned.

Federal Grants to the States

The practice of making land grants began in 1785 when Congress decreed that a portion of the public domain in what was then the Northwest Territory should be set aside for the maintenance of public schools. In 1787, Congress provided "that land not amounting to more than two townships be given perpetually for the purpose of a university" to each state, and it soon became the custom to give each new state, upon its admission into the Union, the two townships permitted for this purpose. This policy was regularly followed until 1889. More than half a million acres of land have been transferred to the states to be used as seats of government or to defray the costs of erecting public buildings.[66]

[64] Extract from *Congressional Globe* (33rd Congress, 1st session, May 3, 1854), pp. 1061-63. Quoted by Breckinridge, *op. cit.*, p. 221. Compare statements by President Hoover and Mr. Gifford in Part II, Chapters 3 and 4.

[65] See Part II, Chapters 5 and 6, for arguments for and against Federal relief.

[66] More than seven hundred thousand acres of national lands were turned over to the newly created State of Ohio by an Act of 1802, and since that time every state in the Union has benefited by Congressional generosity. See MacDonald, Austin F., *Federal Aid*, Thomas Crowell Co.,

In 1862, eight years after the failure of Dorothea Dix's effort to secure Federal land for the care of the insane, the first college land-grant act was passed by Congress and signed by President Lincoln. This act provided for the endowment and support of state agricultural colleges. In 1887 the Hatch Act authorized agricultural experiment stations for which $15,000 a year of Federal funds was appropriated to each state and territory. Since that time and particularly during the last quarter of a century, the growth of the Federal subsidy system has been phenomenal and has kept pace with the rapid and necessary centralization of government aided by fast transport and communication. In 1912 total payments from the Federal Treasury to the states were approximately $8,000,000. In 1921 the payments amounted to two and one-half times the subsidies of the preceding year, and by 1925 they had risen to $147,000,000, an increase of more than 1,700% over 1912. These grants to the states were made for a number of different purposes. Highways and the National Guard took the largest amounts, vocational education and agricultural extension work came next, then the agricultural colleges, the experiment stations and funds appropriated under the oil leasing act. Smaller sums went to the states also for vocational rehabilitation, forest extension and fire prevention, and in 1927 nearly $900,000 for maternity and infant hygiene, appropriated under the Sheppard-Towner Act of 1921.[67] This appropriation for health work with mothers and children financed a program which touched the field of relief more closely than any of the others. It was pre-eminently "welfare work," the first Federal measure of the kind since the futile appeal of Dorothea Dix. In 1929 the Act lapsed because Congress failed to continue the necessary appropriations.

New York, 1928; *Agricultural Extension System of the U. S.*, by C. B. Smith and M. C. Wilson, 1930; *A History of Agricultural Education in the U. S., 1785-1925*, by A. C. True, 1929; and *Survey of Land-Grant Colleges and Universities*, Agricultural Extension Service, 1930.

[67] The following year, 1928, $1,585,000 of Federal funds were spent under this Act, which was administered by the Federal Children's Bureau.

For a discussion of the American subsidy system see Austin F. MacDonald, *op. cit.*, from which these figures are taken. See also Bibliography for other references on this subject.

Emergency Appropriations

The Federal records before 1933 show many Congressional appropriations for relief but in every case the funds were granted for a specific purpose to meet an immediate emergency need.

Beginning in 1827 with an appropriation of $20,000 for "Sufferers from fire at Alexandria, Virginia," Congress made 31 relief appropriations, totaling $11,128,500 during the ensuing one hundred years for the direct aid of sufferers from flood, fire, cyclone, earthquake, Indian raids, grasshopper plagues, scourges, epidemics, and drought. Also in 1867 and 1868 funds were appropriated for general relief purposes in behalf of the destitute in the southern states.[68]

Numerous efforts were made in vain by members of Congress to secure some form of Federal aid for unemployment relief in the depressions of 1893-4, 1914 and 1921-2. In the second Cleveland Administration (1895-99) Senator Peffer, of Kansas, introduced a bill for the immediate relief of want and destitution throughout the country. In discussing this measure the senator prophesied that the time would come when for all such purposes as relief "state lines must be utterly abolished." Other bills were introduced without success to provide employment and to investigate the causes of the depression. During the two Wilson administrations, vain attempts were made to provide a system of employment offices, unemployment and old-age insurance, and a system of public works.

The most significant bill, in view of the adverse stand on the subject taken by the Federal Administration in the early

[68] In addition to these appropriations for relief within the United States a number of grants were made for sufferers in foreign countries, notably the sufferers from the earthquake in Japan, and from disasters in the World War. Large sums were made available to the American Relief Administration for food to relieve the distress of war sufferers in Eastern Europe. See also Part II, Chapter 3. A list of these Federal appropriations and other "relief" legislation (1803-1931) was incorporated in the Congressional Record in February, 1933, as part of the hearings on Senate Bill 5125, *To provide Federal aid for unemployment relief.* The appropriations for direct domestic relief are given in Appendix A. See also Part II, Chapter 4, below.

years of the recent depression, was a measure [69] providing for public works which was introduced during the Harding Administration. The bill, which resembled in many respects some of the proposals made in 1931 and 1932, was favored by Mr. Hoover, who was then the Secretary of Commerce, and Chairman of President Harding's Conference on Unemployment.

Federal Welfare

Although there was until 1933 a consistent denial of Federal responsibility for relief to persons in need, many departments of the Federal Government had developed welfare activities which involved a wide variety of service functions. In addition to the programs which involve grants-in-aid to the states, there were the correctional and penal institutions for Federal offenders; provisions for Indians who live on United States reservations and over whom the states have no jurisdiction; care for disabled soldiers and sailors who have served the United States; provision for those afflicted with some contagious disease, e.g., leprosy, not found in sufficiently large numbers to justify state provision. Pensions for veterans might also be included, but since they are not necessarily awarded on a basis of need they probably should not be considered in the same category as the others.[70]

The Children's Bureau of the Department of Labor stands out as undoubtedly the most important welfare activity of the Federal Government before the recent depression. Created in 1912, it was directed by Congress "to investigate and report . . . upon all matters pertaining to the welfare of children and child life among all classes of our people." From the first the Bureau has served as a clearing house of information. One of its major functions has always been research and the conducting of field studies on all phases of child health and child welfare.[71]

[69] S. 2749.
[70] For list of Federal welfare activities and expenditures, see *Recent Social Trends in the United States*, McGraw-Hill, 1934. Vol. II. Page 1259 ff.
[71] *The Children's Bureau: Yesterday, Today, and Tomorrow.* Government Printing Office, Washington, 1937. See also Part I, Chapter 2.

The establishment of the Children's Bureau was practically coincident with the first Mothers' Aid laws, and the Bureau rendered invaluable service to the states in advising upon every aspect of this program, as well as upon the subsequent development of state departments of welfare concerned with child care and protection. It has given distinguished service in the fields of child labor, child health and juvenile delinquency.[72]

The Social Work Year Book of 1929 listed no less than 21 [73] offices, bureaus and departments of the Federal Government which were then responsible, in the opinion of the editors, for some form of welfare work. Not one of these activities, however, involved relief to persons in need,[74] unless a portion of the expenditures of the Indian Bureau might be put under this heading.

It is therefore no exaggeration to say that until the recent depression, Federal relief has been limited to relatively few emergency appropriations for disaster sufferers in this country and abroad. The tradition of local responsibility was faithfully kept. State governments had done little to supplement local funds; the Federal Government had done practically nothing at all. The principles embodied in the English Poor Law of 1601 and the interpretation which President Pierce had given in 1854 to the "welfare clause" in the Federal Constitution, were still effective in 1929.

[72] The Children's Bureau administered the first Federal Child Labor Law, 1917-18; and the Federal Maternity and Infancy Act, 1921-29.

[73] Immigration, Education, Home Economics, Industrial Housing and Transportation, Labor Statistics, Mines, Naturalization, Veterans' Administration, Public Health, Standards, Census, Vocational Education, Children's Bureau, Employment Service, Forest Service, Indian Affairs, Dept. of Justice, National Park Service, Conciliation Service, Women's Bureau, and Civil Service Commission.

[74] Outside of the District of Columbia.

Chapter 2

Private Versus Public Responsibility

~~~~~~

The Case Against Public Outdoor Relief

Throughout the nineteenth century the theories of the English economist, Malthus, had a marked effect upon American thinking and practice in regard to the poor. Malthus held that the poor were responsible for their own misery and destitution, that they had no "right" to public relief, and should be left to the mercies of private benefactors to whom they should "be bound by the strongest ties of gratitude." [1]

In American experience with early public relief this philosophy was reinforced by the fear and suspicion engendered by ill-equipped officials and the harsh methods which they used in administering local relief. Each of the depressions which have followed in a chain since the Industrial Revolution added to relief expenditures, to the evident abuses of the system of administering aid and to the general distrust in which public relief was held, not only by the charitable organizations formed by private citizens but by the general public.

Even in the depression of 1857 administration of public relief either through an already established public agency, as in Boston, or through an emergency set-up, as in Chicago, raised doubts in the minds of those concerned. Each system involved danger of political patronage, which resulted in suffering on the part of the needy. Inadequately equipped public officials were entrusted with the expenditure of large relief funds. The controversy over the superior advantages of public or private relief, which was to be prolonged over many decades, had already begun.[2]

---

[1] Abbott, Edith, "Abolish the Pauper Laws," *Social Service Review.* March, 1934. See also Report of the Royal Commission on the Poor Laws, 1834, and the English Poor Law Amendment Act of 1834.

[2] Feder, Leah Hannah, *Unemployment Relief in Periods of Depression: A Study of Measures Adopted in Certain American Cities.* Russell Sage Foundation. New York. 1936. 384 pages. Chapter II, p. 23.

This belief in the superiority of private over public relief was held by the early private charity organization societies founded in this country in the 1870's after the model of the London society.[3] Their development was coincident with and probably in large measure a reaction to the spread of abuse and corruption in public relief which followed the depression of 1873. The manifest evils which prevailed, particularly in the large cities, only served to reinforce the notions that private agencies were superior, that it was useless to try to reform public administration and that, therefore, outdoor relief should be abolished. And it *was* abolished during the last quarter of the nineteenth century in eight of the largest cities in the country,[4] not to be undertaken again in most of them on any considerable scale until the beginning of the great depression in 1929.

Belief in the adequacy of private agencies was further strengthened by the apparent and unexpected negative results of this drastic action which took place in Brooklyn, in the middle of the winter of 1879. When relief was cut off there appeared to be no additional suffering and there was no sudden influx of appeals to the private societies. The unforeseen and extraordinary experiences of Brooklyn and Philadelphia, in which much the same thing happened, are discussed at some length by two outstanding social welfare leaders of that day, Seth Low, of the Brooklyn Bureau of Charities, and Mrs. Josephine Shaw Lowell, a member of the New York State Board of Charities, both reaching the same conclusions.

Until 1879, public outdoor relief was given by the county [Kings] to the amount of $100,000 or more yearly; it was then cut off in the middle of winter, without warning, without any substitute being provided, and the result was—nothing.

In fact, except for the saving of the money and the stopping of petty political corruption which had been carried on by means of the relief, and the cessation of the spectacle of hundreds of people

[3] The Buffalo Society was founded in 1877. 15 others were organized before the end of 1879. See Family Welfare Societies, *Social Work Year Book, 1929*, Russell Sage Foundation, 1929.

[4] Brooklyn, New York City, Baltimore, Philadelphia, Washington, St. Louis, Kansas City, San Francisco. See Johnson, Fred R., "Public Agencies for Needy Families," *Social Work Year Book, 1929*.

passing through the streets with baskets of provisions furnished by the public, it would have been impossible to discover that the relief had been stopped.[5]

The stoppage of public out-door relief, wonderful as it seems, appears to have thrown absolutely no additional burden upon the only general relief-giving society in Brooklyn, the Society for Improving the Condition of the Poor. . . . Both in Philadelphia and in Brooklyn, out-door relief was attacked primarily because it was prostituted to political ends, and was demoralizing in its administration. In neither city has there yet appeared the slightest cause for regret at the abolition of the system. . . . Of Philadelphia, as of Brooklyn, it may be said that the public out-door relief has been found to be unnecessary. . . . No reason . . . occurs to the writer why a similar experience would not follow the abolition of out-door relief in any city or town sufficiently large to enable private benevolence to organize and act in concert . . . and that out-door relief, in the United States as elsewhere, tends inevitably and surely to increase pauperism; that in towns and cities it is not needed; that even in villages it can probably be dispensed with. . . . Whenever society has agents enough to organize relief, it can give, through private sources, all the out-door relief needed.[6]

The persistence of this doctrine and the extent of its influence upon the philosophy and practice of charity societies can best be shown by a succession of statements made at intervals since the 1870's by leaders of the private organization movement and by public officials and others interested in the welfare responsibilities of government.

First of all, it is worth noting that, as the depression of 1873-4 was largely responsible for the establishment of the permanent private agencies of the powerful charity organization movement, it also saw the first of that series of annual meetings of state public welfare officials which was to grow into the National Conference of Charities and Correction and become still later the National Conference of Social Work. In view of the fact that this conference was for many years before the recent depression dominated by private social work

[5] Lowell, Josephine Shaw, *Public Relief and Private Charity*, G. P. Putnam's Sons, 1884, New York. 111 pages.

[6] Set forth by Mr. Low in 1881 before the National Conference of Charities and Correction.

interests and philosophy, it is most significant to recall that it was started by state public welfare officials in 1874, as a Conference of Boards of Public Charities under the auspices of the American Social Science Association.

At the first conference in New York, September, 1874, attended by representatives of four state boards of public charities,[7] the delegates discussed at length The Laws of Pauper Settlement, and the Best Mode of Administering Poor Law Relief. Similar broad questions, such as The Causes and Prevention of Pauperism, Municipal and Private Charities, Organization of Charities in Cities, Poor Farms and Pauperism, Public or Private Outdoor Relief, Outdoor Relief in Relation to Charity Organization, are among the subjects given prominence on the annual programs during the following twenty-five years.

During these years relatively few speakers agreed with the lone official who stated in 1877, "I would have the attention of the community directed to the proper use of outdoor relief and to the methods of improving it. I don't think the youngest of us will live to see it abolished," [8] or with the official who maintained in 1891 "that relief should be dispensed by public authorities only."

. . . all relief afforded the poor should be public and dispensed under the authority of the people, through their representatives elected or appointed. The funds for relief should be gathered by assessment of taxation, thus making the burden equal among rich and poor.[9]

The great preponderance of opinion was in favor of private charity and followed the arguments set forth so eloquently by Mr. Low and Mrs. Lowell, already quoted.[10]

[7] Abbott, Edith, *Some American Pioneers in Social Welfare,* University of Chicago Press, 1937, p. 177. See also Part I, Chapter 1.

[8] *Proceedings* of the National Conference of Charities and Correction, 1877, p. 59. F. B. Sanborn, delegate from the State Board of Massachusetts.

[9] Conference of Charities and Correction, 1891, Indianapolis, p. 28. Arguments in Favor of Public Outdoor Relief, by Isaac P. Wright, St. Paul, Minnesota.

[10] See p. 40.

In 1891 at the National Conference of Charities and Correction, C. R. Henderson, of Detroit, made the following statement in which the influence of Malthus is noticeable:

The system [outdoor relief] tends to excite hostility to the State itself. First, relief educates a large class to look to government for help; and, when this is received, the feeling of dependence increases. The poor man has become a pauper, a beggar. A willing pauper is near to being a thief. As the State excites hope which it cannot fulfil, a time comes when the pauper is a public enemy. It is in this class that the worst foes of order are found, the only real proletariat we have. As the State cannot distribute its funds fairly, discontent is aroused in the neighborhood where aid is given. One poor man cannot see why he is not aided as much as his next-door neighbor, since he is quite as poor and has more children.

Having been educated by the State to be a beggar, he turns upon the State because it does not recognize his demand for support to be based on "natural rights."

None of these considerations weigh against personal and voluntary charity, which is a favor and not a legal obligation, and which may be suspended when the demand is made in the name of right.[11]

The depression of 1893-4 revealed the strength of the private agencies which, in the cities at least, "had outstripped the public relief agencies in the interval since the last depression."[12]

Public Relief Defended

A powerful reaction to this defense of private charity came from another quarter. Labor and the friends of labor became strong advocates of "public assistance as a means of rescuing thrifty workingmen from demoralization at the hands of sentimental almsgivers." Miss Feder gives citations on this point, which are worth quoting at length not only to light up the historical sequence but because of the illumination they gave to issues which have been raised during the recent great depression.

[11] *Proceedings* of the National Conference of Charities and Correction, Indianapolis, 1891. Public Outdoor Relief, by C. R. Henderson, Detroit, Michigan.
[12] Feder, *op. cit.*, p. 126.

Stanton Coit, the founder of one of the earliest settlements in the country and a staunch supporter of the early trade union movement, thus writes on the subject:

"It is to be deeply deplored that . . . the people who started the Charity Organization Society were tainted with laissez-faire doctrines and extreme individualistic theories. They did not see that the organization and unification of all relief agencies and methods cannot possibly be brought about by private efforts. The results of years of work by the Charity Organization Society may be swept away in one season of unusual distress by sentimentalists and by newspaper advertising schemes for relieving the poor. Scientific philanthropists will some day learn that charity organization is a distinctive municipal function. Who but the city can prevent the dispensing of free bread, and can limit the relief of each agency to a given district, so that there shall be no waste or overlapping? Who but the city can gather, week by week, full and accurate statistics of the condition of the unemployed? . . . Who but the city can compel every agency to follow careful methods to avoid fraud? In short, the city should grant licenses to relief agencies and regulate their methods." [13]

Miss Feder continues:

Although charity organization societies were set up to reach all groups in society, labor, both skilled and unskilled, regarded these agencies with suspicion and dislike, holding that most of their clients were the "chronic, if not vicious, poor," and that one of their primary purposes was to prevent imposition upon charitable givers. It was perhaps not surprising that some held this to be the chief function of the agencies and criticised the private agencies for their lack of helpfulness in other directions:

"The ordinary charitable institution as now constituted is not in touch with the industrial conditions. Such societies are organized for the relief of pauperism. They are so well accustomed to deal with the degraded or particularly unfortunate class that they necessarily lose a certain sort of tact and generous discrimination which is needed in dealing with men and women, who, under ordinary conditions, are steady wage-earners. Although probably by far the larger number of visitors or agents utilized by these societies perform the work of investigating with praiseworthy discrimination and appreciation of the difficulties of the honest needy, still, the inquisitorial and repellant attitude assumed by those who

[13] Feder, *op. cit.* Quotation from *The Forum*, Vol. 17, May, 1894.

apparently regard the chief duty of a relief body to detect imposition reflects unfortunately upon the work of a relief association as a whole." [14]

Most relief workers on either the private or public side were chiefly bent on destructive and critical comment regarding the opposition. In fact, constructive proposals and helpful statements regarding public outdoor relief hardly appear in the discussions of social welfare leaders before 1897 when the so-called "reforms" of the Indiana Poor Law were reported and discussed with much interest.[15] At that time Professor Charles R. Henderson, of the University of Chicago, who had, six years before, expressed a radically different point of view, called attention to the fact that:

. . . of all agencies for the relief of the poor, governmental agencies are by far the most important. The State assists more widows, orphans, defectives, prisoners, aged persons and sick than all church and private persons combined.[16]

As though in answer to this advocate of public relief, George S. Wilson, of Washington, D. C., reported to the National Conference in 1900 that he had been corresponding with workers in some twenty-two smaller cities, nearly all of whom were heartily in favor of private rather than public outdoor relief. Many, in fact, favored wiping out the latter, though no one believed that his own community was quite ready for this step!

Mr. Wilson's own major objections lay in the fact that "people look upon public outdoor relief as a right and learn to depend upon it in a manner entirely different from that in which they regard private relief. . . ." He gave the following incident as an illustration:

Some two years ago in Washington our Associated Charities was called upon to distribute the sum of $1,000 of public money, the same being a balance in the hands of the public authorities from the appropriation made for medical relief. In some way or other the poor people learned of the presence of this fund even before it was

[14] Feder, *op. cit.* Report of the Massachusetts Board to Investigate the Subject of the Unemployed, March 13, 1895. Part V.

[15] See p. 24.

[16] *Proceedings* of the National Conference of Charities and Correction, Toronto, Ontario, 1897. Poor Laws of the United States.

known to all of our agents, and they quickly made demands upon it. They came with the old story that the money was for the poor. They were poor: therefore, they had a right to a share of it. The administration of this fund of $1,000 caused us more trouble than would have been caused by the administration of $5,000 of private relief funds, and the effect upon the poor was wholly unsatisfactory.[17]

Private Agencies Organize Nationally

The first years of the twentieth century saw the beginning of a movement which was to have far-reaching effects upon the development of private relief and family welfare agencies throughout the country. Mr. Francis H. McLean was then the Superintendent of the Brooklyn Bureau of Charities.[18] His interests extended far outside his own city, however, and had brought him into close touch with a small group of charity organization leaders who had formed a committee and interested themselves in extending charity organization throughout the United States. In this connection Mr. McLean conducted a wide and painstaking correspondence with cities which sought his advice about the organization of their charitable work.

But correspondence was not enough. Miss Mary Richmond gives the following account of the way in which the new movement grew out of this advisory service by mail:

. . . letters at their best are a poor substitute for personal contact. The committee counted itself fortunate when, in the autumn of 1907, it was enabled, by a contribution from the Russell Sage Foundation, to induce Mr. McLean to become its field secretary, and devote his whole time to the study of local conditions in city after city, submitting to each a suggested form of organization or reorganization, and serving each, so far as possible, in working the proposed plan out. No visit was paid without an invitation from those locally interested, but many invitations were forthcoming, and the results achieved were so practical and far-reaching that the Russell Sage Foundation decided a year ago (October, 1909) to establish a Char-

[17] Wilson, George S., "Outdoor Relief in Relation to Charity Organization," *Proceedings* of the National Conference of Charities and Correction. Topeka, 1900.

[18] A private agency. See p. 40 above, for Mrs. Lowell's account of the discontinuance of public outdoor relief in Brooklyn in 1879.

ity Organization Department devoted to extension work and to kindred endeavors.[19]

From the Charity Organization Department, thus established by the Russell Sage Foundation, under the directorship of Mary Richmond, was to develop five years later the national organization [20] now known as the Family Welfare Association of America. Mr. McLean became its first Director.

In this first pamphlet on charity organization, the introduction to which has just been quoted, Mr. McLean's advice to small cities was confined to methods and plans for setting up private charitable agencies. The "public relief officers" were mentioned only among the many people in the community with whom the new society would necessarily have to deal. In regard to public funds he gave the following warning:

Avoid entangling alliances in the form of money from public sources. You will find in the long run that such aid will hurt rather than help you. Private citizens are far more disinclined to give if they know that you are drawing from the public crib, even if you are drawing only a quarter of what you need. There is not so serious an objection to accepting free office space in the city hall, and this is often done.

While this development was taking place in the family welfare field, powerful influences were at work in behalf of children and these were winning growing recognition of the responsibility of government for their welfare.

The Controversy over Mothers' Aid

James E. West, Chief Executive of the Boy Scouts of America, himself an orphanage boy, led a movement on behalf of

[19] Introduction by Mary Richmond to *The Formation of Charity Organization Societies in Smaller Cities,* by Francis H. McLean. The Charity Organization Department of the Russell Sage Foundation, New York, 1910. See also later pamphlets by Mr. McLean: *The Organization of Family Social Work Societies in Smaller Cities,* 1923; *Organizing Family Social Work in Smaller Cities,* 1932. Published by the Family Welfare Association of America. New York.

[20] American Association for Organizing Charity. The name was changed in 1919 to American Association for Organizing Family Social Work and in 1929 to Family Welfare Association of America.

child welfare which resulted in the calling of the first White House Conference on Dependent Children by President Theodore Roosevelt in 1909. This Conference aroused a national interest in child welfare which bore lasting fruit in the creation of the Federal Children's Bureau. Moreover, the principle enunciated by the Conference, that poverty alone was no excuse for the separation of children from their mothers, led directly to the movement for mothers' pensions. Two years later the first mothers' aid laws were passed in Illinois and Wisconsin.[21]

This move to entrust to the government a special responsibility for allowances to young children in their own homes, did not proceed, however, without strong opposition from the charity organization movement. Leaders in social work were split into two distinct camps. The publications and conference discussions of the period are filled with arguments for and against. All the distrust and suspicion of governmental agencies which had accumulated in the general charity organization movement during fifty years of bitter experience came to the fore. Already private agencies were giving allowances to mothers of thousands of fatherless children. Miss Richmond claimed that these children were receiving far better care than they possibly could if they became the charges of politically appointed public officials.

True to the individualistic philosophy of the case work field, of which she had become the acknowledged leader, she maintained that the type of care which each family and child received was far more important than the auspices of the agency from which they received it. She held no brief against the public agency as such, but insisted that no responsibility of this kind be given to any governmental body until it was prepared to provide an administration with standards of social case work comparable to approved practice in charity organization societies.

The advocates of mothers' aid legislation were the spiritual successors of Dorothea Dix, who had vainly tried, sixty years before, to obtain help for the insane from the Federal Govern-

[21] See pp. 26 and 38.

ment.[22]   They believed in the responsibility of government for the welfare of all its citizens, and especially of the poor and helpless. Recognizing the weaknesses of the local poor relief systems, they proposed to make the states partly responsible for the care of fatherless children, and by special laws create for them a new category to be dealt with on a level above that of ordinary public outdoor relief. Undoubtedly the agitation for mothers' aid legislation was to some extent responsible for a most interesting change of attitude on the part of the private agencies which took place at about this time. They began to study seriously the methods of poor relief administration and to recognize, in a practical way, that they might be improved.

The First Local Departments of Public Welfare

After 1890 there had for a period been relatively little discussion of public outdoor relief at the National Conference of Charities and Correction. But in 1915 the Conference came back to the subject in earnest. One of the reasons for this awakened interest was no doubt the fact that within five years no less than twenty-eight states had enacted mothers' aid legislation! Amos Butler, secretary of the Indiana State Board of Charities, summed up the situation in his address on "Official Outdoor Relief and the State."

From 1876 until recently the work of private charities has been magnified. While we are all proud of what private relief has accomplished, it as yet does not seem able to do all that is required.

Now the pendulum seems to be swinging to the other extreme and there appears a demand for more official relief, though that is not what it is called. There are "funds to parents," "mothers' aid," "widows' pensions," "old age pensions," "pensions for the blind." To my mind there is no essential difference between grants from public funds such as these and what we have always known as official outdoor relief. Certain persons are set in a class apart, yet they are all poor persons, and assistance given them in their homes, from public funds, call it what we will, is in reality official outdoor relief.

There is undoubtedly a place for official relief. What we need to do is to correlate it and administer it in the least harmful way.

[22] See p. 33.
See also Abbott, Grace, *The Child and the State*, Vol. II, Sec. IV, Mothers' Aid. University of Chicago Press, Chicago, 1938.

Is it not probable that much of the disrepute into which it has fallen is due to the fact that it has been looked upon as a local problem, while we have concerned ourselves mainly with the betterment of our state charities? Yet it is from local conditions that our state charges come. The state needs to recognize this fact and to extend its supervision to include the local charity, which, unwisely administered, is but a feeder for the larger state institution.[23]

In spite of this change in attitude, improvements in the administration of public outdoor relief came about very slowly. Many municipal agencies became "public welfare departments." They began to invite criticism of their efforts and were promptly told that their relief work was inefficient. Some of them attempted to set up new standards, to place emphasis on "good investigations," and references to "trained social workers" appear more frequently in their reports.[24] The ideal seemed to be that public welfare departments should use the methods of social case work developed by private agencies, as far as was consistent with the conditions under which they operated.

The Department of Social Welfare of the City and County of Denver was the first municipal agency of any considerable size to employ as director a social worker of training and experience gained in a private social agency of recognized standing. Miss Gertrude Vaile, a former District Secretary of the United Charities of Chicago, came to the 1915 Conference in Baltimore from Denver where she had been appointed secretary of the City Department. Miss Vaile not only stated her belief in the responsibility of government for the relief of persons in need, but announced that distinct progress had been made in her public agency in the application of the methods of social case work as practiced under private auspices. She said in part:

[23] *Proceedings* of the National Conference of Charities and Correction, Baltimore, 1915. "Official Outdoor Relief and the State," by Amos W. Butler.

[24] For a review of developments during this period see: *Social Forces*, Vol. X, No. 3, March, 1932. University of North Carolina Press. "Public Welfare and Social Work. Trends in Municipal Administration of Public Welfare: 1900-1930," by Mary Phlegar Smith, Ohio University.

I believe that the principle of poor relief by public authority is absolutely right. Not only should a government, in the mere exercise of its police power, be prepared to see that no one shall be driven to desperation for lack of the necessities of life; and not only is the whole burden of relief unduly heavy to be borne by a generous few, —but in the search-light of the modern spirit another fact stands out with glaring distinctness. The poor and suffering are so, not only by their own fault or peculiar misfortune, but also by the fault of us all. Government permits working and living conditions which create poverty and sickness—yea, even licenses some of them; and it is only just that organized society as a whole should struggle with the responsibility and pay the cost.

It would seem necessary, then, to find some division of the field that is clear and convincing. In the past, this division has come upon the quality of the work done and the element of personal service which was given by the private and not ordinarily by the public administration. But if that difference is to be removed, as I think it must be, and soon will be, what useful divisions remain? [25]

This question is evidence of a turning point in the discussions of public and private relief. In cities where such "socialized" public welfare departments developed during the next fifteen years, social workers no longer concerned themselves with the *rights* of persons in need to public relief; they no longer discussed whether or not public outdoor relief should exist. The questions at issue now revolved chiefly about the division of work between the public and private agencies and which types of cases each should accept.

Public and Private Agencies in the 1920's

During and after the World War the rapid and wide expansion of Home Service in both urban and rural areas by the American Red Cross threw the weight of professional interest again into private social work. This was continued and intensified to such an extent by the development of group organization of private agencies such as community chests and councils of social agencies in the larger cities that, by the end of the 1920's, the majority of city social workers in private agencies

[25] Vaile, Gertrude, "Principles and Methods of Outdoor Relief." *Proceedings* of the National Conference of Charities and Correction, Baltimore, 1915. University of Chicago Press.

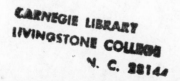

no longer gave much thought to the welfare activities of government.

Throughout these years of armistice, nevertheless, public welfare kept up a steady development. Under the leadership of the Children's Bureau many state departments of welfare were progressing with programs for child care and protection, and almost every state enacted mothers' aid legislation. The Federal and state agencies had little or no official relationship with local public outdoor relief, and therefore little contact with the city public welfare departments. The task of "socializing" these local departments, therefore, was assumed by the private family welfare societies. To a large extent the family agencies took this responsibility upon themselves with mingled reluctance, condescension, and missionary zeal. For instance, in 1918, the American Association for Organizing Charity passed resolutions urging its member societies to take advantage of opportunities to socialize public charities, and to agree upon a division of work with socialized departments based on types of family problems, rather than upon differences of function.

In spite of these improvements, however, the family welfare leaders continued to be skeptical of both the soundness and practicability of public aid. This conservative position, which continued well into the unemployment emergency of the 30's, was set forth again in 1923 by Miss Richmond, who restated in this new problem the principles she had already laid down as one of the arguments against mothers' aid legislation.

Miss Richmond maintained that the most important single thing about relief:

. . . is not whether it is paid for out of public funds or out of private funds, but whether its recipients are being helped to effective living or not.

There are a few public outdoor relief departments in the United States of which it can be truthfully said that they are advancing the permanent welfare of the families that are their clients. All of these few are exposed to the danger that a change of administration may wipe out the gains they have laboriously made. The best protection they have is the private agencies in their several communities, when these agencies are also doing good social case work in families and understand, therefore, the conditions necessary to make such work a success in the public departments.

The day may come when public family welfare departments can assure a greater continuity of policy (and that policy progressive) than the private agencies can. When that day arrives, I shall favor making a large part of our present family social work activities public. Meanwhile I must continue to favor extending public activities cautiously and as steadily as local conditions permit.[26]

The Annals of the American Academy of Political and Social Science for January, 1923, was devoted to discussion of "Public Welfare in the United States." It carried an article on "The Cooperation of Private and Public Welfare Agencies," by Joseph C. Logan, an outstanding southern representative of the charity organization movement, who was at that time manager of the Southern Division of the American Red Cross. Mr. Logan's observations were prophetic since they took a common-sense and clear position little held until ten years later:

The community of interest in public welfare shared both by the voluntary social agency and the political authority have not always prevented the private agency from viewing the government as an inimical and antagonistic body opposed to the constituents of the private agency, instead of being their political creature and the medium of the democratic expression of their ideals and purposes. On the other hand, the political authority has too often failed to recognize the voluntary agency in the field of social work as an indispensable ally. . . .

When the political authority concludes that any given service should be extended to all as a measure of public welfare, it *must* assume final responsibility for funds and administration. . . .

Much better relations would exist between the public and voluntary agencies if the elements of superiority in the voluntary agency were not regarded as inherent and therefore permanent. They have already been acquired, in some instances, by the public agencies. This will become increasingly the case with the development of efficiency in public service and with the right kind of cooperation on the part of voluntary agencies.

This issue of *The Annals* listed fourteen out of a possible forty city departments of public welfare in the country. Not

[26] *The Family.* Vol. III, No. 10, February, 1923. pp. 239-240. American Association for Organizing Family Social Work. New York.

more than half of the departments listed were actually administering outdoor relief. In fact, *The Annals,* as a whole, gave
relatively little space to the subject, being chiefly concerned
with the transition from the era of "charities and correction"
to that of a "public welfare" program which was not only
chiefly institutional, but also covered the fields of education
and health with which charity and poor relief had previously
had little to do. In fact the articles contain little to offset the
questioning and somewhat suspicious attitudes of the strongly
intrenched private family welfare leaders.

Although the "socializing" of public relief agencies by private organizations had been going on since 1910 when Mr. I. A.
Halbert was appointed superintendent of the newly created
Board of Public Welfare in Kansas City, no one of them was
given recognition by a national standard-setting agency until
1922. In that year the Denver City and County Bureau of
Charity was admitted to membership in the American Association for Organizing Family Social Work, which since its establishment in 1911, had admitted only private agencies. Undoubtedly the acceptance of the public agency in Denver was
due to the fact that the employment of a director from the
charity organization field seemed to offer assurance of the
maintenance of private agency standards.

The relationship of this national Family Welfare Association, with its private agency traditions and philosophy, to the
slowly developing field of public welfare, is indicative of the
general private-public attitude during the twenty years which
preceded the recent depression. This relationship is typified
in the membership policies of the Association.

Until 1926 the membership requirements were so worded as
automatically to exclude public agencies. The few which were
admitted up to that time came in as exceptions. Only since
1929 has equal consideration for membership been given to
public and private agencies and, even so, the Association included in February, 1939, only 12 public agencies in a total
membership of 230.[27]

[27] Bureau of Public Welfare, Denver, Colorado; Public Assistance Division, Washington, D. C.; Duval County Family Welfare Agency, Jackson-
ville, Florida; Cook Co. Bureau of Public Welfare, Chicago, Ill.; Webster
Co. Welfare Association, Fort Dodge, Iowa; New Orleans Department of

Public and Private Relief Just Before the Depression

By the late 20's Chicago, Detroit, Los Angeles, Boston, among the large cities; Nashville, Tennessee; Forth Worth, Texas; Syracuse, New York, and Louisville, Kentucky, of the middle group, and a number of smaller cities and rural counties had "socialized" departments of public welfare which administered outdoor relief. Nevertheless these public ventures were in the minority and the social work world was still dominated by private agency attitudes, philosophy and methods which so influenced public opinion that, when the depression came, community after community logically looked to the private agencies to meet the overwhelmingly increasing demands for relief. Community chests and financial social federations which had developed in most of the larger cities during the same period, therefore, bore the brunt of this community expectancy. It is undoubtedly true that wide dissemination through the years of arguments in favor of private charity and against public relief, expressed by such people as Malthus, Warner, Seth Low, Josephine Shaw Lowell, Mary Richmond and Francis McLean, who are quoted in the foregoing pages, had conditioned public opinion to a far greater extent than was realized even by many of the family welfare leaders themselves. This accounts for the wave of unbelief which swept over the social work world when the reports from the newly established Bureau of Social Statistics first made their appearance in 1929. The figures showed that in 1928, 71.6 percent of all relief in fifteen important cities was from public funds. The director of the new statistical agency presented them to the National Conference at San Francisco with these ominous words:

Whether we like it or not, government is already in the field of social work in a big way—on a scale so colossal, in fact, that even the

Public Welfare, New Orleans, Louisiana; Social Service Division, Department of Public Welfare, Detroit, Michigan; Kent Co. Welfare Relief Commission, Grand Rapids, Michigan; Department of Public Welfare, Cleveland, Ohio; Department of Health and Welfare, Fort Worth, Texas; Social Service Bureau, Danville, Virginia; Social Service Bureau, Petersburg, Virginia.

enormous efforts of the private societies seem dwarfed by comparison.[28]

The amazement with which this information was received and the significance attached to it are shown by the extent to which the figures are cited in the literature of the period. They appear like a refrain, in conference papers and reports, magazine articles, statements of policy and recommendations for programs put out by national and local agencies, both public and private. They are quoted with satisfaction and triumph by proponents of public welfare and with some consternation and trepidation by private agency executives.

This statistical evidence immediately and finally took the whole question of public versus private responsibility for relief out of the realm of conflicting theory into that of hard fact. During the next three years the increasing needs of the new mass of unemployed accomplished whatever was still needed to settle this public-private controversy of just one hundred years standing, from the time of Malthus in 1834 to the Federal Emergency Relief Administration in 1933.

The 1929 returns to the Bureau of Social Statistics confirmed the earlier report, by showing that "the lion's share of the rising burden of relief in at least twenty-two American cities, is borne by the taxpayers." [29] In spite of the general consternation aroused by these reports, few people probably realized at the time how truly the figures represented the relief situation throughout the country.

Although no system for gathering nationwide statistics was set up until the FERA was established in 1933, still, certain sources of information [30] already existed in 1929 which were

[28] *Proceedings* of the National Conference of Social Work, San Francisco, 1929. "Some Statistical Comparisons of Public and Private Family Social Work," by A. W. McMillen, Director, Registration of Social Statistics, University of Chicago.

[29] "Taxes and Private Relief Funds," A. W. McMillen, *Midmonthly Survey*, November, 1930.

[30] U. S. Department of Commerce, Bureau of the Census, annual reports, Financial Statistics of Cities Having a Population of Over 100,000, 1911-1931.

U. S. Department of Commerce, Bureau of the Census, special report,

later assembled and analyzed.[31]   These post-facto analyses revealed significant trends over the preceding twenty years not only in the percentage of public relief, but in the number of local units and total funds spent.   The figures, covering 1910 to 1935, showed that there had been a steady increase in the amounts spent from both public and private funds after 1910; this increase had been far more rapid than the growth in population during the same period.   The rate of increase in public relief, at least in the large cities, was much greater than the rate of increase of all governmental expenditures combined. The most rapid expansion had occurred in mothers' pensions (aid to dependent children).   For example, in New York City, in spite of the fact that there had been no general outdoor relief expenditures since 1879,[32] the major share of the total relief load had, for 14 years before the depression, been paid for out of public funds, in the form of relief to special classes, chiefly mothers with dependent children.

Although the peak in expenditures reached during the depression of 1920-22 had been followed by a temporary recession, relief had still continued to mount, giving evidence that the level of need was rising progressively year after year. Therefore the sharp upturn in expenditures which began in the fall of 1929 represented an acceleration of a tendency which was already manifest throughout the preceding two decades.[33]

The Case for Public Relief

Even before the momentous announcement of high percentages of public relief expenditures and months before the ex-

Relief Expenditures by Governmental and Private Organizations, 1929 and 1931.

Winslow, Emma A., Trends in Different Types of Public and Private Relief in Urban Areas, 1929-35, Publication No. 237. U. S. Department of Labor, Children's Bureau, 1937. The Urban Relief Series was transferred to the Social Security Board as of July, 1936.

Study made in 1926 by Ralph G. Hurlin, of the Russell Sage Foundation, "The Mounting Bill for Relief," *The Survey*, November 15, 1926. pp. 207-9.

[31] Geddes, Anne E., Trends in Relief Expenditures, 1910-1935. Division of Social Research, Works Progress Administration.

[32] See p. 40 above.

[33] Geddes, Anne E., *op. cit.*, pp. xiii, xiv, p. 1.   See also Appendix B.

treme pressures of the recent depression began, a few far-sighted social workers in private agencies raised their voices in defense of governmental relief. They challenged the skepticism and scorn with which private agencies in general regarded the public field, and they announced their own prophetic and socialized philosophy of governmental responsibility.

They believed that there existed a "collective responsibility for the inadequacies of a badly functioning economic system," and that public provision for persons in need was "socially mandatory." They deplored the fact that:

Opposition to the entrance of the state into the field hitherto occupied by private philanthropy is not limited to the taxpayer. Mistrust of the honesty and efficiency of the governmental machinery is often shared by the social worker. He is naturally alarmed at the entrance of the state as a competitor for fear that it would destroy the significant achievements of scientific social work. Hence, for instance, that opposition of prominent social workers of New York City to the widows' pension movement twelve years ago, which many of us are trying so hard to forget. Hence the surprising indifference of the rank and file of the professional social workers to such proposals as old-age pensions.[34]

They went so far as to claim that the future of social work lay in the public welfare field and that social workers themselves should be the first to deny that a generous government policy would have a dampening effect upon social work.

To bolster these claims and assertions they compared the conditions existing in Buffalo, Boston and Detroit, where public outdoor relief was extensively administered, with the situations in Cleveland, Baltimore, Philadelphia and St. Louis where the anti-public philosophy of the early charity organization leaders had prevailed. The conclusions drawn from the comparison were heavily in favor of the cities which were carrying the major relief burden through their public welfare departments.

These conclusions, made in the summer and fall of 1929, seemed extreme at that moment to the private social work field. In retrospect, however, they mark the turning point in

[34] Rubinow, I. M., "Can Private Philanthropy Do It?" *Social Service Review*. September, 1929.

the general social work philosophy and attitude toward public relief. During the following two years, as community chests and family welfare societies found it more and more difficult to carry the mounting relief load, their executives discovered it was almost as difficult to surrender deep-seated traditions in the face of needs which could be met only by the resources of government. That they did finally retreat before the inevitable is evident from the active support which they gave to public officials in their efforts to secure funds for unemployment relief from local and state governments and also from the Congress of the United States.

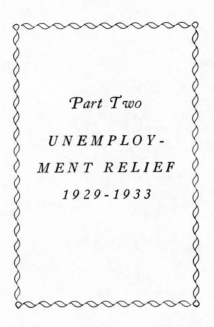

Part Two

U N E M P L O Y -

M E N T R E L I E F

1 9 2 9 - 1 9 3 3

4 *M*

Chapter 3

The President's Emergency Committee for Employment and the Struggle of Local Agencies

～～～～～～～～～～～～～～～～～～～～～～～～～～

The story of relief in the first few years of the 1929 depression is told in some detail because within that short period were concentrated a rapid succession of events which brought about important and dynamic changes in the philosophy, policies and programs of social work and public welfare. The forty-two months from the fatal October day in the New York Stock Exchange to the beginning of the Federal Emergency Relief Administration had more significance for the future of public welfare in this country than had any twenty-year period before that time.

The rapid and, to many, terrifying increase in the army of unemployed, the rising relief expenditures and the pressures upon inadequate and unprepared social work machinery, brought to a focus and into the national limelight the much debated and vital questions of governmental responsibility and sources of funds; the place of private agencies and community chests in relation to unemployment relief; the responsibility of state and Federal governments; and Federal loans versus grants-in-aid to the states.

During the first two years, 1929-1931, the private family agencies made a valiant attempt to carry staggering loads and, under the greatest pressure, to justify the faith of their leaders in the superiority of their methods over those of the public "dole" sysem.

In the midst of, and undoubtedly because of, the losing struggle to raise adequate funds and to care for the growing army of unemployed, the change in attitude toward public aid, which had begun in the 20's, moved rapidly to an almost com-

63

plete reversal of position. In the acknowledgment of governmental responsibility the private agencies and the community chests concurred. Public relief and public welfare had arrived, and had come to stay. Throughout the entire depression there was a continuous development of public relief agencies, at first, uneven, sporadic and entirely local; later, becoming stronger and more orderly during 1932 and 1933 as one state after another, and finally the Federal Government, went into the business of unemployment relief.[1]

The Beginning of the Depression

The first warning of coming disaster had already appeared in the spring of 1929 when the usual seasonal decrease in relief expenditures did not occur. At that time there were already 2,860,000 unemployed men and women in the United States.[2]

Throughout the summer, figures collected by the Children's Bureau from 120 cities showed that expenditures remained ominously higher than the levels of relief during the corresponding months of the year before. In October the sharp up-

[1] When the Federal Emergency Relief Act was passed in May, 1933, 22 states had appropriated funds for unemployment relief.

[2] According to estimates made by Robert R. Nathan for the President's Committee on Economic Security. All unemployment figures are from Estimates of Unemployment in the United States, 1929-35, by Robert R. Nathan, International Labour Office. Geneva. 1936. There are no official government estimates of unemployment but several organizations have prepared estimates. In addition to the Nathan estimates, the National Research League, the Alexander Hamilton Institute, the Cleveland Trust Company, the American Federation of Labor and the National Industrial Conference Board have prepared unemployment estimates. These estimates show the peak of unemployment to have been reached in March, 1933, ranging from the National Research League estimate of 17,920,000 to the National Industrial Conference Board estimate of 13,300,000. These various estimates of unemployment follow similar methods of computation. They are all derived from employment data. The total number of gainful workers is computed from 1930 Census data kept up-to-date by adjustment for the estimated increase in the working population. Then the total number of persons estimated from current employment series to be actually working is deducted from the estimated number of gainful workers. The remainder is the number of workers estimated to be unemployed. See Hopkins, Harry L., Spending to Save, p. 13. W. W. Norton & Co. New York.

turn began. December not only exceeded November but was nearly twice as high as the preceding December.[3]

The increase in the number of unemployed was even more spectacular. By January, 1930, it had jumped to over four million, nearly double the 1929 figure. In March, 600,000 more people were out of work. August was worse than March and the early summer seasonal work caused relatively little decrease in the monthly totals. Five million were unemployed in September, nearly seven million by the end of the year, eight million in the spring of 1931, and then a practically steady increase to the peak of thirteen to fifteen million in the spring of 1933.[4]

Public relief continued to carry an increasing share of the load.[5] In 1930 it more than doubled the amount spent in 1929 while private funds had increased only fifty percent. The following year they both tripled the totals for 1930.

For the first few months after the stock market crash, both public and private agencies took the increasing load in their stride. By spring they became alarmed. The Association of Community Chests and Councils and the Charity Organization Department of the Russell Sage Foundation sent out questionnaires to local chests and to family welfare agencies. Many agencies had spent all the money which had been budgeted for the entire year, others had used reserves, incurred deficits, or secured additional funds in one way or another. Demands for relief continued to increase. The general public, thoroughly conditioned to do so, expected that these needs would be met by the private agencies, and they in turn assumed the burden as a logical part of their job.

During the winter several governors had organized committees to review the relief situation. Government officials and industrial leaders tried to reassure the bewildered people, telling them that the "emergency" would not last long. In fact, they predicted an immediate come-back. Unemployment increased, however, and the situation was aggravated in the

[3] McMillan, A. W., "Taxes and Private Relief Funds," *Survey Midmonthly*, Nov., 1930.

[4] Nathan, 15,071,000. Other estimates range from 13,300,000 to 17,-000,000.

[5] See p. 57.

spring and summer by the first of a series of droughts which brought distress to several agricultural states hitherto not seriously affected.

In August, 1930, President Hoover called a conference of governors and appointed a national committee. The governors in turn appointed state committees. The American Red Cross set up a special fund to be spent through local chapters for drought relief.

At the Boston National Conference of Social Work in June, the American Association of Public Welfare Officials had been organized. The beginnings of this association, which was to play such an important part in the development of public welfare, seemed to have little relation to the growing unemployment emergency. Their early minutes and reports are concerned with the permanent program and there is no statement regarding the unemployment emergency until their first annual meeting in June, 1931.[6]

The Concern of Private Social Agencies

In September the Charity Organization Department of the Russell Sage Foundation called a conference of private family welfare agency representatives to discuss ways and means of meeting the relief needs of the coming winter. The *Survey Midmonthly* carried a report of the discussion which included the following:

If private contributions cannot carry the load, the family agencies should push for the establishment of public departments giving both service and relief. Since it has been demonstrated that good standards can be maintained under public auspices, this seems a logical position for them to take in such circumstances, and is the only statesmanlike way of forestalling the setting up of temporary emergency relief measures, the results of which often hampered their work for years after past emergency periods. . . .

[6] The American Association of Public Welfare Officials as established in 1930 had no staff at all. No funds were available until the summer of 1931. Consequently there was very little activity. The officers of the Association all held full time jobs in other agencies and it was only occasionally that small groups got together to discuss future plans for the Association. The name was changed in 1932 to American Public Welfare Association. See p. 85 below.

In the discussion, it was shown that public departments, including mothers' aid, are already carrying over three quarters of the relief burden in a group of the largest cities, and that the threat to standards of work lies in a wholesale and unplanned development of public relief, and not in the smaller sums raised and disbursed by private agencies. The need of immediate efforts toward joint planning was stressed by representatives of both groups.[7]

"Both groups" evidently refers to the chests and family welfare agencies, since no one was present from any public welfare agency.

At the conference a representative of the chest movement, after citing the alarming increase in public relief, said:

. . . these facts point to the most serious problem for the family welfare field to consider. Unless they "get busy" about it the Association of Community Chests and Councils will have to establish a department for dealing with the drift to public relief. Since the overturn in the public department in Los Angeles, the situation has gone from bad to worse, with 3 million expenditure in public relief. Such situations present the most serious threat to standards, which are likely to go all to pieces, with relief being taken over on such a scale and at such a rate by the public.

The executive of one of the largest private family welfare agencies in the country remarked that he thought:

. . . there was some naiveté in the assumption that what the private agencies could not do the public agencies could. Not even both together will be able to cover the job that needs to be done this winter. It would be a hopeful approach to reality to recognize that fact. It tends to bring the public and private agency together on common ground, and pave the way to conference on what, together, they can do. It is an opportune time to start a public welfare department where none exists, or where one is in being, to sit down together and discuss standards of work.

An even more conservative attitude toward governmental responsibility for relief was shown in a volume, *Community Planning in Unemployment Emergencies*, published at about the same time under the same auspices. Its recommendations are based almost entirely on the experience gained in the de-

[7] Colcord, Joanna C., "Facing the Coming Winter," *Survey Midmonthly*, Nov., 1930.

pressions of 1914 and 1921. The section on fund raising deals only with voluntary contributions, and the attitude taken toward public responsibility is shown by the following:

The situation in each community must determine whether the bulk of the relief burden in a time of unemployment shall be carried by the private family agencies, supported by contributions directly or through the Community Fund, or by the public tax-supported body (Department of Public Welfare, County Commissioners, Overseers of the Poor, as they are variously called).

The creation of a centralized relief agency under public auspices is not necessarily a part of the city government's fulfilment of this responsibility, which can to a large extent, in the absence of regularly established public out-door relief, be delegated to voluntary organizations.[8]

This attitude of the leaders in private social agencies was reflected in the position taken by the Federal Government that voluntary contributions to community chests could take care of the situation. Even the 60,000,000 bushels of wheat which were in the possession of the Federal Farm Board in the fall of 1930 were not devoted to the relief of the unemployed until 1932.

The President's Emergency Committee for Employment

In October, 1930, President Hoover appointed Colonel Arthur Woods to be responsible for developing a program to deal with unemployment. Colonel Woods organized a nonpartisan group called the President's Emergency Committee for Employment. The name was chosen deliberately both to indicate the emergency nature of the situation and to avoid reference to the discouraging term "unemployment." The purpose of the committee was to supplement and encourage the activities of state and local communities upon which was placed the primary responsibility for meeting the emergency.

With funds only for its own expenses and with a limited staff, the Committee acted as a clearing house for measures found effective in

[8] Community Planning in Unemployment Emergencies. Recommendations Growing Out of Experience, Compiled by Joanna C. Colcord, Director, Charity Organization Department, Russell Sage Foundation, New York, 1930.

the emergency, gave assistance on specific problems, and reinforced state and local efforts:

"A. by cooperating with the departments of the Federal Government in their activities concerned with the emergency.

"B. by pointing out the value of expediting necessary public and semi-public construction already planned in providing employment in the emergency.

"C. by working with industry to spread employment and otherwise increase employment opportunities, to care for laid-off employees, and to develop stabilizing policies.

"D. by indicating specific ways and means by which the individual citizen could personally provide employment for his less fortunate neighbor.

"E. by cooperating with national organizations concerned with these problems.

"F. by supporting by publicity and otherwise to enable states and communities better to provide employment and relief." [9]

A few days before Colonel Woods was appointed, President Hoover had said publicly, "As a nation we must prevent hunger and cold to those of our people who are in honest difficulties." [10]

The President's Committee consistently maintained its position that local resources should be depended upon to meet relief needs, and it placed great emphasis upon the importance of private agencies. The Association of Community Chests and Councils and the Family Welfare Association of America were asked to secure information on local conditions and methods. The President's Committee backed both the chest drives and also the Red Cross campaigns for drought relief which, unfortunately, competed with each other in many local communities.

In a news release issued shortly after the Committee began operating, Colonel Woods stated:

Increased funds for local relief and social agencies are needed if human suffering is to be prevented. Various community chests, non-

[9] Hayes, E. P., *Activities of the President's Emergency Committee for Employment, 1930-1931.* The Rumford Press, Concord, N. H. 1936. pp. 3-4.
[10] *Ibid.*, p. 2.

sectarian and sectarian, are financing this direct and indirect burden of unemployment. They should be encouraged.

Hospitals and dispensaries must receive more free patients; children's organizations will be more crowded as broken homes are increased in the strain of hard times, agencies providing for the wholesome use of leisure will be thronged by idle people.[11]

The literature sent out by the Committee, part of which was prepared at its request, described methods used in the two previous depressions, and assumed the validity of local and pre-eminently private agency endeavors to meet unemployment relief needs.[12]

The Committee slogans seemed to be "give a job" and "spread the work." Subsistence gardens and food conservation were encouraged; industry was urged to spread work and give temporary employment. A recommendation for a large Federal Public Works Program made by the Committee was not approved by the Administration, which continued to claim that the normal process of recovery was sufficient to effect recovery and that while there might be an emergency committee, no unusual measures were necessary.

The fall questionnaire of the Association of Community Chests and Councils, sent to cities in which there were community chests, revealed the considerable extent to which public funds were being used for unemployment relief. The private agencies seemed to realize for the first time that no one community resource could be counted on to meet the needs of the coming winter. Public funds had been appropriated for unemployment relief for the first time in a number of cities, and appropriations had been increased in others. Chests planned to conduct supplementary campaigns if necessary, and in many cases had the assurance of future help from the city

[11] Hayes, E. P., *Activities of the President's Emergency Committee for Employment, 1930-1931.* The Rumford Press, Concord, N. H. 1936.

[12] The following publications, among others, were sent out by the Committee: published by the Russell Sage Foundation: *Emergency Relief in Times of Unemployment,* by Mary E. Richmond; *The Burden of Unemployment,* by Philip Klein; *Community Planning in Unemployment Emergencies,* by Joanna C. Colcord; published by the F.W.A.A.: *The Administration of Relief in Unemployment Emergencies,* by Margaret E. Rich; *Care of the Homeless in Unemployment Emergencies,* by Harriet E. Anderson and Margaret E. Rich.

governments. It was evident that chests were looking to public funds as merely another supplementary resource. This increase in public expenditures for relief, however, and the consequent drain upon city treasuries, came at a time when tax returns were falling off. The inability of private citizens and corporations to pay taxes on real estate swiftly depleted city funds, curtailed budgets, increased unemployment, stepped up demands for relief, and thereby created a vicious cycle of threatened municipal bankruptcy and human suffering. City officials, private citizens and congressmen alike began to urge the appropriation of Federal funds for unemployment relief.

President Hoover, clinging to the notion that the depression was no more than temporary, in his annual message to Congress on December 2, 1930, made his position on this point clear by favoring still further temporary expansions of activities already begun in relief of unemployment. He warned against commitments extending beyond six months, and asked for an appropriation of $150,000,000 to provide employment in the various Federal departments, to be applied to works already authorized by Congress. The only mention of relief was, according to the old pattern of emergency, in connection with the drought which extended beyond the borders of the Potomac, Ohio and Mississippi Rivers:

In order that the Government may meet its full obligation toward our countrymen in distress through no fault of their own, I recommend that an appropriation should be made to the Department of Agriculture to be loaned for the purpose of seed and feed for animals. Its application should, as hitherto in such loans, be limited to a gross amount to any one individual, and secured upon the crop.

Relief Needs Throughout the Country

The situation, particularly in the drought states, was so serious that a few weeks later the U. S. Senate voted an appropriation of $25,000,000 for unemployment relief to be administered by the American Red Cross. While the appropriation was being considered by the House, the Red Cross Central Committee passed a resolution refusing to undertake such a responsibility. The House defeated the appropriation bill in January. In March the states raised $10,000,000 for Red Cross drought relief by the device of securing contributions of one day's pay from state employees. In April President Hoover declared the drought to be officially ended.

During the winter several states [13] had made provision for emergency disaster relief—drought, storms, floods, etc. This relief was limited to disasters known as "Acts of God." Massachusetts also made available nearly $3,000,000 for construction of public buildings to "alleviate the present unemployment emergency."

Illinois had one of the most serious unemployment problems in the country, most acute in Chicago, but also extending through the state from the South Chicago Stock Yards to the coal mines in the southern counties. In spite of this, however, Governor Emerson's biennial message to the General Assembly on January 7, 1931, did not ask for an appropriation but reported with evident satisfaction the work done by private citizens. He told the legislature that on October 15, 1930, he had appointed the Governor's Commission on Unemployment and Relief. Since then, he said, busy executives had given time unsparingly. A large headquarters had been fitted up and equipped, and hundreds of employees loaned by industries and business houses and put to work, without spending one dollar from the state's purse for overhead.

Through the public schools an orderly record had been made of persons (132,000) out of work. 45,000 of these were found to be in need of immediate relief. "To date more than 20,000 of those needing relief have been distributed among the organized charities and work is being found for many thousands in addition." To supplement the funds of existing agencies, $3,000,000 had been raised by the "gifts" of corporation employees giving regular monthly donations out of their pay checks, and by state employees giving one day's pay a month.

Regular legislative sessions were exceptional during the latter part of 1931 but, nevertheless, there was a clear trend towards assumption of responsibility by the states. State after state called a special session of its legislature to consider unemployment relief.[14] During the first few months of 1931

[13] West Virginia, Arkansas, Louisiana, Minnesota, Missouri, and South Carolina.
[14] APWA, Recent Developments in Legislation for Public Relief of Unemployment. Dec., 1931. Multigraphed.

Oklahoma appropriated $300,000 to be distributed to the
counties for direct relief, and an equal amount for seed; California set up a contingent fund of $1,500,000; New Hamp-
shire appropriated $75,000 for extension of mothers' aid bene-
fits because of unemployment conditions; Maryland set aside
$24,000 license fees from four racing days held under the au-
thority of the State Racing Commission.   Other states took
action permitting local units to issue bonds for relief or to
utilize funds designed for other purposes.[15]

While the states were beginning to take action and the
municipalities were struggling with increasing demands for relief, the President stated clearly the position of the Federal
Administration in his Lincoln Day address. He said in part:

The evidence of our ability to solve great problems outside of government action and the degree of moral strength with which we
emerge from this period will be determined by whether the individuals and the local communities continue to meet their responsibilities.

Throughout this depression I have insisted upon organization of
these forces through industry, through local government and through
charity, that they should meet this crisis by their own initiative, by
the assumption of their own responsibilities. The Federal Government has sought to do its part by example in the expansion of employment, by affording credit to drought sufferers for rehabilitation,
and by cooperation with the community, and thus to avoid the
opiates of government charity and the stifling of our national spirit
of mutual self-help.

National Agencies Take Action

The Woods Committee had asked the Association of Community Chests and Councils to find out what they could about
local needs and resources, and the Family Welfare Association of America to study the effects of unemployment on people, the deterioration of family morale, and the values and
dangers of various types of made work. They asked the
Bureau of the Census to secure figures on relief expenditures
for the first 3 months of 1929 and 1931 in order to discover

[15] Notably the Pringle-Roberts law in Ohio. See State Legislation for
Unemployment Relief from Jan. 1, 1931, to May 31, 1932, by Rowland
Haynes, the President's Organization on Unemployment Relief. U. S.
Gov't Printing Office. Washington, 1932.

the effect of the unemployment emergency on the total of obligations assumed. This was the first attempt to secure nationwide relief statistics, the Bureau of Registration for Social
Statistics having sampled only some of the major cities. The
report was not published until January, 1932, but it shows
clearly what was happening during these first three months
of 1931.

The total expenditures, including cost of administration, reported
by governmental and private organized agencies for family relief
(outside of institutions) and for relief to homeless men, in the areas
for which returns were received, amounted to $22,338,114 in Janu-
ary, February, and March 1929, and to $73,757,300 during the cor-
responding period of 1931. The number of families reported as receiving relief averaged 333,861 per month in the first three months
of 1929 and 1,287,778 per month in the first three months of 1931.
Due to the fact that a number of agencies were providing relief in
most cities, "there was doubtless some duplication in a number of
families and individuals." Furthermore, in the case of many agencies, the cost of administering relief could not be readily segregated,
and only the amount of relief granted was reported. While the
amounts expended were undoubtedly to be taken as understatement,
they afforded the best measure which it had been possible to secure.

Vivid and revealing as these figures are they give no indication of the extent of the need which was not being met nor
of the inadequacy of the relief which was being given. It is
worth noting that in collecting these figures the Bureau of the
Census counted all public subsidies to private agencies as private funds! Without counting these subsidies, 71% of the
$31,000,000 spent in 81 large cities during those three months
was reported as public money.

In April Colonel Woods left the President's Committee and
Mr. Fred C. Croxton, one of the regional advisers, was appointed vice-chairman.

Distress was increasing throughout the country, but it was
particularly acute in the bituminous coal mining areas. The
Children's Bureau had made studies of conditions which
affected the health of children in mining counties of West Virginia, Kentucky, Pennsylvania, Illinois and a number of other
states. The shocking extent of undernourishment and even
starvation, and the pitiful inadequacy of relief, revealed by

these studies, led to the request, made in the spring by Mr. Croxton, that the Friends' Service Committee go into these counties and feed the children, as they had done in Europe after the World War. Later Mr. Pickett, secretary of the American Friends' Service Committee, testified at a congressional hearing that their work of feeding children began in September in West Virginia and Kentucky and later extended to southern Illinois, western Pennsylvania and eastern Ohio.

Senator La Follette, who presided at the hearing, asked Mr. Pickett how the Friends' Service Committee got their money for this work. Mr. Pickett replied:

"We were given $225,000 by the American Relief Administration,[16] and then we have had added to that from gifts from our own people something like $15,000 to $20,000."

The Chairman. "Is that sum the unexpended balance which the American Relief Administration had left?"

Mr. Pickett. "Yes; I suppose it was—at least, they made no extra campaign, although I know very little about the American Relief Administration fund." [17]

The situation was growing worse not only in the rural industrial areas but in the large population centers. It was aggravated by bank failures, and shortages in municipal funds due to tax delinquencies. The President's Committee continued its emphasis upon the use of local resources, although there was now a general acceptance of the major importance of public funds in the relief picture. Another shift in position came with the recognition of the responsibility of state governments "as a second line of defense," and even of Federal aid as a last resort.

In the existing emergency the Committee found itself in general agreement with the position taken by the President, namely, that Federal funds should not be used for relief purposes in the emer-

[16] Organized to administer relief funds in Europe after the World War. Mr. Herbert Hoover, Chairman. The American Relief Administration had received a grant of $100,000,000 from Congress on February 25, 1919, for European Food Relief (Statute, Vol. 40, p. 116).

[17] See Hearings before Subcommittee of the Committee on Manufactures, U. S. Senate on S. 174 and S. 262, December 28, 1931. Statement of Clarence E. Pickett, Philadelphia, Pennsylvania. pp. 56-64.

gency until local and state resources had been used to the maximum. As state taxation was largely an untapped source of relief funds, the Administration and the Committee were of the opinion that before recourse was made to Federal funds, state resources should be developed. In brief the position taken was that local resources, in accordance with established usage, should, so to speak, be the first line of defense; that state resources should constitute the second; and that only in event the emergency developed beyond the power of local and state taxation and private charity, should Federal tax funds be used.[18]

This report of the Direct Relief Activities of the President's Committee also contains the following statement:

The Committee, however, always acted on the policy that relief needs should be promptly met. The information which came to the Committee during the winter of 1930-31, while not entirely conclusive, indicated that the larger cities were meeting their relief needs.

Mr. Hayes says, however, that it seemed apparent to the Committee in the spring of 1931 that even "with a substantial improvement in business" relief needs would be heavy during the following winter.[19]

Mr. Croxton therefore turned to a number of national agencies, including the recently organized American Association of Public Welfare Officials, to "develop a cooperative program which would enable state and local organizations to cope with the situation." [20]

In this way the committee sought to avoid the necessity of developing "new administrating machinery, which being hastily organized would lack solidarity, and which would be sub-

[18] E. P. Hayes, *Activities of the President's Emergency Committee for Employment, 1930-1931.* The Rumford Press, 1936. p. 96. On one occasion Colonel Woods declined a request to testify before a congressional committee to the effect that Federal relief was wrong in principle; for his opinion, as indicated, was that Federal tax funds should be used if local and state tax resources and private charity failed to meet an emergency situation.

[19] *Ibid.,* p. 96.

[20] These agencies also included the Association of Community Chests and Councils, Family Welfare Association of America, Russell Sage Foundation, National Association of Travelers' Aid Societies, U. S. Children's Bureau, National Conference of Catholic Charities.

ject to the seemingly inevitable delays of government agencies." [21]

This mobilization of private national agencies whose interests were centered in local programs meant that the following summer was characterized by frantic efforts to persuade local communities to establish or enlarge upon relief machinery which they did not have resources to operate effectively. The *Survey* described the activities of the Association of Community Chests and Councils as follows:

The Committee has asked the Association first of all to discover the relief needs and resources of 376 cities of 25,000 or more population and to determine how adequate an organization exists for securing necessary relief funds, private and public.

Where organization is inadequate the Association proposes to offer the services of an enlarged field staff to advise on methods of improving such emergency organization as may be necessary to secure funds. Where local leadership lacks vigor or the community seems unaware of its obligation the Association plans to make available speakers of national influence to put the situation squarely before the citizens. Much of the Association's effort will be directed toward a national publicity campaign through newspapers and magazines, by means of advertising, the radio and special pamphlets, all aimed to create widespread understanding of the necessity of using every possible local resource, public and private, for essential relief, at the same time emphasizing the need of continuing the all-round program of welfare services.[22]

The Association of Public Welfare Officials and the Children's Bureau were the only national agencies primarily concerned with local public relief for the unemployed and which recognized the importance of state governments in the relief picture.

More and more emphasis continued to be placed upon the need of state funds to supplement inadequate local resources. Several cities went into the hands of receivers. The chests planned nevertheless to redouble their efforts in the coming campaigns, in the face of reduced dividends, cut salaries, part-time jobs and failing corporations. As a result of these efforts,

[21] *Op. cit.*, p. 115.

[22] Springer, Gertrude, "Funds for Another Bleak Winter," *Survey Midmonthly*, June, 1931.

relief expenditures from private funds reached their peak during the following year.

Community Chests and Relief

Even in the midst of planning for the chest drives of the fall and winter, the Association of Community Chests and Councils faced the fact that their relief budgets could not possibly meet the demands, and begged for some national declaration which would stimulate the appropriation of local public funds. The Association took this position, however, with reluctance and only when it became inevitable. The community chest had built its prestige and reason for being upon the assumption of responsibility for all community needs. Contributors to the chest were guaranteed immunity from further solicitation by any other charitable agency. The relief appeal, the easiest way to reach the community pocketbook, had been used almost exclusively, although most of the chest agencies spent their money for administration, "service," and "character building" and not at all for relief. Having failed to give to their contributors an understanding and appreciation of the non-relief functions of their member agencies, the chests now saw in the growing recognition of the responsibility of government for relief, not only the loss of their most productive money-raising appeal, but a threat to their very existence.

At this point, as the chests entered the final chapter of the public-private relief controversy, it is well to review their position in the field of social welfare. The development of the community chest had been a logical outgrowth of the function of the private relief and service agency and of the responsibility accepted by the individual private citizen for the less fortunate members of the community. It was an admission of community liability for philanthropy and social work, a voluntary method of self-taxation. It recognized relief as a community obligation and the right of the person in need but at the same time made the act of giving just as impersonal as the city tax levy.

Having guaranteed immunity from relief appeals, and having accepted this community obligation, the chest and its member agencies could not very well refuse aid and send on rejected applicants to some other agency. At the same time, it had no power to enforce collection of the funds it needed to discharge its obligation. Acting for the community, it had no power to compel the community to do its duty. Only the public agency, the legal authority has such power. Undoubtedly, the effort of the Association of Community Chests and Councils and the local chests to carry the load, backed as they were and encouraged in every possible way by the President's Committee, had a deterrent effect upon city officials, at least in the first two years of the depression. The failure of many city governments to act during that early period may have been due to a sense of freedom from responsibility fostered by the very existence of the community chests.[23]

Perhaps the position of the private agencies during the summer of 1931 can best be given in the words of two prominent executives, Mr. C. M. Bookman and Mr. Linton B. Swift. The first, director of the Cincinnati Community Chest, was later (in 1933) called to Washington by Mr. Hopkins to assist in setting up the Federal Emergency Relief Administration:

Unemployment relief can be handled best by local communities, and if we plan wisely I do not believe that it will be necessary to make or to take national or state grants for direct relief. However, I should not hesitate to sanction them if no other way can be found to feed the hungry. It should be made clear that there is nothing unsound socially, governmentally or economically in appropriating taxes for unemployment relief purposes and that government organized to protect and promote the welfare of people has an inescapable responsibility to handle unemployment relief. The present emergency has reached the point when all of us should see with clearness that it takes the combined resources of government, business, private philanthropy and all other social forces to cope even inadequately with the present calamity.[24]

The second executive, as director of the Family Welfare Association of America, represented the family welfare agencies which were then attempting to carry so large a part of

[23] Rubinow, I. M., "Can Private Philanthropy Do It?" *Social Service Review*, September, 1929. Vol. III.

[24] Springer, Gertrude, "The Challenge of Hard Times," *Survey Midmonthly*, July, 1931. Quotation from speech given by Mr. C. M. Bookman.

the relief load. Many of these organizations were the direct descendants of the charity organization societies whose leaders had waged bitter war upon public relief during the last quarter of the nineteenth century.[25] Taking as his cue for discussion "the statement reiterated several times by President Hoover during the past Winter, to the effect that the American method of assisting the unemployed is through private charity," this family welfare leader made the following interesting comment:

Many of us sharply disagree with this statement, not merely because it is not true, but because of its implications. If the President had said that our American philosophy favors local or state action in preference to federal action wherever possible, in relief as well as in other problems, he might have found wide agreement. Many of us are convinced that responsibility should be centered as much as possible in local and state governments, where the people may be more continuously aware of its implications. Because of that conviction most of us would agree that federal appropriations for relief of unemployment should be only a last resort.[26]

These statements show clearly that, bit by bit, the doubts and fears regarding public relief had diminished under new and powerful pressure probably because the inability of private agencies to meet these increasing needs had become more and more apparent. People stopped talking about the relative merits of public and private administration and the demoralizing effects of indiscriminate relief giving, because it was so obvious that unemployment relief had to be public.

The End of the Public-Private Relief Controversy

The Minneapolis National Conference of Social Work in June, 1931, saw perhaps the last symposium on the pros and cons of public versus private relief. At what must have been the climax of these discussions, an elected public official, a woman, delivered a challenge which should go down in history

---

[25] See Part I, Chapter 2.

[26] *Proceedings* of the National Conference of Social Work, 1931. University of Chicago Press, Chicago. "The Future of Public Social Work in America: From the Point of View of the Private Agency," by Linton B. Swift, Executive Director, Family Welfare Association of America, New York City.

as a veritable public welfare bill of rights. The following
vivid account is of interest:

Just when brain-fagged delegates were reaching exhaustion in their
struggle to see what lay before social work in its plunge into public
administration, a woman's voice cut through the fog and dissipated
a whole phalanx of straw-men. The voice was that of Ruth Taylor,
deputy commissioner of public welfare of Westchester County, New
York:
   "Public welfare is here. And we public welfare officials are here.
We are up against a staggering situation which we are as anxious to
meet adequately as you are to have us. We are just as worried as
you are. The situation is forced on us just as it is forced on you.
We are people just like you. Some of us are good and some not so
very good. Most of us are honest, but some of us are not. But we
are all desperately anxious for help with the enormous task that has
been thrust upon us. Where should we look for help but to you?
We need and want you. Of course if you come with a superior air we
shall not like you and may not get on very well with you. But if
you bring with your help a faith in our good faith and a patience
with our limitations you will find us deeply appreciative of all you
can give us. Don't treat us as upstarts. Treat us as partners." [27]

   Less dramatic but equally realistic in rounding out Miss
Taylor's statement was the following argument for public relief. The points are just as valid in 1940 as they were 9 years
ago:

To explain the public development as a transfer to governmental
agencies of functions formerly supported by voluntary contributions
is, in my opinion, an indication of failure to grasp its more important implications.
   The magnifying of private charity as an essential method of dealing with the problems of family dependency was the natural accom-
paniment of such a philosophy. It was accepted as a cardinal principle of social work that the problem of poverty was not the direct
concern of the entire community but only of those who desired to
be charitable. This was corollary to the belief that poverty was an
indication of incompetence if not of personal abnormality. How un-
comfortable many of us must have been during the present year to
find these ancestral beliefs of social workers repeated by President
Hoover and by other governmental and industrial leaders as a justi-

   [27] Springer, Gertrude, "The Challenge of Hard Times," *Survey Midmonthly*, July, 1931.

fication for thwarting emergency public measures for the relief of the unemployed.

We have progressed sufficiently from this untenable philosophy of economic individualism so that the present tendency toward public relief may be set forth as a definite step toward collective responsibility for the inadequacies of a badly functioning economic system. . . .

The philosophy of private benevolence has failed to stimulate machinery for the creation of an adequate social work program for the particular sections of the country which are most in need.

The development of public relief may be considered as a definite reaction against the validity of the principle of private responsibility for poverty. It is no accident, therefore, that the most important development of public relief which we have experienced in the last two decades has been not in the establishment of general case work and relief services in imitation of private family service, such as are to be found in a few socialized municipal departments of welfare, but in the establishment through state action of new forms of relief for dealing with destitution by categories.

The drift to public relief is, in my opinion, a progressive and thoroughly justifiable development in family social work. If we remain conscious of the values and of the shortcomings of public relief, and continue to measure it in relation to a more ideal goal, our drift into public relief may prove to have been a desirable forward step. We may come to consider it as a real contribution made by family social work in the evolution to a modern economic and social program.[28]

The Minneapolis National Conference ended on June 20. The following day in Washington the representatives of several national agencies and two Federal bureaus met in Mr. Croxton's office.[29] The minutes record a discussion of serious need, alarming health conditions, exhaustion of family resources, inadequacy of local relief; of drought; of the increase of transiency and the need for uniform settlement laws. There was a decided emphasis upon the importance of public agencies and the need of increased appropriations. The Asso-

[28] *Proceedings* of the National Conference of Social Work, 1931. U. of Chicago Press, Chicago. "The Drift to Public Relief," by Harry L. Lurie, Director, Bureau of Jewish Social Research, New York City.

[29] On this same day a news release from Mr. Croxton's office announced the Woods Committee Program for Organization of Local Relief Resources. See Appendix C.

ciation of Community Chests and Councils planned to emphasize in local communities not only chest drives, but the policy
that "local predilections as to methods of money raising must
govern." Several members of the group felt that Federal aid
was inevitable, and the Rev. John O'Grady, Secretary of the
National Conference of Catholic Charities, urged them to formulate their ideas on Federal administration in order to be
ready in case they were called before congressional committees during the following winter.

Throughout the summer petitions for help poured into the
White House from local welfare officials, city councils, labor
unions, in widely separated parts of the country. It was evident that some new move was in order, and, on August 19,
Mr. Walter S. Gifford was appointed as Director of the President's Organization on Unemployment Relief.

His activities were to be directed primarily towards the relief aspects
of the unemployment situation during the coming winter. The
President stated that the work "so splendidly directed" by Colonel
Woods during the past year would be "continued under the direction
of Mr. Fred C. Croxton as part of the new organization, including
its work on employment problems." [30]

Looking ahead to the third consecutive winter of continuing
unemployment, Mr. Gifford acknowledged in press conferences
the need of state aid for local communities and also admitted
that there might be a few states unable to meet their relief
needs during the coming winter, although he had yet no definite information on these situations. On the whole he believed
that each state would be able to care for its own.

Five months later he described his organization, methods
and principles at a congressional committee hearing. His
committee took solidly the position that it must leave the responsibility for all relief activities squarely upon the states
and localities. States and local communities were encouraged
in their efforts to raise both private and public funds, and were
advised as to methods of administration. Industry was urged
to "spread the work," and local public works were encour-

[30] Hayes, E. P., *Activities of the President's Emergency Committee for
Employment, 1930-1931.* The Rumford Press, Concord, N. H. 1936.
p. 16.

aged.[31]   Mr. Gifford and Mr. Croxton continued to use the services of the same national and Federal agencies. Every effort was still being made to counteract the growing persistent campaign for Federal aid.

[31] S. 174 and S. 262, pp. 309-333.   January 8, 1932.

Chapter 4

The President's Organization on Unemployment Relief; State Governments Rise to the Emergency

~~~~~~

The American Association of Public Welfare Officials

In the summer of 1931 the American Association of Public Welfare Officials rose to new importance in the unemployment relief situation. At the first annual meeting of the Association in June of that year a committee was appointed to work for increased public relief appropriations, especially in distressed rural areas, and to promote better standards of administration "that the self-respect of those aided" might be maintained.[1] In August a grant of $40,000 was secured from a Foundation "to educate public opinion regarding the fundamental importance of public welfare work in present-day government" and to assist public officials in dealing with the immediate problems of unemployment relief.[2]

In September, Mr. Frank Bane, State Commissioner of Public Welfare of Virginia, became the first Director of the Association and at once established an office in Washington. Mr. Bane and his staff worked closely with the President's Organization on Unemployment Relief which had been appointed in August by President Hoover. A report made five months later to the Spelman Fund gives a summary of these early activities:

[1] Letter from Mr. Fred Croxton, Acting Chairman of the President's Emergency Committee for Employment, to the Association requesting cooperation. 1931. The phrase quoted in the text is the first anti-Malthusian note to emanate from a Federal official.

[2] Correspondence of the American Association of Public Welfare Officials with the Spelman Fund of the Rockefeller Foundation.

Field studies as to the actual conditions of relief needs and public relief measures have been promptly made available to the President's Organization on Unemployment Relief. The Association has responded to the many requests for advice and conference with Governors, Legislators, and public welfare officials of many states. It has promoted the organization of local resources and assisted State Departments and other public welfare organizations to develop effective procedures in administering relief.

In connection with the general program of the Association we have cooperated with and are now working with governmental research organizations, Legislative Commissions or Governors' Commissions in making detailed studies of State governments, and particularly in the development of State Welfare Departments in the following states: Mississippi, Kansas, Kentucky, South Carolina, and Alabama.

From this time on the Association of Public Welfare Officials [3] was a powerful factor in the unemployment relief picture. In fact, the Association, undoubtedly, has had during the past nine years more influence than any other one agency or group of people upon the sound development of emergency relief, and permanent social security programs by Federal, state and local governments.

When the Association was first organized in 1930, its platform had been based upon a deep concern for standards in the *total* and *permanent* public welfare program, state and local. Its work was intrusted to volunteer committees on Interstate Relations; Research and Statistics; and Uniform Settlement Laws and Transfer of Dependents. Its functions were to be the gathering of data, facilitating exchange of information between agencies, and stimulating a gradual improvement of public welfare standards. Although suddenly confronted with the exigencies of the depression and the critical issues presented by unemployment relief, the Association has never lost sight of its major objective, the development of the total permanent public welfare program.

In the fall and winter of 1931, the Association's work with unemployment relief agencies was carried on in close conjunction with the Family Welfare Association of America and the

[3] In 1932 the name was changed to American Public Welfare Association.

Association of Community Chests and Councils. During this period all three Associations agreed in recommending that local funds, both private and public, should be used to the fullest possible extent, and that state governments should be asked for appropriations only if local funds proved inadequate. They also advised that local agencies which were already established should be used to administer relief to the unemployed, whether these agencies were private or public. It was considered unwise to create new agencies in the emergency, provided those in existence could be sufficiently expanded and strengthened.[4]

The Family Welfare Association of America and the Community Chests and Councils were primarily interested in the private welfare field since their membership was made up of private agencies.[5] The American Association of Public Welfare Officials, however, was inherently public, in membership and objectives, and naturally turned to other national associations of governmental agencies and officials. Co-operation and consultation with such organizations as the Public Administration Clearing House and the International City Managers' Association[6] helped to clarify the policies and strengthen the position of the new association. The result was a clearer definition of the place of public welfare in relation to other functions of government. Gradually, as public funds and governmental administration came to play a more and more important part in unemployment relief, the Association became completely identified with the interests of the national organizations which were concerned with public affairs, and, by the same token, found it less necessary to consult with the private

[4] Organization and Administration of Unemployment Relief, pamphlet published by the American Public Welfare Association. Nov., 1931.

[5] A few public welfare departments belonged to the Family Welfare Association of America. See p. 54 above.

[6] Mr. Bane's report, May, 1932, states: "Close cooperation will be maintained with the following associations affiliated with the University of Chicago: Public Administration Clearing House; American Municipal Association; American Legislators' Association; International Association of Comptrollers and Accounting Officers; International City Managers' Association; Bureau of Public Personnel Administration." (The office of the American Association of Public Welfare Officials was moved to Chicago April 1, 1932.)

national agencies. During the years of the unemployment emergency, critical years in public welfare development, the leadership of the American Association of Public Welfare Officials was consistently forward-looking, courageous and sound. Minutes, reports, and published papers show that definite policies were adopted during this period upon many important points, including the responsibility of state and Federal, as well as local, governments for relief to persons in need; the principle that public funds should be spent by public and not by private agencies; the policy that work is the only satisfactory answer to the need of the unemployed; the importance of adequate relief grants; the demand for qualified personnel and the adoption of a classified Civil Service; a uniform settlement law for all states; interstate agreements regarding care of dependents. Not the least interesting is the recommendation made by the Committee on Reports and Statistics which looked toward "standardization of state and local statistics; the preparation of a model law for the establishment in each state of a central state agency, and the development of such statistical tests of administrative efficiency as will make it possible to gauge the relative cost and value of various kinds of welfare activity." [7]

Mr. Bane's appointment was heralded in September by Mr. Gifford in a news release which puts the President's Committee on record as recognizing the major importance of using public funds for relief [8] and the value of securing the co-operation of organized public welfare officials. Through the medium of this release, the American Association of Public Welfare Officials urged public welfare officials to redouble their

[7] Typed minutes of annual meeting June 18, 1931, Minneapolis. The recommendation is particularly interesting in view of later developments in research and statistics in Federal and state programs. See Part III, Chapter 9; also Appendix D, for the statement made in August, 1931, regarding its emergency program.

[8] On Jan. 8, 1932, Mr. Gifford testified before the Senate Committee on Manufactures (S. 174 and S. 262, p. 326) as follows: "In theory, I like the tax resources better. We have, however, built up the system the other way. We have in normal years community-chest campaigns and a great to-do about it, and in view of the grave situation we are in today, I think it is a dangerous thing to change the practice, whatever the final evolution may be."

efforts to extend relief to people in need; emphasized the principle that work is the only satisfactory method of providing for the unemployed; stressed the importance of competent personnel; pledged co-operation to organizations engaged in stimulating relief from private sources; recognized the necessity for statewide planning, and offered assistance to state welfare departments in preparation of relief budgets and consideration of relief policies of states and local subdivisions.[9]

State Unemployment Relief

During the summer and fall months the obvious inadequacy of local relief funds, and the serious financial condition to which local governments were rapidly being reduced, brought increased pressure upon state governments. In New York State a Joint Committee on Unemployment Relief of the State Board of Social Welfare and the State Charities Aid Association had made two extensive surveys of conditions in December, 1930, and July, 1931. Governor Franklin D. Roosevelt called a special session of the New York Legislature to consider the findings of these surveys and the recommendations of the Joint Committee.

The Governor in his message, on August 28, 1931, made the following statement of policy:

Our government is not the master but the creature of the people. The duty of the State towards the citizens is the duty of the servant to its master. The people have created it; the people, by common consent, permit its continued existence.

One of these duties of the State is that of caring for those of its citizens who find themselves the victims of such adverse circumstance as makes them unable to obtain even the necessities for mere existence without the aid of others. That responsibility is recognized by every civilized nation.

While it is true that we have hitherto principally considered those who through accident or old age were permanently incapacitated, the same reseponsibility of the State undoubtedly applies when widespread economic conditions render large numbers of men and women incapable of supporting either themselves or their families because of circumstances beyond their control which make it impossible for

[9] News Release, September, 1931, President's Organization on Unemployment Relief. See Appendix E for full text.

them to find remunerative labor. To these unfortunate citizens aid must be extended by government—not as a matter of charity but as a matter of social duty.

On September 23, 1931, the New York Legislature appropriated $20,000,000 for state aid to the localities for unemployment relief, the money to be raised by a fifty percent increase in the income tax. This sum was intended to last from November 1, 1931, until June 1, 1932, on the basis of 40 percent reimbursement to local public welfare agencies for relief expenditures.[10] This sum was so nearly exhausted by the end of the winter that $20,000,000 additional was appropriated on March 31.

The Act clearly recognized the primary responsibility of local governments but at the same time declared state aid a necessity because of the inability of local resources to provide adequately for the unemployed.

The public health and safety of the State and each county, city and town therein being imperilled by the existing and threatened deprivation of a considerable number of their inhabitants of the necessaries of life owing to the present economic depression, such condition is hereby declared to be a matter of public concern, State and local, and the correction thereof to be a State, county, city and town purpose. While the duty of providing aid for those in need is primarily an obligation of the municipalities, nevertheless, it is the finding of the State that in the existing emergency the relief and assistance provided for by this Act are vitally necessary to supplement the relief work accomplished or to be accomplished locally.[11]

The administration of the act was vested in the Temporary Emergency Relief Administration consisting of three unpaid members, who were appointed by Governor Roosevelt. It was entirely separate from the State Department of Social Welfare. In October Harry L. Hopkins was made Executive Director and Douglas P. Falconer Associate Executive Director, and on November first the agency began to function. A report made in January, 1932, by the Administration to the Governor says:

[10] Relief Today in New York State, Report of TERA, October, 1933, p. 11.
[11] New York Special Session Laws of 1931. Chapter 798.

These two efficient and trained workers organized the headquarters, engaged a field staff of experienced men and women, and have labored literally day and night to put relief measures in operation. But for their devoted and capable direction, the Administration would have been unable to extend relief as promptly as it did. Their acquaintance with the organizations carrying on important social service in the State enabled them to call upon many workers, volunteers as well as paid, who assisted in setting up this temporary machinery.

The attitude of the Legislature toward the relief problem as essentially temporary and emergency is clearly reflected in the title which was given to the administration by that body.

This New York State program is peculiarly significant, not only because it was the first state emergency relief administration to get under way, but because it set standards of relief and personnel; established principles, policies and procedures, and adopted far-sighted imaginative methods of administration which were later carried over into the Federal program when Mr. Roosevelt became President of the United States and Mr. Hopkins was appointed by him as Federal Emergency Relief Administrator.

A study of the activities and policies of the New York TERA during the seventeen months prior to June, 1933, will show striking similarities to the Federal program which followed. During that year and a half experiments were tried out, theories were tested, and principles were established which were to be applied for these very reasons with much more confidence and to much greater advantage in the Federal Emergency Relief Administration.

Lessons learned about state-local relationships proved to be of great value later in the relationship of the Federal Administration to state governments, in the handling of discretionary grants, and in the value of a carefully chosen staff of field representatives. Precedents were set also in such vital matters as standards of relief; the purposes for which emergency relief funds could be spent; a definition of eligibility consistent with the intent of the law; the principle that there must be no discrimination on grounds of political creed, religion, race, color or non-citizenship; the policy of work relief for the able-bodied; employment of trained social work personnel, many of whom secured leave from private agencies; the policy that local expenditures for Old-Age Pensions and Mothers' Aid were not reimbursable; the refusal to reimburse for hospitalization costs; the inception of work projects to meet the needs of professional and other "white-collar" unemployed; the beginning of education projects and other special programs; the inception of a system of accurate and prompt reports and statistical data on relief funds, needs, case loads and expenditures.

The director of the TERA found it necessary to reconcile as best he could certain conflicts which were inherent in the situation and which persisted throughout the later Federal and state programs:

The problem of preserving local autonomy in the administration of relief and yet assuring a fair standard as to adequacy, impartiality and efficiency and the problem as to what constitutes "adequate" relief came up at these early meetings. The conflicts in work relief between the desire to get work done efficiently and the desire to give a maximum of relief, the conflict between the desire to have worthwhile projects and the desire not to interfere with regular employment, the determination that work relief should not operate to depress wage scales in regular employment, all had full consideration. The necessity for an accurate knowledge of the extent of the problem versus the unreliability of figures to be obtained through a census also was thrashed out. Closest to the present perhaps, was the disappointment expressed at an early session upon reports from places where industry had improved without need for additional labor.

The question was raised as to whether adequate relief would pauperize. One answer given in the early discussion was that it was the flat $2 a week that pauperized. "Of course," it was added, "if the depression were to last ten years with adequate relief given, there would be a pauperizing effect without question. But whatever pauperization resulted would result from the long continuance of unemployment." [12]

The Act not only provided for a reimbursement from state funds to the cities and counties of 40 percent of their unem-

[12] *Five Million People, One Billion Dollars:* Final Report of the Temporary Emergency Relief Administration, November 1, 1931–June 30, 1937. 67 pp. pp. 25-7.

ployment relief expenditures, but empowered the State Administration to "make and enforce rules . . . which will best
promote the efficiency and effectiveness of the relief which this
act is intended to furnish." The authority to reimburse and
the power to enforce rules gave to the TERA a powerful lever
for the improvement of standards of relief, methods of administration and personnel. The rules required that each local
agency should have at least one trained and experienced investigator on its staff; that prompt investigations should be
made; contact should be maintained with relief recipients
through periodic visits; and no investigator should carry more
than one hundred "cases." In regard to adequacy of relief the
rules required that "the amount of relief to be given each applicant and his dependents shall be . . . sufficient to provide
for the estimated needs in so far as the family is unable to
do so from its own resources."

The personnel policies and practices of the TERA are of
special significance because they established a powerful precedent for the recognition by government of the principle that
the administration of relief is a social work function.[13]

The state administration was specifically authorized by the
Act to reimburse the cities and counties for salaries of certain
types of employees in Home Relief and Emergency Work
Bureaus. Under this provision the salaries of Home Relief
supervisors and investigators with social service experience
could be reimbursed in whole or in part. This made it possible for the state administration to set personnel and relief
standards and to play an important part in the selection of
qualified social work personnel. An official report issued in
January, 1932, stated their position as follows:

The Administration has come to appreciate how important training
and experience are in the field of social work. Those in distress are
naturally sensitive and the approach by untrained or unsympathetic
workers, or the promiscuous mingling with long lines of applicants
. . . tends to aggravate that distress. The Administration desires
to record the tactful and efficient methods of trained social workers
and to express the hope that most, if not all, of the communities
with which it has been in contact are of a similar mind, and will

[13] See Part III, Chapters 9, 10 and 11; also Part IV, Chapter 15.

wish in the future to include among their executives trained personnel to handle social problems.[14]

Reimbursements from state funds were made to the localities on the condition that the rules were observed in so far as was practicable and reasonable. The result was a notable increase in the amounts of relief given to families and individuals, a general improvement in methods of administration and in personnel standards in almost every part of the state. An important precedent was thus established by the TERA in the handling of the relationship between a state agency and its local units in the administration of a relief program.

New Jersey was the second state to set up an emergency relief administration by action of a special legislative session on October 13, 1931, when nearly $10,000,000 was appropriated for unemployment relief for a period of six months.[15] Here again local autonomy was respected in a state which had 21 counties and 572 municipalities. Each municipality and county desiring state funds was required to submit a program for both "dependency and employment" relief to be undertaken subject to the approval of the state director. Funds for work or "employment" relief were granted partially on a population basis and municipalities were reimbursed 40 percent of the cost of "dependency" or direct relief.

In Pennsylvania, as in New York State, a study of conditions, needs and resources was made by committees of prominent laymen and social workers.[16] Their report to Governor

[14] The members of the Administration were Jesse Isidor Straus, Chairman, Philip J. Wickser and John Sullivan. See Social Service Personnel in Local Public Relief Administration: Research Bulletin, TERA Division of Research and Statistics. Emma O. Lundberg, Director. February, 1935. p. 30. This report states further that:
"Prior to November 1, 1931, only four or five of the largest cities in the State had any trained service for investigation of applications and supervision of relief. By October 1, 1932, 71 welfare districts—43 cities and 28 counties—had requested and received assistance from the State Administration in providing such workers."

[15] Laws, Special Session, 1931. Ch. 394.

[16] John L. Hanna, Arthur Dunham, Edwin O. Solenberger, Jacob Billikopf, Helen Glenn Tyson, J. Prentice Murphy, Horace Forbes Baker, chairman; Governor's Planning Committee on Unemployment Relief. See report published in *Social Service Review*, Dec., 1931, "Relief Needs and Conditions in Pennsylvania, Aug., 1931."

Pinchot described distressing conditions in about half the
counties of the state. They found unusual unemployment, an
abnormal amount of part-time employment, reduction of
wages, exhaustion of both public and private funds, and an
almost complete lack of private agencies outside of the large
cities. The need was most acute in the coal fields, where there
was intense suffering and an alarming amount of malnutrition.

The Governor later gave this vivid summary at a congressional committee hearing:

Every county has some grave unemployment problem.
Fifty-five counties give cause for grave concern.
Nine counties only are well organized and know their problem.
Seven of these counties, though not acutely distressed, have certain
known districts presenting serious problems.
Thirty counties are so poorly organized that they have but little
idea of the extent of their problem.
Nineteen counties are distressed counties in dire need.
County treasuries, community chests, can not meet the need.[17]

The report was presented in August, 1931. Early in November, Governor Pinchot called a special session of the legislature and proposed to them a plan which called for additional appropriations to increase the facilities of the regular
state departments of welfare, health and labor. Funds for
relief of the unemployed were to be obtained by asking private citizens for contributions. This resort to private relief
funds was suggested by the Governor because the Attorney
General had ruled that the State Constitution forbade the expenditure of state funds for relief. The legislature, however,
discarded the Governor's plan and appropriated $10,000,000
for unemployment relief on the ground that it was needed in
order to safeguard the interests of the citizens and that the
Constitution provided this right of protection to the members
of the commonwealth as part of the "general welfare," independently of the limitation regarding relief.[18]

[17] Hearings before a Subcommittee of the Committee on Manufactures
of the U. S. Senate on S. 174 and S. 262. Page 218. Testimony of Governor Pinchot, January 4, 1932. Govt. Printing Office, Washington,
D. C., 1932.
[18] The Act was declared constitutional by the State Supreme Court on
April 8, 1932.

Governor La Follette called a special session of the Wisconsin legislature in November, 1931. No appropriation for unemployment relief was made until February, but before the end of the year Wisconsin passed the first Unemployment Compensation Act in the United States.

In November, Rhode Island appropriated approximately $2,500,000 for relief. This fund was made available to be loaned to the towns and cities of the state. Illinois made an appropriation in February, and Ohio in March. Thus seven states with great industrial populations and increasing unemployment undertook their first responsibility for emergency relief during the seven months from September, 1931, through the following March.[19]

Never before in the history of the United States had state governments invested so heavily in relief for any purpose. These unprecedented appropriations established once and for all the responsibility of state government for relief of persons in need, not only in *this* unemployment emergency but in *any* emergency; not only in any emergency but for permanent programs of public assistance.

During 1932 and 1933 the majority of the states followed the example set by the first seven. The question at issue, however, regarding these later appropriations revolved not about the principle of state responsibility but about constitutional and fiscal limitations and the unawareness, or refusal to be aware, of the relief problem on the part of legislators and governors. It was during the early period of state action in the winter of 1931-32 that the crucial issue of state responsibility for relief was finally argued and settled.

The most telling factor in favor of state funds was the obvious inadequacy of local funds to meet the demands for relief. Local funds came out of real estate and other property taxes. Practically every cent contributed to relief by people

---

[19] See p. 73. Early in 1931 the following states appropriated smaller sums: Oklahoma and New Hampshire in January, Maryland and California in April; and in March, Ohio passed the Pringle Roberts Act which permitted localities to issue bonds. For summary of legislation during these 15 months see: State Legislation for Unemployment Relief from January 1, 1931, to May 31, 1932, by Rowland Haynes; The President's Organization on Unemployment Relief. U. S. Government Printing Office, Washington: 1932. 74 pp.

of small means, either directly by private contributions or in-
directly through taxes, meant a decrease in consumption. Decrease in consumption meant the slowing down of industry.
Hence a vicious cycle was created consisting of mounting unemployment and relief expenditures, increasing tax delinquencies and the bankruptcy of one local government after another. The logical answer to this dilemma was to fall back
upon the broader borrowing and taxing power of the state.

The proponents of state relief also argued that local areas
were inarticulate about their needs, and often the counties and
municipalities, where the need was the greatest, were most inarticulate and had the smallest resources. They pointed to
the precedent set by the use of state equalization funds in the
fields of education and health and held that the state should
carry the major responsibility of maintaining standards and
adequacy, with such guidance as the Federal Government
could give.

Studies made by the Children's Bureau of conditions in coal-
mining counties gave exceptional force to this argument:

Poor relief in Kentucky is voted by the county court and administered by the county judge. As a rule, county funds had in the past
been used only for the support of the aged, blind, and chronically
sick, and had been inadequate for that. . . .

This failure to expand the public relief was not because of a lack
of appreciation of local needs. It was due, first, to limited county
resources; second, to the fact that county relief funds had been used
in the past only for those who were permanently incapacitated; and,
finally, to the practical impossibility of meeting the local needs with
local taxation. County C is not a populous county. Its little hill
farms had been injured recently by drought and flood. Mining was
practically the only industry. The county was seriously in debt. . . .

With local public resources inadequate, public assistance should
come from the state. The most striking fact in these counties was
the completely different way in which the health and the social services for the poor were viewed in Kentucky. The public health services were being supported by federal, state, and local funds. The
public relief was entirely local. The former were organized with the
help of the State Department of Health, and in the event of special
need the county health officer felt free to call upon the State Department for advice or the loan of personnel. In other words, while

the local health unit was locally administered, it had had from the beginning outside financial and professional assistance.[20]

The opponents of state relief still continued to protest. They feared the implications for the future, warning that when once a state started in the relief business it would stay in it, not just for the "emergency" but for five, ten or perhaps twenty years. And on this point time proved that they were right! They called upon tradition, and the common law and the principle of local responsibility embodied in state laws and constitutions. They claimed that the availability of state funds would stultify local initiative and dry up public and private financial resources.

In spite of these protests and arguments, which had back of them the influence of the Federal Government and the Gifford Committee, state after state went into action. Even the Gifford Committee conceded the fact that, after local funds were entirely exhausted, the state might come to the rescue. However, on the question of spending Federal funds for relief, the committee was adamant. Witness Mr. Gifford's own statement in a Congressional hearing: "The central organization in Washington—my organization—was not to do anything other than to encourage the states to do the work; in other words the responsibility was to be left squarely with the states, counties and communities." [21]

The Mobilization of Local Resources

President Hoover in his message to Congress on December 8th told the nation that the Federal Government must not encroach upon nor permit local communities to abandon their "precious possession of local initiative and responsibility." He said further:

Through the President's Organization for Unemployment Relief, public and private agencies were successfully mobilized last winter to provide employment and other measures against distress. Similar organization gives assurance against suffering during the coming win-

[20] Abbott, Grace, "Improvement in Rural Public Relief: The Lesson of the Coal-Mining Communities." *The Social Service Review*, June, 1932, p. 219.

[21] Hearings on S. 174 and S. 262, p. 310.

ter. Committees of leading citizens are now active at practically
every point of unemployment. In the large majority they have been
assured the funds necessary which, together with local government
aids, will meet the situation. A few exceptional localities will be
further organized. . . .

I am opposed to any direct or indirect government dole. The breakdown and increased unemployment in Europe is due in part to such
practices. Our people are providing against distress from unemployment in true American fashion by a magnificent response to public
appeal and by action of the local governments. . . .

The Committee on Mobilization of Relief Resources, headed
by Owen D. Young for the President's Organization on Unemployment Relief, conducted a national drive for local contributions to Community Chests, in co-operation with the Association of Community Chests and Councils.[22] Every type
of publicity was used on a national basis: radio, newspaper,
periodical, billboard advertising; benefits given by motion picture theaters and college football teams.

The methods used in this campaign were called into question during the Hearings on the Senate Relief Bills 174 and
262, as is shown by the following excerpt from Mr. Gifford's
testimony:

Senator Costigan. "In an advertisement extensively carried in the
press during your October campaign for funds, there appeared such
statements as these over the signatures of yourself and Mr. Owen
D. Young:

" 'Between October 19 and November 25 America will feel the
thrill of a great spiritual experience. In those few weeks millions
of dollars will be raised in cities and towns throughout the land, and
the fear of cold and hunger will be banished from the hearts of thousands.'

"First, let me ask you whether you feel that the fear of cold and
hunger has been banished from the hearts of thousands?"

Mr. Gifford. "Undoubtedly; not of everyone but of thousands.
That is a very modest statement, I think."

Senator Costigan. "Does it still remain in the hearts of thousands?"

Mr. Gifford. "I think so. There is no doubt about that."

Senator Costigan. "Is it your feeling that we, as a people, ought

[22] Part IV, Chapter 16.

to follow the practice of advertising ourselves into the thrill of great spiritual experiences?"

Mr. Gifford. "You were comparing this campaign carried on a little while ago to the war. We certainly did it in the war. I do not know that I like it, but, as I say, it is more or less the established practice, and we are faced not with a theory but a practical question—how are we going to get what we need?" [23]

The policy of the committee was to "gain the benefits of coordination for private philanthropy without accepting Federal responsibility for the unemployment problem." Doubt was cast upon the reasonableness of this policy by the wit of one of America's great humorists. The late Will Rogers, broadcasting for the Gifford Committee in November, said:

Mr. Owen D. Young and Mr. Gifford asked me to annoy on this program. You just heard Mr. Gifford, the biggest hello man in the world, a very fine high caliber man, but what a job he has got! Mr. Hoover just told him, "Gifford, I have a remarkable job for you; you are to feed the several million unemployed."

"With what?" says Gifford.

"That's what makes the job remarkable. If you had something to do it with, it wouldn't be remarkable." [24]

Perhaps it was because Mr. Gifford had "nothing to do it with" that he found it necessary to learn so little about the problem. He told the Senate Committee in January that he had made no estimates of the extent of need in the country and that he had collected no data upon which such estimates might be based. Local conditions changed so rapidly that he had no definite information about the standards being used in the administration of relief, but thought they were "fairly all right." He thought conditions were probably 50 percent worse than when the Census Bureau relief report was made for the first three months of 1931.[25] The chests had budgeted 58 percent more for relief for 1932 than for 1931. However, he said that he was not officially obliged to be concerned.

Mr. Gifford counted heavily on what he called "invisible" relief. To quote again from his testimony:

[23] S. 174 and S. 262. p. 327, January 8, 1932.
[24] Quoted by Hopkins, Harry L., *Spending to Save: The Complete Story of Relief.* W. W. Norton and Co., New York, 1936, pp. 62-63.
[25] See Part II, Chapter 3.

These public and private funds, however, do not include what is called "invisible" relief. I refer to the cash aid and the board and lodging extended to relatives, friends, and neighbors; to the aid given by religious, fraternal, labor, and other organizations; to the voluntary or involuntary remission of debts by merchants, landlords, and others; and to the aid—quite real in this depression—extended by business concerns to former employees. These are only a few of the items, but it seems clear that if the total of this invisible relief, which is obviously incalculable, were known it would be found that the private contributions very greatly exceed the public.[26]

The Drive for Federal Relief

As winter approached, the pressure for Federal relief became more and more insistent. On October 13, Mr. William Hodson sent an open letter to President Hoover in which he stated his own position, which was virtually the position held by a representative group of social workers. Mr. Hodson was then executive Director of the Welfare Council of New York City and later New York City Commissioner of Public Welfare. He had acted as chairman of the Sub-Committee on "The Federal Government and Child Welfare" of the White House Conference, which in 1930 had recommended Federal grants-in-aid for child welfare services.[27]

Mr. Hodson's letter urged that facts be secured about the unemployment situation and be used instead of opinions as a basis of planning. He assumed that the facts would reveal the inadequacy of local funds and the necessity of Federal aid. His argument must be quoted at length because of the strong position which he took in favor of public as against private funds for relief, and because of his clear presentation of the case for Federal responsibility:

The power of the federal treasury must be used to help the destitute communities outright, to aid the more prosperous localities according to the particular measure of their need and to stimulate all the local governments to the utmost of which they are capable. We must establish a productive partnership which calls forth the best which the national and the local partners have to offer, thus swelling the total relief by the full contributions of each partner. If in-

[26] See Mr. Gifford's testimony. Senate Committee Hearings S. 174 and S. 262, pp. 309-333.
[27] See Part I, Chapter 1.

stead of this, millions of dollars are appropriated to be distributed on some rough measure of equity, like population, and without the most careful and discriminating type of administration, local effort will be paralyzed and the federal treasury will be substituted for the treasuries of the local governments, thus in the end decreasing the total available resources. . . .

As the report of the Committee on the Federal Government and Child Welfare points out, the demonstrated advantages of federal partnership with the states through grants-in-aid are many, and the first one is that the principle of local administration of local affairs is preserved—there is no real danger of federal bureaucracy. The initiative of the states is insured and their active acceptance of local responsibility encouraged by requiring them to match federal appropriations with their own. Moreover, without jeopardizing local autonomy the federal government through its visitation and inspection can focus upon local administration the broad experience and expert knowledge of a central authority.

Grants-in-aid can be appropriately extended to unemployment relief and the difficulties of "pork-barrel" legislation avoided, provided broad authority coupled with wide discretion is vested in the administering federal agency with only such general limitations and restrictions as experience with this type of aid has proved to be necessary and beneficial. Obviously, however, the usual requirement that the locality match federal appropriations dollar for dollar must be modified by leaving the manner and amount of matching to the discretion of the administering authority.[28]

[28] "An Open Letter to the President on Federal Relief Appropriations (Oct. 13, 1931)," *Survey Graphic,* Nov., 1931, pp. 144-145.

Chapter 5

The Battle for Federal Relief Begins

∽∽∽∽∽∽∽∽∽∽∽∽∽∽∽∽∽∽∽∽∽∽∽∽∽∽∽

The Costigan and La Follette Bills

When Congress convened in December, 1931, Senator Costigan introduced a bill [1] which provided for Federal aid to the amount of $125,000,000 for the remainder of the current fiscal year, and $250,000,000 for the following year. These funds were to be administered by the Children's Bureau under a Federal Board for Unemployment Relief, consisting of the Chief of the Children's Bureau, the Director of Extension Work of the Department of Agriculture, the Chief of the Vocational Rehabilitation Service of the Federal Board for Vocational Education. Forty percent of the funds were to be granted to the states on the basis of population, the remainder on the basis of need, except amounts needed for Federal administration.

Senator La Follette, of Wisconsin, also introduced a bill for Federal aid with somewhat similar provisions.[2] Both bills were referred to the Committee on Manufactures and hearings were conducted by a subcommittee of which Senator La Follette was chairman; the other members were: Henry D. Hatfield, West Virginia; Bronson Cutting, New Mexico; Bur-

---

[1] S. 174. Seventy-Second Congress, First Session.

[2] S. 262. Seventy-Second Congress, First Session. This bill provided for $250,000,000 to be immediately available to be allotted to the several states for preliminary studies of need, for 50% of initial administrative costs, for additional grants based partly on relief expenditures and partly on need. Administration to be vested in the Children's Bureau under a Federal Emergency Relief Board of three members, to be appointed by the President and to receive $10,000 a year each.

In view of later disposition of surplus commodities it is worth noting that both these bills provided for the purchase of wheat from the Grain Stabilization Corporation, its conversion into flour and transportation to the localities where it was most sorely needed.

ton K. Wheeler, Montana; Edward P. Costigan, Colorado.

The first session opened with a statement by Senator Costigan which explained the purpose of the bills, and the detailed investigation of the relief situation upon which they were based. Spoken two years and a half before the passage of the Federal Emergency Relief Act, his words embody the essential philosophy upon which that administration was based:

Unemployment throughout the United States has been widespread and acute since October 1929. It is to be remembered that we have entered the third winter of distress, and that known resulting conditions are sufficiently disturbing to arouse the concern of all informed, humane, and public-spirited citizens. Extraordinarily faithful and generous efforts to meet the emergency have already strained charitable resources and have heavily taxed the facilities of existing social agencies. It has been apparent for some time that the funds heretofore provided and otherwise available are inadequate for the rapidly increasing and urgent needs of our hopeless unemployed and their helpless dependents.

The economic storm which has swept America and the world continues practically unabated, and though legislative plans are now maturing for the restoration of confidence and prosperity, it is evident that before beneficial results may be expected from any such program distress in the United States will have exacted an incalculable toll unless emergency relief on national lines is promptly enacted by Congress. . . .

Some difficulties in attempting to deal uniformly with nationwide distress are apparent. Only a few states, which are listed on a chart available here for the committee, have already acted through their legislatures to extend relief. In this connection it must be remembered that some States have constitutional prohibitions against the appropriation of State funds to assist counties to meet their home-relief problems. Some States are on the verge of exhausted tax possibilities. Others are prevented from taxing incomes. In some States the limits of the general property tax have almost been reached. . . .

The investigations to which I have referred have persuasively demonstrated that nothing short of Federal assistance, early provided and efficiently and constructively extended, can possibly satisfy the conscience and heart and safeguard the good name of America. With advancing winter at our doors, human suffering is becoming more definite and desperate. Long-established standards of social relief are breaking down and it is obvious that the intelligence and good will of the Nation must be organized through the cooperation of Federal, State and other local agencies to deal with the public emergency.

The hearing, which is about to open, is designed to be informative. Social workers and public-spirited citizens of wide experience have been invited to testify. Without attempting to forecast what they will say, I am convinced by inquiries, which were conducted disinterestedly, that their testimony will disclose grave inadequacies, not only with respect to our estimates of the extent of present destitution as a result of prolonged unemployment, but also in respect to provisions for dealing with it without prompt and substantial supplementary Federal assistance. It will, I am sure, be established that legal and economic impediments in different parts of the country call for Federal unification and standards in relief work under trained administrative authority, assisted by skilled workers, and fortified by sufficiently flexible powers to deal with every phase of the present crisis.

One further remark may be required. In the tragic economic era in which we move no one desires to load unnecessary responsibilities either on individuals or on the Nation. Least of all are we concerned with theories. Instead we must face actualities. The facts, if developed here, should establish that the hour has passed for reliance on incurable optimism and that our Nation must grapple with characteristic thoroughness with the realities of the present crisis.

Objection will be taken in some quarters to the measures before us on the ground that they contemplate a "dole" rather than charity. By "dole" is undoubtedly meant that the measures look to public as distinguished from private aid. That objection should be and can be squarely met. Americans must not starve while we quibble over words, for be it remembered that this country has never hesitated to deal with such underlying facts. Throughout our country's past, even in colonial times, public money has been used to provide for the poor. Today, far the larger part of our efficient social work is sustained and assured through State and local taxes. . . .

Nationwide unemployment is today breaking the hearts and lives of friends and neighbors who are inheritors with us of Anglo-Saxon aspirations and traditions. Already many of them have suffered with extraordinary patience throughout a period as extended as that of our participation in the World War. The people of Belgium, San Francisco, Tokio, and the Mississippi Valley, to whose respective plights Congress promptly, sanely, and efficiently responded, did not suffer more severe or uninvited visitations than today afflict several millions of Americans.[3]

The record of these hearings of December, 1931, and January, 1932, together with those of the following winter on the same subject, constitutes what is probably the most vivid, the most telling and the most accurate picture in existence of the unemployment relief problem; the extent of the destitution during the early years of the depression, and the struggles of local public and private agencies to meet increasing needs with inadequate funds.

The testimony included detailed descriptions of conditions in such widely separated parts of the country as California, Mississippi, Chicago, West Virginia, Philadelphia; reports on relief loads, standards, unmet needs, financial resources in cities, counties and states: stories of landlords on relief; families broken up, children passed around among neighbors; mounting numbers of suicides, mental failures, the increase of disease, sick people uncared for, families of four trying to live on $5.50 a week, 6 families crowded into a six-room house.

For the first time in the history of the United States, social workers and labor leaders who had first-hand knowledge of the deprivations and needs of the underprivileged third of the population were called in to testify before a Committee of Congress and were listened to with serious attention. They were asked to bring all the facts they could gather and to put them in the *Congressional Record* to be considered in the formation of a new and far-reaching Federal policy.

A tremendous amount of detailed material was incorporated in the *Record* by the American Association of Social Workers, the Family Welfare Association of America, the Association of Community Chests and Councils, the American Association of Public Welfare Officials, the National Catholic Welfare Conference, the National Conference of Catholic Charities, the Russell Sage Foundation and the Federal Children's Bureau. Executives or other staff members of these agencies testified personally.[4]

[3] Hearings on S. 174 and S. 262, pp. 7, 8 and 9, Dec., 1931.
[4] Reports printed in record of hearings: Budget of Jewish Social Serv-

The executive secretary of The American Association of Social Workers presented a report of conditions throughout the country, compiled from material sent in by chapters of the Association. The director of the Family Welfare Association of America testified on behalf of 4,000,000 people served by the association's 230 member agencies. Much of his testimony was based upon monthly summaries made in the national office of the experience of 100 public and private agencies which were administering relief to the unemployed.

Mr. Frank Bane, of the American Association of Public Welfare Officials, gave a quick summary of the relief situation in the 48 states. He reported that only 12 presented no severe problems. This summary was based upon the findings of the Association's field staff which had worked closely with Senators Costigan and La Follette during the fall of 1931, and had in fact obtained considerably more information about the state of the nation than had been secured by Mr. Gifford and his staff.

Other prominent social workers came from Philadelphia, Cleveland, Chicago, and New York, representing councils, chests, private service agencies, and Foundations. Labor was represented by John L. Lewis, of the United Mine Workers of America, Donald R. Richberg, Counsel for the Railway Labor Executives Association, and Sidney Hillman, President of the Amalgamated Clothing Workers of America. City managers came from Dayton and Cincinnati, Ohio, and the mayor, Frank Murphy, from Detroit. Members of Congress from Washington and Alabama testified of need and inadequate resources in the states which they represented.

Perhaps the most distressing testimony was given by Mr. Pickett, of the Friends' Service Committee, which had been feeding children in the mining counties of West Virginia and

ice Bureau, Chicago. Use of A and B Budgets ("Temporary and Regular"), October, 1931, pp. 39-42.

Report on conditions in each state made by Mr. Frank Bane of the Association of Public Welfare Officials, pp. 106-9.

Relief charts and statistics presented by the Russell Sage Foundation, pp. 162, 167, 168, 173-6.

Statement and statistics regarding "Relief Work in Catholic Agencies in 1931." Presented by the Reverend John O'Grady, p. 180.

Comparative tax rates of 290 cities over 30,000 for 1931, pp. 296-308.

Kentucky at the request of the Children's Bureau and the President's Committee.[5]

From the Philadelphia Federation of Jewish Charities came telling data showing the increase in malnutrition among children; in tuberculosis; in hospital cases; in mental diseases; citing reliable medical authorities which contradicted the favorable report on health conditions referred to by Mr. Hoover in his message to Congress on December 9, 1931:

The evidence of the Public Health Service shows an actual decrease of sickness and infant and general mortality below normal years. No greater proof could be adduced that our people have been protected from hunger and cold and that the sense of social responsibility in the Nation has responded to the need of the unfortunate.[6]

The editor of the *Survey*, Mr. Paul Kellogg, made the following comments upon the situation:

To my mind the "great American dole" is such "unearned" income as has been paid in 1931, as was paid in 1930, to American investors not out of the earnings of American industry in those years but out of accumulated surpluses. . . .

When you scratch the outcry against "the dole," you find that it merely echoes propaganda put out in high places, reflects some childhood teaching, is a defense for the wealthy, or is a serious fear lest we undermine local responsibility, or set up a pork barrel that will be worse than any we have known in pensions or river and harbor appropriations. . . .

We turned to municipal help, but that throws over onto real estate the brunt of an industrial risk at a time when landlords are shy on rents, when business is stalled and when home-owners run the risk of losing their equities. This left-handed blow at middle-class incomes gives another twist to the downspiral of purchasing power. Moreover, the resources of hundreds of American municipalities will be cramped for a long time to come because of their relief bills last winter and this.

Slowly we have begun to realize that local taxation will not afford enough money. In New York, Governor Roosevelt has turned to the State income tax to carry a part of the load; in Wisconsin, Governor La Follette has pushed a rounded program; in Pennsylvania,

[5] See Part II, Chapter 3.
[6] S. 174 and S. 262, etc., pp. 116-123. See also Hopkins, Harry L., *Spending to Save*, pp. 79-83.

Governor Pinchot has been trying to get through a prosperity loan; in Rhode Island the State contemplates underwriting the emergency relief bonds of municipalities. Other States have acted; but in general my impression is that the States have failed to really grapple with the situation as a whole. They may have waited for national leadership which has not come. General unemployment relief is not a load the Red Cross has attempted. The President's commission has given spirited support to chest campaigns throughout the country—but they only reached cities of over 25,000 and not all of those. No one knows the full situation in smaller communities. And this stimulation of charitable giving has not been paralleled by an equally resourceful campaign to elicit and strengthen public appropriations by cities, counties, and States.

We enter 1932 next week, therefore, or this week, without any adequate appraisal by any national public body or by any national private body of what relief needs are throughout the country or what relief resources are. I would like to underscore that. We enter 1932 without any adequate appraisal by any national public body or by any national private body of what relief needs are throughout the country or what relief resources are.[7]

The forces which opposed Federal relief were represented by the Sentinels of the Republic, the United States Chamber of Commerce, the Woman Patriot Publishing Company, the People's Lobby, the Detroit Board of Commerce, and the President's Organization on Unemployment Relief.

The Sentinels of the Republic repeated the same views which they had expressed against public relief in the depression of 1893. The United States Chamber of Commerce had taken a straw vote and, on the basis of the returns, reported that 2,479 against 194 recommended that private funds supplemented by state and local public funds would be adequate to meet all unemployment relief needs.

. . . numbers of cases of distress of a kind suitable for charitable relief are brought to light in times of business depression and may be confused with unemployment distress. That the funds for adequate care for all such cases of distress will be forthcoming there is every assurance. The spontaneous generosity of our people has never failed, and it will be supplemented by city, county, and state funds on a larger scale this year than last. Preparations are under way to assist every city with suggestions. For that purpose, the

[7] S. 174 and S. 262, pp. 80, 83, 84. Dec. 29, 1931.

President has set up a national committee, with distinguished personnel in its officers, its advisory board, and its committees. There will thus be a coordination of relief measures.[8]

Pros and Cons of Federal Relief

The same arguments for and against Federal relief funds which were brought out in these first hearings in the winter of 1931-32 were reiterated in subsequent hearings and on the floor of Congress during the following eighteen months.

Headed by the Federal Administration and the President's Organization on Unemployment Relief, opponents of Federal relief claimed that it would seriously impair the credit of the Federal Government and make it impossible to balance the budget. They claimed that this would retard the restoration of normal business and serve to increase unemployment; and that there was a limit to the Federal borrowing power and to higher income, estate and corporation taxes.

They held that the very idea of Federal relief was contrary to the Constitution of the United States and violated American principles of local responsibility. The Federal Government had appropriated no funds in other depressions, why should any action be taken now? Nothing should be done to lessen the responsibility of citizens or give them an excuse for shirking. Private generosity, energy and initiative could be counted on to restore prosperity unaided. Federal relief would actually render a disservice to the unemployed by encouraging local governments to saddle their burdens on the Federal Government rather than to develop state and local resources.

Federal appropriations would end, to a very great extent at least, the efforts and labor of the thousands of charitable and public-spirited citizens who are working ceaselessly without pay in the various organizations for relief. It would end the community chest and like efforts. It would stop all city, county, and State appropriations. It would remove the final discretion in the apportionment of funds from close and local supervision of those who intimately know their various conditions, to the seat of government at Washington.
It would weaken the morale and the fiber of every individual,

[8] S. 174 and S. 262, p. 378. Quotation from U. S. Chamber of Commerce Referendum No. 58.

community, and state. It would establish another great and growing bureau at Washington with agents, investigators, and representatives going forth, at Federal expense, into every locality of the Union. It would cause delay rather than expedite action, and it would add another tremendous sum to the huge cost of the National Government.[9]

States' rights were said to be in danger of violation by Federal control. The self-respect of states was at stake. They wished to take care of "their own." In fact, the Connecticut Chamber of Commerce issued a statement to this effect which was read on the floor of the Senate by Senator Bingham of Connecticut:

Mr. Bingham. Mr. President, I have received from the executive vice-president of the Connecticut Chamber of Commerce a telegram setting forth the attitude of the Connecticut Employment Commission on the pending bill—

Hartford, Conn., Feb. 5, 1932

Hon. Hiram Bingham
    Senator from Connecticut:
La Follette-Costigan direct Federal unemployment relief bill arouses definite and widespread opposition in Connecticut. The Connecticut Unemployment Commission, which has been in close touch with unemployment in every community in this State, has given assurances to our governor and to the President that Connecticut not only wishes to but is able to take care of its unemployment situation without Federal aid. This organization deplores Federal appropriations for direct aid which we hold should emanate from states and communities where needs originate and exist.—The Connecticut Chamber of Commerce, H. E. Hasty, Executive Vice-President.[10]

This argument was further reinforced by the President of the Sentinels of the Republic who cited the following statement "from one inaugural address of former President Coolidge":

I always like to quote this because it seems to me to state a principle as clearly as it can be stated.
    "The greatest solicitude should be exercised to prevent any en-

[9] Congressional Relief Programs: A Record of Action in the Congress of the United States, 1803-1933. Compiled by Adelaide R. Hasse. *Congressional Record*, Vol. 75, pp. 4016-17.
[10] Feb. 5, 1932, p. 3414, Seventy-Second Congress, First Session.

croachment upon the rights of the States or their various political subdivisions. Local self-government is one of our most precious possessions. It is the greatest contributing factor to the stability, strength, liberty and progress of the nation. It ought not to be infringed by assault or undermined by purchase. . . . It does not at all follow that because abuses exist it is the concern of the Federal Government to attempt their reform." [11]

The opponents of Federal aid also maintained that the states would supplement local funds if necessary. There was no such thing as a helpless and pauper state. No legislature had made a formal appeal for help to the Federal Government. No evidence existed that local resources were insufficient to prevent actual starvation anywhere. Also, if an attempt were made to do more than prevent actual starvation and even to raise standards of relief and standards of living by the use of Federal appropriations, the cost would be huge and the effort would only result in sinking huge sums into a bottomless pit.

Federal relief was referred to as a "dole," although it was not clear why this label was not applicable to local relief. European experience was cited as a warning of the danger which would result from creating a new group in the population similar to the veterans, who would demand "largess" from the Federal Government. To begin giving relief to such a group would be like taking the lid off Pandora's box. Demands for help would be bound to increase "as the inevitable demoralization resulting from public handouts" progressed.[12] Federal aid once started would be difficult or impossible to stop. The spirit of paternalism would be fostered, and the system would create permanent wards of the nation in the place of self-reliant citizens.

It was further declared that the administration of Federal relief would involve an enormous bureaucratic set-up, which had proved "a failure or worse" wherever it had been tried on such a large scale. The attempt to apply one Federal rule to so many widely different local situations would "break the

[11] S. 174 and S. 262, p. 358.
[12] See statement of Mary G. Kilbreth, Chairman Board of Directors, Woman Patriot Corporation, Washington, D. C. Hearings on S. 5125, pp. 478-488, Jan. 14, 1933.

thing down." Untold risks would be involved in administering a program at such a distance from the beneficiaries. Ex-
travagance and waste were bound to occur when spending was
so far removed from local controls, and such a regime would
necessarily be more subject to political interference. Local
citizens knew local conditions best. The nearer the administration of relief was kept to the community affected, the
sooner its evils would be detected and checked, and the less
serious would be the "moral and economic consequences of unwise and unsound policies." [13] Thus the opponents of Federal
aid summed up their case.

On the other side, the most powerful argument in favor of
Federal aid offered by its proponents was the record of the
actual experience of local communities as they had struggled
to meet the increasing needs, and relieve the dire distress of
1930 and 1931; the stark facts of suffering and demoralization which were the result of unemployment, and the inadequacy of local and even of state resources to cope with the
problem.

A national disaster, they declared, arising from causes
deeply rooted in the national economic structure, demanded a
national remedy. Business and industry were organized on a
national scale and to some extent on an international basis.
Relief should not be thrown back upon industrial communities—the very areas which had been hardest hit by the depression. Factories and mines, owned by thousands of investors scattered throughout the country, had shut down. The
communities in which they happened to be located should not
be required to relieve the resulting distress.

The "welfare" clause in the Federal Constitution was for
the first time given a new, although unofficial, interpretation.[14]
If government had any responsibility at all for the welfare of
"society," should that "society" be limited by state boundaries,
or did it exist in terms of a national entity?

Plenty of precedent existed for the assumption of such responsibility by the Federal Government. Moreover, in a democracy the people can always empower their government to

[13] S. 174 and S. 262, p. 354. Resolution adopted by the Sentinels of
the Republic, Mr. Frank L. Peckham, Vice President.
[14] See pp. 33-34 above.

do what they wish. To back up the appeal to precedent, a member of the Senate had read into the *Congressional Record* a list of 31 Federal appropriations made between 1803 and 1921 for emergency and disaster relief of distress due to flood, fire, earthquake, cyclone and drought.[15] Mr. Hoover himself had advocated Federal aid for county health work in 1929, and in 1930 the White House Conference on Child Health and Protection, which he had called and officially sponsored, had recommended Federal grants-in-aid to the states for child welfare.[16] And for many years, the Federal policy of grants-in-aid to the states for highways and agricultural purposes had been well established.[17]

The vicious cycle of depleted buying power, delinquent taxes, bankrupt municipalities and inadequate relief appropriations served as a powerful argument for state aid. It was used even more effectively on behalf of Federal relief because of the power of the Federal Government to impose income, inheritance and corporation taxes. Governor Pinchot drove home this point in a forceful article published by the *Survey Graphic* in January.

In 1929 the National Bureau of Economic Research made a careful study of all the incomes in this country for 1926. They found that four and a half thousand people received that year an average of almost $240,000 apiece. And at the bottom of the heap, forty-four million people had incomes of about one thousand dollars each, or less than one-half of one percent of the separate incomes of those at the top.

Most recent figures are yet more amazing. In 1929 the per capita income in this country was $700 for every man, woman and child. But according to the Treasury Department's preliminary estimate, over five hundred persons had in that year incomes of over a million dollars a piece. Their total income was $1,185,000,000. They received, these five hundred odd, the average shares of 1,692,000 people.

In other words, in the eight-year period between 1920 and 1929, while the total national income increased less than 10 percent, the

[15] See p. 36 and Appendix A.
[16] White House Conference on Child Health and Protection. Vol. IV A. *Organization for the Care of Handicapped Children.* The Century Co., New York, pp. 275-283.
[17] See pp. 34-35.

number of men with incomes of over a million dollars increased over 1400 percent, or one hundred and forty times as fast. And the amount of money these men made in one year increased 1300 percent, or one hundred and thirty times as fast as the total amount of money made by everybody in the whole of the United States. They certainly got their share!

The same astounding concentration of wealth and power is seen in the industrial world. A study of corporate wealth and of the influence of large corporations was published this year in *The American Economic Review*. The conclusions reached are eye-openers. In 1927, there were over 300,000 industrial corporations in this country. Two hundred of the 300,000, less than seven-hundredths of one percent, controlled 45 percent of the total wealth of all these corporations. The same two hundred received over 40 percent of all corporate income, and controlled over 36 percent of all business wealth. Furthermore, about 20 percent of the wealth of this entire nation was in the hands of those two hundred corporations.

Truly the growth of these two hundred giant corporations has been almost beyond belief. In the ten years up to 1929 their assets grew from under 44 billion to 78 billion dollars, an increase of 78 percent. The author of the study, Prof. Gardiner C. Means, asserts that if their indicated rate of growth continues in the future they will own within twenty years virtually half of our national wealth. Professor Means then emphasizes an extremely important fact. He says that in 1927, less than two thousand men were directors of these two hundred corporations. Since many of them were inactive, the ultimate control of more than one third of industry was actually in the hands of a few hundred men.[18]

Before the Senate Committee on January 4, 1932, Governor Pinchot voiced his conviction regarding unemployment relief. He declared "the problem can not be met, in my opinion, without Federal aid. In the second place, it ought not to be met without Federal aid, because Federal aid is the only way by which the people who ought to meet this problem can be made to meet it."[19]

On the floor of the Senate, Senator La Follette called attention to the fact that $2,160,000,000 had already been provided by Congress and the Federal Administration during the depression for the relief of those who own property and securi-

[18] Pinchot, Gifford, "The Case for Federal Relief," *Survey Graphic*, Jan., 1932, pp. 348-49.

[19] S. 174 and S. 262, p. 219.

ties of banks, railroads, insurance companies, and industries. Since large sums had been borrowed for the relief of business, would not the Federal Government be equally justified in borrowing for the relief of the unemployed? Was not the danger of destroying individual initiative as great in the one case as in the other?

Federal aid had been labeled "the dole" by its opponents, but a new definition of the dole as an inadequate fixed amount of relief was brought forward in the Senate Committee hearings:

Senator Costigan. "Referring to your use of the word 'dole,' do you have in mind the inadequacy of the relief which is being afforded?"

Mr. Swift. "Primarily."

Senator Costigan. "Is that why you used this word?"

Mr. Swift. "The inadequacy; and also the fact that, being inadequate, with the impossibility of basing it upon the individual needs of the families, it becomes a more or less fixed amount. In other words, in many instances the giving becomes more or less automatic.

"I wish to make clear my conviction as a social worker that proposals for Federal aid have no relation to the establishment de novo of a dole. A dole is a dole, whether it is given by an individual, a private charitable agency, a city, a State, or the Federal Government. It is a dole whether given in cash or in kind." [20]

The brief experience with state relief in two or three states during the winter of 1931-1932 was drawn upon to furnish support for Federal aid. During the following months as one state after another went into the relief business the arguments based on the insufficiency of state funds were reinforced rather than weakened. A number of the more important points were presented to the Senate Committee exactly two months after the New York TERA began to function.

In New York State, there was a disposition at first to regard the $20,000,000 relief fund, to be drawn from the State income tax, as easy money to be had by local political units for the asking. It is turning out the other way. It is proving a force which is melting township, city, and county appropriations which were frozen before. To get the State funds, they must do their part; they must demon-

[20] S. 174 and S. 262, pp. 102-103. Testimony of Linton B. Swift, Executive Director, Family Welfare Association of America.

strate needs and resources. The emergency system will bring to the
rescue of the unemployed of New York State three or four times the
money provided by the State act itself. More than that, it is lift-
ing the standard of relief to a level which our civilization can stand
for. A few beans and a dollar now and then do not qualify under
the New York act. It has uncovered areas where conditions were
neglected and desperate. It has provoked constructive action by
big industries and public officials. It has called for an entirely new
caliber of investigation and social service in dealing with the cases.
It is a modern social installation to meet an emergency.[21]

The states needed leadership. Many of them were backward in social legislation and welfare programs; their social
policies were conservative; their legislatures and leaders
lacked social vision and were reluctant to increase taxation
and expenditures and to undertake additional responsibilities.
Many states in which standards were low and where suffering
was acute had the most meager resources and the least progressive leadership. A number of states had constitutional
limitations on their power to borrow, or on their power to appropriate money for relief purposes. These constitutional provisions could not be changed easily or quickly, even if the legislature and the voters were so disposed.[22]

For these reasons, Federal aid appeared to its proponents to
be essential if the unemployed were to be cared for with any
semblance of adequacy. Also the very fact that Federal funds
and Federal supervision involved considerable Federal control,
promised to bring some uniformity into a relief world where
for the most part each local community was still a law unto
itself.

Many of these arguments, both pro and con, were summed
up in a document published in January, 1932, called *A Social
Work Study of Federal Aid for Unemployment Relief*. This
was the report of a group of social workers which had been
organized the preceding October as a "Social Work Conference on Federal Action," in order to bring social work knowledge and experience to bear upon Federal unemployment relief legislation. The members of this conference, most of

---

[21] S. 174 and S. 262, p. 85. Testimony of Paul Kellogg.
[22] Heisterman, "Constitutional Limitations Affecting State and Local
Funds," *Social Service Review*, March, 1932, pp. 1-20.

whom were leaders in the private social work field, had testified in the Senate Committee hearings on Federal aid and had been asked by members of the Senate Committee to make suggestions for a Federal relief program and to give advice on the framing of Federal legislation. Most of the principles recommended by the conference in its report had already been incorporated in the Costigan and La Follette bills. This same group of social workers were to testify again and carry the battle for Federal relief through the 1932-33 session of Congress until the Federal Emergency Relief Act was passed in May, 1933.[23]

Increasing Pressure for Congressional Action

On January 15, 1932, Senators Costigan and La Follette combined their original bills and reintroduced the consolidated bill which authorized the expenditure of $375,000,000.[24] It was voted on in the Senate on February 16 and failed to pass. Exciting debate with crowded galleries preceded the voting, in which party lines were shot to pieces.

The bill had provided for outright Federal grants to the states. Throughout both sessions of the Seventy-Second Congress Senators La Follette and Costigan continued to introduce bills providing for unemployment relief. The bills either died in committee or failed to pass, although the hearings continued to bring out the dreadful conditions of distress which prevailed throughout the country. Measures providing for public works, for an employment system and for transient relief were introduced by other members of Congress and were also rejected.[25]

Senator La Follette sent out a questionnaire early in Feb-

[23] *A Social Work Study of Federal Aid for Unemployment Relief.* Report of Steering Committee, Social Work Conference on Federal Action on Unemployment, pp. 1-2. Members of Committee: Frank Bane, Howard S. Braucher, Allen T. Burns, C. C. Carstens, Joanna C. Colcord, Helen Crosby, John A. Fitch, David H. Holbrook, Paul U. Kellogg, H. L. Lurie, John O'Grady, Walter M. West, Linton B. Swift, Chairman; Benson Y. Landis, Secretary.

[24] S. 3045.

[25] See Hopkins, Harry L., *Spending to Save*, Ch. III. Also list of bills and Joint Resolutions, Dec., 1931-May, 1933, Hasse, *op. cit.*

ruary to mayors of cities all over the United States asking these seven questions:

(1) What increase has there been in the number of unemployed persons in your city compared with December 1930? With December 1929?

(2) How much have the city appropriations for the unemployed and the poor increased this year over 1930? Over 1929?

(3) In your judgment how many additional persons will need relief during the winter months?

(4) What proportion of the emergency burden is being carried by private relief agencies? How much have their expenditures increased compared with 1930? With 1929?

(5) Can you state the amount of relief given weekly to the average family (two adults and two children)?

(6) Is your city in a position to float further bond issues in the event that your present income is insufficient to meet adequately the relief needs of the community?

(7) Do you favor a Federal appropriation to assist the local governments in meeting their emergency relief burdens, and do you feel that such an appropriation would be of aid in providing more adequate relief for the needy or in lessening the burden on local taxpayers? [26]

The replies gave overwhelming evidence of widespread distress and demand for Federal aid. Senator La Follette had them read into the *Congressional Record*.[27] The answers said, in effect, that practically every municipality in the United States was on the verge of bankruptcy. They were now administering relief on a starvation basis and were ready to stop it entirely in order to save themselves from becoming insolvent.

The *Record* also contains, under date of February 2,[28] a report submitted by the Federal Children's Bureau on the "Effects of the Depression on Child Health and Child Health Services." This was another disheartening account, presented under such topics as nutrition and general health, consumption of milk, relief standards and the increasing demands which were being made upon existing health agencies.

No one could find out the extent of the relief problems, the

[26] *Congressional Record,* Volume 75. Page 3067.
[27] *Ibid.,* pp. 3068-3260.
[28] *Ibid.,* p. 3095.

number of persons receiving relief, or the demands which were being made upon relief agencies. Estimates made later put the relief rolls at 4,800,000 families, approximately 20,000,000 people, one in six of the population of the United States. Because of the unequal distribution of distress, in certain areas 35 percent of the population were on relief. There was reason to fear an outbreak of riots and violence, especially in the mining counties and in the drought areas. In February, Congress finally passed a Joint Resolution, which was not this time vetoed by President Hoover, authorizing the distribution of government-owned wheat and cotton to the American Red Cross and other organizations, to be distributed in distressed rural communities.[29]

Because it seemed impossible to secure favorable action on direct Federal aid, a substitute plan providing for loans and advances to the states was proposed and supported initially in the Senate by Senators Buckley and Wagner and in the House by Representative Rainey. Senator Buckley gave this explanation of the bill over a nationwide broadcast early in February:

A Democratic substitute will be offered, differing not at all from the La Follette-Costigan bill in the underlying purpose to relieve suffering and hardship, but differing fundamentally in the placing of responsibility for the relief and its administration.

The substitute provides for loans to the States rather than for direct contributions from the Federal Treasury. Under it a loan may be made to any State upon the certificate of its governor that the amount of the loan is necessary for emergency relief, and that it cannot be otherwise obtained.

Our substitute is preferable to the La Follette-Costigan bill fo four outstanding reasons:

First, because it provides work in addition to relief;

Second, because it does not provide a dole nor a gift nor invitation to relaxation of local effort, but it does make available substan-

[29] In March, 40,000,000 bushels of wheat, and not to exceed 350,000 bales of cotton. July, 45,000,000 bushels of wheat and 500,000 bales of cotton. For report on distribution see statement of Hon. John Barton Payne, Chairman American National Red Cross. Hearings before subcommittee of Committee on Manufactures, S. 5125, Part I, pp. 427-438.

See p. 68. A similar measure had previously been vetoed by President Hoover.

tial sums as loans to States wherever the needs justify such help;

Third, because it gives the States the right to administer the relief through those experienced agencies which are already handling the situation, without any bureaucratic red tape and Federal domination of local administration; and

Fourth, because it avoids a direct initiation to a presidential veto by avoiding the La Follette-Costigan provision for the giving away of Federal money to displace what ought to be raised by local responsibility.[30]

In March Senator Wagner, of New York, introduced a bill [31] providing for Federal advances to states which were to be deducted from "moneys payable under regular apportionments made from future Federal grants-in-aid of States for construction of highways." This bill was favorably reported out by the Committee on Manufacturers but in the Senate it was ordered to "lie on the table."

Vigorous debate continued throughout the session on the relative merits of Federal grants and advances to the states. There was also much discussion of the basis on which Federal aid might best be distributed. The weight of opinion seemed to be against distribution of Federal funds on the basis of population, and partial to some form of reimbursement or grant-in-aid dependent upon the expenditures made by municipal, state, and *private* agencies. The inclusion of private agencies in the discussion was symptomatic of the favorable attitude still prevalent at that time toward private local responsibility for unemployment relief. In fact, expenditures for relief by community-chest agencies in the spring of 1932 averaged 200 percent of their expenditures one year earlier. The proportion of these chest funds which were being spent for unemployment relief varied from 10 to 35 percent of the total amount raised in any one city, whereas before the depression not more than 10 percent had been normally spent for relief. These unusual amounts of private relief were budgeted for the entire calendar year to last from January to December, but in almost every city they were exhausted in March or April. 1932 was the last year in which private funds carried any large part of the unemployment relief burden.

[30] *Congressional Record,* Vol. 75, pp. 3574-76.
[31] S. 3676.

While the pros and cons of Federal grants and loans were being debated in Congress, the Illinois Legislature passed five measures between February 6 and March 1 appropriating a total of $20,000,000 for unemployment relief. Wisconsin appropriated $7,000,000 in February for work and relief. In March, Ohio appropriated $9,000,000 and New York made available the second $20,000,000 and extended the life of the TERA. The following month, Pennsylvania made its second appropriation, $12,000,000; and the New Jersey Legislature also acted, having been told by Chester I. Barnard, the State Administrator, that "double the present relief must be undertaken" and that the share of the state government should be 75 percent of the total cost.

The President's Organization on Unemployment Relief was still urging industry to "spread the work," and local agencies to carry the relief load with state assistance where absolutely necessary. Business could not get credit from the banks, and bank failures were becoming frequent in most small cities and many large ones.

In March, 1932, there was a serious riot in Dearborn, Michigan, and reports of hunger marches in more than one industrial center. Red Cross drought funds were almost exhausted. Reports from localities to the Family Welfare Association of America and the Association of Community Chests and Councils told of a decrease of 40 percent in average relief grants to families and a 40 percent increase in applications.

The very states in which large state appropriations had been made reported the most acute conditions and the most inadequate relief. Testimony at Congressional committee hearings pictured the continuation and aggravation of conditions described the preceding December and January. An account of the situation in 44 cities in 25 states was presented by the American Association of Social Workers.[32] The report is filled with tales of hunger and exposure, of bread lines, of separation of families, of the shutting off of gas and electricity, of evictions, even of the eviction of the same families two or three times during the year. Not only were relief grants lower, and

[32] Hearing before Senate Committee on Manufactures. S. 5125, p. 9. Testimony of Harry Lurie, Chairman of Sub-committee on Unemployment of the American Association of Social Workers.

relief spread thinner and thinner, but cuts were being made to an alarming extent in the budgets of the non-relief agencies. There had been already a dangerous curtailment of cultural, recreational, health and child welfare services, and funds were being diverted from education. No one knew how far such cuts would be made by states as well as by local governments, unless Federal funds could be secured for relief.

The deep concern of public officials all over the country is voiced in this significant statement made by Senator Borah during the consideration of the Revenue Bill (H. R. 10236):

We cannot longer expect the States or the cities or the local communities to deal with a situation which is national in all its significance, and which, in my judgment, must be dealt with as a national problem. In order to do that we must necessarily incur additional expense, regardless of what the plan may be. Some outlay upon the part of the Government must necessarily follow; and we had just as well face it, acknowledge the responsibility, and proceed to the completion of a Federal unemployment program. . . .

So far as I am concerned, I am opposed to the Federal Government shirking its responsibility and undertaking to lend to the States or the cities money with which to discharge its grave responsibility. The Federal Government owes a duty itself direct to the citizen. The responsibility is now ours, and we must meet it directly. The States have already incurred heavy responsibility, the cities have incurred heavy responsibility, and it would not be sufficient for the Government to do nothing more than to provide for loans to the States or cities.

It is a dangerous, inefficient, and unfair program, this program of loaning to the States or cities. . . . I am not willing in view of the awful conditions, to intrust them with the Federal money.[33]

More than once the relief offices in Philadelphia had been forced to close for lack of funds.[34] Late in June relief was exhausted in Chicago and important business men wired Washington: "Stations must close tomorrow night." They urged Congress to authorize loans to the state without delay, in order to make some Federal money available at once, because they saw a dangerous situation rapidy growing worse.

[33] *Congressional Record,* Vol. 75, pp. 10252-53.
[34] S. 5125, pp. 115-16.

Chapter 6

Federal Loans

~~~~~~

The Emergency Relief and Construction Act

The Wagner-Rainey Bill providing funds for public works and authorizing the Reconstruction Finance Corporation to make loans and advances for unemployment relief finally passed both houses of Congress and was vetoed by President Hoover on July 11, 1932. The President objected to the appropriation for public works. He questioned its effectiveness on the ground that it would employ too few people. He thought the entire bill was unsound because it meant an unbalanced budget and an ultimate burden on the taxpayer.

On July 16 a bill which was almost identical passed both houses, and was signed on July 21. Commenting on the measure in his campaign speech at Detroit the following October, President Hoover said:

Various conferences were carried on in an endeavor to arrive at an adequate relief bill, expanding activities of the Reconstruction Finance Corporation, but the Democratic leaders insisted not upon economy but upon inclusion in it of a new item of $322,000,000 of further expenditures from the Federal Treasury. Ultimately this bill passed Congress, containing not only these provisions but also measures putting the Government into wholesale pawnbroking with unlimited use of Federal Government credit. On July 11th I vetoed this bill and again protested about the item of $322,000,000 requesting at least that such a reservation be made as would hold back the expenditure until it could be determined if the Budget be balanced. In order to secure the relief bill at all, with these very vital provisions in relief of distress, employment, and agriculture, I was compelled finally to accept it with inadequate safeguards to that $322,-000,000, and this expenditure has been forced upon the Government by the Democratic leaders.[1]

[1] Quoted by Hopkins, Harry L., *op. cit.*, p. 90.

During the four days between the passage and the signing of the Act, 30 states unofficially indicated their intention of applying for loans either for relief or public works. Urgent messages came from one governor after another giving distressing details of local conditions.[2] Illinois was the first state to receive funds under the Act, on July 27, to forestall the closing of the Chicago relief stations. Advances to Pennsylvania, Arkansas, Alabama, Kansas, followed in rapid succession.

Title I [3] of the Emergency Relief and Construction Act authorized the Reconstruction Finance Corporation to make available $300,000,000 for advances to the states and territories "to be used in furnishing relief and work relief to needy and distressed people and in relieving the hardship resulting from unemployment." The advances were to be made at interest at the rate of 3 percent and could be (1) advances made to the governors of states upon their certification of necessity and inadequacy of resources; or (2) loans made directly to cities and counties through the instrumentality of the governors. Under the first procedure, the advances were to be repaid to the RFC by means of deductions "beginning with the fiscal year 1935 from future federal authorizations in aid of the states for the construction of highways and rural post roads." Loans made under the second procedure were definite local obligations to be secured by the usual methods. The bulk of the appropriation was eventually advanced to the states under the first procedure, since many cities had already exceeded their constitutional borrowing powers.[4]

[2] Requests from 12 states totaled nearly $175,000,000 in direct relief loans. Illinois asked for $10,000,000. Arizona, Pennsylvania, and New York each indicated requests for the maximum of $45,000,000. Others indicating need for advances were Idaho, Indiana, Kansas, Michigan, Missouri, Utah, West Virginia, and Wisconsin. Some states were prevented from borrowing by constitutional limitations, as was Florida.

[3] "Titles II and III of the Act provided [$1,500,000,000] for the financing of self-liquidating projects undertaken by public bodies and by private bodies for public purposes, for additional loans for agricultural purposes and for banking institutions, and for various federal public works projects." *Financing Relief and Recovery,* edited by L. László Ecker-R. Reprinted from *The Municipal Year Book,* April, 1937. p. 377. International City Managers' Association, Chicago.

[4] See Watson, Donald S., "Reconstruction Finance Corporation," *Financing Relief and Recovery,* pp. 372-81.

The requirement that advances were to be repaid by deductions from future highway grants was waived before it became operative. This was done by the Federal Highway Act, approved June 18, 1934,[5] and the state obligations were entirely canceled by Act of Congress in February, 1938.[6]

Another important clause of the Act provided that no more than 15 percent of the total appropriation could be made available to any one state. This limitation [7] is indicative of the concept which existed as late as 1932 that unemployment and therefore need was distributed evenly among the states. However, only one state, Illinois, received more than 15 percent of the total [8] after the limitation had been removed by Congress.

Between July 21, 1932, and May 29, 1933, when the administration of Title I of this Act ended, approximately $280,000,-000 was made available to 42 states [9] and 2 territories. A little more than $19,600,000 was loaned to political subdivisions within six states.[10] On June 30, 1939, $2,570,400 of the amount loaned to political subdivisions remained unpaid. Most of this amount was due from the city of Detroit.

Only $30,000,000, about one-quarter of the total, had been disbursed by the end of 1932. This seems strange in view of

[5] "No deduction shall hereafter be made . . . on account of amounts paid under the provisions of Title I of the Emergency Relief and Construction Act of 1932 for furnishing relief and work relief to needy and distressed people."

[6] Under the provisions of this Act "To authorize the Secretary of the Treasury to cancel obligations of the Reconstruction Finance Corporation incurred in supplying funds for relief at the authorization or direction of Congress," the outstanding advances and loan balances were cleared from the books of the RFC, and like amount of RFC notes held by the Treasury were canceled and evidence of indebtedness formerly held by the RFC was transferred to the Treasury.

[7] The limitation was removed by Congress on March 31, 1933, when approximately $240,000,000 had been authorized.

[8] Approximately $55,000,000 was made available to Illinois. Approximately 60% of the $300,000,000 went to seven states: California, Illinois, Michigan, New York, Ohio, Pennsylvania and Wisconsin.

[9] The following states did not receive funds: Connecticut, Delaware, Massachusetts, Nebraska, Vermont and Wyoming. No funds went to the District of Columbia, Alaska or the Virgin Islands.

[10] To 20 counties and 13 cities in the following states: Illinois, Michigan, New York, North Dakota, Ohio, Washington.

the pressure which had been brought to bear upon Congress
for Federal aid. The reasons, however, are not far to seek.
A number of states persisted in their reluctance to assume responsibility for relief. Six of them did not borrow at all. A
few governors insisted that the cities take responsibility for
borrowing and many of the cities had exhausted their borrowing power. Governor Roosevelt objected to the principle of a
Federal loan and claimed that the state could not truthfully
certify that it did not possess resources.[11] In other states delays were due to the necessity of securing legislative authority
or because considerable time was required to set up a relief
administration to handle the funds when they were received.

The prevailing note which characterized the RFC relief administration was self-liquidation. It was in effect a device for
the expenditure of state and local, and not Federal money. It
was not part of the original intention, but due to later cancella-
tion of state indebtedness, it actually resulted that all but
about $20,000,000 of the total appropriation represented di-
rect Federal expenditures.

The results of this experience led to the abandonment of
self-liquidating systems of relief, which added little if anything to the total volume of spending. Later relief acts substituted direct grants for loans and also provided a method of
distribution to the states which was more nearly related to
need than the politically conceived percentages of the Emergency Relief and Construction Act.

This was the only Federal relief measure passed during
the Hoover administration. The opponents of Federal relief
grants claimed that, because of the self-liquidating principle
involved in the loan provisions, the Act did not embody the
conception of Federal responsibility; that it did not overthrow
but facilitated the American system of local responsibility and
that the localities were thereby assisted in discharging their
traditional relief function.[12] On the other hand the advocates
of Federal relief who had fought so hard for its passage
claimed that it implicitly recognized the national character of
the unemployment emergency and established a precedent for

[11] New York did not apply for a loan until almost the end of February,
1933.
[12] See Part I, Chapter 1.

the assumption of Federal responsibility, and for this reason was far more significant than the actual amount of money which it supplied.

The Emergency Relief Division of the RFC

After the passage of the Act, the President's Organization for Unemployment Relief ceased to function and Mr. Fred Croxton, the Vice-Chairman, became "assistant to the Directors in charge of the Emergency Relief Division of the RFC." [13]

Responsibility for application was placed by the Act upon the governor of the state, who must certify the necessity for the funds requested and that the resources of his state were inadequate to meet the relief needs. The funds, when they were available, were to be administered under the direction and upon the responsibility of the governor. Federal partnership was limited to the act of making each loan or advance. The Federal funds were solely for the purpose of supplementing state and local resources when they were virtually exhausted and this was made quite clear in the instructions which were sent out from Mr. Croxton's office.[14] The availability of Federal funds was made a basis of stimulating, if not forcing, state appropriations for relief, and the relationship established by Mr. Croxton's office with state and local governments was used for the informal encouragement and improvement of their standards and methods of administration.

In December, well ahead of the sessions of 44 state legislatures, which were due in 1933, Mr. Croxton sent out a letter which was reported in the survey as follows:

From the emergency relief division of the Reconstruction Finance Corporation there issued last month a letter and set of accounting forms that puts teeth into the oft-repeated warning of the corporation that "it is plainly the intent of the emergency relief and con-

[13] See Senate Committee Hearings, S. 5125, Jan., 1933, p. 321, for Mr. Croxton's description of procedures used in making money available to the states and political subdivisions, and for further discussion of the inadequacy of standards and administrative difficulties encountered under the Act.

[14] See Senate Committee Hearings, S. 5125, Jan., 1933, pp. 44-45, for text of Mr. Croxton's letter to states exerting pressure for state funds.

struction act of 1932 that funds shall be made available by the Reconstruction Finance Corporation not in lieu of but merely supplemental to local and State funds and private contributions."

This letter in effect says to the governors of the States that have received aid through the corporation since the act was passed last July, "An accounting is now in order. If you are expecting to come before the corporation for further help after January 1, 1933, tell us now how the money which you have received so far has been spent." Nothing unusual in this. But then comes the paragraph with the punch: "Many States have regular or special sessions of their legislature in prospect by which State and local relief funds can be made available. Therefore, an outline of the legislative program to produce this result is especially important in order that the Reconstruction Finance Corporation may determine its course of action."

Thus does the corporation point up the philosophy under which it has been making available to States the emergency relief funds put at its disposal by Congress.[15]

The Federal Relief Division had no authority to follow through and make rules and regulations. However, its six regional field representatives worked with governors and their unemployment relief committees to help them set up organizations which could administer relief. They went into cities and rural areas to help measure the need, and they assisted the governors in preparing the material upon which their applications would be based. This type of work was done chiefly in the states which had developed no general machinery for the supervision or guidance of local communities in relief administration and where there was little information available to reveal the need which actually existed.

The RFC adopted the policy of making small initial advances for short periods in order to finance studies of needs and resources and allow time for an appraisal of the state situations. In a number of instances advances for short periods were made pending a change in state administration or in order to tide a state over until the legislature was ready to take action. This policy of making funds available for a month

[15] *Survey Midmonthly*, Jan., 1933, New York. Kurtz, Russell R., "American Relief Caravan." Quoted from Hearings before Subcommittee of the Committee on Manufactures: United States Senate, Seventy-Second Congress, S. 5125, Part I, Jan. 3 to 17, 1933, p. 44.

at a time became habitual and caused untold administrative difficulties. It was practically impossible for the states to set up adequate machinery and secure competent personnel without assurance that the program would continue beyond the end of the month.

In the administration of the section of Title I authorizing loans direct to political subdivisions, the Federal Government crossed state lines to deal directly with cities and counties,[16] although the actual applications were made by the governors. This practice tended to weaken state authority and hinder the assumption of relief responsibility by the states. Fortunately, the loans were made in only 33 subdivisions of 6 states, and the provision was not repeated in subsequent relief measures.

Another difficulty arose from the fact that the funds made available by Washington became state or local property and were therefore subject to state laws and local regulations. This fact, and the lack of any Federal supervisory or administrative authority, made it difficult to press for higher standards of relief or of personnel, although in many cases where traditional relief practices were poor and grants were low, the administration did recommend higher standards.[17] In general the policy was not to vary greatly from accepted local standards, and certainly not to reduce them. The funds were also subject to restrictions of state settlement laws, and therefore could not be used in a frontal attack upon the problem of transiency,[18] which had attained alarming proportions since the beginning of the depression.

During the summer and early fall of 1932 after the passage of the Act, when general policies were being decided upon, Mr. Croxton held weekly meetings in his office of representatives of national agencies and of certain Federal departments. These were essentially the same agencies which had been active in connection with the President's Emergency Committee for Employment and the President's Organization on Unemployment Relief; namely, the American Public Welfare Asso-

[16] See p. 125 above.
[17] See Mr. Croxton's testimony: Hearings on S. 5125, Part I, pp. 317-342, esp. 320-23. See Appendix F for Memorandum re Wisconsin advance.
[18] See Part I, Chapter 1. *Settlement.*

ciation,[19] Family Welfare Association of America, Association
of Community Chests and Councils, Friends' Service Association, American Red Cross and the Federal Children's Bureau.
Mr. Croxton added to this group of consultants the National
Association of Travelers' Aid Societies, the Salvation Army,
and the United States Public Health Service.

The Private National Agencies in 1932

The Family Welfare Association of America had in May
issued a report on Governmental Relief, which was the result
of several months' study made by a special staff in collabora-
tion with the Pathfinding Committee on Governmental Relief
Methods which had been appointed earlier by the Association.
This report attempted to summarize the types and extent of
public relief, and explore methods of attacking the problem.
To this end a questionnaire was sent to "167 public welfare
officials, social workers in private agencies and others: 76
effective replies were received, 71 agreed that some study or
concentrated effort was desirable in relation to the field of
public relief." The report recommended: the creation of an
Institute on Governmental Relief to engage in "factfinding,
educational effort and social planning relating to governmental
responsibility for the relief and prevention of dependency and
directed toward effective programs of public relief, local, state
and national." [20] This proposal from the private social work
field seemed to many of the public welfare officials, who were
in the midst of the emergency relief struggle, like trying to
changes horses in midstream. On the whole, however, the plan
met with considerable approval, although it was not possible
to secure funds to put it into effect.

The Association of Community Chests and Councils exerted
more pressure than ever during the fall in its effort to back up
the local chest campaigns. The drives of the winter of 1932-33
represented the supreme and final effort of the private agencies to carry a substantial share of the costs of unemployment
relief. In spite of many chest failures the private relief ex-

[19] The name was changed in June, 1932, from American Association of
Public Welfare Officials.
[20] Public Relief—Where Are We Going? Leaflet published by the Family Welfare Association of America, 1932.

penditures reached their peak in 1932. This was partly due to the fact that the chests cut the budgets of non-relief agencies much more drastically than during the winter of 1931-32, and turned the money thus saved over to the agencies which were administering relief. Even this effort succeeded in producing less than one-fifth of the total amount which was spent for relief in 1932. The other four-fifths came from the newly available Federal loans, from the appropriations made by the legislatures of 22 states, and from the treasuries of counties and municipalities many of which were on the verge of bankruptcy. And still the need was not met.[21] The situation was indeed so serious that the Association of Community Chests and Councils became a strong advocate of greater amounts of public relief as a necessary means of preventing hysteria and panic.

Newton D. Baker, chairman of a citizens' committee on relief within the Association, made an urgent appeal for state appropriations in the form of "A Challenge to Forty State Legislatures to Meet the Winter's Needs."

The preservation of local social services other than relief may appear to be a somewhat remote product of state participation. But to me it is evident that unless this winter's imperative increase in unemployment relief can be lifted from local resources by state activity and hence by larger R.F.C. loans our whole distinctive American organization for human betterment will be crippled if not demolished. I submit that so long as state resources for relief remain comparatively unimpaired it is indefensible to drain the life-blood from our character-building, health and preventive organizations whose service in and out of the emergency no intelligent person can question.

And yet with relief needs mounting, with R.F.C. funds drawn on less than they might be by appropriate state action and with state funds in the balance the tendency is to do an amputation on the total community service funds with the pious hope that the patient will not die under the knife. In my own city of Cleveland our community fund fell nearly half a million short of its goal which represented minimum budgeting for the essential services of the member agencies. To deal with this shortage the fund has cut 12½ percent from the budgets of all but relief agencies for a period of

[21] In 1932 public relief expenditures were 15 times those in 1929, while private relief expenditures were only five times as much.

two months. This allows a little time to see what will happen. If adequate R.F.C. and state funds take the estimated increase in relief load from private funds, the cut need be only temporary. If they do not, a whole range of services will be seriously impaired at the time when the community and its people need them most.

The chest in Washington, D. C., likewise fell short by half a million. Instead of an immediate cut of agency budgets the chest has added half a million to the estimates of needed public-relief funds to be asked of Congress. If the appropriation fails, the relief deficit will probably have to be absorbed at the expense of other services.

It is not only private services that are endangered. Some of our hard-won gains in public welfare are threatened with the knife. From certain up-state New York counties come reports that short-sighted local economists have discovered that it is cheaper to put a mother's-aid case on direct relief than to treat it through the approved methods of the established board of child welfare. The state reimburses 40 percent toward direct relief; it reimburses nothing on account of mothers' aid. By transferring the case the county saves itself some money, but the total relief fund is not increased and a principle is abrogated. As this is written, the governor of New Jersey is proposing to transfer the state's old-age relief cases to the Emergency Relief Administration, thereby cutting into funds available for unemployment relief and changing the pattern of a service which was difficult to establish and which will be difficult to restore.[22]

It was at this time that the community chests began to be acutely conscious that their publicity and campaign methods had always been centered around the relief appeal. Little or nothing had been done in most cities to lay a solid foundation of interpretation and understanding of "service" and "service agencies." This was one of the main reasons why they had felt obliged to get under the unemployment relief burden when the depression began. Now that the burden was about to crush them entirely and self-preservation forced them to shift it to governmental shoulders, they found that they were also relinquishing their relief appeal, which was, in the eyes of their contributors, the chief justification of their exist-

[22] The State Key to Relief: A Challenge to Forty Legislatures to Meet the Winter's Needs, by Newton D. Baker, Chairman National Citizens' Committee for the Welfare and Relief Mobilization of 1932. Reprinted from the *Survey*, Jan., 1933.

ence. One of the lasting effects of the early depression years upon private agencies came from the sudden change which the community chests were forced to make in their entire basis of interpretation of what they were doing and why, in order to rebuild their support upon a new understanding of the non-relief activities and the more or less intangible "services" of their member agencies.[23]

In the fall of 1932, however, the chests were still committed to carry a large share of unemployment relief. Again, in his message to Congress, President Hoover gave them his whole-hearted backing, and voiced his pride in the generosity of private citizens who were prepared to meet such a large share of the need.

While Mr. Hoover was guaranteeing, as he did in his message, that no one should go hungry or suffer from cold, distress was increasing and relief was more inadequate than ever, in spite of the RFC and the 40 state legislatures. Unemployment had jumped to 14,000,000, taxes had dwindled, public borrowing power had diminished. There was growing unrest among the unemployed; they were beginning to organize in protest against fixed commissary rations and low relief grants. The administrative picture was most confused in a majority of the states. There was wide variation in organization and methods,[24] in standards of relief and personnel. There was widespread use of public relief subsidies by private agencies and private relief was still considered an essential part of the picture. Illinois had issued a manual of instruction for county relief committees which said "Extend relief only where actually needed and only after local resources public and private have been provided to the fullest financial ability of the community." [25]

The Conference on Welfare Standards

The American Public Welfare Association increased its field staff in the late summer of 1932 soon after the Federal Emer-

[23] See Part IV, Chapter 16.
[24] See Part III, Chapter 8.
[25] *Relief Guidance and Control.* Manual for County Emergency Relief Committees. Illinois Emergency Relief Commission, Nov., 1932, p. 8.

gency Relief and Construction Act was passed in order to assist the states with their problems of organization. They worked very closely with Mr. Croxton and his regional staff and undoubtedly were in a better position than any of the other national agencies to know the actual situation which existed throughout the country.

On November 18, 19 and 20, this Association, in conjunction with the Public Administration Clearing House and School of Social Service Administration of the University of Chicago, called a conference on the Maintenance of Welfare Standards, in Chicago. It was attended by approximately 40 people from agencies of Federal, state and local governments; Schools of Social Work; private national associations; and organizations concerned primarily with public affairs and governmental management.[26] Mr. Louis T. Brownlow, Director of the Public Administration Clearing House, presided at all the sessions. The purpose of the Conference was "to provide the forum for a free discussion of current problems and responsibilities by the representatives of governmental and private agencies charged with the burden of administering relief and service for those in distress because of unemployment." [27]

Reports were approved dealing with "(1) the need and the means for providing adequate relief for the millions, heretofore self-supporting, who are in present destitution through no fault of their own; (2) the immediate organization of administration of adequate relief in such manner that present efficiency and future progress may be best assured; (3) the provision of financial resources in such manner as to conserve the adequacy of all necessary governmental services and to protect the broad aspects of community well-being; and (4) the care of homeless and transient persons in coordinated services with comprehensive and adequate results." [28] Principles were enunciated and standards defined which set the keynote for the Congressional hearings during the early months of 1933, and which forecast the terms of the Federal Emergency Relief Act and the subsequent policies and methods of the FERA.

There was unquestioned agreement on the following principles:

[26] See p. 87 above.   [28] *Ibid.*, p. 28.
[27] S. 5125, pp. 27-28.

1. The responsibility of government, Federal, state, and local, for relief; based on the theory that all the people are responsible for the destitute within their nation, state, or particular locality. This point had been very difficult to get across because so much had been said during the early years of the depression about private responsibility that many people had forgotten our history of public relief.

2. The ability of government to administer relief and welfare as effectively as it can be administered by other types of organization.

3. Public funds must be administered by public agencies. A system of public subsidies to private agencies on a national scale would set back the development of public welfare in this country three or four decades.

4. Reasonable sums must be provided for administration; witness the experience with education, health, and highway programs.

5. The necessity of employing qualified personnel. The public deserves to have its work done by people who know something about it. It is pointless to think that anybody is capable and has an inherent right to handle a government job or that these jobs should go to the "worthy."

6. State supervision and direction are most important to a sound program. The administration should be as simple as possible; and not so complicated that ten or fifteen years later some commission will have to be set up to study how to simplify it! If the right Federal, state and local machinery could be set up it would not only reduce the present suffering but would save worlds of trouble later.

The Conference came out strongly for direct Federal grants to states instead of the loans being made by the RFC, and advocated Federal, state, and local partnership in administrative as well as financial responsibility; adequate relief grants and provision for transients.

Looking ahead to the relief problems of the coming months it was the opinion of the Conference that Congress would probably make no move toward further appropriations until the 44 state legislatures, which were due to meet early in 1933, had given some evidence of their intentions—in other words, until the legislatures had either taken "pauper oaths" or declared their ability to "take care of their own."

Federal Grants for Relief Versus Federal Loans

Congress convened in December, and, on January 3, hearings began before a Subcommittee of the Senate Committee on

Manufactures on another bill to "relieve the hardship and suffering caused by unemployment." [29]   This bill was to become eventually the Federal Emergency Relief Act.

Senator Costigan again opened the sessions of the subcommittee with these penetrating and stirring words:

We are now in the midst of the fourth tragic winter, each severer than the one before, of our unprecedented depression. The figures of unemployment and destitution are at last known to all intelligent citizens. Approximately 12,000,000 in this country, who were formerly employed, are now totally idle. Another equally considerable number is receiving meager compensation for part-time work. On every hand one may sense the suffering of worthy men, women, and children. Cold, hunger, malnutrition, illness, and ever-menacing starvation from day to day are disastrously shattering self-respect.

The most startling development of this nationwide tragedy has been the demonstrated unwillingness of a large part of our national leadership, both industrial and political, to face the facts; to admit national responsibility, even where personal, local, and State contributions have failed; and to organize with typical American thoroughness to combat and conquer our recognized crisis. This has been no less true in the case of our estimated 2,000,000 of migratory idle, who are drifting ceaselessly from State to State in search of relief, and for whom local poor laws assume no responsibility.

Nothing but hang-over illusions concerning American prosperity and miracles in reserve appear to explain our unaccountable tardiness. The unwillingness heretofore to act and our disposition to proceed with penny-pinching compromises suggest the inefficiency of paralyzed energies. Meanwhile the tide of human misery is rising to dangerously higher levels. It no longer suffices to say that so-called direct relief merely affords a temporary solution. Even while we move to start industrial activities which will provide the means for making our people once more self-sustaining, our National Government can not do less than aid our fellow citizens in the critical emergency, which at this time, after three exhausting years, exhibits no moderating signs.[30]

[29] S. 5125. Hearings before a Subcommittee of the Committee on Manufactures: United States Senate. Seventy-Second Congress, Second Session, Jan. 3 to 17, and Feb. 2 and 3, 1933. Hearings were also held on February 2 and 3 on a Bill to Amend the Emergency Relief and Construction Act of 1932.

[30] S. 5125. Part I, pp. 4-5.

The testimony at these hearings was given by many of the same people who had appeared during the previous winter and spring. It carried the added weight of another year's experience with the problems of unemployment relief. They told essentially the same story, but the evidence was even more striking and the cumulative force of the facts more telling because the suffering had not only continued but grown worse in spite of additional state appropriations and Federal loans.

Bank failures were increasing, relief stations closing, the commissary [31] was growing in popularity because it was supposed to be more economical and efficient; as a rule food was the only form of relief being given and that was on an emergency basis; pellagra and tuberculosis were increasing. For example, the Kentucky reports on tuberculosis showed no improvement for the first time in 50 years; work relief was being gradually abandoned for the cheaper direct relief. People were hoarding money and food. Relief was spread thin or refused to applicants. Reports poured in from governors, mayors, relief committees and field representaives of national agencies.

The testimony of the American Association of Social Workers was based on first-hand information which had been secured from the Chapters of the Association in every part of the country. They reported an increase in the number of persons who were in a state of complete destitution. Approximately one-fourth of the unemployed were on relief. An additional undetermined number were in distress but unable to get relief largely because the agencies did not have enough money. Almost no rent was being paid, and little clothing or medical care were being given. Food was almost the only kind of relief which could be obtained and that was on a minimum subsistence basis at best; emergency rations were still being handed out in the third year of the depression.

In many localities standards had been shot to pieces and good methods of administration had been abandoned. The agencies were reverting to primitive ways of relieving destitution with soup kitchens and bread lines. Work relief in some

[31] A relief store, from which packages of food and articles of clothing purchased in quantities by the relief agency, were distributed to persons in need, who called for them, after waiting in line for hours at a time.

places paid wages so far below the prevailing rates that they threatened to be a factor in forcing further wage reduction in industry.

Public relief appropriations were decreasing. Municipalities found it harder to obtain credit and were making drastic reductions in their recreational, health, and education programs in order to save money for relief. There appeared to be little chance of additional state appropriations and the loans from the RFC were not enough to supply more than a bare subsistence.

Standards of living had been sharply reduced and housing congestion was prevalent. There was growing dissatisfaction and irritation among the unemployed, evidenced by a number of violent outbreaks resulting in destruction of property, injuries and deaths. An undercurrent of resentment, dissatisfaction and threats existed and probably even more serious riots would have occurred if there had been more adequate leadership among the unemployed.[32]

The criticisms of the social workers and the public officials who testified were not aimed at Mr. Croxton and his staff, but at the terms of the Act itself. There was a general agreement that Mr. Croxton had done the best he could with a very difficult situation. The crux of the trouble lay in the sheer inadequacy of funds, the fact that the Federal Government had insisted upon loans instead of direct grants, the failure of most of the states to do their full share, and the insolvency of cities upon which the existing system still forced the chief burden.[33]

Mr. Paul Betters testified for the United States Conference of Mayors which had come into being "for the purpose of devising ways and means to protect the American people from

[32] S. 5125, Part I, pp. 75-77.

[33] In the territory covered by RFC loans (representing 52 percent of the population of the U. S.) 80 percent of the relief expenditures came from the Federal Treasury; the other 20 percent represented the total of local and state funds, private contributions and Red Cross flour.

Between Aug., 1932, and May, 1933, more than a thousand American municipalities were in a condition of insolvency with bankruptcy proceedings apparently the only method of relief. On March 4, 1933, the banks in 36 states were closed. See "City Problems of 1933," *Annual Proceedings* of the United States Conference of Mayors, Paul V. Betters, Editor, Chicago, 1933.

starvation during the fall and winter of 1931-1932." This organization had played an important part in the passage of the Emergency Relief and Construction Act in the preceding summer,[34] and exerted a most effective influence in the spring of 1933, in behalf of Federal relief.

Mr. Betters called attention to one of the chief reasons for delayed applications from states and municipalities. Because Federal relief was in the form of advances against highway funds and because Federal aid for highways was spent entirely on rural roads, and did not reach the cities at all, the governor of a rural state was naturally reluctant to apply for a loan on behalf of a large city when he was responsible to a rurally dominated state and was under constant pressure from his rural constituents not to favor the cities.

The most significant testimony was that of Mr. Harry L. Hopkins who spoke out of his 14 months' experience with the New York TERA.[35] He had found that the cities and towns did not relax their activity nor fall down in their responsibility because state funds were available. After all, the immediate problem was "on the necks" of the local communities. They could not sit back and wait for the state to come in. They had to take care of hungry people. On the other hand, the state stood ready to carry the whole load if the local government was really bankrupt.

Mr. Hopkins considered this unemployment emergency to be the most serious problem this country had ever faced. He believed that the local communities and the states should provide all they possibly could but he was sure this would not be enough without Federal aid. "I think we [New York State] have had as much money available for public relief as any state in the union but, in my opinion, our funds have been inadequate." The Federal Government must help, he declared, if the unemployed were to get anything like a square deal. He was convinced that if half a billion dollars could

[34] The conference was an outgrowth of a meeting held in Detroit in 1932 by the then Mayor, Frank Murphy. It met in the winter of 1933 and again the following May, in Washington. See "City Problems of 1933," *Annual Proceedings* of the United States Conference of Mayors.

[35] Hearings on S. 5125, Jan., 1933, pp. 79-86. See also page 116 above.

be made available in Federal grants to the states, a similar amount could be secured from the states and localities.

He predicted that 3,000,000 unemployed families, or 10 percent of the population of the United States, would require assistance from public funds in 1933. "If they are to receive as little as a dollar per day per family, the total cost of direct unemployment relief will be well over a billion dollars."

He outlined the principles of administration and state and local relationships which obtained in the TERA and which were made possible by the wide powers provided under the TERA Act. He recommended that similar powers be given to the Federal administrator in the bill which was being discussed.

The major points in Mr. Hopkins' testimony had already been set forth in a letter which he had written on December 14 to Governor Roosevelt regarding Federal relief and the changes which he believed should be made in the light of New York's experience with the RFC. He recommended that:

1. Loans should be out and a grant-in-aid plan adopted.
2. The Federal Government should deal with states only.
3. Funds should be of two types:
   a. for reimbursement to states
   b. free funds to be allotted at the discretion of the administrator.
4. The Federal Administration should be an independent agency similar to the TERA. At least it should not be in the RFC.
5. $600,000,000 to $1,000,000,000 should be appropriated.
6. It would be desirable to exert pressure for the passage of the bill in the present session of Congress even though there might be a veto, because it would then be a basis of action at a special session after March 1.

On the last point it is interesting to note a suggestion made elsewhere in the testimony that it might be better if the bill did not pass until the special session, after Mr. Roosevelt's inauguration, in order to avoid having the new Federal agency set up under Mr. Hoover's Administration.

While the hearings were going on, the report of the President's Research Committee on Social Trends [36] was published.

[36] *Recent Social Trends in the United States*, McGraw-Hill, 1934.

The Committee had been appointed by Mr. Hoover and the report came out with his official approval. It is rather significant, therefore, that the Committee went on record as recommending old-age pensions, a 6-hour day, and unemployment compensation.

On March 4, Mr. Roosevelt was inaugurated as President of the United States. The relief bill was then before the Senate, and in the hands of the House Committee on Banking and Currency.

By the end of April it was evident that the $300,000,000 RFC fund would shortly be exhausted. Accordingly, it was necessary either to authorize further advances by the Corporation or devise some other means of assisting the states to relieve the unemployed.

On May 8 and 9 Congress passed the Federal Emergency Relief Act which had been debated at such length. It was signed on May 12 by President Roosevelt who immediately appointed Mr. Harry L. Hopkins as Federal Administrator. On May 22, Mr. Hopkins came to Washington and the Federal Emergency Relief Administration came into existence.

Part Three

*THE FEDERAL
EMERGENCY
RELIEF ADMIN-
ISTRATION*

Chapter 7

Work Relief for the Unemployed

~~~~~~

The National Emergency

The principles and policies which governed the program of
the Federal Emergency Relief Administration can be best understood if they are considered against the background of the
conditions which confronted the country when the Act was
passed in May, 1933.

In his inaugural address in March, President Roosevelt described the situation in these words:

Values have shrunken to fantastic levels; taxes have risen; our ability to pay has fallen; government of all kinds is faced by serious
curtailment of income; the means of exchange are frozen in the cur-
rents of trade; the withered leaves of industrial enterprise lie on
every side; farmers find no market for their produce; the savings of
many years in thousands of families are gone.

More important, a host of unemployed citizens face the grim
problems of existence, and an equally great number toil with little
return . . . and the only thing we have to fear is fear itself—name-
less, unreasoning, unjustified terror which paralyzes needed efforts to
convert retreat into advance.

During the spring unemployment had reached its peak.
Approximately 15 million people were out of work. The fiscal
condition of states, counties and municipalities was becoming
more and more serious. In many places the economic machinery had already collapsed. Essential public services were
being suspended. Thousands of families were losing their
homes and their farms. There was no such thing as security,
whether that meant the assurance of a job, a home, a farm,
shares of stock, deposits in banks, or a life insurance policy.

Four million families representing 18,000,000 persons were
receiving relief from public funds. In some states 40 percent

of the population were on relief; in some counties of these states even 90 percent. This meant that nearly one family out of every six in the United States was dependent.[1] Eighty percent of the money for this relief was coming from Federal loans made to states and political subdivisions by the Reconstruction Finance Corporation.

The Federal Emergency Relief Act

Under the terms of the Federal Emergency Relief Act, Congress made available $500,000,000 "To provide for cooperation by the Federal Government with the several States and Territories and the District of Columbia in relieving the hardship and suffering caused by unemployment and for other purposes." The appropriation was divided into two parts. The first $250,000,000 under subsection (b) of section 4 of the act, was made available to the states on a matching basis. One dollar from Federal funds was provided for each $3 of public moneys from all sources spent in the state during the preceding three months. The other half of the appropriation, under subsection (c) of section 4, was to be used as a discretionary fund from which grants would be made to those states where the relief needs were so great and/or financial resources were so depleted that grants must be made without regard to the matching provisions already described.[2]

The passage of this act came after more than three years of pressure upon Congress for Federal aid. The measure meant drastic changes in Federal relief policy. It meant that the problem of unemployment was thereby recognized as national in scope, and that concerted action had been taken to meet it by a consistent Federal policy and leadership, since the Federal Government was the only agency with sufficient power and credit to deal with the situation. The self-liquidating principle was abandoned and grants to the states substituted for loans and advances. It is most important to note, however, that even this direct aid from the Federal treasury by no means failed to respect the long tradition of local re-

[1] Estimated by the Reconstruction Finance Corporation. See *FERA Monthly Report*, May 22 to June 30, 1933, p. 1.

[2] *FERA Monthly Report*, May 22 to June 30, 1933, pp. 1-2.

sponsibility.   The act provided for Federal co-operation with the states and local units to aid them in meeting the costs of unemployment relief.   The Federal role in the total relief picture was changed from lending to giving what the states and localities could not supply by themselves.

This measure for supplementary aid stood out as one of the most important expressions of a new conception of government which maintained necessity of federal action in the interests of human welfare under an economic system over which the individual has small control.   It was, in effect, a new and social interpretation of the "welfare" clause in the Federal Constitution which had served to restrict Federal relief policy since the middle of the nineteenth century.[3]   In fact, President Roosevelt virtually threw a challenge back over eighty years to his predecessor, President Pierce, when he said to Congress:

If, as our Constitution tells us, our federal government was established among other things "to promote the general welfare," it is our plain duty to provide for that security upon which welfare depends.[4]

The act created the Federal Emergency Relief Administration to make grants and discharge other administrative responsibilities and provided that the RFC act merely as the fiscal agent.[5]

President Roosevelt appointed, as Federal Administrator, Mr. Harry L. Hopkins, who had served as executive director and later as chairman of the New York Temporary Relief Administration while Mr. Roosevelt was Governor of that state. The fact that Mr. Hopkins was a social worker was evidence of the intention of the Federal Government to treat the relief of unemployment as a social problem and to establish a social agency to administer the program.

[3] See page 34.

[4] Message to Congress, June 8, 1934.

[5] The Reconstruction Finance Corporation, under the Act of 1932, had received and passed upon applications for loans and advances.   There had been much criticism of this procedure on the ground that relief was a social rather than a financial problem, and should be administered by a social rather than by a financial agency.

Federal Grants to the States

Mr. Hopkins assumed office on May 22 and the following day approved the first grants from the "matching fund," to Colorado, Illinois, Iowa, Michigan, Mississippi, Ohio and Texas. These grants were made in response to telegraphic applications from state governors.[6] The amounts were equal to one-third of the public funds including Reconstruction Finance Corporation loans and advances spent in these states during the first quarter of 1933. By the end of June, grants had been made to 45 states, the District of Columbia, and the Territory of Hawaii, amounting to approximately $51,000,000.

The June grants were made from both the matching and discretionary funds. The act provided in subsection 4(d) that the matching provisions in subsection (b) could become inoperative by action of the President. Such action was taken on January 6, 1934, when approximately $200,000,000 of the matching funds had been made available to the states. The balance of the 1933 appropriation and all subsequent appropriations were granted on the discretionary basis. The first discretionary grant was made to Texas in the sum of $808,429 on June 27, 1933.

By the end of December approximately $324,500,000 was allocated to 48 states and all the Territories to which the act applied. Six weeks later on February 15, 1934, further funds were appropriated by Congress. From May, 1933, to June 30, 1936, the huge sum of $3,088,670,625 was provided for the Federal Emergency Relief program under five different Acts of Congress.

With the exception of the $500,000,000, appropriated by the Relief Act of 1933, all of this money was allocated or transferred to the Federal Emergency Relief Administration under Presidential direction. A significant characteristic of emergency Federal legislation after 1933 was the appropriation and authorization of relief funds to be used at the discretion of the President. This procedure made possible a financial flexibility which seemed imperative because of the number of govern-

------

[6] "These telegraphed requests were followed by the specific figures and data called for by section 5 of the act." *FERA Monthly Report,* May 22 to June 30, 1933, p. 2.

FEDERAL FUNDS AUTHORIZED FOR THE USE OF OR
ALLOCATED TO FEDERAL EMERGENCY RELIEF AD-
MINISTRATION [7]

(Cumulative through June 30, 1936)

Authorization	Amount
Federal Emergency Relief Act of 1933............	$411,040,000
National Industrial Recovery Act of 1933.........	148,035,000
Act of February 15, 1934......................	605,000,000
Emergency Appropriation Act, fiscal year 1935:	
Title II, par. 1.............................	257,000,000
Title II, par. 2.............................	223,590,000
Title II, par. 3.............................	500,000,000
Emergency Relief Appropriation Act of 1935......	944,005,625
Total	$3,088,670,625

mental agencies concerned and the variable nature of the relief
problem.

Under the stimulus of Federal aid the states increased expenditures from their own funds from $103,700,000 in 1933
to slightly more than twice that amount in 1935. Local contributions showed a similar rise from $196,798,000 in 1933 to
$250,000,000 two years later. The grand total of Federal,
state and local obligations incurred during these three years
was $4,119,000,000.[8]

Federal Objectives

Throughout the life of the Federal Emergency Relief Administration certain objectives, policies and conflicts in philosophy and procedure stand out as important, not only in the
administration of emergency relief, but as vitally affecting the
planning and operation of the later Works Program and still
later permanent provisions for social security and general relief.

From the start in May, 1933, it was unmistakably the intention of the Federal Relief Administration to use the Fed-

[7] *Financing Relief and Recovery,* edited by L. László Ecker-R. Reprinted from the *Municipal Year Book,* 1937, published in April, 1937,
by the International City Managers' Association. p. 404.

[8] *FERA Monthly Report,* June, 1936, p. 171. Figures given above are
taken from tables revised by the Work Projects Administration, Division
of Statistics, February, 1940. See p. 204 below.

eral appropriation for the unemployed who were victims of the depression through no fault of their own. The terms of the act allowed the most liberal interpretation of eligibility. Almost any type of need, suffered by any person, might be considered "the hardship and suffering caused by unemployment." Nevertheless, an attempt was made to distinguish between "employables" and "unemployables." The entire case load was divided into two groups on this basis, although no satisfactory definition of either classification was ever possible; the "unemployables" having been given this invidious label, were always unwanted on the relief rolls, and were finally rejected as recipients of Federal aid.

Help for the unemployed meant work; public works, if no private employment could be secured; work relief,[9] if jobs on public works projects could not be provided fast enough or in large enough numbers. Direct relief was merely a temporary, emergency expedient. It was necessary to keep the unemployed from starving until work and wages in some form could be provided. The "dole," or direct relief, for the able-bodied unemployed was in disrepute, and it was discarded as quickly as possible.

Unemployment as a major nationwide economic problem was the primary concern of the Federal Relief Administration from the beginning of the program. Relief was only a stopgap pending the development of public works or the revival of industry. The army of the unemployed had to be dealt with *en masse*. Social work with its traditional interest in the incompetent, the indigent and the disabled, was dominated by a case work philosophy which interpreted all problems and remedies in terms of individual needs and characteristics. Social workers had been leaders in the Congressional fight which had ended in the passage of the Federal Relief Act and they looked upon the ensuing program as their own. They considered themselves partners with government in an enterprise which would lead to the development of a permanent program of social case work under public auspices. However, this public welfare objective was of secondary importance to the Fed-

---

[9] However, the act itself gave no preference to work relief over direct relief.

eral Administration. Social work was used in the Federal Emergency Relief Administration because it was needed "continuously to investigate families to see that no one obtained relief who could get along without it." [10] Social work, because of its very concern with the individual, was needed to protect the public purse. The known professional integrity of social workers was needed to assure an honest, non-political relief administration. Social workers carried the onus which comes from standing at the point of intake, for they performed the difficult task of deciding who would or would not get relief in every city and county Emergency Relief Administration in the country. They were bitterly disappointed and disillusioned when at the end of 1935 the program was liquidated and the responsibility for general relief returned to the states and localities. The disappointment was due, in part at least, to their misunderstanding of the objectives and philosophy of the Federal Administration. They had not realized the wide cleavage which existed between this Federal philosophy and their own hopes and ideals.

The following brief review of the most important points in the development of the Federal program between 1933 and 1936 will provide ample evidence of these underlying concepts and policies regarding work for the unemployed, eligibility, public welfare and social work. It will also serve as a background for more detailed discussion in the following chapters of the relationship of the FERA to public welfare organization and to the people on relief.

On June 14, 1933, within three weeks of the beginning of the FERA, a conference of state officials was called in Washington at which 45 states, the District of Columbia and Alaska, Hawaii and Puerto Rico were represented. The Governors of Pennsylvania, Virginia, Arkansas, Montana, South Carolina, Rhode Island, New Hampshire and Maine attended. The Federal Administrator interpreted the terms of the act and outlined his administrative policies. President Roosevelt addressed the Conference, and emphasized that the states and local units were expected to do their fair share in meeting the costs as well as the administrative responsibilities of relief. He stressed the importance of co-operation with industry "to

[10] Hopkins, Harry L., *Spending to Save*, p. 101.

secure work opportunities for as many of the unemployed as possible. . . . But until these jobs are available the Federal Government, states and every local community must provide relief for every genuinely needy unemployed person in America."

He left no doubt that this primary objective was to provide work for the unemployed:

The Emergency Relief Act is an expression of the Federal Government's determination to cooperate with the States and local communities with regard to financing emergency relief work.[11]

It is essential that there be effective coordination of relief and public works in all communities. While an important factor in setting up a public-works program is speed, there is no intention of using the public-works funds simply to build a lot of useless projects disguised as relief. It is the purpose to encourage real public works. One function of public works in an emergency is to provide a bridge by which people can pass from relief status over to normal self-support.

The social workers gathered at the National Conference in Detroit heard Mr. Hopkins give the same emphasis to the problem of unemployment and to work. In the same address he made his position clear regarding "unemployables," and the place of relief and of social work organization in the new program:

The whole business of experimentation in this bill is very broad. I am tired of reading unemployment reports which repeat over and over again the terrible situation in this and that place, about miners in various counties who will probably never earn a living again. Here is the chance of a lifetime to do something about some of these things if we have any brains at all. I am for experimenting with this fund in various parts of the country, trying out schemes which are supported by reasonable people and see if they work. If they do not work, the world will not come to an end. However well this

[11] In March and April, 1933, the first steps had been taken, weeks before the FERA was passed, to set up the first of the emergency work relief programs of the New Deal. When President Roosevelt addressed this conference of Governors the camps were being prepared and the young men and boys being selected for Emergency Conservation Work. 276,000 men were enrolled by July 1. The Emergency Conservation Act, popularly known at the time as the Reforestation Act, was approved on March 31, 1933. Seventy-third Congress, First Session, Public Act 5.

thing is administered, this enormous relief business can never be anything more than a make-shift. We had all the power and all the money that we needed in New York. We could hire all the social workers we wanted, and we had some terrible unemployment-relief administrations in New York. But I do not get too upset about it. We propose to see that the unemployed get some relief. Fortunately we do not have to go through this battle alone. The picture has changed, and, whether you believe it or not, the new deal is here. Two acts have been passed: the Industrial Recovery Bill and the Public Works Bill. Nobody knows how the Trade Recovery Act will work out, but my guess is that between now and October 1 at least two million men are going to be put to work through this section of the act.

We have these great armies of government—trade recovery, public-works relief, United States employment service—all marching hand in hand under the direction of the President. Anybody tied up in Washington is part and parcel of the administration. In a unified attack under the President's direction we are doing the work. I believe firmly that we are going to win. That is why I am not too worried about relief. Surely we cannot go on having four million families being handed grocery orders and tickets for clothing. Three hundred people in a city in the United States worked full time and averaged $3.50 per week during the last week in May, and every one of them received relief. The Federal Relief Administration does not intend to subsidize miserably low wages. We do not intend to permit anybody to use relief funds to reduce the standard of living lower than it is now. We are not going to allow relief agencies to starve people slowly to death with our money.

I think we are in a winning fight. We want to do a good job. Our job is to see that the unemployed get relief, not to develop a great social-work organization throughout the United States. Our business is to see that the people who need relief get it, and we intend to do it. . . .

We are now dealing with people of all classes. It is no longer a matter of unemployables and chronic dependents, but of your friends and mine who are involved in this. Every one of us knows some family of our friends which is or should be getting relief. The whole picture comes closer home than ever before. It seems to me that the intent of this act is that relief should be given to the heads of families who are out of work and whose dependency arises from the fact that they are out of work; single men and women who are out of work, and to transient families, as well as the transient men and women roaming about the country. Those are the persons for whom relief is intended. I am not going to hide behind the cloak of the intent of Congress as to what federal funds can be used for. It is my belief that the people who fought for this bill, who tried to get this money, were trying to get it for relief for the unemployed, and not for a number of other perfectly fine and worthy social objectives. So in my opinion these funds were not intended to pay for the board of children, to support orphanages, Travelers Aid Societies, and a dozen and one other activities, many of which are having great difficulty in supporting themselves.[12]

At this early stage in the program Mr. Hopkins thus gave notice of his intention to use Federal funds exclusively for the relief of the unemployed. This was one of the first public statements of the purpose and philosophy which were to prevail throughout the entire emergency period and to motivate the policies and programs which originated in Washington. This goes far to explain the extent to which work and insurance programs have been developed almost to the exclusion of permanent provision for dependent people who are unemployable and therefore not eligible for such benefits.[13]

The People on Relief

The fact remains, however, that the terms of the act admitted the broadest interpretation,[14] and they were so interpreted in practice as the relief program proceeded. After all, the administration of relief financed by a combination of Federal, state and local money, actually took place in the cities and counties of the country. Local interpretations, local pressures, lack of adequate local funds were all factors in putting

[12] *Proceedings* of the National Conference of Social Work at Detroit, Mich., 1933. "The Developing National Program of Relief," by Harry L. Hopkins.

[13] In 1936 Mr. Hopkins said to a Congressional committee that his thinking centered "entirely around the problem of unemployment, to which relief is no answer, whether it is work or the dole, or whatever it is. The longer I have anything to do with relief of unemployment the more I am convinced that it has little to do with reviving employment as such: that it is a palliative. . . ."

Testimony before the subcommittee of the House Appropriations Committee: Hearings on the Second 1936 Deficiency Appropriation Bill. Government Printing Office.

[14] See preamble and Sec. 4 of the FER Act.

upon the local emergency relief rolls [15] a mixture of not only the unemployed able-bodied heads of families to whom Mr. Hopkins referred at Detroit, but also poor relief beneficiaries, "chronic dependents," of long standing, as well as families from mothers' aid waiting lists, the aged, the sick, the infirm, and many others who had needed relief, but who had never had the courage to apply to the "overseer" in the past. People who had jobs got on the emergency relief rolls, because these jobs were paying them only a pittance, hardly enough to keep body and soul together. Thousands of them were working only part time, others worked all day, six days a week.[16] These last were underpaid industrial workers, or farmers; farm tenants and share-croppers, who were trying to scratch a living out of submarginal land.

This was the type of chronic misery uncovered when the Federal Emergency Relief Administration went into action through 4,000 local units in practically every county in the

[15] Undoubtedly many localities spent their money for other purposes and "dumped" their "unemployables" onto the relief administration. This was the situation in most of the states in which practically all of the relief funds came from the Federal Government. In states where a considerable share of the relief expenditures were provided by the states themselves and by the localities, the acceptance of unemployable cases by the relief offices merely meant that the state and local authorities chose to provide for their local charges in this way instead of through separate agencies. See *Social Welfare in Florida,* by Emma O. Lundberg, 1935. Also, *Public Welfare in Oregon,* a study made by the American Public Welfare Association, 1935, p. 32, "the emergency relief administration has taken over most of the responsibility for outdoor poor relief." *Public Welfare in the State of Washington,* by Mildred Buck, 1934, contains the statement that some counties which were hard pressed financially turned over to the state much of their "ordinary relief load of unemployables, aged, mothers with young children; other counties continue to carry alone the entire burden of relief." "Pauper cases are not to be included," Virginia Manual of Relief and Service, Virginia Emergency Relief Administration, 1934.

[16] Full-time workers in industry were not eligible for relief according to a policy issued in Sept., 1934. Many full-time workers were, however, given relief locally. Persons working for themselves, shop-owners, farmers, etc., were eligible if they were judged to be in need. In October, 1933, the Philadelphia County Relief Board gave relief to 217,562 persons; of this number 7.58% were employed; 1.20% full time; 2.02% part time and 4.36% on casual work.

country. The facts began to come in as soon as the nation-wide statistical reporting system got under way and the Research Division set up by the FERA began a series of studies.[17] The reports of these studies were a revelation of need and misery of which the general public and most of the social welfare leaders and public officials were entirely unaware. It put a new and significant meaning into the famous welfare clause in the Constitution and gave to the emergency unemployment relief programs an additional purpose of deep and permanent significance.

The Administration was convinced that no effort should be spared to secure complete information regarding the levels of living throughout the country, because not until such a bill of particulars was in their hands could they "reckon the expensiveness of American poverty or figure out its specific causes . . ."[18] or plan what to do about it!

Public Works and Work Relief

Evidences of the primary interest in work appear, as might be expected, at the beginning of the FERA program. Less than three weeks after taking office, the Federal Administrator informed governors that the passage of a public works bill in the near future was probable,[19] and suggested that a classification[20] of relief cases be made by occupation and ability to

[17] "A Division of research and statistics has been established. The functions of this division will include collection of comparable Nation-wide information concerning the number of families given relief from public funds, the amount of public relief expenditures, types of relief given, and the sources of public funds for unemployment relief. It will go beyond this to include the interpretation of this information in relation to national and local economic conditions." *FERA Monthly Report,* June, 1933.

[18] Hopkins, Harry L., *New York Times Magazine,* August 19, 1934.

[19] The President approved the National Industrial Recovery Act on June 16, 1933, authorizing the appropriation of $3,300,000,000 "to encourage national industrial recovery, to foster fair competition, and to provide for the construction of certain useful public works, and for other purposes."

[20] There was no nationwide occupational classification of persons on relief rolls until the spring of 1935 when the FERA Division of Research and Statistics made such a classification in preparation for the administration of the Works Program.

work in order that prompt action might be taken when calls were made for workers. He added that relief officials "should expect to have only a reasonable proportion of workers taken from relief lists as distinct from those unemployed and not on relief."[21]

The Administrator promptly held meetings during that first month with representatives of the United States Employment Service and of the Federal Emergency Public Works Administration, to discuss the co-operation of the three agencies in their common task of relieving unemployment and to make plans for the correlation of their programs.[22]

In July the FERA undertook to finance, by ear-marked grants to the states, the current expenses of the new re-employment offices which were being established in communities by the National Reemployment Service,[23] "so that there will be full cooperation with the National Industrial Recovery Act in providing work opportunities to the unemployed." The selection of local re-employment managers was to be approved by the State Emergency Relief Administrators.

Beginning in the summer of 1933 the FERA assisted the states with their programs of emergency direct relief and a certain amount of rather poor work relief which was more nearly "work-for-relief." The projects were of limited social value, and the workers, who numbered nearly one million, were chiefly unskilled. The program was uneven and on the whole was poorly conceived and inefficiently executed. Many of the projects were a continuation of work which had been financed during the preceding winter and spring with the aid of RFC funds.[24]

[21] This admonition definitely forecast the employment policy of the Civil Works Administration created on November 9, 1933, under the authority of Title II of the National Industrial Recovery Act.

[22] *FERA Monthly Report*, May 22 to June 30, 1933, p. 4.

[23] The United States Employment Service was created as a bureau in the Department of Labor by Public Act No. 30, Seventy-third Congress, June 6, 1933; the National Reemployment Service was set up on June 22, 1933, as an agency of the U. S. Employment Service. The support of N.R.S. offices was assumed by CWA November 18, 1933, and terminated April 27, 1934.

[24] In March, 1933, approximately two million workers were employed on these local projects, FERA estimate. See *FERA Monthly Report*, June, 1936, pp. 23-29.

Rules and Regulations No. 3, issued on July 11, laid down detailed specifications for the conduct of projects for which Federal relief funds were to be used. The rules included such matters as conditions of work, eligibility for employment, rates of pay, hours of work.

Provision was made for work relief projects on Federal property, under Federal Departments as early as August, 1933. It marked the beginning of a huge program of federally sponsored projects which was to reach its full development in 1936-38.

In September the initiation of the emergency education program recognized the needs of unemployed teachers. This was the beginning of extensive work relief projects for professional people, greatly expanded during the following winter and continued under the subsequent Emergency Work Relief Program and the Works Progress Administration. The first regulations for education projects provided that teachers be subjected to the same type of investigation or "means test" which was applied to all other beneficiaries of the program. This involved a searching inquiry into the resources of each applicant to discover whether or not he had the "means" of subsistence. If not, he was considered to be eligible for relief. From the beginning of the Civil Works Administration and throughout the subsequent Emergency Work Relief Program, teachers and other professional persons were for the most part exempted from this stringent investigation.

There was constant conflict between the desire on the one hand to do away entirely with the "means test," to assist every unemployed person in need, to reach all the "marginal cases" who were too proud to apply and be questioned and, on the other hand, the urgent necessity of making available funds go as far as possible in helping the most needy who could be discovered only by applying the measuring-stick of eligibility. There were also conflicts between the desire to get work done efficiently and the desire to give a maximum of relief to the greatest possible number of people. Direct relief was undesirable, but it was the least expensive method of aiding the destitute. Hastily planned devices by which the unemployed could work for their relief grants were less costly than socially useful projects which paid a regular security wage. Most expensive of all were public works projects in which the contractors employed and paid the workers regardless of their need for the job or their eligibility for relief.

At no time did the funds available even approach the amount which would have been needed to finance a public works program for all of the unemployed. Almost continuous shortage of funds and constant uncertainty regarding the time and amount of future appropriations by Congress accounted in part at least for the many shifts and changes between the less satisfactory methods of providing work and relief.

The Civil Works Administration

On November 9th, five months after the establishment of FERA, the Civil Works Administration was launched.[25] The new program was intended to remedy the defects of the FERA work relief program, to meet the critical unemployment needs of the winter and to promote recovery through the injection of purchasing power into the economic system within a short period.

Half of the workers to be employed were to be taken over from the emergency work relief rolls. The other half were to be people who needed jobs and who were to be asked for no proof of need. They were not to be investigated or submitted to a "means test." One purpose of the CWA was obviously and admittedly pump-priming. The program was very

[25] Created by Executive Order under Title II of the National Recovery Act on Nov. 9, 1933. On November 8, 1933, a communication to State Emergency Relief Administrators announced that the President was creating the Civil Works Administration and appointing as its Administrator the Federal Emergency Relief Administrator. "The purpose of this agency is to provide employment to 4 million persons able and willing to work, now unemployed. The first task of this agency will be to provide regular work at regular wages for the 2 million now on so-called work relief. The Federal Emergency Relief Administration will name its State and local emergency relief administrations as State and local Civil Works Administrations." See *Chronology of the FERA:* May 12, 1933, to December 31, 1935, p. 27.

The CWA was federally operated and was distinct from the FERA and State ERA's. In many respects CWA forecast and established precedents for the later Works Program.

costly [26] and lasted several months. The peak load was reached in January, 1934, when 4,260,000 workers were employed; liquidation was announced in January, begun on February 15 and the program was officially closed on July 14. It stopped as quickly as it began. The workers were dropped, or transferred to FERA with little pretense of investigation. The emergency relief rolls increased tremendously as a result.

The New Federal Emergency Relief Administration Program

With reduced funds the Federal Emergency Relief Administration was forced in the spring of 1934 to return to a relief program in which the rules prescribed a "means test" for all applicants for direct or work relief benefits. A threefold program was undertaken to meet the needs of different sections of the unemployed population. An Emergency Work Relief Program was set up in urban centers, including all communities of more than 5,000 population. This program took over many of the unfinished work projects of the Civil Works Administration and was by far the most important activity of the Federal Emergency Relief Administration during the following twelve months.[27]

In April, the Rural Rehabilitation Program was established for farmers in distress. It operated in rural areas and communities of less than 5,000 population. The general objective of this program was "the placing of the individual family in a

[26] Total funds allocated to CWA to June 30, 1934: $863,965,000.

[27] Approximately two-thirds of the expenditures of the Federal Emergency Relief Administration were made in ten industrial states. Approximately 80% of the relief recipients lived in industrial centers. One-half of Federal work relief funds was spent in 1937 in the 50 largest cities which contain over 25% of the population of the U. S. See L. László Ecker-R., *Financing Relief and Recovery*, p. 372. Reprinted from the *Municipal Year Book*, 1937, published by the International City Managers' Association, Chicago.

This Emergency Work Relief Program of the Federal Emergency Relief Administration lasted from April 1, 1934, to the beginning of Works Progress Administration in the summer of 1935. During that period a monthly average of 2,000,000 workers were kept at work.

The Reports of the State Emergency Relief Administrations on file in the library of the Works Progress Administration are chiefly concerned with the activities of the Works Program.

position to become self-supporting" [28] by means of loans, an advisory service on farming problems, and projects on which they might "work for relief" while they were in process of achieving their independence.

The third section of the program was designed to assist stranded populations, people living in communities in which their one industry was dead and where there was no longer any hope of future employment. For these families an ambitious program of land purchase was undertaken, with the intention of transplanting them to farms either singly or to newly formed and specially organized rural communities.[29]

The announcement of this diversified program reiterated the belief that direct relief is not an adequate way of meeting the needs of able-bodied workers. There was, however, some reflection of the earlier philosophy of "work for relief" in the instructions sent out from Washington. The official bulletin said that work was to be supplied to the needy unemployed "who can give adequate return for the benefits they receive" and who "very properly insist upon an opportunity to render this service to their communities." The instructions regarding the means test also provided an ample loophole for professional, technical and skilled workers by allowing their eligibility to be determined "in cooperation with professional and labor organizations." [30]

The "Unemployables"

The bulletin on work relief was followed early in April by a letter to the State Emergency Relief Administrations from the Federal Administrator:

As you are aware, the emphasis of the FERA program is being placed upon work relief or subsistence activities for normally em-

[28] FERA, RD-1, March 22, 1934.

[29] This was the beginning of the Land Program section of the Rural Rehabilitation Division of the FERA which was on April 30, 1935, transferred to the Resettlement Administration and became the Land Utilization Program of that organization. The inception of this program was forecast in the statement made by Mr. Hopkins in June, 1933, at the National Conference of Social Work. See p. 152 above.

[30] Letter from Mr. Hopkins to State Administrators. FERA, WD-3, March 20, 1934.

ployable people. We feel, particularly now, that it is important that states and localities continue responsibility for various types of chronic cases and also continue and extend such services as pensions for widows, aged, etc.

There has been some intimation that in a number of States many widows with dependent children have gone over to the CWA or ERA rolls, either because more relief was granted than was available under the pension or because pensions were eliminated entirely. I am very anxious to get at the facts in this situation, and I wish you would furnish me with the following information. . . .[31]

The replies to this letter showed that large numbers of widows with dependent children were on the rolls of the local ERA's in state after state. No move was made by the Federal Relief Administration to drop these "unemployables" at the time the information came in. In the fall of 1934, however, a definite plan was made to drop from the rolls in six southern states all of their "unemployables." The order was given through the field representative and passed on to the state administrators. It went into effect on February 1, 1935, in the states which had the least resources to care for this needy group.[32]

The percentage of unemployable persons on the emergency relief rolls was estimated in 1934 to range from 5 percent to 25 percent of the total, depending on the locality. The highest proportions were undoubtedly in the southern states where few other agencies and meager local resources existed to care for them. The fact that these states were receiving from the Federal Government nearly 100 percent of the total amounts which they were spending for emergency relief had a direct bearing upon the order to cut off the "unemployables." It was entirely consistent with the Federal policy that Federal funds were intended for and should be spent for the relief of the able-bodied unemployed. States in which both state and local funds were being contributed to the program in considerable

[31] Letter dated April 4, 1934. FERA, AO-6.

[32] See material in Appendix G. This action anticipated the provision of Federal funds for dependent children under the authority of a Social Security Act. The Social Security Bill was introduced in Congress in January, 1935, about one month before the unemployables were dropped. The bill was not passed until August and no funds were appropriated until the beginning of the following year.

amounts were considered to have a right to make their own decisions regarding the use of their own funds for "unemployables." At least no such drastic order was given in any other section of the country.

The three-fold program announced by the FERA in March, 1934, to succeed the CWA was designed exclusively for the relief of employable people. There was, however a continuation of direct relief to persons in need who for one reason or another could not be employed on the work projects or were not eligible for the loans made by the Rural Rehabilitation Division. Direct relief was also used to a great extent to supplement the wages paid on the work relief program, as well as to eke out industrial wages paid for part-time and full-time work. A large proportion of the direct relief funds continued to be spent for the care of "unemployables."

Planning for Social Security

The Federal Emergency Relief Administration had barely launched this new program of work relief and rural rehabilitation when the first steps in a long range attack upon the problem of unemployment were taken by the Federal Government. On June 29, 1934, the Committee on Economic Security was appointed to "report to the President not later than December 1, 1934, its recommendations concerning proposals which in its judgment will promote greater economic security." The Federal Emergency Relief Administrator was made a member of the committee.[33] Planning at once began for a drastic change in the total program which would involve the liquidation of Federal emergency unemployment relief; the initiation of a huge works program; insurance for unemployment and for old age; and "pensions" or public assistance for persons over 65.

All of the studies and planning undertaken at first by this committee were aimed directly at the problem of unemployment. Even the old-age insurance and "pensions" were intended to remove from the labor market all workers who were

[33] The other members of the Committee were members of the Cabinet: the Secretary of Labor, chairman; the Secretary of the Treasury; the Attorney General; the Secretary of Agriculture.

over 65 years of age.   No account was taken of dependent
children or of any other unemployable persons or of any other
type of disability until the committee was approached in the
late summer and early fall by the Federal Children's Bureau,
the United States Public Health Service and the Office of Education.   In response to special requests made by these agencies, the problems dealt with in four titles of the present social
security act [34] were finally taken under consideration after the
original studies were well under way.

The major concern of the committee was throughout with
insurance against the hazards of unemployment and old age.
These measures were designed to provide economic security
for that section of the population who are actually employed
and able to contribute.   The plans for a works program were
undertaken by the staff of the FERA and were aimed at the
provision of a certain degree of security for the able-bodied
unemployed.   Only partial consideration was given, however,
to that large section of our population made up of the people
who are in greatest need because some disability or other unfortunate circumstance has deprived them of the capacity or
ability for work and self-support.   These "unemployables"
were never considered as a whole by the committee as presenting a problem of economic security to be dealt with by the
Federal Government.   Instead certain categories were selected
to receive Federal assistance through grants-in-aid to the
states.   No such provision was recommended for the aged and
for dependent children who did not fit the special requirements
of eligibility recommended in the committee report, and no
account whatever was taken of the thousands of people who
were equally unemployable for other reasons such as physical
and mental disabilities and who were known to be in dire need.
The tenor of these recommendations was entirely consistent
with the emphasis put by the Federal Government upon the
problem of unemployment, yet they failed by a wide margin
to provide that security for the men, women and children of

[34] Titles for Aid to Dependent Children; Maternal and Child Welfare;
Public Health Work; Vocational Rehabilitation.   The title for Aid for
the Blind was added to the bill while it was being considered by Congress.   See Chapter 13.

the nation which the President had placed first among the objectives of his administration.[35]

The report of the Committee on Economic Security was transmitted to Congress by the President in the special message of January 17, 1935. The Social Security Act was introduced at that time and became law on August 14, almost seven months later. The Social Security Board, as the permanent agency to administer the Act, came into operation in October. Not until February, 1936, however, more than a year after the bill had been introduced, were funds for the program appropriated by Congress.[36]

The Federal Works Program

On January 4, 1935, President Roosevelt presented to Congress the plan for a works program which was embodied in the Emergency Relief Appropriation Bill introduced shortly afterward. In his message the President explained his reasons for requesting that work be provided for the destitute unemployed.

The lessons of history, confirmed by the evidence immediately before me, show conclusively that continued dependence upon relief induces a spiritual and moral disintegration fundamentally destructive to the national fibre. To dole out relief in this way is to administer a narcotic, a subtle destroyer of the human spirit. It is inimical to the dictates of sound policy. It is in violation of the traditions of America. Work must be found for able-bodied but destitute workers.[37]

Approximately 5,000,000 families and single people were then on the emergency relief rolls. Estimates made by the FERA had separated these people into two general categories: those who were unemployable and those who belonged to families in which at least one member was able and willing to work. Of these two groups the President said:

About one million and a half of these belong to the group which in the past was dependent upon local welfare efforts. Most of them are unable for one reason or another to maintain themselves inde-

[35] Message to Congress, June 8, 1934.
[36] See Chapter 13 for more detailed discussion.
[37] FERA Monthly Report, April, 1935.

pendently—for the most part, through no fault of their own. Such people, in the days before the great depression, were cared for by local efforts—by States, by counties, by towns, by cities, by churches, and by private welfare agencies. It is my thought that in the future they must be cared for as they were before. I stand ready through my own personal efforts, and through the public influence of the office that I hold, to help these local agencies to get the means necessary to assume this burden.

The security legislation which I shall propose to the Congress will, I am confident, be of assistance to local effort in the care of this type of cases. Local responsibility can and will be resumed, for after all, common sense tells us that the wealth necessary for this task existed and still exists in the local community, and the dictates of sound administration require that this responsibility be in the first instance a local one.

There are, however, an additional 3½ million employable people who are on relief. With them the problem is different and the responsibility is different. This group was the victim of a Nationwide depression caused by conditions which were not local but national. The Federal Government is the only governmental agency with sufficient power and credit to meet this situation. We have assumed this task and we shall not shrink from it in the future. It is a duty dictated by every intelligent consideration of national policy to ask you to make it possible for the United States to give employment to all of these 3½ million employable people now on relief, pending their absorption in a rising tide of private employment.[38]

The Emergency Relief Appropriation Act of 1935 was approved on April 8, 1935. It appropriated $4,880,000,000 "to provide relief, work relief, and to increase employment by providing useful projects." The fund was to be used "in the discretion and under the direction of the President. . . ." Its clear objective was to furnish employment on useful public projects and thus to effect a substantial reduction in the emergency relief rolls.[39] It was obvious that if the 3,500,000 "employables" on relief were to be put to work, the new program must give preference to the unemployed who were already receiving relief.

If there had been any possibility of securing enough funds to put all of the unemployed to work, the Administration

[38] *FERA Monthly Report*, April, 1935, pp. 2-3.
[39] *FERA Monthly Report*, April, 1935, p. 1.

would gladly have set up a huge program of public works without a means test or any form of relief certification. One estimate actually made for such a program called for the appropriation by Congress of $10,000,000,000! Another plan called for $6,000,000,000 to provide direct employment, at the peak, for 6,000,000 persons. The actual appropriation of $4,800,000,000, large as it was, was divided up to finance public works projects under a number of Federal agencies, and nearly a billion dollars was spent in the liquidation of the Federal Emergency Relief Program. As a consequence the Works Progress Administration received approximately $1,400,000,000 with which to finance "small useful projects" for the needy unemployed who were on relief.[40]

In considering this change of program it is most important to remember the total unemployment figure. In the spring of 1935 eleven to twelve million people were out of work. Approximately half of them were members of the 5,000,000 families who were on the relief rolls of the FERA.

It was with the greatest reluctance that the administration faced the necessity of excluding from the program the unemployed who were not on relief. This appeared to be the only practical way to make certain that the benefits would go to the people who were in the greatest need. It seemed essential that the new relief funds be used for that part of the army of unemployed who could not provide for themselves, and it was perfectly obvious that if the program were thrown open equally to all the unemployed those who were on relief would have the least chance to get the jobs. This was the basis for the order given in June, 1935, to transfer some 3,500,000 people from "relief rolls" to work; from the grants of the FERA to the security wages to be paid by the Works Progress Administration.

The Rural Rehabilitation Division of the FERA ceased to function on June 30, 1935. On that date its responsibilities were finally transferred to the Resettlement Administration which had been established by the President two months earlier under the authority of the Emergency Relief Appro-

[40] Statement of agencies and amounts. See Appendix H for Treasury Report.

priation Act of 1935.[41]   Between two and three hundred thousand [42] rural families and single persons who received, in June,
advances for subsistence or capital goods were included in this
transfer.[43]

In keeping with the President's statement in his January
message to Congress that "the Federal Government must and
shall quit this business of relief" and in accordance with his
proposal made at that time for the care of "unemployables"
by the states and localities, the Federal Emergency Relief Administration gradually withdrew its assistance to state relief
administrations by making final grants during November and
December.

Transfers from relief rolls were pushed and the employment
on WPA projects rapidly rose to the desired 3,000,000 [44] by
February, 1936.   This represented the maximum achievement
of the Federal Government in providing work relief for the
unemployed.   The program was not straight public works, but
a compromise; the projects were handled on "force account," [45]
not by contract; the men were certified as in need of relief and
not selected solely because of their fitness for their particular
jobs.   Yet the projects were socially useful, the work was
real, not "made" work, the wages were not based on a budget
deficiency, but amounted to a guaranteed "security" sum each
month.   Above all, once on WPA a man was actually dropped
from relief rolls, and the "case was closed."   Reviews and re-
investigations, reapplications and check-ups came later, but
only in contradiction to the preferred policies of the Administrator who would gladly have continued to employ every

[41] Executive Orders 7027 and 7028, April 30, 1935.   *FERA Monthly
Report,* April, 1935.

[42] Total cases under care by the FERA Rural Rehabilitation Division
April, 1934, through June, 1935, were 397,130; cases receiving advances
in June, 1935, were 203,418.

[43] Responsibility for this program is now carried by the Rural Rehabilitation Division of the Farm Security Administration in the Department of Agriculture.

[44] Another half million were employed at that time by other Federal
agencies.

[45] A term applied to the direct employment of day labor by the relief
agency, as over against the system of letting contracts for the work to
be done and the employment of the necessary labor by the contractors.

man and woman who needed and wanted to work if Congress
had been willing to supply the funds such a program would
have required.

Unmet Needs

The Works Program has never put to work all of the needy
able-bodied unemployed. It has fallen far short of caring
for those who were actually eligible for relief and receiving
relief in the states and localities. Since the early months of
the program thousands, even hundreds of thousands, of eligible,
desirable workers have made up the waiting lists for project
assignment. The individuals on these lists have constantly
changed, but the totals have remained large and disquieting
in their significance.

In a number of states the relief officials took the position
that since the Federal Government had assumed responsibility
for all of the needy unemployed, therefore, all state and local
assistance should be refused to every able-bodied person who
applied for relief. Such drastic policies were actually enforced
for months in many areas, and the practice has been consistently followed since 1936 in the District of Columbia.

The failure to give employment to all of the employable persons who were on relief or seeking relief; the return to the
states and localities of responsibility for people who were unable to work; and the liquidation of the Federal Relief Administration, brought a storm of protest from state and local
relief officials and from leaders in social work and public welfare agencies.

They claimed that the distinction between "employables"
and "unemployables" was cruel and unjust and in fact impossible to make. Thousands of the so-called "unemployables"
were just as much victims of the depression as the able-bodied
people who had weathered the storm. Numbers of them suffered from disabilities incurred during the depression—the results of malnutrition and nervous and mental strain. They
were not the time-honored chronic dependents. Many of their
disabilities were temporary. With a little help large numbers
of them could get back into the employable group. Thousands
of others were able-bodied but were out of reach of the work
program because of unusual occupations or because they lived

in remote or isolated places. Why should the Federal Government discriminate against all these people?

The social workers were bitterly disappointed that the FERA had not become a Federal public welfare department empowered to assist the states and localities in developing integrated programs which would provide public assistance to all types of persons in need. They maintained that such general relief was essential to prevent suffering and to aid all destitute persons fairly and without discrimination.

Much of the bitterness and resentment was undoubtedly due to a failure to understand that the primary objective of the Federal Relief Administration was throughout to provide work for the unemployed; [46] that relief was despised as a "dole" and tolerated as a temporary emergency expedient made necessary because people were starving or in danger of starving.

The Federal Emergency Relief Administration served its purpose as a stopgap for the unemployed until the Federal Works Program was established.

[46] Mr. Hopkins made it clear in his talk before the National Conference of Social Work (Detroit, June, 1933) that the "big show" at Washington was National Recovery and that he hoped to have his act crowded off the boards by the success of the main performance. "Until such happy event comes to pass, he wants relief to get through to the people in prompt and adequate fashion." See *Survey*, Aug., 1933, p. 284. See also pp. 152-4.

Chapter 8

Organization and Administration: Public Responsibility in an Emergency Program

∽∽∽∽∽∽∽∽∽∽∽∽∽∽∽∽∽∽∽∽∽∽∽∽∽∽∽

Administrative Powers and Problems

The Act of May, 1933, which appropriated half a billion dollars for Federal relief, also created for a period of two years a Federal Emergency Relief Administration, "all the powers of which shall be exercised by a Federal Emergency Relief Administrator . . . to be appointed by the President, by and with the advice and consent of the Senate." [1] Authority was given the Administrator for the employment of necessary staff and for the use of not more than $350,000 for administrative costs. He was authorized also to make "any investigation pertinent or material to the furtherance of the purposes" of the act and "such further investigations and studies as the President may deem necessary in dealing with problems of unemployment relief." [2] The decision of the Administrator as to the purpose of any expenditure was to be "final." [3] Grants were to be made to the several states [4] "to aid in meeting the costs of furnishing relief and work relief and in relieving the hardship and suffering caused by unemployment in the form of money, service, materials, and/or commodities to pro-

[1] FER Act of 1933, Public No. 15. Seventy-third Congress. Sec. 3(a). The life of the FERA was continued by successive relief acts during the following four years. It expired June 30, 1938, having been liquidated by the Works Progress Administrator, in accordance with the provisions of the Emergency Relief Act of 1937, Public Act 47, Seventy-fifth Congress.

[2] FER Act, 1933, Sec. 3(b) and (c).

[3] *Ibid.*, Sec. 4(e).

[4] *Ibid.*, Sec. 7. "The term 'state' shall include the District of Columbia, Alaska, Hawaii, the Virgin Islands and Puerto Rico, and the term 'governor' shall include the commissioners of the District of Columbia."

vide the necessities of life to persons in need as a result of the present emergency, and/or to their dependents, whether resident, transient or homeless." [5]

The purpose was to enable the Federal Government to "cooperate more effectively" with the states. Applications must be made by the governors, and grants were not made until the Administrator had certified his approval to the Reconstruction Finance Corporation which acted as fiscal agent. The Act specified that the applications must set forth the amounts spent for relief from both public and private sources within the state, as well as "the provision made to assure adequate administrative supervision" and "suitable standards of relief." They must also describe purposes for which the funds requested would be used. The governor was required to file with the FERA monthly reports of the disbursements made under the grants.[6]

The Act provided further that the Administrator might "under rules and regulations prescribed by the President, assume control of the administration in any state or states where, in his judgement, more effective and efficient cooperation between the state and Federal authorities may thereby be secured in carrying out the purposes of this Act." [7] This was the only authorization given for the assumption of direct Federal control. It is highly significant in that it recognized the final responsibility of the Federal Government for the welfare of its citizens.

The preamble of the Act declared that the economic depression had created a serious emergency. Eighteen million persons, nearly one-sixth of the population of the country, were on relief, and in addition an unknown number were uncared for. The Act gave broad powers to the Administrator to exercise a type of Federal responsibility which was without precedent. A huge sum of money [8] was involved, as well as the welfare of millions of people.

[5] FER Act, 1933, Sec. 4 (a).

[6] *Ibid.*, Secs. (5) and (6).

[7] *Ibid.*, Section 3(b).

[8] The original appropriation of $500,000,000 was added to by later allocations and appropriations. The total amount, June, 1933, through June 30, 1936, was $3,088,670,625. See p. 148 above.

When Mr. Hopkins took the oath of office on May 22, 1933, he undertook to administer the biggest single business ever developed in any country. Speed was imperative. The emergency was serious, but the Administration firmly believed that it was also temporary, or at least that the need for Federal relief would be of short duration. President Roosevelt, in asking Mr. Hopkins to accept the appointment, stated that the new Federal agency would be "organized on a temporary basis." He suggested that Mr. Hopkins secure a leave of absence from the chairmanship of the New York TERA, assuring him that New York would be all right in the meantime "with the present administrator and the excellent executive staff." [9]

This belief in the temporary nature of the job; the obvious fact that it was not expected to be as large or last as long as it did; the later administrative uncertainties as to the size and the timing of appropriations were all serious handicaps to long-time planning and accounted to a great extent for the failure to give a sense of security to the state and local administrations and their employees or, finally and most important, to the recipients of relief.

The Reconstruction Finance Corporation, under the Relief Act of July, 1932, had merely received and passed upon applications for advances. As a financial agency, it had not been in a position to encourage better state and local standards or furnish leadership by adopting positive administrative policies. As a result, the relief situation in the states and localities was uneven and confused. Benefits were generally inadequate; standards widely varied, and policies were half-formed, or conflicting and unsatisfactory. Wide variations existed, including every stage of development from highly organized and effective administrations in New York, Illinois and Pennsylvania to the eight states which, in the summer of 1933, still had created no state relief machinery at all.

In contrast to the limited powers of the RFC, the new relief administration was prepared to exercise considerable control over state relief programs in the interest of greater uniformity

[9] Minutes of New York TERA, May 19, 1933. As late as March, 1934, persons appointed to the staff of the FERA were advised to secure leave of absence from their positions.

and better standards. This control was theoretically indirect, since it was based upon the power to withhold grants, or to take over, that is, to federalize, the administration of relief in a state which did not meet requirements. In practice, however, the control was as direct, and involved the exertion of as much pressure upon the states, as was consistent with the terms of the Act.[10] These terms specifically respected state responsibility and initiative. The Federal grants became state funds and were therefore subject to state control. Federal authority hinged upon the implications of the provision that no grant could be made without the approval of the Administrator; and that the application to be submitted by the governor must present "in the manner requested by the Administrator," information on relief needs, provision for adequate administration, for suitable standards of relief and the purposes for which the funds requested would be used. At no point did the act authorize Federal regulation of the program.[11] Nevertheless, many factors combined to make possible a highly central-

[10] "Instead of giving the Federal Emergency Relief Administration complete control over the giving of relief, and instead of directing it to set up a new and elaborate organization throughout the county responsible directly to Washington, Congress in the Federal Emergency Relief Act provided that the Federal Emergency Relief Administration should cooperate with the several states in relieving the distress due to unemployment. It is on this cooperative basis that the Federal Emergency Relief Administration functioned.

"Its interpretation of cooperation is that the cooperation should be constructive, and that insofar as possible guidance and leadership should be exercised with respect to financial responsibility, as well as with respect to other relief problems, and that whenever essential guidance and leadership should be supplemented by as much pressure as the terms of the act would permit." *Expenditure of Funds: FERA*, Gov't Printing Office, Washington, D. C. Letter of transmittal to Senate Committee on Appropriations, p. xvii.

[11] "The Relief Act contained no mandate relating to standards of relief giving nor safeguarding of relief funds. Congress assumed that these were State and local problems and that the State and local governments would continue, as they had in the past, to watch over the details. The act did not even provide for a detailed accounting by the States to the Federal Government for expenditures made from grants to the States, again on the assumption that the States were qualified and prepared to do everything that might be necessary in accounting for and auditing relief expenditures." *Op. cit.*, p. 647.

ized and dominating administration. The most important elements in the situation were the terms of the act just noted, as well as the provisions which put unusual powers into the hands of the Administrator. Other contributing factors were the near panic which existed throughout the country in the face of the increasing unemployment; the depletion of state and local funds which made it absolutely necessary to secure Federal help; the inexperience, insecurity and uncertainty of state and local officials in the face of the tremendous demands for relief and the huge number of people who must be fed. All of these factors combined to make the states turn to Washington for help and caused them to welcome not only financial aid from the Federal Government but Federal leadership, advice, direction and even control.

This was particularly true during the first twelve months of the program. During the second year, in the winter of 1935, the pendulum began to swing in the other direction.[12]

When the FERA first began to function in May, 1933, there were three major administrative tasks which demanded immediate attention. It was essential that sufficient funds be allocated to the states to meet known and pressing needs, and that current information be secured regarding both the number of people on relief and the amount of money being spent. The way in which the first two tasks were met through the early grants to states and the establishment of a system of statistical reporting have already been briefly mentioned.[13] The third job was to ascertain what provisions had been made in the states for getting relief to the people in need. This meant a scrutiny of state and local administrative facilities, the improvement of existing agencies, and the creation of new relief authorities where they did not already exist.

State and Local Administration

Although the Federal Emergency Relief Act did not make the requirement usually attached to Federal grants-in-aid that each state which received a grant must create a state agency to

---

[12] A reaction against the controls exercised by the FERA was clearly shown in the action taken by Congress in eliminating certain standards from the Social Security Act of 1935. See Chapter 13 below.

[13] See pp. 148 and 156 above.

administer the funds received from the Federal Government,[14] it was fairly obvious that the FERA must immediately give attention to the problems of state and local administration.

Relief was then being administered in local offices by local officials. Nothing in the new Federal Act was meant to change that local responsibility, nor did the Federal Administrator have any intention of doing so. Furthermore, the Act clearly put upon the state governments the responsibility for adequate administrative supervision.[15] This responsibility was clearly recognized by the FERA which throughout its existence, worked entirely with and through state officials and the state relief administrations, and did not cross state lines by dealing directly with local units.

From the beginning of the program the Federal Administrator placed the greatest emphasis upon the importance of a "competent and businesslike [state] administration, entirely free from partisan politics."

Obviously the governors of the states must delegate such cooperation to properly constituted commissions. To cooperate with the Federal Administration, such a state body should represent the state and oversee the details of administration on a non-partisan basis.

A state relief organization should consist of a full-time properly qualified state director, an adequate force of field supervisors to visit frequently the local relief units, and an auditing staff responsible for checking local relief expenditures and making sure that every dollar of relief funds is properly accounted for.[16]

[14] "The following conditions in varying forms are usually attached to all grants-in-aid. First, the State legislature must accept the Federal Act and create a State agency with power and assets adequate to execute the work involved. Secondly, the State agency must project a plan for carrying on its activities which meets with Federal approval. The State originates the plan and is responsible for its proper execution." *FERA Monthly Report*, May, 1936, p. 5. The Titles of the Social Security Act which provide Aid for Dependent Children, the Blind and the Aged make somewhat similar requirements.

[15] See p. 172 above. "Each application . . . shall . . . present . . . the provision made to assure adequate administrative supervision." FER Act, Sec. 5.

[16] Hopkins, Harry L., *Proceedings* National Conference of Social Work, Detroit, 1933.

The situation in most of the states at the time was far from meeting the standards which Mr. Hopkins set forth. In order to obtain a better picture of the primitive and confused conditions which did exist, it will be worth while to review briefly the main points in the development of state and local relief machinery during the preceding two years.

As stated in a previous chapter seven states [17] appropriated and began to distribute funds for unemployment relief between September, 1931, and July, 1932, when the Emergency Relief and Construction Act was passed. Five of these states set up emergency relief agencies to disburse and supervise local administration. The other two used state agencies already in existence: Pennsylvania distributed $10,000,000, appropriated by the first Talbot Act, through the State Department of Welfare to the local poor boards,[18] and Wisconsin used its State Industrial Commission to distribute funds and supervise local administration.

The effect of the passage of the Emergency Relief and Construction Act, in July, 1932, was to bring 33 more states into the relief business during the succeeding ten months.[19] Thus, when the Federal Emergency Relief Administration was created in May, 1933, forty states had made some provision for the statewide administration of relief.[20] In 1933 relief on a large scale was almost as much of an innovation in state governments as in the Federal Government since, at that time, most of the state relief administrations had been in existence for less than ten months.[21]

[17] New Jersey, New York, Rhode Island, Pennsylvania, Wisconsin, Ohio, Illinois.

[18] See p. 95.

In August, 1932, the second Talbot Act was passed by which the legislature created a State Emergency Relief Board and County Boards to administer a new appropriation of $12,000,000.

[19] Six states created relief administrations in July and August, 19 in September and 8 in October, 1932.

[20] The following states organized after the creation of the Federal Emergency Relief Administration: Iowa, Connecticut, Maine, Massachusetts, Utah and Vermont in June; Nebraska in July and Wyoming in December, 1933.

[21] On June 30, 1933, 42 states had received advances from the Reconstruction Finance Corporation; Connecticut, Delaware, Massachusetts, Nebraska, Vermont and Wyoming received no loans or advances under

Thirteen of these 40 states had originally entrusted all or part of the responsibility for the administration of emergency relief to existing state welfare agencies as follows:

Alabama .... The State Department of Child Welfare
California .... The State Department of Social Welfare
Florida .... Made the Commissioner of Public Welfare
                    Director of Relief
Georgia .... The State Department of Welfare
Maryland .... The State Board of Aid and Charities
Michigan .... The State Department of Welfare
Minnesota .... The State Board of Control
New Mexico .... The Bureau of Child Welfare
North Carolina ..... The Board of Charities and Public Welfare
Pennsylvania .... The State Department of Public Welfare
West Virginia ...... The State Department of Public Welfare
Wisconsin .... The State Industrial Commission

It is significant that among the thirteen were included the states which had been engaged for a number of years in developing county units of public or child welfare. Many of these states conceived of their early unemployment relief programs as an integral part of their plans for county welfare units, and as a stimulus to the extension of permanent local public welfare agencies. So much interest in public welfare was in fact created by the rapid development of relief administration that bills providing for permanent state programs were introduced into the legislatures of Colorado, Kansas, Nevada and New Hampshire early in 1933.[22]

The other 27 states had set up emergency relief administrations. These special agencies were created by executive action, either by appointment, proclamation, special order or by some other form of authorization. Very few were created by legislation. As a rule, the states in which administrative machinery was authorized by statute were those operating entirely or in part on funds appropriated or made available by their legislatures; while the states which operated on funds borrowed from the RFC used administrative machinery cre-

the Emergency Relief and Construction Act of 1932. See Part II, Chapter 4.

[22] See *Public Welfare News*, March, 1933. Published by American Public Welfare Association, Chicago. See Part I, Chapter 1.

ated by executive action. The names of these agencies varied widely, although the words "emergency" and "relief" appeared with great regularity. There were also differences in size and form of the governing commission, committee or board. In a few states a director or administrator was made directly responsible to the governor without any board or commission.

The situation in the political subdivisions was even more varied and confusing. It was also an older and more stubborn problem, because local agencies had been struggling with unemployment relief long before the first state appropriation was made.[23]

The Confusion in Local Administration

The extent to which the localities had developed emergency programs depended upon the seriousness of their unemployment problem. During 1930 and 1931 the need was greatest in the industrial centers. This involved most of the cities and those rural areas where the population depended upon employment in mines and textile mills. Public welfare departments, poor relief offices, private agencies, special emergency relief commissions, were all used to administer unemployment relief, alone or in various combinations. The distribution of state appropriations, and of the Federal loans which became available in 1932, tended on the whole to increase rather than decrease these variations in local administration.[24]

During the ten months preceding the FERA most of the cities continued whatever relief machinery was already in use, whether permanent public department or private agency, or one of the many forms of emergency relief commission. At the same time the practice of making large subsidies of public funds to private agencies increased rather than diminished.

As state after state undertook responsibility for relief administration, however, a fairly rapid expansion into rural areas

[23] See Part II, Chapter 3.

[24] New York and Pennsylvania had fairly uniform systems: New York used the existing local public welfare machinery for home (direct) relief and set up special Work Bureaus for work relief. The latter were later put under the public welfare administrations. Pennsylvania created County Emergency Relief Boards which were separate from all other local agencies.

took place. Here, even more than in the cities, the program had to reckon with a deep-seated sense of local independence, the desire for self-government and local option, and with the wide differences between the towns of New England, the all-important counties of the South and West, and the complicated combinations of township and county jurisdiction in the middle western and south central states.

The existence of county welfare units in certain of the states [25] also added to the diversity of local administration. Eleven states [26] had countywide child, or public, welfare units of one kind or another. The proportion of organized counties in a single state varied from 100 percent in Alabama to one out of 21 counties in New Jersey. Altogether probably no more than 500 counties had developed welfare units under public auspices. Approximately half of these had no paid staffs but depended entirely on volunteer board members. The remaining 2,000 rural counties in the country had practically no social agencies, either public or private. Unemployment relief in these counties had to be entrusted either to the officials who were regularly responsible for poor relief, or to special emergency agencies created for the purpose.

The result of the rapid expansion of relief administration into these rural counties in 1932-1933 was a mixture of special emergency agencies, welfare units diverted from their usual functions to administer relief, and poor relief officials who had been suddenly given vaster responsibilities than they had ever carried before. These forms of local administration varied not only between states but within states, from county to county and from city to city.

This meant that the unemployed were receiving relief either from public officials or from private citizens employed by private agencies, depending upon the setup. The agencies were either public or quasi-public or private, and each agency might have any one of a number of official or semi-official relation-

[25] See Part I, Chapter 1.

[26] Alabama, California, Florida, Georgia, Minnesota, New Jersey, New York, North Carolina, Virginia, West Virginia, Wisconsin. In addition, Iowa and New Mexico had organized county programs which combined public and private agencies.

ships with the local government, or no relationship at all except that it received money from the public treasury.[27]

There was considerable variation also in the type of relationship which the local administration bore to the state agency. This connection ranged all the way from the definite supervision given by the New York Temporary Emergency Relief Administration, fortified as it was by the right to withhold the grants with which the state reimbursed the localities for 40 percent of their relief expenditures, to the often unfortunately complete independence of local units in a number of states in which the state relief agency was practically no more than a disbursing agent and exercised little, if any, supervisory responsibility.

The administration of unemployment relief, both state and local, was, therefore, in a highly experimental stage. With the exception of the few states which had been longest in the business, the country was full of new, hastily established, or older, ill-adapted agencies, for the most part managed by people who were accustomed to small programs and who had no experience with handling relief or conducting any other enterprises on such a tremendous scale. They were, for these reasons, usually trying to operate an enormous business within a petty framework of restricted social philosophy, narrow local limits, and according to old methods.

This was the situation in May, 1933, when the Federal Emergency Relief Administration was created, and began requiring that governors submit for approval, with their applications for grants, information to show "the provision made to assure adequate administrative supervision" and "suitable standards of relief." These apparently simple phrases actually involved an approval by the Federal Administrator of all that was necessary to safeguard the spending of Federal funds in a way that would best meet the needs of the unemployed. With this end in view the staff of the FERA undertook to assist the states to organize or reorganize, where necessary, relief administrations in every one of the 48 states as well as in the territories included in the terms of the Act.

---

[27] See Appendix I for description of different types of agencies in existence at this time, ranging from the duly established public agency to the independent private agency which receives a public subsidy.

Emergency Relief Separated from Permanent Agencies

Eight states set up emergency relief administrations under the stimulus of the Federal Emergency Relief Administration [28] between July 1, 1933, and the end of that year. A tremendous amount of reorganization also took place in most of the other states. Perhaps the most significant feature of this reorganization was the gradual separation of the state emergency relief programs from direct connection with permanent state agencies in all but one of the thirteen states [29] in which emergency relief had been originally connected with established state agencies. Maryland [30] was the only state which did not eventually set up an Emergency Relief Administration which was independent of the permanent state welfare program. This seems to have been entirely in line with Federal policy since the eight new state administrations were all set up without any connection with permanent welfare agencies. Attention has already been called to the emphasis placed upon the emergency and temporary character of the New York State administration when it was organized in the fall of 1931 during the governorship of Mr. Roosevelt, and to the belief which he expressed later as President, at the beginning of the Federal Emergency Relief Administration, that the Federal relief program was of a temporary nature.[31]

To have put a program of such an emergency and temporary character under a regular, established governmental agency would have carried implications of permanence and have created probabilities of continuing Federal relief which the Federal Relief Administration was evidently anxious to avoid. Also it is true that relatively few states had welfare departments which would have been willing to administer relief or able readily to modify their programs in order to assume extensive new responsibilities.[32] Those welfare depart-

[28] See footnote on p. 177 above.

[29] See p. 178 above for list.

[30] Maryland continued to administer relief under the State Board of Aid and Charities throughout the life of the Federal Emergency Relief Administration.

[31] See Part II, Chapter 3, and p. 173.

[32] The only such departments in a number of states were central authorities responsible for state institutions. See p. 23.

ments which did temporarily undertake to handle the relief job found that their regular functions were seriously crippled thereby.

Another factor undoubtedly entered into the decision to establish separate administrations. This was the probability that independent emergency agencies would more readily conform to the pattern set by the Federal Relief Administration; would be more susceptible of control, and particularly would be able to move more rapidly than the permanent agencies which, having been established by law, were bound in numerous ways by statutes, administrative rulings, and tradition. The size of the relief job, and the speed with which it had to move, required agencies which were free from such limitations, and also agencies of Federal, state and local governments which were all part of one closely-knit system.

This separation of the emergency relief administration from poor relief and permanent public welfare programs was highly significant on at least two counts. It was indicative of the intention of the Federal Administration to maintain the relief program on an emergency, temporary basis, as merely a stopgap for the unemployed until positive measures could be taken to insure economic recovery.[33] It was also important because it put this momentous adventure of government with relief administration in a position where it could not, or at least did not, directly affect permanent programs in the sense of bringing about changes in the public welfare and poor relief systems by direct action. Whatever influence was exerted was necessarily indirect. The nature and extent of this indirect influence and some of its favorable and unfavorable effects upon public welfare and poor relief will be discussed in later chapters.[34]

The Problem of Public Subsidies to Private Agencies

No less significant than the separation of the emergency relief administration from established public relief and welfare programs was the early ruling of the Federal Administrator that Federal funds were to be administered by public agen-

[33] See Part III, Chapter 7.
[34] See Part III, Chapters 10 and 12, and Part IV, Chapter 13.

cies. This ruling effectively separated the emergency program from the whole field of privately sponsored social work since it put an abrupt end to the subsidies which were being made from public treasuries to a large number of private agencies.[35]

The practice of granting public subsidies to private agencies for relief purposes had been fairly common before the beginning of the recent depression. In the struggle to handle the huge unemployment relief load between 1930 and 1933, subsidies had increased to a considerable extent, both in number and in amount. The exhaustion of private relief funds in city after city had forced one private agency after another to turn for help to the public treasury of the city or county. When state unemployment relief funds were distributed to the localities, subsidies were usually continued where the practice was already in effect. In Illinois, for instance, established private local agencies were formally recognized as possible recipients of subsidies from the state relief allocations. The manual of instructions, issued in 1932 by the Emergency Relief Commission of that state, provided that the county committees might in their discretion allocate state funds to either public or private agencies, although the state commission required that wherever practicable, qualified public agencies were to be used.[36]

The practice of making public relief subsidies continued during the ten months when loans and advances were being made by the RFC. These advances became, of course, the property of the state or political subdivision which borrowed them, and they were allocated according to the pattern already established in the cities and counties in which they were to be spent. Probably the chief effect of the RFC funds upon subsidies was only to increase them in many cases, because a larger total amount of money was available for relief.

The commonly applied principle that, in times of depression, new machinery for emergency relief should be avoided and established agencies used was responsible for the great extension of subsidies during the first three years of the depression. The advocates of this principle, who were leaders in the field of private social work, interpreted it to mean that

[35] See Part I, Chapter 2.
[36] See Part II, Chapter 6.

the *best qualified* established agencies should carry the load. On this basis subsidies to large numbers of private agencies were thought to be justified, and the corresponding city or county governments were thereby relieved of the necessity of developing agencies of their own.[37]

In June, 1933, the first full month of the FERA, there were in the 71 cities (in 32 states) reporting relief expenditures to the Federal Children's Bureau, 175 private agencies which received and spent public funds for relief. There are no figures to show how many more subsidized agencies were operating at that time in other places. Under the heavy pressures of the emergency job many, if not most, of these private agencies had so diverted their staffs, operating facilities, and funds to the job of administering relief to the unemployed that very little was left of their regular programs. Moreover, the public subsidies had become such a large proportion of the total budget of many agencies that even to suggest the withdrawal of public funds was to threaten their very existence.

Public Funds Administered by Public Agencies

The first rule [38] issued early in June by the Federal Administrator was a definite pronouncement on the question of public responsibility:

Grants of Federal emergency relief funds are to be administered by public agencies after August 1, 1933.

Just as all State commissions responsible for the distribution of Federal and State funds to local communities are public bodies, so in turn should those local units be public agencies responsible for the expenditure of public funds in the same manner as any other municipal or county department.

This policy obviously must be interpreted on a realistic basis in various parts of the United States. Hundreds of private agencies scattered throughout the land have freely and generously offered their services in the administration of public funds. It would be a serious handicap to relief work if the abilities and interests of these individuals were lost. But these individuals should be made public officials, working under the control of public authority. Thousands

[37] See Part II, Chapter 6.
[38] In a letter which was sent to the states early in June, and on June 23 issued as the first section of Rules and Regulations, No. 1.

of these workers are serving and will continue to serve without pay, but, if paid, they should be compensated in the same manner as any other public servant.

It is not the intention of this regulation to instruct the several States to make hasty changes in agreements which the State Administration may have made with the private agencies. Adjustment, however, to this policy is to be made no later than August 1, 1933.

This ruling prohibits the turning over of Federal Emergency Relief Funds to a private agency. The unemployed must apply to a public agency for relief, and this relief must be furnished direct to the applicant by a public agent.

This regulation, like the other rules issued by the FERA, applied only to Federal funds. However, since Federal, state and local funds were all administered by the same agencies, the Federal regulation actually determined the administrative auspices of every state and local agency in the entire program.[39]

This policy was epoch-making in that it established once and for all a clean-cut principle and a broad philosophy of governmental responsibility for relief. It clarified and settled a question regarding which there had been much confused and rationalistic thinking and discussion for a great many years. Its practical effects were to create consternation in the ranks of private social workers and to start a process of reorganization wherever the subsidy system was in effect.

Many private agencies now found themselves faced with the necessity of making immediate and radical adjustments. A number of them, having come to depend almost entirely upon public funds, were now headed for disaster because they had failed to continue and safeguard their regular functions. Other agencies were better prepared because they had established separate divisions for unemployment relief to administer their public subsidies. They were ready to turn these divisions over to governmental control and devote their attention to their regular programs which had been carried during the emergency in parallel divisions. For example, a segregation of function had been undertaken some months earlier by the Associated Charities of Cleveland in anticipation of just such

[39] A few counties scattered through several states never received Federal funds, and therefore were not subject to this rule.

a shift to public auspices. When the Federal Emergency Relief Administration order came, the county commissioners set up a relief committee which was approved by the Ohio State Relief Commission. The Associated Charities turned over to this county committee the entire emergency division, including the staff and case load. Moreover, the secretary of the Associated Charities resigned to become director of the new public relief agency.

Adjustments in most of the other subsidized private agencies were not so easily effected. Considerable difficulty and delay were encountered in a number of other large cities.[40]

The Family Welfare Association of America,[41] with a membership of more than 200 of the largest private family welfare agencies in the country, was more directly concerned with the effects of the new Federal rule than any other of the private national agencies. Approximately one-fifth of the member agencies of the Association were faced with serious difficulties requiring immediate and radical readjustments. The following summary of the situation appears in a report made by the Association in July:

About twenty-five of these [37] agencies have recently been relying wholly or in large part upon federal funds with no apparent provision for the taking over by a public agency of the part of their work thus financed, and with no adequate safeguards for the preservation of their other functions as private agencies. In many instances, their private support has almost entirely disappeared, and unless such support can be immediately developed upon the basis of their special functions as private family case work agencies, they face their transformation into the governmental agency or a more or less temporary suspension of activities.

Of the twelve or more agencies, subsidized from public funds, which are to some extent prepared for the new federal policy a few have created or are developing a separate unemployment relief division financed by public funds, which can be taken over by public

[40] Baltimore, Kansas City, Birmingham, Memphis, Toledo, St. Louis, Houston, Texas; Des Moines, Iowa; Omaha, Nebraska; Little Rock, Arkansas; Portland, Oregon; were the most important larger cities which transferred their unemployment relief programs from private to public auspices. In most of these cities there was considerable delay and confusion.

[41] See Part I, Chapter 2, and Part II, Chapters 3 and 4.

authorities (including unemployment relief commissions) without destroying a real nucleus of work and support for the private agency. Most of the twelve, however, are prepared only in the sense that the executive has been appointed a public official, and in that capacity is administering public funds through the private agency. In such instances also, thoughtful and immediate adjustments will be necessary if the family case work functions of the private agency are to be preserved.

We consider it to be the duty of this Association to assist member agencies affected by this order in making such adjustments as may be necessary to assure a reasonably adequate future administration of relief funds, conserving in public and private agencies the values which may have been built up over a period of years in case work and administrative procedures. All of this is primarily in the interest of the families served, and involves the most loyal cooperation between public and private agencies.[42]

So much misunderstanding and confusion developed in the attempt to apply the rule abolishing subsidies that, on July 11, Mr. Hopkins found it necessary to define the terms "public agency" and "public agent or public official" and to clarify his meaning in regard to the use of private agency personnel. He ruled that a "public agency" might be an established public welfare department or an emergency unemployment relief administration. The latter might be authorized by legislation or created by executive action. But, however established, it must be vested with full governmental authority to spend state and Federal funds. It must also have the full sanction of the state ERA and conform to its rulings.

A public official must be "a member of the official staff of the public agency responsible to the chief executive employed by the public agency to administer the entire organization of unemployment relief. This relationship must be made official by definite appointment and acceptance of such appointment." [43]

Personnel loaned by private agencies must become an integral part of the public agency. This must be shown by hav-

[42] "Bulletin to all Member Agencies," Family Welfare Association of America, July, 1933, Mimeographed. Compare with Miss Richmond's statement on pp. 52-53.

[43] FERA Monthly Report, May 22, 1933, to June 30, 1933, p. 9.

ing the name of the public agency "on the office door so that clients may know that they are applying to a public agency for relief." In all respects, including the handling of order forms, receipts, identification cards, and payment of bills, transactions were to be conducted as from the public agency. Evasion of the rule was provided against in the final section which read as follows:

It is expected that on other matters than the determination of relief there will be cooperative relationships established between public agencies and private agencies, but the public agency shall not pay for supplemental services so rendered by private agencies.[44]

These definitions which were issued by the Federal Emergency Relief Administration as the first section of Rules and Regulations No. 3, made clear the fundamental proposition that the unemployed who were to be helped from Federal funds should be able to apply to government offices for government aid and their requests should be dealt with by public officials according to governmental policies and procedures. The Federal Emergency Relief Administration would not countenance subsidies to private agencies and the resulting confusion between public and private policies and controls. Local governments could no longer evade the assumption of direct responsibility for the public administration of relief to the unemployed.

August first had been set as the deadline in the original ruling on public administration, permitting somewhat more than a month for the transfers, but the necessary reorganization took much longer in many places. Reports to the Federal Children's Bureau show that in the 71 cities reporting relief expenditures, 20 private agencies stopped spending public funds in June, 1933; 50 more stopped in July, August or September and 18 other agencies stopped during the last three months of the year. The reports do not show which of these agencies received Federal funds. It is probable, however, that the negligible percentage of agencies which reported subsidies after September were spending funds which they had received from local public treasuries.

[44] *Ibid.*, p. 10.

Significance of These Two Policies

This FERA ruling on public responsibility established a principle and a precedent. Not only in the administration of unemployment relief but in all subsequent programs for public relief and categorical assistance, Federal, state and local, that precedent has been followed without question. The financing and administration of public benefits for persons in need was definitely established as being the responsibility of government and not of private citizens, however organized or however charitably disposed.

This was the second of the two important aspects of the process of organization and reorganization which took place under the FERA. The first, which has already been discussed, was the establishment throughout the country of a system of state and local public emergency relief administrations which were in the state pattern entirely separate from established agencies, and in the local pattern separate in most of the states from poor relief machinery on the one hand and, on the other, from welfare units and agencies administering Mothers' Pensions and other statutory benefits.

During the summer and fall of 1933, a tremendous amount of work was done by the states and localities under the leadership of the FERA to bring order out of what was very near chaos in many areas. The result was the achievement of an amazing amount of uniformity in an exceedingly short time.

It is no exaggeration to say that more changes were introduced in a few months in the administration of unemployment relief than had occurred during the preceding three emergency years. It is also indisputable that the changes made under the FERA taken together with those which had occurred during the administration of RFC loans, revolutionized the system of public relief which had been practically unchanged for more than three hundred years.

Chapter 9

Federal-State-Local Relations

∽∽∽∽∽∽∽∽∽∽∽∽∽∽∽∽∽∽∽∽∽∽∽∽∽∽∽∽∽∽∽

With a commission from Congress to assist the states in providing relief as promptly and as adequately as possible for
some twenty million people, the Federal Emergency Relief Administration undertook the biggest enterprise in the history of
the United States, if not in the world. It touched the lives of
people in every corner of the country from the crowded slums
of great cities to isolated mountain camps and jungle clear-
ings. It reached into Puerto Rico, the Virgin Islands, Hawaii
and Alaska.

Because the emergency relief organization was practically
uniform throughout the country and independent of the permanent structure of government with its manifold restrictions,
it could function with speed and effectiveness. Because its
funds must be spent by public agencies, clear lines of responsibility were established through local and state officials direct
to the Federal Administrator, who was in turn responsible to
the President and to Congress.

Because the essential function of the Federal Emergency
Relief Administration was to co-operate with and assist the
states, it followed that the relationship maintained by the Federal Relief Administration with the state governments and the
state emergency relief administrations constituted the very
core of its existence.

The actual granting and receiving of relief went on in the
localities: counties, townships, cities, and villages. The state
relief administrations supervised these local operations and
were responsible for their effectiveness to the Federal Administrator, insofar as Federal funds were involved, upon whom
in turn rested the responsibility for co-operating with and assisting the states in achieving the purposes of the Federal Act.

The assistance given the states fell under three general head-

191

ings: (1) the allocation of Federal funds to supplement the state resources which were available to meet estimated needs; (2) helping the states to provide adequate administrative supervision; (3) determining policies and rules to safeguard the expenditure of Federal funds, and to assist the states in establishing suitable standards of relief.[1]

All of the policies, rules and regulations, activities and organization of the Federal Emergency Relief Administration grew out of the need to give these three types of assistance to the states and at the same time to safeguard the spending of Federal funds. Broad policies were set forth regarding public responsibility for public funds, and concerning standards of efficiency and adequacy of the relief provided by these funds. Rules were issued regarding such matters as the specific purposes for which Federal funds could be spent, qualifications of personnel, and the methods by which relief might be administered whether direct or work relief, cash or kind. Divisions and special services were set up within the Federal Relief Administration to meet specific needs of the program as it developed. These divisions implemented the relationship between the Federal Administration and the states.

Field Representatives

A field staff, which later formed the nucleus of the Division of Relations with States, was appointed by Mr. Hopkins immediately after he took office.[2] It was imperative that the Federal Administrator should have a staff to go out as his official representatives into the states, to keep in close and constant touch with the state program, to interpret Federal policies, to report to him on conditions, needs and resources, in order that he might have a sound basis for the allocation of funds. They were also needed to advise the states on their pressing problems of organization and reorganization and to assist them in establishing efficient methods of administration and supervision.

[1] See p. 171; also Federal Emergency Relief Appropriation Act, Section 5.

[2] This was practically the same staff which had been serving in a similar capacity under the direction of Mr. Fred Croxton in the administration of loans and advances to the states by the RFC. See p. 128 ff.

Mr. Hopkins, in his report to Congress in 1935, describes the field staff as follows:

The Federal Emergency Relief Act of 1933 provides that the Federal Government shall cooperate with the several States "in furnishing relief to their needy and distressed people." Power is given to the Administrator to "conduct any investigation pertinent or material to the furtherance of the purposes of this act. . . ." The Federal Emergency Relief Administration takes this responsibility very seriously and has divided the United States into 10 regions with a field staff in each region for the purpose of advising and consulting with the States to the end of providing the most effective relief administration possible in each State.[3]

Administrative Divisions

This Division of Relations with States was central to the whole administrative structure. It was in fact the only division of the FERA which dealt with the states on general administrative matters. The other divisions were set up to perform technical specialized services either in relation to the entire program, as in the Division of Research, Statistics and Finance or in relation to only one type of activity, as in the Work Division.

These two divisions were made responsible for approving, on behalf of the Administrator, the corresponding technical services which were set up in each state relief administration. Their relationship to the states extended beyond approval or disapproval to actual assistance in organizing the services and to continuing supervision and consultation in the interests of sound administration.[4]

The Work Division was established almost at once after the creation of the FERA because work relief for the unemployed was specifically mentioned in the act and was also the major objective of the Administration.[5] Moreover, work relief projects were already in operation in many localities and had

---

[3] Expenditure of Funds, FERA, *op. cit.*, p. xvii.

[4] In general the State Emergency Relief Administrations followed the pattern of the FERA, as far as the services were needed. County ERA's were similarly organized wherever the size of the relief load or the need of a diversified program justified special divisions or services.

[5] See Chapter 7.

formed an increasingly important part of local relief programs during 1931 and 1932.

Within the first two weeks of the FERA a statistical and reporting service [6] was developed which later became the Division of Research, Statistics and Finance. This service grew out of the immediate necessity of securing factual information about state and local expenditures, resources and needs upon which decisions could be based regarding the size of grants to the states or the reasonableness of state applications. Such a system was absolutely necessary because most of the states had few or no definite facts or figures to present. There were in existence few satisfactory state systems for reporting the numbers of relief recipients and the amounts of expenditures. As a result, a vague uncertainty prevailed concerning the size of the relief problem. After nine months of RFC administration there were still no adequate figures in Washington to show the volume of current state and local relief expenditures nor the size of the relief load throughout the country.[7] Little was known about the characteristics or composition of the relief population.

Under this Research Division a uniform, nationwide system for the regular reporting of relief statistics was established for the first time in the history of the United States. The information secured from these early reports and from the subsequent studies undertaken by the FERA research staff, or financed by FERA funds, revealed the existence of certain groups and classes of the population whose needs could not be met through the ordinary relief channels and for whom special programs were required. This information was used as the basis of the later planning and development of Federal programs, not only for emergency work relief and permanent public assistance but for social insurance, housing, farm security and other fields with which the New Deal was concerned.[8]

During the first eight months of the FERA additional services were set up within the three major divisions which have already been mentioned. Early in July, 1933, a service was

[6] Beginning on June 6, 1933. See p. 156 above.
[7] Expenditure of Funds, FERA, *op. cit.*, pp. 650-6. Exhibit U. "Unemployment Relief" by Corrington Gill.
[8] See Part III, Chapter 7.

established under the Work Division to assist the states in developing self-help co-operatives. At about the same time a Transient Bureau was established to co-operate with the states "in establishing permanent policies and standards of service." [9] These programs were undertaken in accordance with provisions of the act which specifically authorized grants to the states for self-help co-operatives and for "needy persons who have no legal settlement in any one state or community." [10]

Two months later, in the fall of 1933, the Emergency Education Program was organized in the Division of Relations with States to assist in meeting the needs of unemployed teachers. In October, 1933, the Federal Surplus Relief Corporation was organized as a joint undertaking of the FERA and the Department of Agriculture, and the Work Division of the FERA established a service for the distribution of surplus commodities to persons who were receiving relief. During the same month a Federal Director of Women's Work was appointed. In April, 1934, the Rural Rehabilitation Division was created, as the fourth major division, to assist the states in developing a diversified program for the rehabilitation of rural people in distress.

In April, 1934, nearly a year after the creation of the FERA, a Social Service Section was established within the Division of Relations with States to give technical supervision to the Social Service Divisions which had been operating in the states and localities since the beginning of the program.[11]

During the summer and fall of that year other services and specialists were added to the FERA staff, notably a medical director and a dental adviser, who were appointed in October. Medical relief had been authorized a year earlier,[12] but the states had been left to set up their own medical care programs without professional advice and assistance from the Federal Relief Administration.[13]

[9] Rules and Regulations, No. 3. Issued July 11, 1933. The Transient Bureau was in the Division of Relations with States.

[10] Federal Emergency Relief Appropriation Act. Section 4(c).

[11] See Part III, Chapter 10.

[12] See Rules and Regulations, No. 7. Issued September 10, 1933. *FERA Monthly Report.*

[13] See Part III, Chapter 10.

When the medical director was appointed he was made responsible not only for directing policies and activities in the field of medical relief, but for advising on health and sanitation matters, and assisting in "developing work-relief projects which promote health." [14]

The Federal Emergency Relief Administration developed on a national scale many of the programs and special services which had already been in operation under the New York TERA. A study of the structure, methods and policies of the state relief administrations of 1931 and 1932 in New York, Pennsylvania and Illinois shows the profound influence which those early programs exerted upon the policies, activities and practices of the FERA and consequently upon state and local emergency relief administrations throughout the country.[15]

By November, 1934, the organization of the FERA was well developed with four major divisions, a highly diversified program of work and rural rehabilitation, and numerous special services which had been set up to meet special needs. The process of developing these special services had followed no consistent organization plan. Many of them were put into divisions with which they had no particular functional relation. The line-up was determined often by a particular interest of a division director in the new service which was being established. In short, the Federal organization was fairly loose-jointed. It was also, by reason of its emergency nature, happily much less rigid and formal in its interoffice relationships and communications than the permanent bureaus of the Federal Government. This informality made possible a flexibility which was highly desirable in such a rapidly moving program.

Purposes, Policies and Plans

The Federal Administrator and his assistants were not content with a routine job of providing relief for twenty million people. They went back of the needs to discover causes; and they went beyond the twenty million who were already on re-

[14] *Chronology of the Federal Emergency Relief Administration,* p. 67, AO-20. October 29, 1934.

[15] See Appendix J for summary of relief administrations in Illinois, New York and Pennsylvania, West Virginia and Wisconsin, issued by the Family Welfare Association of America, April, 1933. Mimeographed.

lief to explore the unmet needs of the millions in that unde-
fined marginal area which lies between stark destitution and
decent living conditions. They really cared that people were
in distress, not because they knew them as individuals, but in
spite of the fact that they knew them only by thousands, by
hundreds of thousands and by millions. They cared what
happened to the unemployed on relief although they saw them
only as figures and lines and shaded areas on statistical reports
and charts.

Out of the offices of the FERA in the Walker-Johnson
Building in Washington came the original conception, the planning, and the first experimental operation of an amazing number of programs which later attained to independent status or
were transferred to and continued under other governmental
departments or agencies.[16]

These programs began as part of an effort to provide a constructive answer to the problem of unemployment. They continued in an endeavor to translate into actual fact the theory
of governmental responsibility for the welfare of *all* citizens,
of whom at least one-third were living or rather existing on a

[16] Among the programs for the inception of which the FERA was
wholly or partially responsible may be mentioned the following:

Civil Works Administration, in many respects the forerunner of the
Works Program and the Works Progress Administration. The latter con-
tinued the diversified work program already begun under the FERA:
Projects for professional people: Adult, Parent, Workers' Education;
Recreation, Music, the Arts and Writers' Projects. The Works Progress
Administration was renamed Work Projects Administration and made
part of the Federal Works Agency on July 1, 1939.

Rural Rehabilitation, resettlement of farm families living on submarginal land; purchase of submarginal land; rural organized communities:
now under the Farm Security Administration in the Department of Agriculture.

The Federal Surplus Commodities Corporation which is now under the
Department of Agriculture.

The National Youth Administration which is now in the Federal Security Agency.

Some idea of the extent to which the FERA diversified its program
may be gained by the following list of Federal agencies which operated
projects financed entirely or partially by FERA funds, or which participated through other means directly in the FERA program: Agricultural
Adjustment Administration, Biological Survey, National Park Service,
Bureau of Indian Affairs, Corps of Army Engineers, etc., etc.

level far below any reasonable standard of decency and health. The planning was motivated by a sincere desire to restore and conserve human resources, to make decent living possible where it had never been known before and to give people a break who had never had one.

The manifold diversification of the program to fit the varied needs of people and the almost continuous changes, additions and adjustments to specific situations in the field, required that a vital, close and constant relationship be maintained between the Federal Relief Administration and the states. The broad policies which were the backbone of the program and the basis of this Federal-state relationship were formulated and announced at the very beginning. They were set forth in the Rules and Regulations [17] and in a few early letters from the Federal Administrator. They embodied well-thought-out principles which stood the test of time and remained valid and intact through all the exigencies to which the program was later

[17] Published as follows:

RULES AND REGULATIONS

Date	No.	Subject
June 23, 1933	1	Rules governing expenditures of Federal emergency relief funds
July 1, 1933	2	Additional rules governing expenditures of Federal emergency relief funds
July 11, 1933	3	Supplement to Rules and Regulations No. 1 and rules governing adequacy of relief, investigation and service, direct relief, relief to transients, and self-help projects
July 21, 1933	4	Conditions of employment on work-relief projects
July 21, 1933	5	Employment of personnel on administrative pay roll under the Federal Emergency Relief Act of 1933
Aug. 11, 1933	6	Purchase of supplies in compliance with NRA codes or provisions of the President's Re-employment Agreement
Sept. 10, 1933	7	Medical care provided in the home to recipients of unemployment relief
Nov. 6, 1933	8	Organization and operation of transient service bureaus

See *Chronology of the Federal Emergency Relief Administration. May 12, 1933, to December 31, 1935.* Works Progress Administration, Division of Social Research, p. 108.

subjected. Since Federal funds were allotted to the states to be spent in a unified program with state and local money, it was essential that the Federal Administration should take its stand and announce its policies before the states could be expected to determine their positions on any important aspect of the program.

A uniform minimum wage was established. There was to be no discrimination "because of race, religion, color, noncitizenship, political affiliation, or because of membership in any special or selected group." [18] Public agencies were to be responsible for the expenditure of public funds.[19] Personnel, though employed by the states, was to be approved by the Federal Relief Administration. A definite stand was taken in favor of adequate relief and standards of investigation and administration. The general policy that the funds were to be used for emergency unemployment relief was emphasized again and again.

These policies and rules provided for a fair degree of uniformity throughout the country. Many of them were purposely left vague in detail to permit their adaptation to local circumstances and conditions. The states were responsible for interpreting the rules to their local administrations since the Federal Administration dealt with the states and did not cross state lines to establish direct relations with local units.

Relations with the States

As has already been said, the Division of Relations with States was the focal point of contact with the state relief administrations on all major matters of policy. The FERA established a new record in the use of its field staff and in its general conduct of Federal-state relations. There was no precedent for a Federal agency administering relief grants to the states. There was certainly no precedent for the business crisis and the huge unemployment problem. The states needed and wanted advice and assistance badly. Questions were constantly arising, at a great distance from Washington, concerning Federal policies and their interpretation which had to be settled at once because large sums of money and great num-

[18] Rules and Regulations No. 3. Issued July 11, 1933.
[19] See Part III, Chapter 8.

bers of people were involved. It is therefore not difficult to understand why the field representatives were given considerable authority and responsibility in their dealings with the states, and why and how the states were brought nearer to Washington than they had ever been and into intimate relationship with the Federal Relief Administration.

The specialized divisions which were responsible for the approval and supervision of technical services also sent their staff members into the states. The immediate result was confusion in the field and an inevitable crossing of lines of responsibility and authority. In order to clarify the situation and establish definitely the functions and relationships of the staff members of various divisions who visited the states, the Federal Administrator announced on May 3, 1934, a reorganization of the field service. The United States was divided into regions each of which included several states, a field representative was placed in charge of each region and made responsible for all state relationships which in any way affected administrative policy and operation.[20] A staff member from each of the more important special divisions or services was assigned to each chief regional representative. This staff member had a.double responsibility. He was under the administrative direction of the regional representative to whom he referred all matters involving policy and organization. At the same time he was directly under the technical supervision of his special division in the Federal office and consequently referred to that division all matters which concerned the distinctly technical aspects of his job of supervising the specialized state service for which he was responsible. This type of field staff relationship continued throughout the existence of the FERA and was used, although with distinct modifications, in the WPA to which agency many of the FERA field staff members were later transferred.

In May, 1934, when regional offices were first established, a field examiner [21] was assigned to each region from the Division

---

[20] *Chronology of the Federal Emergency Relief Administration*, p. 56.

[21] "Attached to each regional field staff is a field examiner whose duties include a regular examination of the system of auditing and accounting and statistical reporting in each State in his region to see that the methods used are adequate for insuring properly authorized expenditures of

of Research, Statistics and Finance, a social worker from the Social Service Section of the Division of Relations with the States, an engineer from the Work Division, and a Rural Rehabilitation adviser from the newly organized division of that name. A research supervisor was added to each staff somewhat later.

Throughout the entire staff, the size of the job, the heavy responsibilities, the speed and the unusual pressures, as well as the caliber of the personnel, all combined to create a morale and an *esprit de corps* which was most unusual. This staff morale was not limited to the Federal and state offices. It existed to an amazing degree on the firing line where thousands of hastily recruited people, who had little or nothing in common except the job of administering emergency relief, worked under unbelievable difficulties, for long hours, under exhausting pressures, for moderate and often pathetically inadequate pay. Their loyalty and integrity were outstanding. Approximately 120,000 people were employed on Federal, state and local emergency relief administration staffs, the country over. More than $2,500,000,000 was spent in the first two years. On May 1, 1935, the Federal Administrator reported to Congress that 1,000 complaints of misuse of funds had been investigated, and that of this number only 130 were found to

funds and for setting forth a complete and accurate picture of financial transactions. He also has the duty of ascertaining that the relief funds are properly safeguarded by proper bonding of depositaries and officials.

"The field examiner cannot act as an auditor; the responsibility for auditing is upon the States. However, he does aid the States in maintaining effective systems of auditing and accounting for funds. If necessary, he may supervise a detailed audit, and on occasion may find it necessary to recommend that an auditor be removed. . . .

"The regional examiners represent the Division of Finance and Statistics in the field, and consequently upon them rests the responsibility for regular examination of the financial and statistical work and records of the States to make sure the methods used are adequate for insuring the properly authorized expenditure of relief funds. Theirs is also the responsibility of seeing that the States report correctly all financial transactions and relief statistics from each county. The examiners see that regular bank reconciliations are made, that officials handling relief funds are qualified to do so and are properly bonded, and that relief funds are safeguarded in every possible manner."

See *Expenditure of Funds, FERA, op. cit.,* pp. xviii and 649.

be true charges. "The record shows that the thousands of public officials and public-spirited citizens in every locality throughout the United States spent this huge sum wisely, honestly, and effectively." [22]

Federal Grants to the States

Since the only reason for the existence of the FERA was to co-operate with the states in furnishing relief to their needy and distressed people, it was clear to the persons who framed the act and supported it in Congress that the states' end of the business of co-operation would vary drastically. It would depend upon such complex and unmeasurable factors as local standards of living, attitudes towards "the poor," economic and social conditions, the willingness or ability of legislators to appropriate funds and, most serious of all, the deep-seated American tradition of local responsibility for relief.[23]   Because these factors were unmeasurable, one-half of the original Federal appropriation was made a discretionary fund to be allotted to the states on the basis of need in amounts to be decided by the Federal Administrator.[24]   This method, therefore, virtually involved submitting the states to a "means test." It placed the Federal Administrator in somewhat the same relation to the states as a relief investigator is to an applicant for relief. In this relationship were involved the simliar and familiar dangers of creating dependency in the states; discouraging effort to produce resources of their own because Federal funds were easy to get; and encouraging the tendency to spend money freely because it had been given to them by the Federal Government.

These unmeasurable and intangible factors in the state situations together with the practical difficulties of securing satisfactory data on economic conditions and fiscal ability, reduced the Federal Relief Administration to the point of often making empirical and impulsive decisions regarding amounts of grants to the states. Numerous critics called attention to the fact that the rate at which the grants were apportioned among the states bore no direct relationship to the distribution of the un-

[22] See *Expenditure of Funds, FERA, op. cit.*, p. 650.
[23] See Part I, Chapter 1.
[24] See Part III, Chapter 7.

employed or of the relief load nor to any other definite current data. This criticism was undoubtedly often justified. There is no question but that the intangible factors prevailed over the tangible in guiding the decisions regarding allocations of funds. A tremendous amount of fiscal and economic data was continuously being gathered, compiled and interpreted by the Municipal Finance Section which had been set up for that purpose in the Division of Research, Statistics and Finance. Their reports were regarded as a relatively minor element in the total situation. The final decisions were more likely to be based upon the recommendations of the regional representatives and the results of discussions with state administrators, governors, members of Congress and state legislators.[25]

It is worth recording, however, that the total amount granted to each state in monthly allotments throughout the first twenty-two months of the FERA, when compared with the

[25] "Discretionary grants depend upon numerous factors, no one of which is definitive. Matching grants have the alleged advantage of inducing local and state financial support; discretionary or equalization grants, designed to compensate for state variations in need and in ability, have the advantage of flexibility. Inasmuch as relief needs and the ability to finance relief activities tend to vary inversely, much can be said against the matching provisions. It is probable, however, that a federal-state financial arrangement which made use of both matching grants and limited discretionary grants would be somewhat more satisfactory than an exclusively discretionary arrangement." . . .

"Thus there is need for an equalization technique which will take account both of variations in need and of variations in ability to meet that need. In the absence of such a technique, America has found it necessary to place the distribution of its federal funds either at the discretion of administrators or on some mechanical matching basis, both admittedly unsatisfactory. The former suffers from variability and uncertainty, the latter from excessive rigidity. Some may, of course, be content with the practice of delegating the task of equitably apportioning federal and state funds among the lesser units to administrative authority. Democratic government, however, is not compatible with the placing of large public funds at the discretion of selected individuals, irrespective of their separate or collective integrity. We are not concerned with righteousness of character but with wisdom of public policy. The latter dictates that even a poor formula is preferable to no formula."

Financing Relief and Recovery, edited by L. László Ecker-R., pp. 398-99, 374-75. See also *FERA Monthly Report*, December, 1934, pp. 1-33. "Federal Emergency Relief Administration Grants."

total of all Federal relief grants made during that period, proved on analysis to follow closely the percentages which the population of the same states bore to the total population of the United States in the Census of 1930.[26]

State and Local Funds

The pressures which were brought to bear on the states by the Federal Relief Administration, however unevenly they may have been exerted, resulted in a steady and notable increase in the total amount of state and local appropriations for unemployment relief during 1933, 1934 and 1935.

The state totals for 1935 were double those for 1933 and local appropriations increased 27 percent in the same period. The greatest increase was, however, in Federal relief funds which totaled almost $494,000,000 in 1933, jumped to more than twice as much or over one billion dollars in 1934, and nearly tripled in 1935. This predominance of Federal funds accounts for the percentages given in the following table:

TABLE 2

Amount of Obligations Incurred for Emergency Relief *

By Sources of Funds, by Years—January, 1933, through December, 1935

Continental United States [27]

Calendar Year	Total	Federal Amount	Percent	State Amount	Percent	Local Amount	Percent
Total ...	$4,119,004,631	$2,918,701,248	70.9	$519,445,598	12.6	$680,857,785	16.5
1933	794,535,689	493,996,282	62.2	103,741,319	13.0	196,798,088	24.8
1934	1,489,861,759	1,066,551,303	71.6	189,421,902	12.7	233,888,554	15.7
1935	1,834,607,183	1,358,153,663	74.0	226,282,377	12.3	250,171,143	13.7

* Includes relief extended to cases under the general relief program, cost of administration and special programs; beginning April, 1934, these figures also include purchases of materials, supplies and equipment, rentals of equipment, earnings of non-relief persons and other costs of the Emergency Work Relief Program.

This steady increase in the actual amount of Federal grants as well as in the proportion which Federal funds bore to state and local expenditures, becomes even more significant when the figures and percentages for each state are examined.

[26] See Table in Appendix K. See *Expenditures of Funds, FERA, op. cit.*, p. 637. Exhibit Q.

[27] Federal Works Agency, Work Projects Administration, Division of Statistics, February 20, 1940.

From January, 1933, through December, 1935, the Federal Government supplied to eleven states over 90 percent of all the money which those states and their political subdivisions spent for unemployment relief. Only three states received less than 50 percent of their total expenditures.

Alabama 94.6	Louisiana 96.9	South Carolina 97.9
Arkansas 96.5	Mississippi ... 96.2	Tennessee 90.5
Florida 91.8	New Mexico .. 94.1	Virginia 90.2
Georgia 94.2	North Carolina 93.7	

Connecticut .. 43.9	Delaware 42.6	Rhode Island 37.9

During the three-year period six states spent either nothing at all out of their state treasuries or a negligible amount, less than one-tenth of one percent of the total unemployment relief bill in the state.[28] Twenty-five states appropriated amounts ranging from one-tenth of one percent in Virginia, to nine and nine-tenths percent in Connecticut. The remaining seventeen states ranged from 10 percent in Iowa to 38.1 percent in Delaware, as follows: [29]

Arizona 14.0	Michigan 15.3	Pennsylvania . 24.1
California 16.3	Missouri 10.9	Rhode Island . 26.9
Delaware 38.1	New Hampshire 20.1	Texas 16.9
Illinois 20.1	New Jersey ... 29.3	Utah 14.1
Iowa 10.0	New York 15.0	Washington .. 12.1

Maryland 24.9	Ohio 15.4

During this period (1933-1935) 42 state legislatures enacted a total of approximately 350 measures directly concerned with unemployment relief, most of which carried appropriations. Georgia, Mississippi, North Carolina, South Carolina, Vermont and Virginia took no legislative action on relief during this period.

Local funds ranged from 2.1 percent in South Carolina to 47.4 percent in Massachusetts. All of the New England states, in fact, spent relatively high percentages of local funds. This

[28] These six states were Georgia, Louisiana, Nebraska, North Carolina, South Carolina, South Dakota.

[29] Federal Works Agency, Work Projects Administration, Division of Statistics.

was to be expected in view of their long tradition of local responsibility.[30]

The fact remains that the Federal Government contributed during the 36 months, from January, 1933, through December, 1935, nearly three billion dollars or 70.9 percent of the total cost of unemployment relief; [31] the states 12.6 percent and local governments 16.5 percent. Aside from the problems of allocation which have already been mentioned, two other important factors partly accounted for the high percentage of Federal funds. These factors were first, the difficulty of using the power of withdrawal of grants, which was the only effective lever which the Federal Administrator could use to force state contributions; and second, the extent to which "Federalizing," or setting up Federal machinery to administer relief in a state, discouraged state and local appropriations to the program.

Federal funds were intended to supplement, not supplant, the expenditures of the states "in furnishing relief to their needy and distressed people." When pressure was brought upon a state to do its share in this co-operative task, and the state failed to make an adequate effort to meet its responsibility, the Federal Administrator was empowered by the terms of the Act to withdraw Federal funds from that state.[32] Such a procedure involved a threat which was not easy to make nor

[30] See p. 5. Throughout the emergency relief period all the direct (home) relief expenditures in New England were made from local funds. The Federal grants were used only for work relief and special programs. The local funds included the customary poor relief as well as direct relief to the unemployed.

[31] One effect of pouring this huge sum of money into the cities and counties, was to restore gradually the financial status of municipalities, many of which had been bankrupt or on the point of bankruptcy. See Part II, Chapter 6.

[32] "The responsibility of the FERA, however, to make sure that funds are properly spent and accounted for is too obvious to need explanation. The real power of the Federal Government in exercising this responsibility rests only in its power to refuse further grants of money to any State which fails to give relief in accordance with sound relief principles, which fails to employ competent and honest persons in the administration of relief, which diverts relief funds to illegitimate purposes, or which permits actual dishonesty or graft." *Expenditures of Funds, FERA,* Letter from the Administrator, p. 647.

to carry out. The Administrator used this power in very few instances, because, in the very states where a threat of this nature seemed necessary, it was only too evident that "the stoppage of Federal funds as a means of forcing state officials to do their duty would have no other result than to reduce the people on relief rolls to starvation." [33] Rather than penalize the unemployed who would have been the only people to suffer, grants were made on numerous occasions rather than force appropriations from state legislators who were able but not willing to contribute. Every time this happened the percentage of Federal funds was increased. Mr. Hopkins comments on this type of situation as follows:

Unfortunately, in some instances, State authorities, because of failure to familiarize themselves with the Federal Emergency Relief Act or for other reasons, have taken an attitude in complete reversal to that assumed by Congress in passing the Act. These authorities have assumed that it was the obligation of the Federal Government to bear all or substantially all of the relief burden and accordingly, have resented insistence by the Relief Administrator that their States contribute a fair proportion of relief expenses even when the determination of that portion was based upon consideration of economic conditions, total amount of relief required, existing revenue systems, attitude towards relief, and other factors that might affect a State's proper contribution.[34]

The second lever in the hands of the Federal Administrator, the authority to assume direct control, was not used to induce larger state appropriations, but to safeguard from abuse the expenditure of Federal grants and to insure to the unemployed a sound administration according to the purposes of the act.

Under the usual procedure the grants became state funds once they had been accepted by the governors who were held responsible for their proper and effective use. The Federal Administration considered that "co-operation" on the part of the governors and state administrators consisted in observing the Federal rules and regulations and in providing at least the minimum standards of administration which were con-

[33] *Ibid.*, p. xvi.

[34] *Expenditures of Funds, FERA,* Letter from the Administrator, p. xix.

sistent with the purposes of the act. This meant a reasonable assurance that the suffering and distress within a state would be relieved and that the money made available would be used in good faith for this purpose and this purpose only.

The Power to Federalize Relief in a State

To guard against the violation of these requirements on the part of a state government the following provision had been incorporated in the Federal Emergency Relief Act:

The Administrator may, under rules and regulations prescribed by the President, assume control of the administration in any State or States where, in his judgment, more effective and efficient coopera- tion between the State and Federal authorities may thereby be secured in carrying out the purposes of this Act.[35]

This provision established an entirely new principle in Fed- eral grants-in-aid. It equaled in significance the precedent which the Federal Emergency Relief Act established in the acceptance by the Federal Government of responsibility for re- lief. The power which was given to the Administrator to as- sume control of the administration of Federal funds in a state constituted, in effect, a recognition by the Federal Government that the citizens of this country are Federal citizens and have rights which transcend state lines and the jurisdiction of state governments.

This power was used by the Federal Administrator only as a last resort, in time of crisis, when co-operation with a state had

[35] FER Act, Sec. 3(b).

This power was further defined in the Act of February 15, 1934, which provided "that nothing contained in the Federal Emergency Relief Act of 1933 shall be construed as precluding the Federal Emergency Relief Administrator from making grants for relief within a state directly to such public agency as he may designate." This additional provision was made necessary by the fact that the FER Act of 1933 provided that application for funds must be made by the state governor and grants made to the states. The Federal Administrator could not "assume con- trol" as long as the Federal grants had to be made to the governor. The provision in the 1934 act made it possible to allocate funds direct to an agency in the state which had been made a state branch of the FERA. See FERA Monthly Report, March, 1934, p. 17.

completely broken down; when efforts to insure reasonable standards of relief giving and financial control had failed.

Control was assumed, that is, relief was "federalized," in six states during the life of the FERA. The reasons were varied.

States	Date of Federalization
Oklahoma	Feb. 23, 1934
North Dakota	Mar. 1, 1934
Massachusetts	Mar. 7, 1934
Ohio	Mar. 16, 1935
Louisiana	Apr. 8, 1935
Georgia	Apr. 19, 1935

Control of relief in Oklahoma was returned to the state on February 15, 1935; and in North Dakota on December 15, 1935.[36]

The work relief program in Massachusetts was federalized because of the existence of state statutes under which the governor could accept Federal grants only on condition that the money be allocated to the towns on an arbitrary basis, irrespective of need. Direct relief continued to be financed from local funds.[37]

In Oklahoma the governor announced early in 1934 that he would not accept Federal funds unless he could spend them without regard to Federal rules and regulations. Louisiana and Georgia were federalized for much the same reason. In North Dakota evidence was uncovered that employees of the state relief administration were being assessed for contributions to a political campaign. In Ohio the legislature refused to appropriate what the Federal Administrator considered to be the state's fair share of funds and the newly elected governor was found to be using the Relief Administration for political purposes.

The method by which authority was given to the Administrator to assume control of a state relief administration is shown by the following communication:

[36] *Financial Procedure in the Federally Operated Relief Administrations in Six States*, by F. S. Bartlett, *FERA Monthly Report*, June, 1936, p. 134.

[37] See p. 206, footnote 30.

The White House
Washington, March 16, 1935
My dear Mr. Hopkins:

I have examined the evidence concerning corrupt political interference with relief in the State of Ohio. Such interference cannot be tolerated for a moment. I wish you to pursue these investigations diligently and let the chips fall where they may. This Administration will not permit the relief population of Ohio to become the innocent victims of either corruption or political chicanery.

You are authorized and directed forthwith to assume entire control of the administration of Federal relief in the State of Ohio.

Very sincerely yours,
(Signed) Franklin D. Roosevelt.

Hon. Harry L. Hopkins, Administrator
Federal Emergency Relief Administration,
1734 New York Avenue, Washington, D. C.[38]

This authority applied only to Federal funds; state and local funds remained under the same jurisdiction as before. The Federal Administrator created a state branch of the FERA to spend Federal funds and appointed an administrator who with all of his staff became Federal employees [39] and took the Federal oath of office. Applications for funds were made by, and grants paid to, the administrator of the federalized agency rather than to the governor, as formerly. The funds were subject to the rules and regulations of the Comptroller General of the United States. A Federal office under the supervision of the district system of the United States Treasury was established to handle all disbursing of Federal funds.[40]

While the power to assume Federal control of the administration of federal funds within the boundaries of a state was unprecedented in the long history of Federal grants-in-aid, it was undoubtedly inserted in the Act as a concession to the emergency which existed in the spring of 1933. The Works Program which followed the FERA was, and continues in 1940 to be, entirely Federal in spite of numerous efforts to return work relief as well as direct relief to the states and localities.

---

[38] *FERA Monthly Report,* March, 1935, p. 18.

[39] This personnel was for the most part the same as that of the state relief administrations.

[40] *Expenditure of Funds, FERA,* p. 648. See footnote 36, p. 209.

The Federal grants-in-aid which were provided by the Social Security Act of 1935, however, followed essentially the model established by similar measures prior to the depression, and there was no repetition of the power to federalize which was provided in the Federal Emergency Relief Act. On the contrary, the Social Security Act imposes certain restrictions on the Federal authority which appear to have been inserted as a result of an adverse reaction to the authoritative nature of the FERA. This reaction against Federal control in the administration of relief was but one aspect of the general reaction of the states, and assertion of their "rights" in the face of the unusual authority and powers which had been exerted by the Federal Government since the beginning of President Roosevelt's Administration in March, 1933.

The Authoritative Element

The Federal Emergency Relief Administration was authoritative not only in the exercise of its power to assume control of funds, but in its ordinary relations with the states in which the Federal grants became state funds and in which the states were responsible for the administration of relief according to the general provisions of the Act. This was contrary to all tradition in the history of Federal grants to the states.

It is difficult to analyze the factors which entered into this authoritative relationship. Nothing in the terms of the Act implied it. The precedents established by other Federal agencies which administered grants-in-aid programs were of a mild supervisory and advisory nature. The Federal Emergency Relief Administration found it exceedingly difficult to follow these precedents, and to avoid undue centralization in the face of the perpetual problem of securing, at the same time, minimum standards within the states as well as a certain degree of uniformity throughout the country, which would insure to people in need the share of Federal benefits due them as citizens of the United States. There was a consistent effort to strike a balance between the minimum level of decency to which the FERA could subscribe and the maximum level of adequacy which could be provided by all available funds. The Federal Administrator considered that the state and not the Federal Government was "the arbiter as to what amount of relief will be given per capita to its citizens." Also the state was held responsible for standards in the counties. It was for the state to decide whether or not local standards should be a matter of local determination.[41] The problem was further complicated by the fact that in the actual administration of relief in the states and localities Federal, state and local funds were combined and spent under the same regulations and procedures in the same agencies and by the same personnel. The policies and rules which the Federal Administration issued to safeguard Federal funds were, therefore, applied generally to all funds spent for relief. State or local funds could be and often were spent for purposes for which Federal money could not be used, but on the whole Federal policies and regulations governed the entire program.

That the FERA was considered not only authoritative but dominating by outside observers is shown by the references in current social work literature to its "position of dominance," its entrance into local communities as a "foreign agency" and to the belief that local communities were subject "somewhat to local traditions but yielding to Federal-state direction on essential issues of policy, standards and procedure." [42]

There was much also in the general situation throughout the country during the early months of the FERA that contributed to the development of this authoritative element in its relationship with the states. Financial and industrial disorganization had reduced the country to a state of near panic.[43] Fear was very near the surface. The numbers of unemployed and the relative inexperience of the people who were responsible in the states for administering relief, and who were working in an uncharted area in which there were no precedents; the huge sums of money for which these same people were accountable to their legislatures and to Washington, all helped to engender a state of mind which not only welcomed leadership, rules and instructions but constantly asked for more. During the first few months, and to some extent during the first year of the FERA, the majority of the states conformed so

[41] *Expenditure of Funds, FERA*, p. xv.
[42] Kurtz, Russell, *Social Work Year Book, 1935*, published by Russell Sage Foundation, New York.
[43] See p. 145.

readily to the Federal pattern that the danger lay in too great dependency, and an almost complete lack of initiative. The speed with which the program had to be set up and the rate at which the operations had to proceed only intensified this attitude. There was no time to question or deviate from a given set of procedures.

Speed was imperative not only because millions of people were involved, but because the program was being conducted in the public eye. The enaction of each legislative measure which appropriated funds, or set up a new part of the program, or authorized a change in policy, was immediately given wide publicity by the press. Relief was news. It was extremely difficult even to keep the latest Administrative decisions out of the newspapers until adequate preparations had been made to put them into effect. On each occasion the publicity brought demands from the unemployed and from the public in general for immediate action on the new policies or procedures which had been authorized. These demands had to be met at whatever cost, and, to do it, the emergency staffs set new all-time speed records in relief administration! The frequency with which this was done helped to establish a rapid tempo in the relief offices which became an emergency habit and was carried over into the administration of the later permanent programs.

The tempo was kept up also by sudden changes in procedure or in matters of minor policy which were often made in Washington and issued to the states without much, if any, notice being given in advance of the releases made to the press. Instructions of this kind were usually the work of staff members of the specialized Federal divisions who had never done a local job, who had had no experience in working directly with people on relief and who could not visualize or anticipate the difficulties which their instructions created for the local staffs, or the hardships and injustice they often brought to the recipients of relief.

On the other hand, the staff members in both state and local offices were often at fault in their interpretation of the instructions and in the spirit in which they received them. They sometimes failed to distinguish between permissive, suggestive material from Washington and mandatory instructions. There was an unfortunate tendency to consider most or all of the material as mandatory. A literal-mindedness developed which failed to distinguish between the intent and general administrative basis of the program described in a given bulletin and the detailed specifications for its execution, although many if not all of the latter might have been left entirely to the option of the state or locality.

There was great difference in this respect among state administrators. Many of them appreciated the wide latitude in administrative matters allowed them within the underlying intent of the law and the basic policies of the Federal Relief Administration, and operated their programs accordingly. Other state administrators were almost afraid to move on any point on which no specific Federal ruling had been made, without asking permission of Washington. Such requests were often embarrassing to the Federal office as the Administration was reluctant to take a definite position on a matter of detail for fear that the decision might create difficulties in some other state or locality, even though it might be entirely permissible under the law. The Federal Relief Administration constantly faced the critical problem of framing policies and rules which were broad enough and subject to sufficiently general application and interpretation to meet the needs of 48 states and more than 4,000 local administrative units with every variety of climate, industry, law and tradition.

A kind of deference toward the Federal Administration developed in the states. This, together with the tendency to literal-mindedness, caused undue weight to be given to the pronouncements of every visitor from the Federal office. Especially in the first few hectic months of the program an emissary from Washington, no matter what his technical qualifications were, nor what division he might represent, was asked by the state staff members about any matter which happened to need attention at the time. More often than not the emissary's answer was seriously given and as seriously accepted as Washington's verdict and beyond appeal.

This disposition to defer to Washington faded considerably as the program progressed and as the state staffs acquired more facility on their jobs and more confidence in themselves. They also learned to use more discrimination in their use of the Washington office. However, as long as the FERA lasted, the influence and authority of the Federal Administrator was unquestioned and his requests as well as his instructions were treated with respect and confidence.

The Temporary Element

A major administrative difficulty lay in the fact that Federal grants were made on a monthly basis with no assurance given to the state administrations as to how much they could count on from month to month. Planning ahead, and the type of economy which goes with it, was practically impossible. The personnel were employed and the program functioned on a temporary, emergency basis, with no certainty and no security. This had a direct consequent effect upon the relief recipients who were subject to unexpected changes in the amounts of their grants and were always in danger of being dropped from the rolls without notice.

This hand-to-mouth method of dealing with the states was necessarily repeated in the allocations of funds by the states to their political subdivisions. Each state determined the basis for these allotments, but the total amount of money available for each month was not known until the Federal grant had been decided upon in Washington.

State-Local Relations

The basis for local allotments was determined by legislation in a few states [44] but in the large majority of states the distribution of funds was left to the discretion of the state administrators. This financial relationship between the states and the local units tended to develop in the counties the same attitude of dependency toward the states as many of the latter had toward the Federal Government. The authoritative element was also repeated in the state-local relationship, depending somewhat upon the size and importance of the local unit and its traditions of local autonomy.[45]

[44] In New York State the TERA Act provided that state funds should be used to reimburse the local units for 40 percent of their relief expenditures. See Part II, Chapter 2, Part III, Chapter 4; also *FERA Monthly Report*, December, 1935, pp. 1-33. "FERA Grants."

[45] There was, for instance, little state authority exerted in New Eng-

The emergency relief administration was in many respects a foreign and superimposed program in local communities, particularly in rural areas. Where local autonomy was strong, as it was in most of the rural counties, the result was conflict and resistance. The fact that large amounts of Federal and usually of state money accompanied the "foreign" program, was often the only reason why it was accepted. It was especially unwelcome because it deprived the locally elected officials of a function which they felt should have been theirs. The speed with which the program moved and the pressure under which the staffs had to work made it difficult to use committees and volunteers, the channels through which social agencies ordinarily interpret their activities.[46] The consequent lack of community participation meant that there was built up little real understanding of the program on the part of the average citizen.

The objections and prejudices which developed in local communities, whether or not they were justified, undoubtedly played an important part in the general reaction to Federal jurisdiction which imposed certain definite restrictions upon the powers of the Social Security Board when that permanent agency was authorized by Congress in 1935.[47]

In the last analysis the attitudes of citizens and the reception of the relief administration in local communities and neighborhoods depended to a great extent upon the way in which the needs of the unemployed were met, the methods used, and the treatment given day by day to the people who came to the offices to apply for relief, to receive their grants, to secure information or to make complaints. The quality of this day by day job and the spirit in which it was done depended almost entirely upon the kind of people who made up

land over local programs. New York City, Philadelphia, Chicago, Los Angeles and other large cities were also relatively independent of state control.

[46] Notable exceptions were the County Relief Boards in Pennsylvania, the local boards in Maryland, Alabama and a few other states.

[47] Social Security Act: "Section 2(a). A State plan for old-age assistance must . . . (5) provide such methods of administration (other than those relating to selection, tenure of office, and compensation of personnel) as are found by the Board to be necessary for the efficient operation of the plan." See Chapter 13.

the staffs in the relief offices, and particularly in the Social' Service Division.   These were the people to whom was entrusted the actual execution of the purpose of the Federal Act, to relieve "the hardship and suffering caused by unemployment" and "to provide the necessities of life to persons in need." [48]

However uneven the results may have been, this was the ultimate objective of all of the dealings of the FERA with the state relief administrations.

[48] FER Act, Sec. 4 (a).

Chapter 10

How Relief Was Given—I

~~~~~~

The Social Service Divisions

The Social Service Divisions served as the point of intake for the entire relief program since their primary function was the determination of individual and family eligibility for relief. Here the applicants made their requests for help, and, even though they might later be assigned to projects under the supervision of the Work Division, they were continuously in touch with the social service staff until they ceased to receive relief. The duties of this staff included not only the receiving of applications and the establishment of eligibility but the determination of the amount of relief to be given to a family or individual, the actual administration of that relief, and the regular visiting of the recipients to see that their needs were being met or that relief was discontinued if they were no longer eligible. Heads of families and individuals who were able to work were certified to the Works Division of the local emergency relief administration for assignment to work projects in order that they might earn the amount of their relief grant. The Social Service staff also recommended eligible families to the local Rural Rehabilitation Division for assistance under that program after it was set up in the spring of 1934.

Rules and Regulations No. 3 issued by the Federal Relief Administration on July 11, 1933, included a section on "Investigation and Service," with the following provisions:

To carry out the purposes of the Federal Emergency Relief Act of 1933 the investigation of all applicants for direct and/or work relief is required. . . . (1) Each local relief administration should have at least one trained and experienced investigator on its staff; if additional investigators are to be employed to meet this emergency, the first one employed should have had training and experience. In the larger public welfare districts, where there are a number of investigators, there should be not less than 1 supervisor, trained and experienced in the essential elements of family case work and relief administration, to supervise the work of not more than 20 investigating staff workers.[1]

These rules constituted the Federal authority for the operation of Social Service Divisions wherever Federal emergency relief funds were administered throughout the country. Such divisions were already set up and were administering state and Reconstruction Finance Corporation funds when the FERA was established. The rapid development of the service in the rest of the country was part of the program of organization which was carried out under the leadership of the FERA during the last half of 1933.[2] The work of the local offices in the counties, towns and cities was supervised by Social Service Divisions in the state relief administration offices and these in turn by the Social Service Division of the Federal Emergency Relief Administration.[3]

The functions discharged by the local Social Service Divisions involved direct contact with the people who were in need. For this reason it was necessary that the division offices be located so that the staff members would be able to reach the homes of the unemployed as easily as possible and so that the unemployed would have ready access to the relief offices. In urban areas a city-wide plan of district offices was established, the location of the branch offices being determined by the areas in which the unemployed were found in greatest numbers. In rural areas the problem was complicated by distance and by the inaccessibility of many of those in need. A county seat was usually the headquarters for a county-wide office, with branches wherever centers of population existed. In many sparsely populated areas, a single office often served as a central point from which the staff made visits over a wide area, sometimes including several counties.

[1] Compare New York TERA rules, see Part II, Chapter 4.
[2] See Part III, Chapter 8. Local Social Service Divisions administered relief in political subdivisions.
[3] The FERA Social Service Division was not established until April, 1934; see Part III, Chapter 9.

In the rural districts the workers exerted great effort to reach families in their own homes rather than to force them to travel long distances to visit the relief offices. Many of these people were not well enough fed or warmly enough clothed to tramp miles in wet or bitter weather to apply for relief. In the cities, however, the offices were almost too accessible and were continually crowded with applicants and relief recipients, especially during the first months of the emergency program.

The provision of adequate office space constituted a serious problem. It was extremely difficult to secure sufficient waiting rooms, essential privacy for interviews, and adequate space for staff offices. Federal funds could not be used for rent,[4] but the State Administrations borrowed or rented stores, warehouses, banks, schools, church buildings and other structures which were made over into more or less satisfactory offices. It was thought at the time to be undesirable to spend large amounts of state or local money for these offices in view of the temporary, emergency nature of the program. In the early days of the relief administration it was not unusual to see long lines of people waiting patiently at the doors and in the corridors, and sometimes lined up far down adjoining streets. As the program continued, however, better and more evenly distributed offices were provided by many of the state and local relief administrations, with the result that the crowded waiting rooms and the long lines of applicants became less and less frequent.

The rapid expansion of the emergency relief program into practically every county and township in the country brought social workers and the methods of social work into hundreds of rural areas for the first time.[5] In more than three thousand county administrative units and in over a thousand additional town and municipal units, social service staffs were

[4] Rules and Regulations No. 2.

[5] The only other rural social work program at all comparable to this had been the extension of Home Service to soldiers and their families by the American Red Cross fifteen years earlier, during and after the first World War. See Josephine C. Brown, "Rural Social Work," *Social Work Year Book*, 1935. Russell Sage Foundation, New York.

rapidly built up to a total of approximately 40,000 [6] by October, 1934, to administer relief to from four to five million families.

It was not possible to find qualified social workers to fill even a fraction of these positions. In accordance with the Federal Emergency Relief Administration rules an effort was made to secure for the staff of each local unit "one trained and experienced investigator," but the words "trained and experienced" were subject to many different interpretations. Social work as taught and practiced in different parts of the country was in many stages of development, and there were wide variations in methods of work, attitudes towards people, social philosophy and economic theory. These differences in point of view and training were brought into the state and local emergency relief administrations by the many "trained and experienced" social workers who came chiefly from private agencies. In fact, very few of them had had anything but private agency experience prior to their employment to administer emergency relief. These workers were given heavy responsibilities as supervisors or even as administrators of local relief units. The great majority of visitors or investigators who constituted the rank and file of the social service staffs, on the other hand, had to be recruited from non-social work sources.[7] They were local people who brought into the administration of relief, in varying degrees, the local poor relief traditions and attitudes which had persisted from colonial and pioneer days.[8] As a result, the actual practice which was followed in determining eligibility and in giving relief in any city, town or county was the product of a combination of forces represented by the mores of the community itself, the philosophy and methods of social work advocated by the supervisor or director, and over all the Rules and Regulations from Washington which attempted to supply some degree of uniformity and of justice in the expenditure of Federal funds.

Relief Philosophies, Attitudes and Methods

The philosophies, attitudes and methods of social workers have played such an important part in the relief picture of

---

[6] This figure does not include clerical staff.

[7] See Part III, Chapter 12.   [8] See Part I, Chapter 1.

the past decade that it is advisable to review them briefly in order to see more clearly their effect upon the administration of emergency relief and upon the later programs of public assistance and social insurance.

This historical background begins with the colonial adaptations of the Elizabethan Poor Law.[9] The deterrent, repressive practices used in dealing with the poor and the stigma attached to poverty persisted in varying degrees throughout the intervening three hundred years and naturally would not suddenly be stopped from carrying over into unemployment relief at the beginning of the recent depression.

Helen Wright, in her article on "Dependency" in the *Encyclopedia of the Social Sciences,* says that it remained "for the new religious ideas of the seventeenth and eighteenth centuries and the concomitant economic changes to destroy almost entirely any concept of dependency not resulting solely from the fault of the dependent. For as economic prosperity became the mark of the Lord's approval and poverty a sign that the victim has incurred His anger, it followed that those too poor to live without alms must be sinners in need of punishment." And she adds: "This view of dependency persisted long after its underlying religious sanctions had lost their vitality."

The poor were looked upon as lazy, shiftless and incompetent and their condition was blamed upon their failure to exert themselves. They were told that they could get work to do if they wanted it, and since they preferred relief it must be made as disagreeable as possible in order to force them to support themselves and get out of the "pauper class."

The charity organization movement which developed during the last quarter of the nineteenth century [10] introduced a much more humanitarian element into the giving of relief. The poor were still believed to be in difficulty because of disability or lack in themselves or because of some inadequacy in their immediate circumstances. But distinction between the "worthy" and "unworthy" poor gradually gave way to a greater understanding which resulted from an ardent search for the "causes

[9] See Part I, Chapters 1 and 2.

[10] See Chapter 1; also, Richmond, Mary, *Social Diagnosis,* 511 pp., 1917, and *What Is Social Case Work?* 268 pp., 1922. Russell Sage Foundation, New York.

of poverty." Each "case" was analyzed in terms of possible causes. A diagnosis was made of the problem and plans worked out for the "rehabilitation" of the family. The investigation which was necessary in order to determine the causes of the family's difficulty was thorough and "scientific." It used legal methods of weighing evidence and evaluating testimony. It followed up "clues" revealed in the course of conversations which the investigating social worker had with the unsuspecting members of the family. The social worker's consultation or correspondence with "references," that is, with former employers, former neighbors, and relatives both near and far, often proceeded without the consent and sometimes against the wishes of the family whose affairs were being discussed. A certain maternalism on the part of the social worker seemed to justify these practices on the score that a social worker was in a position to "see all around" the family situation and would, therefore, know what to do for them and how to plan much better than the members of the family themselves.

The theory of the individual inadequacy of the poor and the practices of making plans for the clients, as applicants to relief and welfare agencies came to be called, and of using the "interview of persuasion" to get the clients to accept these plans, were accompanied by a moralizing philosophy and a tendency to dictate to them and an attempt to control their lives. The power which is inevitably in the hands of the giver of relief was used conscientiously to get the clients to do what the social worker thought was "right." This regulation of other people's lives extended not only to what they should eat, what they should wear, and where and how they should live, but it also attempted to tell them how they should order their relationships within the family group, with their relatives, neighbors and friends.

An appeal for a temporary loan of money to pay a month's rent or the request for a pair of shoes for one of the children was considered by the charity organization worker as a symptom of a serious "maladjustment" or series of "maladjustments" within the family circle, and was honestly taken as a sign that the social worker had a duty to investigate, analyze, diagnose, plan for and treat all the problems which could be uncovered. "Skill in case work was for a time largely the achievement of adequately tactful ways of getting people to fall in with what the case worker thought best for them." [11]

Relief in kind, that is, food, grocery orders, clothing, instead of the cash with which to buy these necessities, was still believed to be the wisest way in which to help most of the families to whom aid was given.[12] The average client family was not thought to be capable of spending money wisely and economically for the things they needed. Since they could not be trusted to do this, the planning and sometimes the buying was done for them for their own protection and for their own good. Even unusual families who were given money after careful budgets had been worked out and detailed instructions given regarding expenditures, were required to turn in at regular intervals, an itemized account of every penny spent. This account the social worker carefully scrutinized and commented upon.

The "work test" was still used as a means of diagnosis in certain cases, especially with homeless men. The wood yard of the charity organization society had by no means disappeared. The test was used to discover whether or not a given individual was "work shy." The best practice, as defined in 1922, required that the work used as a test be so simple that no one could pretend to lack the skill to do it, and severe, yet not too severe for the ordinary strength.[13] In a milder form than the compulsory labor of the workhouse,[14] it was also em-

[11] Reynolds, Bertha C., "Re-Thinking Social Case Work," published by *Social Work Today*, New York, 1938, 32 pp.

[12] The influence of this attitude toward relief in kind is seen in the provision made in the Wicks Act which established the Temporary Emergency Relief Administration in New York State in 1931, that all "home" or direct relief should be in kind while work relief should be paid in cash. "In addition to the abhorrence of the dole, there was considerable feeling that no one should receive public money without putting forth suitable effort in return and a substantial fear of potential abuse of the procedure of distributing cash without work in return—the latter finding expression in the prohibition in the original Wicks Act against cash home relief." *Work Relief in the State of New York,* a report by the Governor's Commission on Unemployment Relief. Albany, New York, 1936, 113 pp.

[13] See Watson, Frank Dekker, *The Charity Organization Movement in the United States,* p. 121, The Macmillan Co., New York, 1922.

[14] See Part I, Chapter 1.

ployed as a deterrent to the willfully idle and as a prerequisite to receiving relief.

The philosophy underlying this work test practice was based on an acceptance of the status quo in our modern competitive economy, in which a third if not one-half of the population live in a state of near destitution or at least of perpetual insecurity. The function of social work was to apply remedial measures to maladjusted families and individuals who were for the most part victims of this economic system. The famous definition given by Mary Richmond: "Social case work consists of those processes which develop personality through adjustments consciously effected, individual by individual, between men and their social environment," [15] put the primary emphasis upon the individual in need of adjustment and considered the environment only in relation to the individual. There is a direct connection between this definition and the early conception which made poverty and failure a matter of individual responsibility. Undoubtedly poverty and failure were and still are often traceable to individual disability and inadequacy, but, even in ordinary times, there are many cases in which this is not so. The millions of unemployed, thrown out of work by the economic depression of the 1930's, offered the best possible illustration of poverty which was not due to individual failure and inadequacy. Yet the earlier conception persisted among many social workers in the family welfare field which had inherited part at least of the philosophy of the charity organization movement.[16]

The traditional attitudes and methods of social case work

[15] *What Is Social Case Work?* Russell Sage Foundation, New York.

[16] "Social work when it dealt with but a small portion of the population incidentally developed a method of control of the client's life, whose evil effects, though real, were not striking enough to be dangerous. But when 10 to 20 percent of the families of the nation live only where they are told to live, in houses not of their own choosing, are clothed with hand-me-downs that violate self-respect, are compelled to eat whatever is given, and, in many instances, are moved from place to place without having any voice in their own disposition, democracy has been about as completely destroyed as it has ever been in any status short of slavery." From Presidential address of Frank J. Bruno, *Proceedings,* National Conference of Social Work, Detroit, Michigan, June, 1933. See also footnote 11, p. 224.

as practiced by most of the charity organization societies during the first two decades of the twentieth century underwent drastic changes in a number of the larger cities following the World War. These changes were partly due to the effect of the Home Service program of the American Red Cross which offered service to thousands of families of soldiers who had to adjust to living without their men. "For the first time in the history of organized philanthropy, it was *we* giving to *ours,* not one group handing down something to another which was outside its self-defined community."[17] "This was not 'charity' but the due of those who had given their all [as the sentimental post-war phrase put it]. Even the poorest had some part in giving, if only to sew, knit or farm. Democracy was getting into philanthropy, and the latter could never be the same again."[18]

Psychiatry was an even more potent force in effecting changes in the social case work world. "Out of the necessity of treating cases of 'shell shock' in the army, there came to be applied to personal problems a body of more or less scientific data which was soon seen to be equally valid for personal difficulties in civilian life."[19] The use of this scientific data by social workers in dealing with human problems demanded an approach to the client on the basis of respect for his dignity and worth as a human being. It engendered humility. The psychiatric case worker did not attempt to control or dictate or assume a position of superiority. He saw himself as only one of the many forces which might influence the client's feeling and action.

A Democratic Philosophy in Unemployment Relief

This new democratic approach to people, an approach radically at variance with the traditional assumptions of the older case work methods, had taken a strong hold upon the teaching and practice of social work in certain of the more progressive schools and agencies during the late 20's. The stock market crash in the fall of 1929, and the subsequent struggle of public and private agencies to administer relief to the constantly increasing thousands of the unemployed, gave ample opportu-

[17] Reynolds, Bertha C., *op. cit.*   [19] *Ibid.*
[18] *Ibid.*

nity to test in practice the validity of the new principles. Here the average relief applicant was so obviously competent and accustomed to managing his own affairs and supporting himself in a normal way that it was utterly useless and absurd to pretend that he was at fault, and a self-made pauper.

The new philosophy was articulated by Virginia Robinson in *A Changing Psychology of Social Case Work* which appeared in 1930. "It crystallized the growing revolt against authoritative methods in this fashion: 'The case work relationship is a reciprocal relationship in which the case worker must accept herself and the other equally, in which all of her attitudes towards the client would be such that she would be content to be at the other end of such a relationship herself.'"

Social workers who sat at application desks in unemployment relief offices during the first hectic months of the depression realized with a new and vivid understanding the meaning of these words. They discovered that whatever they had to do with the unemployed had to be done "hand in hand, not handing down." They could do it in no other way. Too many of the applicants were people like themselves, with much the same or sometimes better cultural background, education and previous earning capacity. They knew very well that only chance or Providence had put them on the social work side of the desk instead of on the applicant's side.[20] They also knew that although many of the applicants must have had other problems in their lives, they came to the office for relief and not usually for help and advice in other connections. The thoughtful social worker who had accepted the democratic

[20] "The new poor are different from the old poor in that their poverty is clearly the result of outer social circumstance and not of their individual inadequacy. . . . Yet in times of peace and prosperity we have seen dependency so often associated with personal inadequacy that we have come to pay great attention to studying the person and trying to remedy his situation through himself. . . . Now, when all persons, strong as well as weak, are either fallen or threatened, when nobody knows what day his turn in the bread-line will come, attention is forcibly directed to the dependence of every person upon the network of social relations within which he lives. Poverty and dependency take on new meaning for us as citizens and for us as social workers." M. Antoinette Cannon, "Recent Changes in the Philosophy of Social Workers," *The Family,* October, 1933.

principles of the changing psychology of case work did not think it was his duty, nor had he time, to try to uncover these other problems which might exist but on which the applicant obviously was not seeking advice.

This democratic philosophy of social case work developed just in time to serve as preparation for the administration of unemployment relief by governmental agencies. It fitted perfectly the tenets of the Federal Government which maintained in the spring of 1933 that government, local, state and Federal, had a direct responsibility for the welfare of all its people and a direct interest in what happens to the individual. Each person in need had a right to share in the provision made by the government to meet the ravages caused by the breakdown of the American economic system. Because of this right an applicant for public relief incurred no stigma, asked no favor, and was expected to express no gratitude. He, as well as his application, were treated with respect, and his eligibility was to be determined impersonally in the light of legal requirements, available funds, and fairness to others who were also in need of assistance.

Just as the democratic approach in social case work had been accepted chiefly in the larger and more progressive schools of social work and in the more advanced social agencies, so the practice of the same philosophy in public unemployment relief was limited to those state and local relief administrations where there was unusual leadership and where there were directors and supervisors who had received their training and had secured their experience under the influence of this modern case work philosophy.

Great numbers of social workers were loaned or released in 1931, 1932 and 1933 by private social agencies to administer public relief. Most of them stayed in the public field. They brought with them, as has already been said, the philosophy, attitudes and methods of work which were characteristic of the social agencies and schools where their experience and training had been secured. Therefore, the social service divisions of the relief administrations throughout the country represented virtually every type of practice and philosophy. Every stage of development was present from the most primitive poor relief customs, through the various aspects of the charity organization movement, to the new, democratic, thoroughly *public* approach just described.

In spite of these differences, however, the fact remains that the administration of public unemployment relief under the Federal Emergency Relief Administration marked an epochal turning point in social work philosophy and practice as applied to relief. Not only was the responsibility of government established once and for all, but public relief was recognized as a right of people in need, and their worth and dignity as human beings respected.

In order to define the position of the Federal Emergency Relief Administration and offer a guide in the practice of relief administration to the state and local social service divisions which were bewildered by the older and less democratic methods of relief giving, the Federal Social Service Division issued a statement in April, 1935. This statement pointed out that the administration of unemployment relief was a form of social work which used certain of the methods of social case work, but was not identical with it, as that term was commonly understood.[21] It was directed toward a problem which is society's own, outside the individual and beyond his control. In this area social work found it necessary to create its own new methods. Its clientele presented a common, mass, economic need; a common problem, unemployment; and demanded a common treatment, relief. The unemployed might have other problems but it was not the function of the public relief administration to inquire into or treat them.

If the unemployed request advice and assistance with these other problems, the relief administration may furnish social treatment as an additional public welfare function, but only when there are workers available who are well equipped to give it.[22]

The statement outlined the method by which the social worker as an agent of the government should administer re-

[21] This referred to the common assumption that social case work practice included the treatment of problems which are inherent in individuals and families; their inadequacies, their failures, their personality difficulties.

[22] "Social Work in the Administration of Unemployment Relief," Federal Emergency Relief Administration, 5314, Multigraphed, April 30, 1935.

lief, according to essentially democratic principles and with the utmost respect for the dignity and worth of the applicants. The determination of eligibility and of the extent of need were to be undertaken jointly by the social worker and the applicant as necessary procedures in the equitable distribution of public funds. References and information regarding living expenses and income were all to be considered on an impersonal, businesslike basis. Relief was to be given in cash in order that the recipient might be free to spend it as he had spent his wages when he was employed, a marked reversal of past practice. He was finally to be asked to report any change in his circumstances which might affect his eligibility or the amount of relief he needed.

The Federal Emergency Relief Administration was a mass relief program. It involved social planning and social action on a large scale. The social service divisions and their social work staffs had a peculiar responsibility to recognize and deal with individual needs in relation to the principles and policies of the mass program. It was the social workers' peculiar function to safeguard human values and to interpret these values to the other divisions and to the community. In discharging this function the social workers profited greatly from an exchange of knowledge and experience with the staff members of the Works Division, the Divisions of Research, Statistics and Finance, Education, and Rural Rehabilitation. These divisions planned the highly diversified work program, put the relief recipients to work, paid them, counted them and studied their needs and their problems. The social workers broadened their education and deepened their insight in observing the work of the engineers, accountants, statisticians, research workers, educators and business men; the methods of each of these in handling people and the type of thing each did for the clients. One of the outstanding contributions which the emergency relief program and the later Works Program made to professional social work was the enrichment of content, the broader perspective and the greater understanding of the methods and objectives of other professions which came from this close and continuous association with well-qualified people in other fields.

Eligibility for Relief

The work of the Social Service Divisions centered largely around the determination of eligibility. The broad principles laid down by the Federal Relief Administration provided that relief should be given

. . . to all needy unemployed persons and/or their dependents. Those whose employment or available resources are inadequate to provide the necessities of life for themselves and/or their dependents are included.

This imposes an obligation on the . . . emergency relief administration . . . to see that no relief is given to persons unless they are actually in need. . . .

There shall be no discrimination because of race, religion, color, non-citizenship, political affiliation, or because of membership in any special or selected group.[23]

Each state relief administration and to some extent each local unit interpreted, applied and added to these definitions of eligibility. Within the general framework of the Federal rules there was a wide variety of practice, due not only to the differences in philosophy, attitudes, and traditions which have already been discussed but to differences between rural and urban areas as well as in racial, political and industrial conditions.

Because of these variations in practice, no attempt will be made here to discuss in detail the work of the Social Service Divisions. It will be sufficient to mention some of the problems and significant developments of a fairly general nature.

A number of the more important problems involved in the determination of eligibility are clearly stated in a report of the "Background, Development and Use of Standards of Eligibility in the Philadelphia County Relief Board":

The local administration recognized its dual responsibility, both to the client and to the taxpaying group, of which the client never ceases to be a member.—A report of the Committee of the Community Council of Philadelphia includes a clear statement of eligibility. "A sound relief program—would clearly define and candidly announce (a) the specific conditions under which any individual or

[23] Rules and Regulations No. 3. *FERA Monthly Report,* May 22 through June 30, 1933.

family becomes eligible for community help; (b) the specific schedule of relief allowances available under varying conditions; (c) the procedures by which eligibility and need will be determined by the community's agents. It would thus seek to make its service available to all who truly need relief according to these objective standards, including those who may be too proud or sensitive to seek it in time to save themselves from irreparable injury; at the same time it would save unnecessary trouble, expense and disappointment for those who now seek aid in vain because, despite their limited means and hard struggles, they still do not fall below that level which the community deems a minimum standard of living in this emergency." [24]

This emerging concept of eligibility suggests a middle ground between the two conflicting viewpoints of relief: one, of imposing "the most drastic safeguards in order to make sure the recipients are worthy and in order that there will still be an incentive for the poor to work for a living"; the other, "those who would use relief as an instrument for equalizing wealth."

When the local administration first acknowledged its responsibility in establishing the specific conditions under which an individual or family becomes eligible for assistance—it was impossible to realize the diversity and complexity of the problem of meeting this self-imposed charge. Out of the day to day experience, came questions which challenged and continued to challenge the thinking of the standards formulating group. What should be the organization's position in relation to the property owner? Is his real estate to be considered routinely as a resource? Should the public relief agency accept the application of those for whom the community has planned in another way, but for whom there are no available funds? Is the individual on the waiting list of another public agency the proper charge of the relief administration? Should all resources be exhausted before the applicant asks for relief? Whether or not the individual may be found eligible when it is his expressed intent to retain certain limited resources for burial expenses, etc., is another typical question that came before the Board. Should the fact that an applicant is a striker influence his eligibility? Applicants with small businesses of their own raise a whole series of questions concerning standards. . . . What should be the administration's position in relation to the family whose traditional way of living has been berry picking in an adjoining state, and who in the past has managed to exist during the winter months? The deserted wife

[24] Quoted from "A Plan for the Treatment of Unemployment." *The Survey*, March, 1933.

whose court order is insufficient to meet her needs, the deserted child, the applicant without work references, the non-resident individual or family, the unemployed father who claims no income from his work-ing children, suggest the need for the formulation of standards. . . . Why does an agency need to formulate detailed standards of eligibil-ity? The very fact that the relief administration dispenses public funds provides one reason. In the interest of many whose applica-tions must be considered, an underlying uniformity of approach is essential. The scarcity of professionally equipped personnel has given rise to the need for more specific statements of principle than might otherwise be necessary—the general intent in any policy or standard of eligibility is in the interest of justice and in providing a guide to the agency representative.[25]

This report emphasizes the primary importance of a clear statement by the relief administration regarding standards and policies which embody the conviction of the agency. Modifi-cations in these standards might be necessary because of changes in amounts of money available or other administra-tive factors, but the intent and basic policy of the agency would always be clear. On the other hand, the lack of a defi-nite agency standard and policy resulted in confusion and "wide variation in interpretation of policy and standard, or no interpretation at all." [26]

Standards of eligibility varied greatly throughout the coun-try. They were influenced by the available funds in each state and locality, the numbers of people receiving relief, the poli-cies of the relief administrations and the local traditions and concepts regarding the amount of relief a dependent family ought to receive. They also depended to some extent upon the standards of living and the prevailing rates of wages.

Although the average monthly relief grant to families and individuals is only a rough indication of the standard of eligi-bility in any community or state, these averages may be used to show the wide differences in benefits which existed between

[25] "Background, Development and Use of Standards of Eligibility in the Philadelphia County Relief Board," under the direction of Elizabeth H. Collins, 1937, Monograph, Multigraphed. Under auspices of the Com-mittee on Social Security of the Social Science Research Council. The study covers the period from September, 1932, to March, 1937.
[26] *Ibid.*

regions and states at different periods under the Federal Emergency Relief Administration.[27]

For example, the average monthly benefits ranged in May, 1934, from $6.78 in Kentucky to $45.12 in New York. This meant that all families of average size (4) having non-relief incomes of from five to six dollars were not eligible for relief in Kentucky, while at the same time a family of four could have four or five times that much income and still be eligible for relief in New York State. Also the lowering of the standard at any given time meant increasing the number of eligible families by hundreds, if not by thousands. This was one of the reasons why the relief rolls did not at any time begin to reveal the extent of need. The standards were always and everywhere arbitrary. The artificial definitions of eligibility kept an undetermined number of needy people off the rolls. The Federal Administration was always sure of the existence of this marginal group, but could never discover its size or devise a satisfactory way of reaching its members.

The desire of the Administration to include these "marginal" people in the relief program has already been mentioned.[28] The original FERA rules, which required a "means test" for the determination of eligibility, were relaxed in favor of certain groups, and thus a part but by no means all of the marginals were brought in.

Eligibility for enrollment in the Civilian Conservation Corps determined by local relief agencies under the supervision of Selecting Agents,[29] in the State Relief Administrations, was limited, for about a year, from July, 1934, to July, 1935, to boys in relief families. During the first year of the Civilian Conservation Corps, which was organized in the spring of 1933, and since July, 1935, boys from "marginal" families

[27] See Appendix L, Average Monthly Relief Benefits per Family, May, 1933, May, 1934, May, 1935. Also *FERA Monthly Reports*, June, 1935, March, 1936, and June, 1936. Figures in text revised since 1936 by WPA. See also p. 250 below.

[28] See Part III, Chapter 7.

[29] The Selecting Agents were appointed by the United States Employment Service which was responsible for the selection of all boys who were enrolled in the Civilian Conservation Corps.

have been admitted in accordance with a rather generous eligibility policy.[30]

The selection of students who were to be beneficiaries in the Student Aid work relief program was left, by the FERA Education Division and later by the National Youth Administration, entirely to officials of the colleges and universities which received funds for this purpose. Eligibility requirements had no relationship to a possible relief status of the students' families. Reference has already been made to the freedom with which teachers were admitted to the Education Program beginning in the fall of 1933 under the FERA.[31] Designation by the head of the State Department of Education or by a committee of the state or local educational association as being in need was sufficient to admit teachers to work relief jobs. The device of certification by committees of professional associations or unions was followed quite generally during the first year or eighteen months of the FERA in many localities. Artists, actors, musicians and clerical or so-called "white collar" workers were admitted to relief jobs in this way. A number of relief units established separate offices to which "white collar workers" might apply, in order that they might avoid incurring the stigma of mingling with "ordinary" relief applicants.

The CWA, during the winter of 1933-34, employed one-half of its 4,000,000 project workers without any qualification except the need of a job and fitness to do the work to which they were assigned. At the end of this program in March, 1934, only those workers who were eligible for relief were supposed to be transferred to the FERA Work Relief Program. However, the speed with which the CWA was liquidated made it impossible for the social service division staffs to investigate adequately and determine eligibility of all the workers who applied for transfer. The result was that thousands of people were included in the new relief rolls who were never subjected to the means test. This was particularly true in the larger industrial centers where the relief load was especially heavy.

This general transfer from the CWA accounts, in great part,

[30] See Part IV, Chapter 15.
[31] See Part III, Chapter 7.

for the increase in the relief load in the spring of 1934, at a time of year when it might be expected to decrease.

However, the increase in the case load would undoubtedly have been much greater if it had not been for the order issued by the FERA to close all rural cases on April 1, 1934, and re-open them only after reapplication and the re-establishment of eligibility. This occasioned a reduction in the relief loads in many of the states which had a high proportion of rural cases.[32]

The total number of families and single persons receiving relief in March, 1934, was nearly 3,700,000. In April it had jumped to nearly 4,500,000. Other factors, however, undoubtedly played an important part in this increase. The depression was then in its fifth year. The resources in savings, credit, and in assistance from relatives upon which thousands of the unemployed had been living were reaching the point of being exhausted, and many people, who had held out until this time, were forced to apply for relief. The growing usualness of relief and the fact that so many self-respecting people were receiving it, helped to remove the stigma and thus weakened the proud antipathy of many new people to the thought of making application. The administration of the program had improved. Better personnel as a rule received applications and established eligibility. There was greater diversification in the types of work relief available, and the employment policies of CWA had encouraged applicants to look upon the Federal program as offering "jobs" rather than relief *per se*.

The FERA rules specifically designated the needy unemployed and the inadequately employed as eligible for relief. Yet, as the program progressed, it became more and more apparent that hundreds of thousands of unemployable persons had found places on the relief rolls. The acceptance of these unemployable people as beneficiaries of the unemployment relief program was due to a number of factors. In the first place it was not easy for Social Service Divisions to decide who was employable and who was not. On what basis should a choice be made between an able-bodied housewife, who had never

[32] The case counts in the following states were lower in April than in March: Arkansas, Delaware, Georgia, Kentucky, Mississippi, New Mexico, North Carolina, Tennessee, Vermont, Virginia and West Virginia.

done any work for pay, and a man with a wooden leg who had been a night watchman for years before he lost his job? Or should both be accepted? According to one theory everyone might be considered employable except the idiot who was a complete and helpless cripple; another theory excluded everyone who had not lost a *bona fide* job during the current depression. Actual practice tended toward putting on relief people who were in need regardless of their status or possibilities for employment.[33]

Direct Relief and Work Relief

The Rules of the FERA provided for both "Direct Relief" and "Work Relief":

Direct relief . . . shall be in the form of food, shelter, clothing, light, fuel, necessary household supplies, medicine, medical supplies, and medical attendance, or the cash equivalent of these to the person in his own home.

A liberal interpretation of direct relief . . . must be controlled by the rule of reason and public policy. Under no circumstances shall an allowance be made which makes provision for other than the emergency needs of the immediate family. . . .

Direct relief does not include relief—where provision is already made under existing laws—for widows or their dependents, and/or aged persons. There is further disallowed the payment of hospital bills or institutional care, and the costs of the boarding out of children.

Federal funds had been used for all of these purposes under the Reconstruction Finance Corporation in 1932-1933. The ruling of the FERA caused much consternation and great pressure was brought to bear upon the Administrator to change the policy, without success.

Work relief was allowed only to those who were employable. The others were to receive direct relief. Work relief wages could be paid by check, in cash or in kind and the payment was to be made at a "fair rate" for the work performed. The worker, however, was to work only just enough hours or days at this "fair rate" to earn the amount of relief to which he was entitled. This amount was called his "budget deficiency" and

[33] See Part III, Chapter 7, for further discussion of the FERA policy in regard to "unemployables" including mothers' aid, etc.

was estimated by the Social Service Division as the sum which was sufficient to meet the weekly needs of the worker and his family to that extent to which the family was not able to meet them from its own resources. In other words, the wages earned on the work relief job were supposed to be equal to the difference between the total budget needs of the family and any other income which they might be able to count on. There was great variation throughout the country in the standards used in estimating budget needs. In many cases where relief funds were low the relief grants were decided upon without the use of budget estimates.

The provision that work relief wages might be paid in kind,[34] that is, by orders for groceries, clothing, etc., or by the commodities themselves, was a recognition of the fact that, in the summer of 1933, many local work relief programs were being conducted on this basis. Not until March, 1934, at the beginning of the Emergency Work Relief Program, was the order issued that "all wages must be paid by cash or by check." This order also provided that "no person shall be employed in work divisions less than 54 hours a month for unskilled or 30 hours per month for other labor, or less than 3 days in any one week for any labor. Persons whose budgetary deficiency is less than this shall receive direct relief." [35]

The early "fair rate" provision was wholly unsatisfactory. It resulted in low wages, particularly in the southern states where the prevailing rates were as little as 10 cents an hour in rural districts. On August 1, 1933, the FERA established a 30-cent minimum rate and provided that the prevailing rate should be paid in those areas where it was in excess of 30 cents per hour. This policy placed work relief benefits on an hourly basis. It involved an equality of payment for unskilled labor which made race discrimination impossible, or at least much more difficult than it had been under the vague "fair rate" ruling. The 30-cent minimum was abandoned, however, in November, 1934, in favor of the local prevailing rates, which were

[34] "Kind" meant the actual food, clothing, etc., instead of money with which to buy them.

[35] The CWA, with cash wages (see Part III, Chapter 7), absorbed the FERA work relief program so that the rule allowing wage payments in kind was in effect only from July to November, 1933.

to be ascertained in each community by a committee representing the relief administration, organized labor, and the business or professional group.   This placed the responsibility for determining wage rates squarely upon the localities themselves, an interesting return to recognition of local autonomy.

The program was operated locally by the staff of the Work Division who assigned the workers to their jobs, supervised their work, and were responsible for the completion of the projects.   The Social Service Division certified employable persons who were found to be eligible for relief to the Work Division and designated the amount of each budget deficiency, which was the relief to be earned.

In the selection of relief recipients for certification and in assigning them to projects there was undoubtedly a certain amount of discrimination in spite of the Federal rules to the contrary.   Local pressures and prejudices were powerful forces which influenced the treatment of Negroes, aliens, and members of political and labor groups, to a greater or less extent in many areas.

In the early months of the program, during the summer and fall of 1933,[36] there existed throughout the country every type of work relief, exemplifying all the stages of its historical development, beginning with the most punitive forms reminiscent of the "work test" and the compulsory labor of the workhouse.[37]

The most common type, known as "made work," had been organized in most of the large cities since the winter of 1930-1931 after the pattern adopted in earlier depressions by both public and private agencies.[38]   This consisted in providing projects which were invented as an excuse for work, obviously made for the purpose of creating means whereby the recipients of relief could make some payment for what they received.

[36] See Chapter 7.

[37] See p. 224 above and Part I, Chapter 1.

[38] "The last previous depression during which work relief was practiced on any large scale was that of 1914-1915." Colcord, Koplovitz and Kurtz: *Emergency Work Relief*, Russell Sage Foundation, New York, 1932, 286 pp. See also *Unemployment Relief in Periods of Depression*, by Leah Hannah Feder; "Work Relief Wage Policies, 1930-1936," by Arthur E. Burns, *FERA Monthly Report*, June, 1936, p. 22.

The projects were usually of questionable value. Most of them required only common labor.

Wide differences in philosophy were back of this method of helping the unemployed. Many people who were not willing to give outright relief to the needy, believed in making them work for what they received, so that the community would have a return for the money expended. They even insisted that the needy should "work," although this might mean no more than putting them through the motions, as was the case on many a "leaf-raking" project. On the other hand there were many of the needy who were not willing to take public aid and give no return. They believed that if they earned their relief they would avoid the stigma of the detested "dole."

This strong abhorrence of the "dole" was one of the basic forces operating in favor of work relief when the Wicks Act was written which set up the Work Bureaus of the New York TERA in 1931.[39] "The opposition to direct relief or the 'dole' was so strong during this period, both because of its supposed disadvantages to the recipients and to the community, that relatively little consideration was given to possible disadvantages or defects in the work relief principle."[40]

A more enlightened theory considered the made-work program as one designed primarily for the well-being of the relief recipient, to help him preserve his morale and his working skills for future employment. It regarded work as a human need apart from its relation to subsistence, and recognized its value to the community in the accomplishment of public work which would not be done without relief labor.

The extremes in actual practice are illustrated by the establishment of the Work Bureaus in New York State as entirely separate from the Home Relief offices because of the "stigma" attached to the latter; and the workhouse psychology which was carried over into many county offices of the Emergency Relief Administration, particularly in the South, where locally recruited staff members in the early months of the program were known to treat their project workers as though they were

[39] See Part II, Chapter 4.

[40] *Work Relief in the State of New York*, a Report of the Governor's Commission on Unemployment Relief. New York, 1936. 113 pp.

working chain gangs of paupers. It was also not uncommon to threaten a relief applicant who was unwilling to work with the refusal of any aid at all unless he accepted a project assignment.

The CWA in the winter of 1933-1934 introduced new principles into unemployment relief. "It emphasized the claim that the unemployed want work and that the abstract right to a job should be supplemented by a public policy and program which provided a job." It employed both those in need of relief and those in need of a job but not necessarily destitute. It paid them, not the equivalent of their budget-deficiency relief allowance, but prevailing rates based on a fixed number of hours per week. It set up projects of social and economic value which were more substantial in character than those devised for the "made-work" programs.[4] In many respects the CWA was the forerunner of the later Works Program,[42] with which it had more in common than the Emergency Work Relief Program of the FERA which immediately succeeded it in April, 1934.

The Emergency Work Relief Program returned to the budget deficiency basis for wages, and limited its employees to persons who were certified by the Social Service Divisions as eligible for relief.[43] It took over much of the unfinished work of the hastily liquidated CWA and profited by the winter's experience with that program which had been more nearly comparable to public works than to work relief. The improvement over the program of 1933 was noticeable in the change from small jobs to large construction projects which had never before been undertaken with force account or non-contract labor. There was more money set aside for materials and better project equipment. Also the projects were more highly diversified in order to give suitable employment to some at least of the wide variety of skills which were found on the relief rolls.

In spite of the provision in the rules that employable people were to be assigned to project jobs, thousands of them received

[41] Haber, William, "Unemployment Relief," *Social Work Year Book*, 1939. Russell Sage Foundation, p. 460.
[42] See Part IV, Chapters 13 and 15.
[43] See Part III, Chapter 7.

direct relief. Many of them were working at small rates in private industry, and their relief was intended to supplement their inadequate wages.[44]   Others did not have budget deficiencies large enough to permit their working the minimum of 54 hours a month and 3 days a week prescribed in the regulations.[45]   Many employable people lived in rural areas where projects were inaccessible, and numbers of them could not be assigned because no jobs were available for which they were suited. This was particularly true of the thousands of domestic workers, small shopkeepers and other persons who had been in business for themselves. Another important factor which kept employable people from receiving work relief was the failure of local communities to supply enough projects, either because of insufficient funds, poor planning and management, or lack of imagination and vision.

Relief in Cash or in Kind

Although work relief was paid entirely in cash or by check after March, 1934, direct relief was given in both cash and kind throughout the duration of the program, depending on the policies of state and local relief administrations. The Federal Administration recommended cash, both because it preserved the normal purchasing function of the family, and because it maintained existing channels of retail trade in small groceries, clothing and fuel. The cash method was also the simplest to administer. A weekly check equivalent to the budgetary deficiency, or to such part of it as could be allotted from available funds, could be mailed to each family. There was supposed to be no attempt on the part of the local relief staffs to regulate the expenditure of the money once the families had received it.[46]

Where relief was given in kind, the usual method of distribution was through orders on merchants issued by the relief office and given to the clients. These orders might specify each item of food and the amount which the grocer was to give the holder, or they might be blanket orders for food of the family's choice up to a designated sum. The orders issued by many relief agencies were redeemable at any store which the

[44] See p. 266 ff. below.   [46] See p. 230 above.
[45] See p. 238 above.

recipient chose.   Other agencies, however, limited their orders to a group of merchants who were willing to grant certain discounts to the relief administration.

The use of cash relief increased markedly during the second year of the FERA.   "Of the total direct relief extended in the Continental United States during December, 1934, about $16,700,000, or 23 percent, were paid in cash as compared with slightly under 10 percent in May of that year."   The system of cash payments was largely concentrated in cities and, by December, was used entirely in Philadelphia, Baltimore, New York, Los Angeles, Detroit, Newark and Jersey City.   The shift to a cash basis was most marked in the industrial states in which these cities were located and in West Virginia which instituted a cash relief system in December, 1934.[47]   Other rural and urban communities followed suit in 1935.   The pronounced trend in the direction of the exclusive use of cash was consistent with the new democratic attitudes toward the people who received relief, and was a recognition of the fact that the large majority of the unemployed had not only been accustomed to spending their earnings without supervision but had never before in their lives been forced to ask for any form of assistance.

Another form of dispensing relief in kind, besides the grocery order, was the commissary.   At the beginning of the depression and during the first year of the FERA this was an unfortunately common form of relief giving, probably because it seemed to be the cheapest possible method.   Central warehouses were established where food and clothing, bought at wholesale by the relief administration, were distributed to relief clients.   The method proved to be clumsy, and uneconomical, and was gradually abandoned.   It caused the recipients of relief to congregate in large numbers and to stand in line for hours, and involved improper storage and delays in the distribution of perishable foodstuffs with inevitable waste.   Most state and local relief administrations gradually discontinued the use of commissaries in their own programs, but the

[47] *Cash Relief and Relief "In Kind": FERA Monthly Report,* January, 1935, p. 16; see also *Cash Relief* by Johanna C. Colcord, Russell Sage Foundation, New York, 1936, for a detailed report on experience with the two forms of relief in nine large cities.   263 pp.

method was employed extensively in the distribution of surplus food, purchased and sent to the states by the Federal Surplus Relief Corporation.[48]

The results of studies made in Allegheny County (Pittsburgh, Pa.) and in Detroit, show clearly the preference of the families themselves for cash. They also raise questions as to the effect on the morale of many families in which a marked dependency may have resulted from long continued receipt of relief in kind with its inevitable supervision by the relief agency.[49]

In Detroit, an experiment was made in October, 1934, in giving food budgets in cash at the same time that it was necessary for the relief administration to make a 5 percent reduction in the grants. After three weeks of the experiment, inquiry was made of 20,000 families and out of this total only 7 families were discovered to have used their money for purposes other than food, and, even in those cases, the money had been spent to good advantage.

Standards of Relief

An entire section of Rules and Regulations No. 3 was devoted to "adequacy of relief." The rules placed "an obligation" on the states and their political subdivisions "to see to it that all . . . needy unemployed persons and/or their dependents shall receive sufficient relief to prevent physical suffering and to maintain minimum living standards." The amounts were to be "adjusted to the actual needs of each individual or family," and were "under no circumstances" to provide for "other than the emergency needs of the immediate family." Food was to be measured "by the number, ages and needs of the individual members of the family in general ac-

---

[48] See Part III, Chapter 11, below.

[49] In February, 1935, the Allegheny County Relief Board visited 3,600 families soon after relief in cash was inaugurated. They found that 78 percent of these families preferred cash, 10 percent had no preference, and 12 percent preferred the order plan, because they liked to have expenditures controlled and had found it difficult to manage with cash. Taken from a typed summary by Margaret Wead, Family Welfare Association of America, May 28, 1935. See also *A Study of Cash Relief in Ohio*, March, 1935. 68 pp. Multigraphed, Federal Emergency Relief Administration in Ohio, Columbus, Ohio.

cordance with standard food schedules." Shelter and household supplies were to be furnished "where necessary," sufficient gas, light, fuel and water "for current needs" and clothing for "emergency needs."

This definition of adequacy in terms of "minimum living standards" was certainly a conservative and realistic statement in view of the position taken by the Federal Administrator before the National Conference of Social Work in Detroit. In June, 1933, on almost the same day on which the rules were issued, Mr. Hopkins assured the Conference that: "We do not intend to let anybody use relief funds to reduce the standard of living lower than it is now. We are not going to allow relief agencies to starve people slowly to death with our money."

There is no question that the intention of the Federal Administration was to make relief as nearly adequate as possible and that great pressure was brought to bear, to this end, upon state relief officials. The figures show that some progress was made in raising relief standards against heavy odds of local tradition and limited funds. The great difficulties of the problem were reviewed by Mr. Hopkins after the liquidation of the FERA:

Probably the worst decisions that we have had to make, and those of the most far-reaching importance, have been those which have determined or affected the adequacy of relief. Each decision had finally to rest with the judgment of a handful of men whose opinion might be no better than that of several others who would have come to a different conclusion. Although for each family it might entail the expense of no more than a few cents, or more than a few dollars, it ran into millions.

Should we pay the rent? There was never a clear cut decision on this. Sometimes we did and sometimes we did not. For a lack of full acceptance of that responsibility thousands of landlords have taken a loss, and millions of families have seen themselves moved from the hill to the hollow; consecutively from good quarters to bad, from bad to worse.

Should we pay hospital bills? This we decided in the negative, and hospitals have been overburdened with the weight of sickness and dependency which fell upon them. We paid for medicine and sometimes for the doctor.

Should we place in institutions those dependents of a family who most obviously belonged there? We decided against this also and families already unsettled with want and strain were further demoralized by the burden.

We made such decisions because the first thing for which our money had to go was food to keep people alive. In more places than could be believed, families had been asked to live on two dollars a month. In spite of the fact that we were able to raise relief from such a sum to at least fifteen dollars, and that we have probably left behind us a basic minimum unprecedented in many communities, we must admit that our prevalent standard had no margin of safety, even after nutrition advisors had educated women as to how to get the maximum nourishment from the food which was allowed them. There have been families who have had less than they wanted to eat and little that they liked. . . .

It is curious that among the almost innumerable criticisms we have experienced, the one most truthful allegation is never made except by the families who depend upon us. *We have never given adequate relief.* We can only say that out of every dollar entrusted to us for the lessening of their distress, the maximum amount humanly possible was put into their hands.[50]

How far removed is this statement from the poor relief doctrine of "less eligibility"! [51]

In the effort to overcome local prejudices against decent relief standards, the Federal Administration was unexpectedly assisted by the local influence of citizens and corporation directors who were heavy taxpayers, when they began to realize that these relief expenditures were being made from Federal funds over which they had no control. The money was bound to be spent somewhere and they decided that it might well be spent in their own communities. They, therefore, stopped trying to depress the standards of relief and instead welcomed more liberal policies since thereby the families on relief in their communities were given just that much more purchasing power.

No Federal relief budget was ever imposed on the states. A schedule for an "adequate diet at minimum cost," prepared for families of various sizes by the Bureau of Home Economics

[50] Hopkins, Harry L., *Spending to Save*, Chapter IV, W. W. Norton and Co., New York, 1936. The italics are the author's. pp. 102-3, 99.

[51] See Part I, Chapter 1, and p. 222 ff. above.

of the Department of Agriculture, was recommended by the Federal Relief Administration but was never insisted upon. Final decisions regarding standards and the items to be included in the budgets were left to the states and localities. The Federal rules named the items for which Federal funds might be spent, but other items could be added by the states if paid for out of their own funds. For example, insurance premiums and union dues were considered in a few states to be legitimate charges against the budgets of families who were on relief but partially self-supporting.

In many of the states the Social Service Divisions used budgets prepared by the State rather than the Federal Bureau of Home Economics in estimating relief needs.[52] Available funds, however, were rarely adequate to permit giving the amount of relief for which these budgets called. Even where food was given according to an "adequate standard diet," it was usually necessary to omit one or more of the other budget items. Rent, clothing, household supplies, utilities, might all be left out of the allowance in order to give enough food to keep the families from near starvation. There is no doubt that food needs were met on a more nearly adequate basis than any of the other requirements. At least the food item was met first and the other needs taken care of thereafter, if possible. However, "Relief administrations which provided an adequate food allowance generally met other minimum requirements for health and decency as well; administrations which were unable to provide an adequate food allowance were almost certain to supply other forms of relief on an inadequate

[52] In December, 1933, the FERA urged the state relief administrations to arrange for the services of nutrition advisors on their state staffs. An Advisor on Food Requirements was added to the staff of the FERA in the Division of Relations with States. Early in 1935 at least 63 home economists were on the staffs of State Emergency Relief Administrations, and 78 nutritionists were in district or area offices and 567 in local units. These figures fall far short of indicating the total number of relief nutritionists in the program and serve only to show the increasing realization of the value of their services. See Mary Aylett Niccl, "Family Relief Budgets," *FERA Monthly Report*, June, 1936, for analysis of practice in the Emergency Relief Administrations regarding the payment of rents, allowances for fuel and utilities, household supplies, medical care, etc.

level. Information on relief food allowances is one important index of the adequacy of relief in general." [53]

The rent policy throughout the country in the summer of 1933 was chiefly one of eviction for non-payment. The usual procedure of the relief agencies after a family had been evicted was to pay a month's rent for them in new quarters, and nothing more until the family was again evicted. Gradually the state relief administrations assumed varying degrees of responsibility for payment of rents. Several of them also instituted work projects to repair houses in return for their use by relief families. Eventually the majority of the states reluctantly adopted the policy of including small regular rent allowances in relief budgets, although they might not actually be able to pay them if funds were short. A few states [54] continued to pay rent only in case of eviction, and in Mississippi no funds were permitted for shelter at any time during the program.

Provision for clothing in the relief allowances was haphazard during the first years of unemployment relief. It depended largely upon private giving, and upon second-hand clothing renovated in emergency work relief sewing rooms. Under the FERA the states began to realize the importance of making regular and adequate provision for clothing upkeep and replacement, and definite allowances for this purpose were added to some of the direct relief budgets and to nearly all of the work relief budgets.

At all times some provision for fuel was made in the cities. Most rural relief families had wood which they could cut for their own use and hence were expected to take care of their own requirements. Gas, light and water were not counted in the budgets at first, but they were included as a rule when standards began to improve. Gas or kerosene was provided on the score that food without fuel to cook it was not food, and light was included because, as one state put it, "inadequate lighting may mean future impairment to the eyesight of the children in relief families."

[53] See Mary Aylett Nicol, "Family Relief Budgets," *FERA Monthly Report,* June, 1936.

[54] Colorado, Delaware, Florida, Illinois (except Cook County), Montana and West Virginia.

Work relief budgets and grants were generally a little higher than those for direct relief. Extra amounts were allowed for additional food, carfare, and for the heavier or better clothing needed by the member of the family who was working. Often direct relief was used to supplement the wages earned on work relief. Surplus commodities [55] and medical care [56] provided by the relief administration were given in addition to the work relief wages or direct relief grants.

The average monthly relief grant per family in the United States was $15.15 in May, 1933, when the Federal Emergency Relief Act was passed. At that time the highest average was $33.22 in New York State and the lowest $3.86 in Mississippi. A year later the average for the country was $24.53 and the highest was still New York at $45.12 and the lowest $6.78 in Kentucky. In May, 1935, before the beginning of the transfer from the FERA to the Works Progress Administration had brought down the averages by adding to the number of short time grants, the highest figure was $52.92 in Nevada, followed closely by over $49.00 in both Massachusetts and California, while the lowest was $11.32 in South Carolina.[57]

The average for the United States had gone up to $29.33 by May, 1935, which meant an increase of $14.18 per month per family during two years of the FERA. The last half of 1935 saw a gradual decrease of average benefits to $23.21 in December. This may be largely accounted for by two factors. During this period most of the cases transferred to the new Works Program received relief during a part of a month. Also the gradual withdrawal of the Federal Government from the field of direct relief during this period may have contributed to the decline of relief benefits.

Changes in average monthly benefits from month to month in any one state and the great differences which existed between states, were due to a number of factors, as has already been pointed out.[58] Also the averages for the country as a whole and for individual states, while significant as a general

[55] See p. 254 ff. below.
[56] See p. 256 ff. above.
[57] See footnote 27; also Geddes, *Trends in Relief Expenditures, 1910-1935*, p. 102.
[58] See p. 233 above.

indication of standards and for broad comparisons over a series of months and between states and regions, are of less value as a gauge of the amount received by any single individual or family because they were a composite of a number of variable factors.

Averages were influenced not only by local traditions and poor relief practice and by the total amount of money available for relief, but by variations in state policies toward such items as rent and clothing; by climatic differences and seasonal changes which affected the need for fuel and clothing; by standards of living and of wages; and by the standard of relief used by a given agency to measure the size of its grants. The figures were also affected by the comparative number of single persons on relief rolls and the predominance of small or large families; by the extent to which non-relief income was supplemented and by the number of families which remained on the rolls only part of any one month.

Another important factor was the practice of the local administration in regard to the treatment of minority groups such as Negroes, aliens, veterans, and non-residents. While the Federal rules forbade discrimination against members of these groups and the state administrations reiterated the policy, yet the fact remained that the actual administration of relief was in the hands of local authorities and the promulgation of a rule by the FERA was not sufficient in many cases to overcome sectional traditions and prejudices in a comparatively short time.[59]

Perhaps the most serious factor in determining the size of the family relief benefit was the method used by the majority of state and local relief administrations in estimating the amount of money which would be needed and the amount for which they should apply to the FERA. Federal funds were allocated on a monthly basis, and estimates had to be made for a month in advance. The current case load was employed as a rough measure of future needs. To this was added probable changes in number of relief grants estimated in the light

[59] See Smith, Alfred Edgar, "The Negro and Relief," *FERA Monthly Report,* March, 1936; Webb, John N., "The Transient Unemployed," *FERA Monthly Report,* January, 1936; "Transient Survey," *FERA Monthly Report,* January, 1935.

of past changes from month to month. Some additional allowance was usually made for emergencies and unexpected additions to the load. Application was then made for funds to provide benefits at the rate per family in use in the state or county at that time. Often the allotment from the FERA was less than the amount applied for on the basis of this estimate. Starting a given month with a smaller fund than had been anticipated, the local administration often found that the intake far exceeded expectations or that some disaster or unforeseen occurrence such as a tornado, a flood or a strike, increased the relief load unduly. The question then had to be decided as to whether the money should be spread thin over the increased number of families or whether enough applicants should be refused to keep the relief benefit up to the standard of the previous month. More often than not the decision was in favor of spreading the money over all the eligible applicants, thus reducing the standard and sending the average down to a new low level. The estimate for the following month was then very likely to be made on the basis of this new level, with possibly a repetition of this downgrading, spreading-thin process month after month. This depressing of benefits was often aggravated by Washington, for, in spite of the desire of the Federal Administration to raise standards, there was a tendency to urge the states to apply for the smallest amount on which they could possibly manage. Consequently, many governors and state administrators took pride in seeing how small they could make their applications and still manage to handle their relief problem. This situation and the resulting reductions in the benefits given to needy people constituted one of the most serious objections to the discretionary basis of allocating funds which was employed throughout practically the entire period of the FERA.[60] The difficulties were emphasized by the fact that so much leeway was given to local judgment and practice in a country where the traditions of local autonomy were strong and deep-seated.[61]

[60] See Part III, Chapter 7.

[61] See Part I, Chapter 1; also Wells, Anita, "The Allocation of Relief Funds by the States Among Their Political Subdivisions," *FERA Monthly Report,* June, 1936, pp. 56-87, esp. 85-87; McCormick, M. Riggs, "Federal Emergency Relief Administration Grants," *FERA Monthly Report,*

The very attitudes of the social service staffs themselves, as well as the tenor of the detailed instructions sent out from the FERA and from the state offices, tended often to have a depressing effect upon standards. Miss Cannon has pictured this struggle between the haves and have-nots vividly in her report on the Texas Institutes:

The relief worker, whether or not he has achieved a degree of detachment from the neighborhood attitudes, is the grain of corn between the millstones of the receiver and the giver. One of the greatest difficulties we encounter is the tendency of the community to split itself apart into these two opposing states of mind. On the one hand, like a nether millstone, those now in need press upward, wanting and needing always more. On the other, an upper millstone, those who still have, represented in neighborhood criticism and in the rules coming from the top of the organization, press down with constant admonition not to spend, reminder that there is a limit to the money that can be spent, that the best office is that which most decreases its load, and that all relief is measured by an average and bounded by an appropriation.[62]

This statement describes pointedly the way in which local and often state social workers allowed themselves over and over again to be pushed into an ever narrower conception of the relief program. It is hard to say how much this was due to the pressure of routine tasks or to the influence of punishing and restrictive community attitudes toward clients. Or it may have been the stultifying effect of unquestioning acceptance of orders from above, accompanied as they often were by warnings about limited or exhausted funds.

Whether the cause was the pressure of community forces, the warnings from above about money saving, or too rigid interpretations of rules, the result was to make the staff "bear down" on the clients, more often than not. The workers seemed to think in terms of how many applicants they could reject, not of how many they could possibly accept under the eligibility requirements. Theoretically they believed in

December, 1935, pp. 1-33; Williams, Edward A., *Federal Aid for Relief*, Columbia University Press, New York, 1939.

[62] Cannon, M. Antoinette, *An Experiment in Providing Instruction for Relief Workers*, Bulletin of the New York School of Social Work, New York, October, 1935.

high standards of relief, but in practice they figured out not how much they could give but on how little a family could possibly manage and how many items could be cut out of the budget. They rationalized the low grants by their professed need to compromise with shortage of funds and their consequent effort to spread relief thin.

On the other hand there were many social service staff members who refused to compromise with these administrative and community pressures and become submissive tools to enforce low standards upon defenseless clients. They made the needs of the people on relief their first concern. They realized that they were in a better position than anyone else to know how badly more money and broader policies were needed. Their efforts to interpret actual needs which existed in their own communities to the state administrative officials, to the legislatures and to the public, resulted, in many cases, in the appropriation or allocation of additional funds and the raising of standards of relief.[63]

The most potent factor, however, in raising standards was the fact that Federal funds were actually allocated with the deliberate intent to effect a gradual leveling up of relief benefits in areas where local and state resources were especially inadequate. As a result, in spite of all the negative factors, the average monthly benefits in June, 1935, were double those of June, 1933, the first month of the FERA.

[63] This was particularly true among the younger, newer recruits, the "rank and file" of investigators and visitors. See Chapter 12.

Chapter 11

How Relief Was Given—II

~~~~~~

Surplus Commodities

The distribution of surplus commodities was gradually geared into the administration of direct relief and occasioned the continuation of the commissary system in many places. Commodities were made available by the Federal Surplus Relief Corporation which had been incorporated on October 4, 1933, "to help solve the paradox of hunger and destitution existing in a country with huge agricultural surpluses." It was "created to serve as the instrument through which price-depressing surplus commodities might be removed from the open market, processed, and distributed to relief clients in such forms as foodstuffs and clothing." [1] The original incorporators were Henry A. Wallace, Secretary of Agriculture; Harold L. Ickes, Secretary of the Interior; Harry L. Hopkins, Federal Emergency Relief Administrator. Commodities were purchased at first by the AAA from revenues from processing taxes, and by the FERA from Federal funds earmarked for this purpose.

This corporation was created six months after the establishment of the FERA but for the twelve months preceding the FERA the American Red Cross had been distributing, through its local chapters and other local agencies, flour made from the wheat and cloth and clothing made from cotton which had been made available to the Red Cross by an Act of Congress. The supply of wheat, 85,000,000 bushels, had been distributed to relief families by June first; the clothing made from 844,000 bales of cotton,[2] however, lasted until the end of summer.

---

[1] "The Federal Surplus Relief Corporation," *FERA Monthly Report*, July, 1935. See also *FERA Monthly Report*, November, 1933.

[2] See *FERA Monthly Report*, February, 1936.

With the establishment of the new surplus commodities system in October of that year the Federal Administration, which was encouraging localities to give direct relief in cash and insisting, in the spring of 1934, that all work relief wages be paid by cash or check, continued to give relief in kind through a program which was financed almost entirely by Federal funds and was entirely under Federal control. This distribution of surplus commodities not only constituted relief in kind, but "package" or "basket" relief handed out through commissaries or at the corner grocery store where the recipients were bound to be publicly marked as "reliefers" to all their neighborhood. In order to regulate prices and take surplus goods off the market, the Federal Administration has been willing for six years to give direct Federal relief of the most demoralizing and stigmatizing type.[3]

Families on work relief as well as those on direct relief received surplus commodities. Strict instructions were issued by the Federal Administration that the commodities be used only as additional, or extra, grants. They were not to be substitued for any part of the usual relief allotment, because such substitution would be equivalent to putting the goods back on the competitive retail market where they would tend to depress prices. As a matter of fact the commodities were used in place of part of the usual relief in numerous localities in spite of the Federal orders to the contrary, even though these orders were reiterated by the state relief administrations. The relief funds were never sufficient for adequate benefits and surplus commodities merely meant that the available money could be eked out in order to give a little less inadequate aid to the same "case load" or to supply the same degree of inadequacy to a greater number of families.

When the FERA was liquidated at the end of 1935 and Federal funds were no longer granted to the states for relief, surplus commodities became the only aid available to thousands of families in communities where no state or local funds were provided for them. Often, in fact, money which these states and localities might have used for relief for these people was

[3] "Of all forms of relief we have seen undertaken since the advent of our administration, I believe the commissary to be the most degrading." Harry L. Hopkins, *Spending to Save*, p. 104.

spent in defraying the expenses of storing and hauling, and on overhead costs of distributing food shipped in by the Federal Government.[4]

Medical Relief

Medical attendance and medical supplies to recipients of unemployment relief were authorized by the FERA in June, 1933. Rules and Regulations No. 7,[5] issued in August of that year, amplified and defined policies and procedures under which medical care might be given. In accordance with the usual Federal policy these rules were drawn in general terms, leaving the states to formulate specific policies appropriate to local conditions. The result was a wide variation in the scope of care considered permissible and possible within state and local budget limitations, ranging from the general medical attention provided in a few states, to emergency care only to which the medical program was limited in the states which interpreted the rules more strictly.

State and local relief administrations entered into working agreements with medical societies and individual physicians for the purpose of obtaining medical care for persons on relief. There was close co-operation with public health agencies. Advisory services of state and local professional organizations were used. Accredited lists of physicians and dentists were limited to practitioners licensed or registered to practice in the state. Physicians and dentists were paid, on a reduced-fee basis, but were expected to give to relief patients the same type of service as they gave to their private patients. Nurses were expected to maintain standards set by accredited local nursing organizations. Much of the nursing service, however, because of widespread unemployment among nurses was provided through nursing work relief projects rather than under the medical care program. The Federal rules provided that at all times the traditional physician-patient relationship be safeguarded. Medical care was recognized as a right and was

[4] Another temporary but important part of the program of the Federal Surplus Commodities Corporation was the purchase and processing of cattle, calves, sheep and goats in drought areas in 1934 and 1935 in co-operation with the State Relief Administrations.

[5] See *FERA Monthly Report*, August, 1933.

accepted as a part not only of local and state governmental responsibility, but of Federal responsibility.

The payment of professional fees out of relief funds was a decided step forward from the earlier depression period when doctors were called upon for free service and gave it under greater and greater difficulties as the number of patients who were unable to pay increased and professional incomes decreased. The extensive use of relief funds, however, necessarily kept the medical care program under the jurisdiction of the relief administrations, when its technical and professional aspects demanded and should have received professional supervision and probably direct rather than advisory administration. As this was realized, public health officials were borrowed, or physicians were employed as medical directors in many states and most if not all of the states made use of professional advisory committees.[6]

The close association of public health officials, physicians and relief workers in the medical care program helped greatly to increase the understanding of social problems on the part of physicians and the knowledge of medical and health problems on the part of staff members of the relief administrations. This mutual understanding was greatly furthered by medical social workers wherever they were employed by the relief administrations, or wherever, as staff members of other agencies and institutions, they worked closely with the medical care program.

Probably the most valuable contribution of the FERA medical care program besides the immediate remedial measures which it made possible, was the public awareness which it created of health needs and of the inadequacy of existing facilities, especially in rural areas. The scarcity of physicians in sparsely settled regions; the absence of clinics, of hospitals, of sanitaria and of facilities for convalescent care became matters of general knowledge and concern. This new awareness of health needs and the wide participation of citizens in the

[6] In October, 1934, Dr. Clifford E. Waller, Assistant Surgeon General of the United States Public Health Service, was loaned part-time to the Federal Emergency Relief Administration as Medical Director, reporting directly to the Administrator. Dr. John T. Hanks was appointed Dental Advisor.

program did much to educate communities to their responsibilities.

As part of an emergency mass relief program for the unemployed, the administration of medical care was subject to all the limitations inherent in such a program. Unemployment was often assumed to be the only problem in a family because small staffs working under heavy pressure had little time or skill to enquire about health conditions, even when they directly affected the wage earner's employability.

Eligibility was limited to relief families and in consequence all so-called marginal cases were ruled out. This was an artificial discrimination made more serious by the great variations in relief standards between states and between rural and urban areas in the same state. As a result, in states with low relief standards, many thousands of families in need of free medical care were excluded from the program who would have been eligible in states with higher standards.

The limitation of funds and the uncertainty of allotments from month to month made planning difficult, and threatened continuity. Also, there was great emphasis on holding expenditures to the minimum consistent with adequate service. This often resulted in too rigid interpretation of the restrictive aspects of the rules. For instance, decisions as to the number of doctors' visits and type of care were too often made with reference to the amount of money available, rather than with regard to needs of patients.

No hospital bills could be paid out of Federal funds. As a consequence, not only hospitalization but care in sanatoria and provisions for convalescence were very difficult to secure. Dental care was restricted to emergency extractions and repairs. Medical care for chronic cases was definitely limited in many areas and practically excluded in others. This was, of course, theoretically consistent with the emergency nature of the program and with the general ruling that care could not be given for conditions "that do not cause acute suffering, interfere with earning capacity, endanger life, or threaten some permanent new handicap that is preventable." This policy, however, laid the administration open to the charge of being wasteful and extravagant, since treatment of disease in the early stages would, in addition to furthering the welfare of the patient and keeping him employable, have saved time and money in the long run.

There was considerable confusion and conflict as to the relative responsibilities of the administrative authorities and the medical authorities. The state and local relief administrations were responsible for final approval of programs, including fee schedules, and for decision as to the eligibility of the patients. Once the authorization for care was given, however, the individual physician was responsible for the type of care (within the scope of the program), and for maintaining high professional standards.

The greatest weaknesses and inadequacies in the medical care program were due first to its emergency nature and last to the fact that a relief agency and not a health agency was finally responsible for the approval of all policies and procedures. There is no doubt, however, that the program created a new favorable attitude toward public medical care on the part of influential members of the medical profession which it might have otherwise taken fifty years to develop. It paved the way for the subsequent provision of Federal Social Security funds for public health work and the further development of the group medical and hospitalization movement. It also helped to make possible the serious consideration in Congress of the National Health Act of 1939.[7]

Relief for Transients

In times of depression the more vigorous and adventurous among the unemployed are likely to "hit the road," to set out on their travels to look for jobs. During the first half of 1931 there was a steady increase in the number of transient unemployed and by the fall of that year many of the communities into which these newcomers were pouring became seriously

[7] For further information on the Federal Emergency Relief Administration Medical Care Program see "Medical Care for Relief Clients," a study made by the American Association of Medical Social Workers, 1935. Published by that organization. Other studies which are typed or mimeographed were made in 1934 by the American Public Welfare Association and by the Division of Research and Statistics of the Federal Emergency Relief Administration and may be found in their reports and files.

alarmed. Looking ahead to what promised to be an even more serious situation in the winter of 1931-1932, the cities appealed for outside assistance to meet the increasing demands. They received little help, however, during the following eighteen months, and it was not until the Federal Emergency Relief Act was passed in May, 1933, that Federal funds were provided for a transient relief program.[8]

A special provision for transient relief was included in the Act:

That . . . the Administrator may certify out of the funds made available by this subsection additional grants to the States applying therefor to aid needy persons who have no legal settlement in any one State or community. . . .

The rules issued in June, 1933, by the FERA defined settlement, for the purposes of the Federal transient program, as residence within a state for a period of one continuous year or longer. They provided that programs of direct and work relief for transients should be set up under the direction of the state emergency relief administrations to be financed by "earmarked" Federal grants as stipulated in the Act. Emphasis was placed in the rules upon the prevention of transiency and the maintenance of morale in the mobile population. A Federal Transient Bureau was established to co-operate with the states in determining policies and standards of service.

The State Transient Bureaus, financed entirely by Federal funds, formed a nationwide network for the care of non-residents under the leadership of the Federal Bureau. By the end of 1933 there were 261 transient relief centers and 63 transient camps in 40 states, and within the next few months every state but Vermont had a transient program in operation.

The use of Federal funds made it possible to give relief to persons who did not have state settlement, without regard to the settlement laws.[9] Persons who had lived more than 12 consecutive months in any state and had not acquired settlement were cared for by the emergency relief administrations, since they were financed in part at least by Federal funds.

[8] See Webb, John N., "The Transient Unemployed," *FERA Monthly Report*, January, 1936, p. 1.
[9] See Part I, Chapter 1.

The Transient Bureaus set up their own relief standards which were usually higher than those of the relief administration in the same city or county. Elaborate facilities for housing and feeding, for medical service and hospitalization, and for education and recreation were developed.[10] Thousands of men and boys were given work relief in camps outside the cities, where they were kept out of the labor market and lived a segregated barrack life.[11]

According to the midmonthly census taken in all transient bureaus, approximately 125,000 persons were cared for on February 15, 1934. The peak load was reached a year later at 300,000, and 250,000 were cared for on August 15, 1935, shortly before the order to close intake was issued by the Federal Relief Administration.[12] The major part of the program was liquidated in the fall of 1935, just prior to the cessation of Federal relief grants to the states.[13] Plans were made to transfer the employable transients to the Federal Works Program, but local prejudices against outsiders made this process slow and unsatisfactory.

The closing out of Federal transient relief left all persons who had no state settlement subject to the eligibility requirements of the same programs, Federal, state and local, which were provided for residents. Transients had to compete with residents for places on the Federal programs and when they applied for relief from state and local funds they were again subject to the settlement laws, which were becoming ever more restrictive and more rigidly enforced.

[10] The program provided for "shelter, food, and clothing, adapted to the individual needs of unattached men, boys, women and girls, and families; medical and health service; transportation either to place of legal residence or other destination . . . ; work adapted to the physical handicaps of the clients, . . ." "Program for Relief to Transients," *FERA Monthly Report,* July, 1933.

[11] For a discussion of transiency and transient relief see "Transiency-Mobility in Trouble" by Elizabeth Wickenden, *Survey Midmonthly,* October, 1937.

[12] See Webb, John N., "The Transient Unemployed," *FERA Monthly Report,* January, 1936; also report of the transient program in *FERA Monthly Report,* December, 1933, and John N. Webb and Jack Y. Bryan, "Migrant Families," *FERA Monthly Report,* February, 1936.

[13] See Part IV, Chapter 13.

Self-help and Barter

Early in the depression, unemployed and destitute people in various parts of the country formed themselves into groups in order to supply their needs co-operatively by bartering their idle man power for various goods and services. When the Federal Emergency Relief Act was passed in 1933, it included a provision which authorized the Administrator "to aid in assisting cooperative and self-help associations for the barter of goods and services."

The rules of the FERA allowed "earmarked" funds to be granted to states upon request "for the specific purpose of establishing the barter unit," on the understanding that the units were to be considered experimental until they had proved that they had provided adequate relief without increasing the total relief expenses. A division of self-help co-operatives was established within the Work Division of the FERA to assist the states and the local groups themselves in developing this part of the program.

Between August, 1933, and October 31, 1936, over $3,000,-000 was granted to 26 states, the District of Columbia, Puerto Rico and the Virgin Islands for this purpose.[14] On the latter date there were 182 active associations with a membership of 10,029. It is estimated that during the entire period approximately 35,000 participating families benefited from co-operative activities. Relief budgets were reduced and some families succeeded in removing themselves from relief rolls entirely. The growing of foodstuffs, canning, fuel-wood cutting, and the making of clothing were activities carried on by most of the groups in addition to a wide variety of other work undertaken where the products or services could be used or exchanged. A partial list of other activities includes dairying,

[14] Included in this total is a grant of $300,000 for co-operative activities sponsored by the Tennessee Valley Authority. For a full report on the FERA self-help program see "Self-Help Cooperative Associations," Exhibit J, pp. 132-141, in Extract from Hearing before the Sub-Committee of the Committee on Appropriations in Charge of Deficiency Appropriations, House of Representatives. Seventy-fifth Congress, Statements of Harry L. Hopkins, Administrator, Works Progress Administration, Washington, 1937; Government Printing Office. Also *FERA Monthly Report,* September, 1935. Also *Inquiry on Cooperative Enterprise in Europe,* United States Government Printing Office, 1937.

butchering, poultry raising, plumbing, fishing, carpentry, operation of bakeries, beauty shops, laundries, and cafeterias, and various handicrafts; the making of soap and cosmetics, maple syrup, jams and pickles; and the repair of automobiles, shoes and radios.

The FERA report states that "on the whole, the program has been beneficial. It has conserved crops that might otherwise have gone to waste. It has reduced relief expense and has provided thousands of people with necessities which, because of the insufficiency of money income, were unavailable through the regular channels of trade. It has built up the morale of the participants by affording them work." The same report also records an estimate that "each Federal dollar used up in this program has helped to create benefits valued at nearly $7."

Clients' Organizations

The inadequacy of relief, the increasing needs and the administrative confusion during the early years of the depression, naturally gave rise to pressure groups of the unemployed, particularly among dissatisfied relief clients. These groups were organized at first on a local basis in the larger industrial centers. Later state and national organizations were formed, culminating in the Workers' Alliance which came into existence in 1935 following the announcement of the liquidation of the FERA, the return of unemployables to the states and localities, and the initiation of a Federal work relief program.[15]

Throughout the life of the FERA the majority of complaints regarding relief decisions and conditions of labor on work relief projects were made to local relief offices by individuals. At no time did organized groups include more than a fraction of the people on relief rolls or more than a very small fraction of the total number of the unemployed.

During the period of the FERA, pressure groups usually took the form of grievance committees or client delegations who came to relief offices to protest against inadequate relief, methods used by investigators, the indignity of the grocery order or the commissary, or conditions under which work re-

[15] See Part IV, Chapter 13.

lief had to be performed. These protests sometimes took the form of demonstrations, hunger marches, or work-relief strikes. Many of the demonstrations centered about the failure of most of the relief administrations to pay rents [16] which occasioned a great number of evictions. "The procedures of class conscious groups centered about the halting of evictions, the sending of large delegations to relief offices, and the staging of demonstrations. The universal eviction technique, which unquestionably dramatized the urgency of the rent problem, involved forcible replacement of belongings into flats from which their possessors had been evicted. . . . Serious clashes with police and numerous arrests occurred."

In making complaints about general policies, similar methods were used. "Relief offices were approached by large committees, numbering ten, fifteen, twenty, and sometimes more persons, which demanded immediate audience, without previous appointment and regardless of staff members' schedules. Where minority race groups constituted a special administrative problem, the committee ordinarily contained representation from the minority group highly out of proportion to the comparative numerical significance of the group. Frequently these large committees were buttressed by neighborhood crowds which gathered outside the relief office and waited while committees within presented 'demands.' " [17]

In the introduction to the report from which these statements are quoted, Miss Seymour says:

Unemployment relief, from its earliest days, has been paralleled by organization among the needy unemployed population. Every large city, most small cities and towns, practically all states, even the national area, have witnessed the growth of relief pressure groups. More recently, pressure organizations have spread to the social security categories.

[16] See Part III, Chapter 10.

[17] Seymour, Helen, *When Clients Organize,* American Public Welfare Association, 1937. A study of pressure groups of clients in relation to relief organizations; a "summarized account of a detailed and documented study made possible by the American Public Welfare Association and the Committee on Social Security of the Social Science Research Council: 'The Organized Unemployed' (unpublished M.A. thesis) by Helen Seymour, University of Chicago, August, 1937."

The Federal Relief Administration and later the Works Progress Administration recognized the right of clients to organize and openly encouraged the movement. They recognized their right to complain and to appeal to the highest authority, and their complaints were heard with fairness and understanding in the Washington office. The direct impact of the pressure was felt, however, chiefly by the local relief offices. It fell to the lot of social workers and investigators to hear most of the complaints and interview many of the delegations. Those social workers who were impregnated with the philosophy of the early charity organization movement and who looked upon the relief recipients as people who needed adjustment because of inherent failings, grew impatient with and irritated by the complaints. Others who administered relief as the right of the needy citizens of a democracy, met complaints with understanding and respect for the difficulties encountered by the helpless victims of the depression. The newer recruits to the staffs of the social service divisions aligned themselves definitely with the interests of these client groups, and, through the rank and file organizations, worked hard for better working conditions on the work programs and for more adequate relief payments.[18] As a whole the social workers who met the grievance committees and delegations week after week and month after month learned a technique of handling pressure groups which proved an invaluable part of their emergency experience. They also acquired a new understanding of labor problems, and of industrial and economic questions, which had never before been a part of a social worker's equipment.

Unquestionably pressures exerted by organized client groups not only succeeded in correcting numerous local deficiencies in the administration of emergency relief but were potent in securing larger appropriations of funds from local, state and Federal governments. The groups developed and improved their own technique, which was used by the Workers' Alliance in Washington with great effectiveness in the programs which followed the Federal Emergency Relief Administration.

[18] See Part III, Chapters 10 and 12.

Relief to People Working in Private Industry

When the Federal Relief Administration analyzed its "rolls" it found that the "employables" on relief were by no means an unmixed group. They consisted of the unemployed who had lost their jobs, the partially employed whose earnings were insufficient and had to be supplemented by relief, the self-employed, such as small storekeepers, who presented problems peculiar to themselves, the seasonal workers, and the full-time workers who were underpaid. The FERA ruled that the last-named group should not receive Federal relief, but despite the rule, full-time earnings were supplemented to a great extent throughout the program. This supplementation, whether of full-time or part-time or seasonal wages, was, of course, a way of giving relief to industry, a form of subsidy which, however, carried no stigma whatever upon the industry but only upon the underpaid employee who was thereby marked as a "failure."

Studies made by the FERA in 1934 and 1935 show that the supplementing of inadequate earnings was a widespread practice.[19] Half a million employed urban workers in private industry, counting one worker to a family, received relief in May, 1934. This number was about 18 percent of the two million cases receiving relief in urban areas during that month. Over half of this number or a quarter of a million workers were estimated to be working full-time in private industry and also receiving relief in addition to their wages.

In the 1935 study about one-third of those who reported wages earned less than $5 a week; 65 percent earned less than $11; and 80 percent earned under $15. The median weekly wage for white workers averaged $9.30 and for Negro workers, $3.50. Although unskilled workers were most heavily represented, large numbers of skilled, semi-skilled and "white-collar" workers were found to be receiving supplementary relief. They were employed in practically all important occupational

[19] Survey of Occupational Characteristics of Persons on Relief in May, 1934, in 79 Cities. Survey of Current Changes in the Urban Relief Population in January, February and March of 1935: FERA and WPA. "Supplementation of Private Earnings by Relief," *FERA Monthly Report,* June, 1935, p. 9.

groups, but there was a disproportionate number of persons in personal and domestic service.

The *FERA Monthly Report* concludes with this statement:

The Relief Administrator has already announced that the Federal Emergency Relief Administration is opposed to supplementing by relief the full time earnings of workers employed in private industry. This policy is based upon the fact that workers with supplementary earnings create a dangerous situation in the labor market. A labor market in which subsidized workers compete with other workers is both unhealthy and undesirable, for all competing employers will be forced, or at any rate encouraged, to lower wages to meet the lower costs of production of the employers with a large number of subsidized workers. Since depressed wages would also tend to spread to competing industries, all possible pressure should be exerted to prevent such a depressing effect upon wage rates, with its threat of demoralization to workers generally.

Supplementing of part-time wages created a problem almost as serious. There was always the possibility that the employer, in expectation of supplementary relief grants, might deliberately run his mill or factory part time. A study [20] of relief given to tobacco workers in Richmond, Winston-Salem and Durham, from January 1 to November 30, 1934, shows a high degree of under-employment. 231 of the 477 cases studied received supplemental relief. 90 percent of the entire group were Negroes. The average length of employment of all of the workers was only 91 days of the 200 or more working days in the eleven months of the study and the average earnings were $144.00 for that period.

A state-wide study made in Pennsylvania [21] revealed the fact that in July, 1936, 43,562 cases or 25.1 percent of the 172,099 cases comprising the state direct relief load were wage-earners receiving supplementary relief at that time.

The underpaid or underemployed worker presented a seri-

[20] Webster, Edward J., "Relief Households Among Tobacco Workers in the Virginia and North Carolina Region," *FERA Monthly Report,* September, 1935.

[21] "SERB Cases Receiving Direct Relief as a Supplement to Non-Relief Income," Pennsylvania SERB, Release, August, 1936. See also *Grants-in-Aid of Wages, A Study of the Problem of Supplementary Relief,* Philadelphia County Relief Board, Philadelphia, Pennsylvania. June, 1937. Multigraphed, 55 pp.

ous problem to the Social Service Divisions. Wages might be adequate on a minimum standard for the small or average family, but impossibly inadequate for the large family. Or the wages might be hopelessly inadequate for any family to manage decently. It was exceedingly difficult to decide whether a given employee was eligible under a broad interpretation of Federal and state rules and, if relief were given, what the effect would be upon him and on his job and on his employer. It was also not easy to decide how much to give since the man who worked had more expenses to meet than the man who was idle.

Closely related to the problem of supplementation was that of the relief recipient who was afraid to accept a job in private industry for fear he might not be able to hold it and, having lost it, might have difficulty in "getting back on relief." He was even more reluctant to accept a short time or "odd job" for fear that he would be dropped from the rolls and left with no income at all, or that the relief office would subtract the pittance he earned from his next weekly relief grant. Many of the relief agencies met this problem by offering a kind of guarantee of reinstatement to the client who took a *bona fide* job and later lost it through no fault of his own. In many localities the practice was adopted of allowing small, intermittent earnings without counting them in the estimate of the "budget deficiency." Also workers were encouraged to refuse jobs which offered working conditions below a reasonable standard, and wages below the prevailing rate for that type of work. This policy led to many of the popular criticisms of so-called "job refusals" in which relief recipients were accused of laziness, of being content to live off relief, of thinking that the world owed them a living, and of refusing all kinds of good jobs because they preferred loafing to work.[22]

The same relief agencies which encouraged the refusal of sub-standard jobs also refused relief or discontinued relief to persons who refused *bona fide* jobs which offered wages at prevailing rates and reasonable working conditions and which were in keeping with their training and experience. For example, in April, 1935, the Job Refusal Committee of the Phila-

[22] See Part I, Chapter 1, and discussion, p. 222 ff. above for reference to traditional English Poor Law attitudes towards dependents.

delphia County Relief Board was organized and formulated the following definition:

An offer of employment will be considered "bona fide" when both the wage offered and the number of working hours requested are the going wages and hours in that industry, providing the working conditions are in accord with the Board of Health regulations and that the performance of duties does not impair the belief (religious or other) of the employee. Reasons for refusing work or leaving employment will be considered "justifiable" whenever work offered or required cannot be classed as "bona fide" employment; the physical ability, previous training, or experience of the employee are not in line with the position offered; the performance of duties will impair the health of the employee or his possibility of returning to his lifetime vocation.[23]

The Federal Emergency Relief Administration made a series of studies in order to follow up specific charges that there were numerous unjustified job refusals, and to ascertain the facts which lay back of the reports. During the spring and summer of 1935, studies were made in five communities [24] where such rumors were particularly prevalent. In these cities out of 603 cases only 20 were discovered "which could be clearly adjudged instances of unjustified refusal of jobs." The investigations showed that "contrary to popular assertion, most relief persons are extremely anxious to 'get off relief' and will take any acceptable job."

On the whole, experience not only confirmed the conviction of the Federal Relief Administration that the unemployed preferred work to relief at any time, but did a great deal to educate public opinion on that point. The alacrity with which the able-bodied unemployed who were on relief in May, 1935,

[23] Cited from *Study of The Background, Development and Use of Standards of Eligibility in Philadelphia,* pp. 77, 78. See also Kahn, Dorothy C., "Problems in the Administration of Relief," *Annals* of the American Academy of Political and Social Science, November, 1934.

[24] Baltimore, Maryland; Alleghany County, Virginia; Washington, D. C.; Memphis, Tennessee; and Buffalo, New York. Hammonton, New Jersey, was also studied but no numerical records were made there. See Arthur, Henry B., "Summary Study of Alleged Job Refusals by Relief Persons," *FERA Monthly Report,* November, 1935, p. 6. Also "Alleged Refusal of Employment by Relief Clients," *FERA Monthly Report,* June, 1935.

accepted jobs on the Federal Works Program only served to bear out the earlier experience.

The position taken by the FERA with respect to labor is exemplified in the policy adopted as early as July, 1933, in regard to relief to strikers which was set forth first in a letter from the Federal Administrator to the Executive Director of the Pennsylvania State Emergency Relief Board regarding a strike in Montgomery County, Pennsylvania:

The Federal Emergency Relief Administration is concerned with administering relief to the needy unemployed and their families. Each case applying for relief to the local emergency relief agencies should be treated on its merits as a relief case wholly apart from any controversy in which the wage earner may be involved.

The FERA will not attempt to judge the merits of labor disputes. State and Federal agencies, as well as courts, exist which are duly qualified to act as arbiters and adjusters in such disputes.

Unless it be determined by the Department of Labor that the basis for the strike is unreasonable and unjustified, the FERA authorizes local relief agencies to furnish relief to the families of striking wage earners after careful investigation has shown that their resources are not sufficient to meet emergency needs.[25]

This policy, which made so clear a distinction between the issues of relief and labor, was adhered to throughout the entire emergency program by the Federal Relief Administration. In many localities, from time to time, there were departures from the general principle and in some cases local officials, yielding to pressures from labor or from industry, gave or refused relief to strikers on some other basis than need. On the whole, however, the Federal policy was followed in local practice and did much to clarify thinking in regard to the relation between the administration of relief and labor disputes. It also had a strong influence on the position of the officials in the later permanent state and local public welfare agencies when it became necessary for them to deal with similar situations.

The Education of People on Relief

The Federal Relief Administration made a distinctive contribution to the education of low income and destitute people

[25] *FERA Monthly Report*, July, 1933, p. 7.

which far exceeded the scope of the formal education work relief program. Ignorance was obviously a major factor in the widespread misery which was uncovered by studies and nationwide statistical reports during the first year of the emergency program, and Federal funds were used to attack the problem in a number of different ways.

During the school year, 1933-34, considerable sums of money were allocated to several of the southern states to provide subsidies for the rural public schools which otherwise would have had to close because of depleted funds in the State Departments of Education. In addition to keeping hundreds of these rural schools open during that first winter the Federal Relief Administration began in October, 1933, a work program to employ approximately 40,000 unemployed teachers who were in need of relief.

By March, 1935, 44,000 persons were teaching 1,723,000 pupils. The classes were free and the pupils were of all ages and all stages of education, from the old men and women who were learning to read and write their first words, to students who were able to stay in college because they could earn a Federal wage every month. The pupils who attended these classes did not have to be eligible for relief. But many of them came from relief families, and even more of them belonged to that marginal group who probably would have been on relief if the local administrations had had a little more money.

In addition to Student Aid which supplied work relief for students who could not otherwise have remained in college, the program provided classes to instruct illiterate adults to read and write English; vocational education and rehabilitation to train the unemployed in practical occupations and to help the physically handicapped to become self-supporting; parent education and nursery schools for preschool children from relief or low income families.

The most significant contribution of the education program was made in the classes for workers who were employed in industry or on the work relief projects. This program, now in its seventh year,[26] is carried on in co-operation with groups

[26] Under the WPA.

of workers in industry and agriculture, to help them gain a broader understanding of their own economic and social problems, in order that they may attempt to solve them through channels of organized labor, legislation, education, community organization and individual citizenship.

At the liquidation of the FERA all of these cultural and educational activities were transferred to other agencies and for the most part their scope was enlarged rather than restricted.[27] This meant a continued recognition by the Federal Government of the principle which had been established by the FERA, that the underprivileged third of our population had as much right to a good education as they had to a decent standard of living.

[27] The Student Aid program was transferred to the NYA in 1935 and the other activities to the Works Program at the same time.

Chapter 12

Social Work Personnel and Training

∽∽∽∽∽∽∽∽∽∽∽∽∽∽∽∽∽∽∽∽∽∽∽∽∽∽∽∽∽

General Personnel Policies

The FERA was established as a social work program, in contrast to the fiscal administration of relief loans under the RFC during the preceding year. One of its outstanding characteristics was the fact that it drew its personnel not only from social work but from a great number of other fields, including business, finance, accounting, engineering, statistics, research and education, yet it remained essentially a social work agency and was the means through which social work became a major function of government.

Technical and professional personnel from non-social work fields were needed in the special operating and service divisions to which reference has already been made.[1] The Social Service Division required social work personnel. The administrative positions were filled, as a matter of general policy, with persons who were thought to have executive ability, capacity for leadership and experience in administration, whether they came from business, or social work, or from some other occupation or profession.

The FERA exercised a general control over personnel in the states and localities. The Act provided that State Administrators should be appointed by the governors subject to the approval of the Federal Administrator. Other appointments were made by the State Administrators but the approval of the Federal Field Representatives was required for all persons who were placed in important positions in the state and large city relief administrations. This approval was considered essential in order to insure efficient administration of Federal funds.

[1] Part III, Chapter 9.

The Federal Administrator, the Assistant Administrator who was in charge of the Division of Relations with the States, the Director of the Transient Bureau, and several of the Field Representatives were social workers. Otherwise no one from the social work field was appointed to the Federal staff until April, 1934, nearly a year after the program had been established, when the Federal Social Service Division was set up to give technical supervision to the State Divisions which had already been functioning for eleven months.[2] At no time during the life of the FERA were there more than twenty social workers on the Federal staff which had gradually increased to over 400 non-clerical employees by July 1, 1935, when the transfer to the WPA payroll began.[3]

About one quarter of the State Administrators who were appointed at the beginning of the program were social workers, although several of them were later superseded by people from other fields. Several states at first followed the practice of appointing social workers as directors of local relief administrations, although many of these positions were also filled later on by men with executive experience who seemed better fitted to handle the increasingly complicated business of administering relief. There were, however, whole states, such as Georgia and Alabama, and many of the largest cities in which social workers remained as directors throughout the program.

This new type of administrative job, with its varied responsibilities for spending large sums of money, managing big staffs, co-ordinating and assuring the effectiveness of several different, highly specialized programs, for planning, interpretation and public relations, made heavy demands upon the capacities and abilities of the available personnel. Social

[2] Part III, Chapter 9.

[3] The *FERA Monthly Report*, December, 1933, contains the following statement regarding the administrative staff in Washington:

"The personnel of the Federal Emergency Relief Administration consists of heads of special divisions, necessary clerical and stenographic assistants, research and statistical experts, field examiners who review the accounts and expenditures of each State administration, and a staff of seven field representatives, who represent the Federal Administrator and are constantly in touch with the State Administrations." p. 5.

In June, 1933, 48 persons were on the Washington staff of the FERA, of which 30 were clerical employees.

workers, trained to deal with individuals and their problems, found these demands particularly exacting since there had been little in their professional education and experience to prepare them for administrative work *per se*. Many of them failed to meet the crucial test of successful administrative performance. Many others proved that they had the native capacity or at least the ability to acquire the necessary skills. Those who made good brought to their jobs a social vision, a skill in dealing with people and an understanding of human values and community relationships which constituted their peculiar contribution as social workers.

A number of the people from other fields who were given major administrative responsibility gained from the social workers on their staffs and from the social work leadership in the Federal office a concept of social action, an appreciation of human values and a belief in standards of personnel and relief which later put them in the front rank as leaders in the development of sound permanent public welfare programs.

The experience of the FERA with social workers in administrative positions had much to do with the introduction of additional teaching material on this subject into the curricula of schools of social work, just as the interest in "career" positions in government has been greatly stimulated by the development of New Deal agencies, and has resulted in a rapid expansion of schools and courses in public administration. There is decided difference of opinion as to whether a public administrator needs to know much or little or anything at all about the technical content of the functions which his agency administers. In other words, should a public welfare administrator be also a social worker, or may he be entirely successful if he merely knows administration?

Personnel in the Social Service Divisions

The Social Service Divisions were considered to be the exclusive domain of social workers, who were regarded by the Federal Administrative staff pre-eminently as "investigators." This was the attitude held by the general public which had not found it easy to understand the constructive, preventive aspects of social work nor its concern with social planning and social action.

The first rules issued in July, 1933, recognized the primary importance to the relief administration of the investigating function:

Each local relief administration should have at least one trained and experienced investigator on its staff; if additional investigators are to be employed to meet this emergency, the first one employed should have had training and experience. In the larger public welfare districts, where there are a number of investigators, there should be not less than one supervisor, trained and experienced in the essential elements of family case work and relief administration, to supervise the work of not more than twenty investigating staff workers.[4]

The official reports of the FERA bear out this original emphasis on investigation. A statement regarding personnel in the December, 1933, *FERA Monthly Report* does not mention the state supervisory social work staffs but records the fact that there were in the local emergency relief administrations, "in addition to the necessary administrative personnel, trained workers, who investigate the needs of applicants for relief and see that only those in actual want are assisted, to the extent of their minimum budgetary requirements." In the report of the Federal Administrator to Congress in 1935, the administrative costs in the states were justified partly on the score that they included the salaries of "the large number of trained social workers who determine the eligibility of persons applying for relief, and who save literally millions of relief dollars for needy persons by preventing persons who have other resources from receiving relief." [5] The same general attitude was indicated in the explanation given of the difference between the work relief of FERA and "a job on a work program such as the Civil Works Administration and Works Progress Administration. To the man on relief the difference is very real. On work relief, although he gets the disciplinary rewards of keeping fit, and of making a return for what he gets, his need is still determined by a social worker, and he feels himself to be something of a public ward, with small free-

---

[4] Rules and Regulations No. 3.
[5] *Expenditure of Funds*, Federal Emergency Relief Administration, p. xviii.

dom of choice. When he gets a job on a work program, it is very different. He is paid wages and the social worker drops out of the picture. His wages may not cover much more ground than his former relief budget but they are his to spend as he likes." [6]

Many states had already established emergency relief administrations before the Federal Emergency Relief Act was passed.[7] Social Service Divisions were functioning, many of them with personnel borrowed from private social agencies before the Federal rules requiring trained investigators were issued. However, the announcement of this policy and the expansion of relief administration into between four and five thousand local units created a demand for social workers which altogether was much larger than the professional field could supply.[8] Prior to the depression one of the most common problems of social agencies had been to find the money with which to employ the social workers needed to do their work. Now, for the first time in the history of social work an agency possessed and was willing to spend money to employ more social workers than could be found.[9]

Most of the state and large city Social Service Divisions filled their key positions with social workers who had training and experience, chiefly in private agencies, but as a rule the local staffs in the smaller places, especially in the rural

[6] Hopkins, *op. cit.*, p. 114.

This attitude toward social work and social workers was in part at least a reaction to the clue-following managerial methods of numbers of social workers who had carried over into the emergency program the traditions and practices referred to in Chapter 10.

[7] See Part III, Chapter 8.

[8] Total state and local Social Service Division staffs in the United States numbered approximately 40,000 in October of 1934. The number in each state ranged from 27 workers to over 10,000. See p. 221 above.

[9] Several of the State Emergency Relief Administrations which had been established in 1931 and 1932 had developed social work personnel standards, job classifications and salary scales, notably New York, Illinois, New Jersey, Ohio, Pennsylvania and Virginia. For the New York Temporary Emergency Relief Administration Classification and Salary Scales for Social Service Staff, see *Temporary Emergency Relief Bulletin* 27, February 15, 1934, and Lundberg, Emma O., "Social Service Personnel in Local Public Relief Administration," *TERA Research Bulletin*, February, 1935.

counties, were necessarily made up of people who were not social workers at all.

Many of these people who were employed by local agencies as investigators, and often as supervisors, had had their training and experience in other professions and allied fields. They included teachers, engineers, nurses, home economists, and others who had, as a rule, good educational background. Efforts were made to secure people whose personal qualifications indicated resourcefulness, ability to work with people, good judgment, tact, capacity to carry a large volume of work, and above all, a deep respect for people and regard for human values. Many of these recruits were young people who had just graduated from college or who had only partly completed their college work.

Selection of personnel was not only affected by the limited supply of social workers in the country as a whole, but was further handicapped in many states by insistence upon state and even in some places upon local residence requirements. There was also a certain amount of prejudice in regard to the employment of married women or of a member of a family in which another person was already employed. An added difficulty arose from the desire to give the jobs to the people who needed them most. Numbers of people were employed because they were in need of relief and work rather than because they were qualified to give relief to other people.

This custom placed many of the social service staff members in certain states and localities on work relief status. This was often done deliberately by the State Administration in order to reduce or conceal administrative costs. Work relief wages were lower than those of the administrative staff and were counted as relief expenditures. This practice resulted in poor work and ill-qualified personnel and was discouraged by the FERA. In order to prevent concealment of real administrative costs the FERA began during 1934 to ask for reports of these administrative-work-relief wages as part of the administrative expenditures. In November, 1933, the New York Temporary Relief Administration, taking the lead in removing staff from work relief status, notified all city and county relief officials that the entire social service staff should be placed on the administrative payroll on a salary basis.   For the two years preceding this date the greater number of investigators and other non-supervisory workers had been employed on work projects and had been paid work relief wages.[10]

Inevitably the social service staffs, then, especially in the smaller places, came to be made up largely of local people who were not social workers by virtue of any previous training or experience and were called social workers or case workers merely because they had been employed to discharge a social work function in the Emergency Relief Administration.   The FERA report on "Social Workers in Rural Problem Area Counties, Summer of 1934" stated that in the 64 rural counties in 23 states included in the study, 91.5 percent of the 324 visitors and 68 percent of the 37 supervisors were untrained and inexperienced; that is, they "had never attended a school of social work, had never had a course in case work, and had never had a paid social work position outside the emergency relief administration of a rural county." [11]

The supply of social workers varied considerably in different sections of the country.   In general the northeastern states, parts of the Middle West and the Pacific Coast comprised the well-developed social work areas, with a high percentage of the total social work strength in the country.   States located in the other sections brought in staff from outside their borders to fill many or all of their key positions and for the rest recruited local material.   States with the larger social work populations drew heavily upon their private agencies and permanent public welfare departments but even then were forced to go outside the professional group for the large majority of their local social service staff members.

Notable exceptions to this general statement were Alabama, Florida and Louisiana.   Alabama had developed a strong social work staff in state and local Child Welfare Departments. Florida and Louisiana had, in 1932, assembled large social work staffs for state and local emergency relief administration,

[10] See Lundberg, Emma O., "Social Service Personnel in Local Public Relief Administration," *TERA Research Bulletin,* February, 1935.

[11] *FERA Research Bulletin,* C-17, February 15, 1935, Division of Research Statistics and Finance.

from northern states. Miss Emma O. Lundberg, reporting on her study of Florida, says:

> In the 67 counties of Florida there are now 578 workers in the social service end of emergency relief: 69 social service directors, 21 supervisors, 56 case workers of senior and junior grades, and 432 "social aides." In the first three groups approximately one-third had some experience in family or children's case work before they were employed in emergency relief activities, and one-sixth had other social work experience. In a large proportion of the counties social workers were an unknown species before the emergency relief period, but in many communities there is evidence of growing understanding of the value of trained social service.[12]

Institutes

It was imperative that these inexperienced staffs be given some orientation in the social work field and as much instruction as possible in procedures, in methods of taking applications, making investigations and administering relief. The situation was further complicated by the scarcity of good local supervisors and experienced field workers to take positions on the state staffs.

Attempts to meet this problem were made by holding institutes for visitors and aides. Most of the states held one or more institutes during the first year, ranging in duration from about one to three or four weeks. These institutes were either on a district basis or attempted to draw together all the visitors in the state who could be spared from their jobs at any one time.

Instructors were secured wherever they could be found, usually from schools of social work, or from private agencies. Few of these institute leaders had had practical experience with much of the material they were asked to present. As a rule they undertook, in consequence, to cover the whole field of social work in addition to the general objectives of the relief program. The institutes were too large, and the visitors who attended represented a wide variety of backgrounds and interests. Supervised field work, or any field work deserving of the name, was out of the question. The result was great

[12] Lundberg, Emma O., "A State Plans Social Welfare Reconstruction," *The Family*, April, 1934.

confusion in the minds of inexperienced visitors; misunderstanding of the methods and meaning of social work and public welfare; failure to distinguish between the relative values of institutes and professional education. Practically the only accomplishment of the institutes was instruction in the general objectives of the relief program and in the mechanical details of the administration of relief.

In the summer of 1934 a few special allotments of Federal funds were made to states to finance institutes planned and conducted with considerably more care at certain universities. In one state where the personnel problem was especially difficult a program combining institutes and supervision was financed over a six month period during the winter of 1934-35.[13]

While a few institutes were sanctioned, the policy of the FERA was to advise against adding to their number, even though certain of the state relief officials advocated the use of local colleges for the instruction of large numbers of workers as more practical than sending a few persons away to a school of social work in another state. In refusing special funds for additional local courses and institutes the FERA took the position that they not only were entirely unsatisfactory from an educational standpoint, but that they were likely to mislead the workers who received the short course "training" into believing that they had thereby acquired some kind of professional status. Most of these workers knew little or nothing of professional qualifications or of the standards of social work education. It was natural that they should believe that credits acquired at institutes which were provided by the government and given at a university would count towards membership in the professional organization, the American Association of Social Workers. Instructions to the contrary notwithstanding, professional sanction seemed in the minds of the worker-students to be inevitably attached to a college course, although they were bound to discover later on that they were mistaken.

[13] Under the auspices of the Dallas Civic Federation and the Texas Relief Commission, October, 1934, to March, 1935: See Cannon, M. Antoinette, "An Experiment in Providing Instruction for Relief Workers," *Bulletin* of the New York School of Social Work, Oct., 1935.

Training on the Job

As a result of this experience with institutes most of the state relief administrations adopted a different approach to the problem of instructing staff members. This took the form of a combination of state supervision and direction of both personnel practice and in-service training, on a full time basis. These state-wide programs were, however, entirely focused upon the immediate administrative need of giving instruction to the staff members while they were on the job, and were not considered to be in any sense substitutes for professional social work education.

Professional Education

In the early summer of 1934 the marked increase in the relief load which had followed the liquidation of the CWA, and the prospect of an even larger load the following winter, with corresponding demands upon the Social Service Divisions, emphasized the inadequacies of the personnel and the desirability of providing further training facilities. After consultation with leaders in the field of social work education and with social workers who held administrative and supervisory positions in state and local relief administrations, a program was adopted which seemed to offer the most valuable contribution to the future development of permanent public welfare as well as to the immediate personnel needs of the FERA.

This program involved sending approximately 1,000 students to accredited schools of social work during the academic year 1934-1935. "Ear-marked" funds, allotted state relief administrations for the purpose, totaled approximately $420,-000, including $30,000 to Puerto Rico. The states sent between 500 and 600 students to school for the first half of the academic year and the remainder for the second half.

Student quotas were allotted to 39 states, ranging from 6 students for each of three sparsely populated states, to 50 students each for Georgia and Texas. The majority of the states received quotas of 16, 24 or 32. In making these allocations the following factors were considered: The number of counties and relief units in a state; the relief load and the consequent need of social workers; the number of trained social workers already in a state in relation to the need; the extent to which the Social Service Division in a state would probably be able to give supervision to the students and help them make the necessary adjustments when they returned from school; the known interest of the state relief administration in maintaining or in developing a high quality of social work; the general background and traditions of a state in relation to social work and professional standards. On the basis of these factors it was decided not to allocate quotas to the following nine states: Massachusetts, Connecticut, Rhode Island, New York, Pennsylvania, Delaware, New Jersey, Maryland and Ohio. The District of Columbia was also omitted. These states had a larger number of social workers. Most of them were definitely interested in standards and put into operation training programs of their own without the stimulus of Federal "ear-marked" funds. It is worth noting that within the borders of these states and the District of Columbia there were at that time ten accredited schools of social work.

Throughout the training program the policy was consistently followed of sending students exclusively to accredited schools of social work. In other words, the program was limited to use of member schools of the American Association of Schools of Social Work. At that time there were 28 members of the Association. Students were sent to 20 of these member schools and to the School of Social Work of the University of the State of Washington which was approved for this purpose by the Association. The selection of the schools was based on location and adequacy of their facilities to accommodate large numbers of students who might be sent by states in the same general areas. No member school was excluded and students were free to request that they be sent to any accredited school in the same general region. A few students made such requests which were granted.

A number of state universities which were not accredited by the Association asked to be included in the program.[14] It

[14] The demand for social workers created by the Emergency Relief Administration brought thousands of young women and young men flocking to take social work and sociology courses at universities and colleges the country over. This stimulated the organization of undergraduate social

would have been impracticable to have granted all these requests, and a choice amongst them would have involved a careful evaluation of the type of training offered by each one. The FERA had no facilities for such an evaluation and it was not feasible to set up such facilities in an emergency program.

The most difficult pressure to meet came from the colleges and universities in which so-called "random courses" in social work subjects had been approved by the American Association of Social Workers as counting towards the students' professional qualifications for membership in that Association. It was difficult for the university faculties to understand that this approval did not accredit their courses with the Association of Schools of Social Work. The two Associations were entirely different in scope and function, but their names were very easily confused. It was also difficult for these educators, and for some of the State Administrators, to understand that training for social work involved more than a course in case work with the addition of one or two supplementary courses in whatever related subjects it was convenient to offer at a given college or university.

In view of these numerous requests, careful consideration was given to the advisability of adding a few carefully chosen and developed training centers to those which were already accredited by the Association of Schools of Social Work. This possibility was given up, however, on the ground that the use of such additional centers, before the capacity of the accredited schools had been tested, would undoubtedly weaken the already accredited schools and would also tend to lower standards because of the difficulty of securing a sufficient number of qualified teachers. Furthermore, the FERA was not in a position to plan for more than one year ahead and it seemed unsound to attempt to develop training facilities on such a short-time basis.

The limitation of the training program to schools which were accredited probably played an important part in the safeguarding of the existing standards of education for social work during the emergency period. These standards might have been

work curricula, the inception of several new schools of social work, and also greatly increased the attendance at accredited schools.

seriously threatened, if not destroyed, if the FERA had spent the entire training fund in institutes, short courses, and the development of special schools devoted to the instruction of workers in the methods of administering unemployment relief.

The response of the Association of Schools of Social Work and its members to the proposal that they accept 1,000 additional students was immediate and cordial. Many of the schools had been for some time deeply concerned over the growing demand for personnel in the relief program, and they had been using every possible means to meet the need through the provision of scholarships, of extension courses [15] and of institutes organized at the request of state relief administrations.

An Advisory Committee to the FERA appointed by the Association gave great assistance in explaining the program to the schools, in supplying information to the Federal Social Service Division regarding capacity and facilities of the different schools, and in advising on questions which related to standards of professional education. The Committee assisted in outlining the points which were given to the State Social Service Directors to be used as the basis of selecting students. The program was designed to be one of graduate study only and the students were expected to meet the regular admission requirements of the schools. At least one school relaxed its exacting admission requirements to admit students from rural states where the educational standards were particularly low, when it became almost impossible to find enough applicants with the stipulated grades and prerequisite courses.

The students were chosen from among recruits for the relief administration staffs as well as from persons already employed, and the selection was, on the whole, made with great care. Mistakes were made, particularly in states in which there was not as yet good professional social work leadership. In the summer of 1934, when the first group of students were chosen, very few of the Regional Social Workers who later made up the field staff of the Federal Social Service Division

[15] Extension courses were provided by a few accredited schools during 1934 and 1935, particularly the School of Social Service Administration of the University of Chicago and the Philadelphia School of Social Work.

were available to advise with the State Directors or interpret the objectives of the training program to them.[16]

It was clear from early reports from the schools that a number of students had gone to school without understanding fully why they were sent. Apparently some of them had not particularly wanted to go, and others had been given little or no interpretation of the training program. There was also evidence that a few of the students had been sent because they had become problems to the relief administration and the training program was looked upon as a solution!

The experience gained with the first group of students helped to refine the selection of the next group. More emphasis was placed upon maturity, mental and emotional stability, potential leadership and capacity to assume greater responsibility upon return to the job. The schools found that students over 40 years of age learned less readily and made the necessary adjustments less easily. One of the schools to which a large number of the students were sent estimated that 75 to 80 percent were qualified to make good use of their training. This proportion was slightly lower than that for their regular graduate students in social work.

In general the students who had had experience in the relief administration or in other social agencies profited more than those without any such experience. They all acquired a reputation for working with greater emotional and mental intensity than the average student and at a more rapid pace. This was undoubtedly a hangover from the swift tempo of the emergency job, but it was also partly due to the fact that they felt a special responsibility for getting the most out of their brief opportunity at school.

Each state relief administration made its own financial arrangements with the students, and, in consequence, there were

[16] On August 18, 1934, the following memorandum was sent by the Federal Social Service Division to the State Directors of Social Service: "We have heard from one of the schools of social work that applications received from prospective students in our training program show some lack of understanding of the purpose for which this training is being given. Will you please at once make clear to all the students in your state who are applicants for this training that it is to prepare for work in the public welfare field only."

decided differences in the amounts of money which students from different states at the same school could spend for living and for incidental expenses. Some students were inclined to consider these discrepancies unjust at first, but on the whole they were accepted philosophically. A few of the states had made living allowances too small for even minimum expenses in a metropolitan center and found it necessary to make adjustments which would provide reasonable comfort and freedom from worry. A school which accepted students from a number of different states reported:

One of the first areas of stress to emerge was in the plans for financing. The realization that there existed marked differences in amounts allowed by the various states for the Fellowships operated to complicate the initial adjustments considerably. The attitudes of the individual students toward this inequality seemed entirely reasonable, and because the reaction was so widespread, there seemed some reason for the School to attempt to clarify the situation. A member of the administrative staff discussed with students from each state the details of financial plans, their budgeted expenses, etc. The School acted only as fact-finder in this problem, attempting to clarify just what the divergences were and how adequate the grants were for meeting living needs, passing these facts on to the Federal Emergency Relief Administration Field Representative for consideration. All but one of the states have now adjusted their stipends.

No arrangements whatever were made for the students to work in order to earn any part of their tuition or living expenses. The time spent at school was so short that it seemed essential for the students to devote all their energies to the task in hand and not consume precious study time and effort in doing work for very small wages. This policy was adopted as assuring the most profitable return on the investment in the training program and the best possible use of the students' time.

The schools which accepted a considerable number of students found it necessary to make many adjustments to meet their needs. In addition to providing more classes and extra field work facilities, the faculties spared no pains to do everything possible in response to the eager demands of the students.

More emphasis was put on the rural aspects of social work

in several of the schools. At least one special course was given on unemployment relief, and one institute was held to "integrate case work training with FERA problems." Several schools arranged additional hours of field work so that the students might qualify for junior membership in the American Association of Social Workers.[17] Brief orientation courses were arranged, and meetings held to explain the training program, the purpose of the courses offered, and the set-up of the agencies in which the field work would be done. At least one school found that "some of the usual field work experiences and methods took on new meaning with FERA students. Group conferences meant opportunity to share experiences and find new methods to apply to problems at home as well as training in how to conduct conferences.[18] Discussion groups were organized on the application of case work methods to supervision and administration. Faculty consultants did yeoman service with discussion groups and in individual conferences. There were informal teas, talks by prominent social workers and (special) formal lectures were given as evident need arose.

Everyone concerned in the program, the students, the schools of social work, the Federal and state social service directors, agreed that half of an academic year was entirely too short a period for any student to secure satisfactory preparation for an emergency relief job, much less for professional social work.[19] Two-thirds of the students wanted to stay through another half-year period and almost all of the others felt the need of more training but preferred to alternate it with periods of practical experience in the field.

It was not surprising that it took the students two or even three months to adjust to a life of study in an academic setting. They had been working at high speed in busy relief

[17] Requirements for junior membership include 300 clock hours of field work. See pp. 281 and 284 above.

[18] Pyles, "Learning with Our FERAs," *The Family*, Jan., 1936.

[19] The Advisory Committee of the Association of Schools had decided that one semester, or two quarters, was certainly the shortest period which could be used to advantage by a student who had had no previous school experience. At the beginning of the program the Philadelphia School of Social Work refused to take students for less than a year, but finally agreed upon half a year against the better judgment of the faculty.

offices with little question as to why they did certain things and with very little understanding of the program.

Many of the state social service directors felt so strongly about the importance of a longer training period that they recommended that the next selection of students should be made from among those who had already had some professional education. They believed it would have been better to have sent fewer students and to have sent them for an entire academic year. A number of students, at their own expense or with the help of the schools, managed to stay through another term. A few of the state administrations continued the training program with state or Federal funds the following year. The State Department of Public Welfare of Washington sent 15 students during the fall and winter quarters, 13 students for the spring quarter of 1935-36 and 12 students in the summer of 1936. An interesting comment on this point came from Georgia in September, 1937, two years after the close of the program:

There has been no careful study, but results would point to the value of longer periods of preparation. Fifty persons were sent to schools of social work for six months under the Federal Emergency Relief Administration training program. Of this group more than one third are now employed as directors of county departments in the developing public welfare program of the State. Of the group given three months' training, either through special courses arranged in Georgia or in schools of social work, only about 15 percent are now employed in the public welfare program.

Some Effects of the Training Program

In May, 1935, after the students who attended school during the first half of the academic year had been back on their jobs for one or two months, an inquiry was made in order to learn, if possible, what the school experience had meant to them in terms of their day to day jobs. Six months later a similar inquiry was made regarding the experience of the second group of students. In making these inquiries questionnaires were sent by the FERA to the thirty-nine State Directors of Social Service, to one-half of each group of students and to the schools which they had attended. Summaries of the replies to these questionnaires were prepared and distributed to the agencies and schools and others who were interested.

An analysis of this material showed that on the whole the training program had been of distinct value to the students, to the state relief administrations and to the participating schools. The students had acquired perspective, some basic knowledge of social work, and considerable insight into their possible contribution to the welfare program; the relief administrations found their services proportionately more valuable and the schools were brought closer to reality and thus greatly stimulated by the experience.

However, the replies to the questionnaires also brought into focus and revealed new angles of many problems and difficulties which had already been realized to some extent. Many of the students felt keenly the drastic change from a rural to an urban setting and from the pressures of an emergency administrative job to the distinctly different and quieter tempo of the classroom and student field work in a city social agency. The case material used at the majority of the schools was entirely urban, and numbers of students reported that they received no help in applying case work principles to rural situations. Students from rural communities likewise found that it took longer to adjust to their new settings. This was particularly true of southern students who went to school in New York, Chicago and Philadelphia.

There was much demand from the students for more help with distinctly administrative and organization problems, and for instructors who had had experience with, and detailed knowledge of, the emergency relief program. For instance, one of the state directors of social service suggested that each school staff "should have at least one member with emergency relief administration experience to bridge the gap between the top speed, hectic pace of Federal Emergency Relief Administration students and the philosophical, studious attitude of some of the teaching staff."

It was evident that a wide gap existed between the theory taught by the schools and the exigencies of the emergency relief job; between the protected seclusion of the offices in which the students' field work was done and the tense, hectic atmosphere of those from which they had come; between the richness of urban social resources and the pitiful meagerness with which they were familiar in the country, especially in those regions in which there were single counties large enough to take in all of New England!

There was also a serious question as to whether an equally wide gap did not exist between the methods of social case work as generally accepted by private social agencies and the practical application of these methods to the administration of unemployment relief; even between the entire content of professional education as it had developed in many of the schools of social work and the vital needs of the new public welfare programs, which gave social work a place as a major function of government.

This problem was directly related to the fact that the greater part of the development of social work in this country had taken place in private social agencies in the larger cities.[20] The schools of social work had grown out of the need of these private agencies for trained personnel. The largest and most important schools were located in large cities. Relatively few were in state universities or had statewide or rural or public welfare interests.

Personnel in the Transition Period

At the end of the training program a number of serious problems presented themselves. The student quotas had been originally limited to the numbers for whom each state could reasonably be expected to furnish qualified supervision upon their return. It was most important that after their short period of study the students should practice what they had learned under supervisors who could continue to teach them and help them to capitalize what they had gained from their school experience. For the same reason it was desirable to protect them as far as possible from too rapid promotion, a hard thing to do in the face of emergency demands. These policies assumed that the students would return to positions under the state relief administrations which sent them to school, and each student had agreed to come back for a year. By implication the state relief administrations had also agreed to employ them all, so far as lay in their power.

[20] See Part I, Chapter 2.

The twelve months of the training program, from September, 1934, to August, 1935, saw many drastic changes which had not been foreseen by the Social Service Divisions when plans were made in the summer of 1934. The President's Committee on Economic Security made its report in January, 1935. Bills providing for the Federal Works and Social Security programs were introduced in Congress during the same month and were enacted in March and August respectively. By July the Works Program had begun operations and preparations were being made to liquidate the Federal Emergency Relief Administration.[21]

In this changing picture no agency could give assurance of future employment to anyone and no worker away at school could feel anything but great uncertainty and insecurity. Many students did not finish their time at school until the end of the summer quarter in August, 1935. By that time orders had already gone to the states from the FERA to make drastic cuts in the Social Service Division staffs since thousands of relief recipients were being transferred each week to projects of the new Works Program from the "rolls" of the FERA.

Even the first group of students who returned to their states and to jobs in February and April of 1935 were met by the growing uncertainties of the transition period. The fundamental objective of the training program had been to prepare them to take part in the development of permanent public welfare programs, and it was somewhat ironical that as they finished their courses they should have been faced with the disintegration of the emergency program and find little assurance that any permanent agencies would take their places.

In spite of the uncertainties, however, the relief administrations needed and welcomed the students who returned from school in the winter and spring of 1935. The need was so great, in fact, that more than half the students were given greater responsibilities than they had carried before they went to school. The students had, therefore, much less opportunity to receive supervision than had been planned for them. There is no question but that many of the younger workers were given far too much responsibility and pushed too fast. Prac-

[21] See Part IV, Chapter 13.

tically the same proportion of the students who returned during the summer were promoted, for much the same reason, because the reduction in the social service staffs did not take place to any great extent until well into the fall of 1935. The relief administrations then tried to hold their best staff members, and, whenever possible, gave preference to those who had been sent to school. As a result a large proportion of the total number of students were employed throughout the transition period.

While preparations were under way to liquidate the FERA, the Federal Social Service Division undertook, in the spring and summer of 1935, to make an analysis and evaluation of the personnel standards in the state and local Social Service Divisions; to analyze the changing functions of these divisions during the transition period, and to assist the state Social Service Directors in their difficult task of staff reduction.

In view of the possibilities of a permanent program under the Social Security Act which had then been introduced in Congress, it seemed particularly important to take stock of the personnel situation in the emergency Social Service Divisions—since they represented the first example of the use of social work by government on a nationwide basis—and make the results of this initial experience available for future guidance. Reduction of staff had even more direct bearing upon the permanent programs in terms of the personnel who were to be held on the state and local staffs during the transition period.[22]

The material on personnel standards sent in by the state Social Service Divisions in the spring of 1935 revealed the difficulties with which the states had contended in meeting their needs for qualified workers. The requirements for the various positions were invariably written in terms of maximum qualifications which represented the amount of education and experience considered desirable by the SERA and balanced by minimum requirements and a provision for the approval of ex-

[22] "Social Service Division Staffs of the State Emergency Relief Administrations, 1935 and 1936," *Research Bulletin,* Works Progress Administration, Multigraphed, 41 pp., containing a report of reduction procedures, functions, personnel standards, trends, prepared by Marjorie Merrill Ocker. Issued October, 1937.

ceptions by the state office. The minimum requirements made definite concessions to local prejudices and their terms were conditioned by the scarcity of trained personnel, the general educational level of the communities, and the necessity of employing a large staff. The maximum qualifications in most of the states required professional social work education and experience to an extent which varied with the positions to which they applied. General agreement on standards was balanced by great difficulty in filling the positions with workers who met more than the minimum requirements.

The analysis of the maximum qualifications shows, however, that a milestone in social work history had been passed with the acceptance of professional criteria by governmental agencies generally throughout the country. The policy adopted by the emergency relief administrations of writing their social work qualifications in terms of minimum and maximum requirements was carried over into the state public assistance programs which later administered Federal funds under the Social Security Act.[23]

Reduction of staff in the state and local emergency relief administrations began in August and continued through the fall and winter. The Federal Social Service Division, in advising the state Social Service Directors regarding methods to be used in reducing their staffs, urged them to keep in mind the fundamental differences between the emergency and the permanent programs. While professional preparation and quality of performance should always be given first consideration in the selection of workers, it declared, the emergency program had necessarily placed special emphasis upon administrative ability and efficiency in organizing a large volume of detailed work. These qualifications need not be considered equally important to the permanent program. The Directors were asked to review carefully their personnel classifications and standards and to revise them if necessary in order that a workable plan might be available to the permanent agency, and to make their selections according to classifications on a state-wide basis in order that the best workers for each type of position might be retained. They were advised to hold the

[23] Part IV, Chapter 15.

professionally trained workers wherever possible and to give preference, in the group without previous training, to those who appeared to be capable of growth and development, who had an adequate educational background and who were interested in preparing themselves for work in the professional social work field.

This process of selection, which was more difficult and more important, because of its significance for the permanent program, than the original recruiting of workers for the emergency staffs, was carried out in the midst of the confusion and uncertainty which existed in state relief offices faced with the withdrawal of Federal funds, drastic changes in the policies and plans of state legislatures, and subject to many forms of community pressure. In spite of these handicaps selections were made in most of the states on the basis of the qualifications of the workers, although considerable weight was given to other factors such as residence, length of service, and need of employment.

Following these months of staff reduction, although the states were still in the midst of the transition from the emergency to the permanent program, the Federal Social Service Division asked for information as to the whereabouts of the Federal students. The replies showed that on August, 1936, a year after the last students had returned from school, 629 out of nearly 1,000 students who had been sent to school held positions in some type of public welfare program. Of this number, 452 were employed in state or county departments of public welfare or emergency relief administrations; 86 were in state or local Divisions of Intake and Certification of the WPA; 51 were employed by the WPA in other capacities; and 40 were employed by the Resettlement Administration.

The Rank and File

The very fact that in the reduction preference was given to persons with professional social work education and experience, meant that the workers most seriously affected by dropping or demotion were those who had been newly recruited for the emergency staffs. Among these workers, in many of the largest cities, unions had been organized which identified the interests of the "relief investigators" with the unemployed and with other organized labor groups. "The Rank and File Movement in Social Work" had begun in a few private agencies before the depression, but, stimulated by adverse working conditions and low relief standards in the emergency agencies, spread to public relief bureaus in New York and Chicago soon after they were first established and later to emergency agencies in other large cities. In 1935 there were 21 of these organized groups, most of them in the large local relief administrations. They campaigned, "often successfully, for standardized salaries, for improved working conditions, and for machinery for the hearing of grievances." They fought for adequate relief standards and "in the course of their development they turned to other groups in the community, including the organized unemployed, for aid in the defense of the joint interests of staff and client." [24]

In November, 1935, representatives of 14 rank and file groups "called upon the Federal Government to continue allocations to the States for relief, to raise relief standards, to assume full responsibility for the transient program and to set up a Federal Department of Social Welfare." There is no question but that both the insecurity of individual relief workers, and the threat to relief standards involved in the policies of Federal and state governments had much influence upon the organizational activity of these social work unions during 1935 and 1936. The staff reductions occasioned group protests and in some cases bitter dissension in the cities where protective associations existed. In two cities the protests took the form of constructive proposals for the reorganization of relief agencies into permanent departments of public welfare.

The growth of the rank and file movement was one of the distinctive personnel developments in the emergency relief administration in certain parts of the country. In the spring of 1936 there were protective organizations in approximately 35

[24] Fisher, Jacob, "Trade Unionism in Social Work," *Social Work Year Book,* 1939. See also Fisher, Jacob, "The Rank and File Movement in Social Work, 1931-1936," published by the New York School of Social Work, 1936.

"The formation of the National Coordinating Committee in February, 1935, was undoubtedly a factor in the tempo of organizational growth that year." *Ibid.*

public agencies and 30 private agencies in 14 states and the District of Columbia, with a total membership of about 12,000.[25] The identification of these workers with the labor movement was a recognition of their position as salaried employees who were allied with wage earners and with them prepared to take collective action in dealing with their employers as the only means of preserving for themselves "their precarious standard of living." [26] Maintaining that "a strong interest in job security and a concern for the larger problems of social work are not mutually exclusive," they brought to the field of social work a realistic, vital, and liberal element which aligned itself much more readily with the programs of social action supported by the leaders of the New Deal emergency agencies than with the essentially conservative interests of professional social workers.

Although the influence of this movement has been important and lasting and its membership large, it existed like most organized movements chiefly in the densely populated and highly industrialized sections of the country and touched very slightly the social work personnel in the rural county agencies in practically three-fourths of the country.

The FERA—A Social Agency

Many of the difficulties which accompanied the development of the rank-and-file movement in the emergency relief administration were inherent in the personnel line-up which included people from such a variety of occupations, professions and fields of work as has been described. The relief administration was a social agency with social objectives and social work leadership in the Federal office. Yet the majority of the administrators of its local units were not social workers, and not many of them came from other professions. They were chiefly persons with business experience or some other form of administrative background who had much to learn about professional standards and about relationships of a social agency with its community, its employees and its clientele. Under the administrators were the supervisory staff, made up, at least

[25] Ibid.

[26] Ibid.; see also for an account of the affiliation of these groups with the national labor organizations.

in the larger cities, of well-equipped professional social workers. At the bottom of the agency structure were the newly recruited investigators who constituted the rank-and-file workers. It is not surprising that difficulties arose under the pressures and strain of administering relief to the unemployed, within an organization where three different types of ideologies and backgrounds had to be directed toward the accomplishment of a common social objective. On the other hand, it is significant that these agencies, in which professional social workers were in the minority and not in control of policies, functioned as social agencies throughout the emergency period and produced a type of social work personnel which could form the nucleus of the public welfare staff in the permanent social security program.

Part Four

THE BEGIN-NING OF A PERMANENT PROGRAM: 1935-1939

Chapter 13

1935—A Year of Transition

∿∿∿∿∿∿∿∿∿∿∿∿∿∿∿∿∿∿∿∿∿∿∿∿∿∿∿∿∿

The FERA was officially liquidated on December 31, 1935.[1] The twelve months preceding this date were a time of transition from Federal Emergency Relief to a Federal Works Program, and to Federal provision on a permanent basis for social security, in the form of categorical public assistance and insurance. The year was marked by a shift from a general relief administration, involving both work and direct relief, in which Federal, state and local governments participated, to a division of responsibility according to categories of need, whereby the Federal Government undertook to provide for the employable unemployed through a direct Federal Works Program, and to assist the states with their responsibility for the "unemployables" by making grants-in-aid for the aged, the blind and children who fulfilled certain eligibility requirements.

These changes were entirely consistent with the original intention of the Federal Administration to attack the unemployment problem by providing work. The FERA was looked upon as a temporary expedient, a stop-gap, to be liquidated as soon as possible. The very fact that the emergency relief structure had been built up and operated independently of the permanent public welfare activities in the states bore out the Administrator's early declaration that the job of the FERA was to "see that the unemployed get relief, not to develop a great social work organization throughout the United States."[2]

The transition from Federal Emergency Relief to the Works

[1] Legally the FERA was continued until June 30, 1938, in order to fulfill commitments made and discharge obligations incurred prior to December 31, 1935, but no new program was initiated after that date. See p. 171, footnote 1.

[2] See Part III, Chapter 7.

Program has already been discussed.[3] This chapter tells the story of the initiation of the permanent program of Federal grants to the states for categorical assistance, and describes the way in which the liquidation of the FERA affected the process of transition in the states from the administration of emergency relief to the establishment of permanent public welfare programs. The more important events and dates in this story are given in the accompanying table.

TABLE 3

President Roosevelt's First Message to Congress on Social Security	June 8, 1934
Committee on Economic Security created by Executive Order No. 6757	June 29, 1934
President's Message to Congress on Work Relief ...	Jan. 4, 1935
Report of Committee on Economic Security submitted to President	Jan. 15, 1935
Report of Committee transmitted to Congress by President	Jan. 17, 1935
Social Security Bill (Economic Security Act[4]) introduced in Congress	Jan. 17, 1935
Emergency Relief Appropriation Bill introduced in Congress	Jan. 23, 1935
Emergency Relief Appropriation Act of 1935, appropriating $4,880,000,000 approved by the President	Apr. 8, 1935
Social Security Act approved by President (no appropriation made by Congress)	Aug. 14, 1935
Social Security Board began operating	Oct. 1, 1935
Federal Emergency Relief Administration final grants to states made	Nov-Dec. 1935
First appropriation made by Congress for purposes of Social Security Act (Public 440, 74th Congress)	Feb. 11, 1936
First Federal grants made to states by Social Security Board for public assistance	Feb. 11, 1936

[3] See Part III, Chapter 7.

[4] The Social Security Bill under the title "Economic Security Act" was introduced in the Senate and House simultaneously on January 17, 1935, as S.1130 and H.R. 4120. Hearings were begun on January 21, before the House Ways and Means Committee and on Jan. 22, before the Senate Finance Committee. Neither bill was reported out of committee but on April 4, a rewritten bill, H.R. 7260, was introduced in the House which later passed both Houses in amended form, and was approved on August 14, 1935, as the "Social Security Act," Public 271, Seventy-fourth Congress.

Federal Planning

The Committee on Economic Security which had been appointed by President Roosevelt in June, 1934, made its report on January 15, 1935. This Committee, as has already been stated,[5] devoted its attention primarily to provisions for unemployment compensation, old age insurance and old age assistance. A recommendation for assistance to dependent children was included in the report, largely at the instance of the Federal Children's Bureau, but material assistance to other persons in need who could not be employed on the proposed work program was definitely not considered by the Committee to be a proper responsibility of the Federal Government. This was clearly stated in their report:

As for the genuine unemployables—or near unemployables—we believe the sound policy is to return the responsibility for their care and guidance to the States. . . . We suggest that the Federal Government shall assume primary responsibility for providing work for those able and willing to work; also that it aid the States in giving pensions to the dependent aged and the families without breadwinners. . . . With the Federal Government carrying so much of the burden for pure unemployment, the State and local governments, we believe, should resume responsibility for relief. . . .

The measures we suggest all seek to segregate clearly distinguishable large groups among those now on relief or on the verge of relief and to apply such differentiated treatment to each group as will give it the greatest practical degree of economic security. We believe that if these measures are adopted, the residual relief problem will have diminished to a point where it will be possible to return primary responsibility for the care of people who cannot work to the State and local governments.

To prevent such a step from resulting in less humane and less intelligent treatment of unfortunate fellow citizens, we strongly recommend that the States substitute for their ancient, out-moded poor laws, modernized public assistance laws, and replace their traditional poor-law administrations by unified and efficient State and local public welfare departments, such as exist in some States and for which there is a nucleus in all states in the Federal emergency relief organizations. . . .

The Federal Emergency Relief Administration is recommended as the most appropriate existing agency for the administration of

[5] See Part III, Chapter 7.

non-contributory old-age pensions and grants in aid to dependent children. If this agency should be abolished, the President should designate the distribution of its work. It is recommended that all social welfare activities of the Federal Government be coordinated and systematized.

In making the recommendation that the "unemployables" be returned to the care of the states and localities, the Committee did not follow the recommendations of their Advisory Committee on Public Employment and Relief which was appointed in November, 1934, by the Secretary of Labor, Chairman of the Committee on Economic Security. This Advisory Committee was made up of representative social workers and leaders in the field of public welfare.[6] They strongly recommended an enlarged work program, without any relief eligibility requirement, for all who needed employment, and Federal grants to the states for general relief for the benefit of all persons in need who could not be provided for on the work program.

On the latter point, the report of the Advisory Committee states that "the social hazards to which millions of persons and families are subjected, are too varied and too complicated to make it safe to assume that work would remove the need. For these, and for any who can work but to whom the employment program does not apply, other security measures will be required. . . . Health problems, the social and personal results of long continued unemployment, lack of adaptability to work available, and other problems would make it unsafe to

[6] Chairman, Miss Dorothy Kahn, Director, Philadelphia County Relief Board. Members: Miss Edith Abbott, Dean, Graduate School of Social Service Administration, University of Chicago; Miss Gay Shepperson, Administrator, Georgia Emergency Relief Administration; Mr. Frank Bane, Director, American Public Welfare Association, Chicago; Miss Elizabeth Wisner, Director, School of Social Work, Tulane University, New Orleans, Louisiana; Father John O'Grady, Executive Secretary, National Catholic Conference of Charities, Washington, D. C.; Dr. Ellen Potter, Director of Medicine, Department of Institutions and Agencies, Trenton, New Jersey; Mr. Prentice Murphy, Executive Secretary, Children's Bureau of Philadelphia; Mr. Jacob Kepecs, Jewish Home-Finding Society of Chicago; Mr. Linton B. Swift, General Director, Family Welfare Association of America; Mr. Walter West, Executive Director, American Association of Social Workers; and Mr. Fred H. Hoehler, Director of Public Welfare, Cincinnati, Ohio.

assume that a work program could absorb more than 50 to 60 percent of the families now on the FERA rolls. If the Federal program should include only old age pensions and mothers' assistance, the needs of a great bulk of the families would be left to the present local poor relief system, the evils of which are well recognized."

The Advisory Committee also recommended that the Federal Government should lend its assistance "to wiping out completely the poor law system of outdoor relief," and voted unanimously in favor of a permanent Public Welfare Department in the Federal Government which would grant funds for public assistance to the states on an equalization basis and co-ordinate Federal, state and local public welfare activities. They believed that this Federal Department should be given authority to require a state to consolidate its welfare functions in one satisfactory permanent department with appropriate local units as a condition to the allocation of Federal funds; and that these funds should be granted not only for unemployment compensation, "but also for old-age pensions, mothers' aid, general home assistance, care of homeless children and adults, and other parts of the unified welfare program." The report added, "The Committee also expresses its belief that no hard and fast line can be drawn between any of these categories." This last statement was inserted out of regard to the opinions of those members of the committee who were opposed to categorical relief. It was intended to emphasize the gaps and overlappings which were bound to be present in any categorical program and the need of general assistance to care for the people who would fall between the categories and the work program; the "employables" who, because of questionable ability or unusual occupations, or because they live in remote or isolated areas, would not fit into the practical work program; the "unemployables" who did not belong to the categories which might be selected for assistance or who, even if they were aged men and women or children under sixteen, could not qualify under the arbitrary definitions which would undoubtedly be set up in the Federal and state laws.

The records of the Committee on Economic Security, then, show in this report just cited that a representative group of social workers and public welfare leaders, including two outstanding emergency relief administrators, recommended Federal grants to the states for general public assistance, and the establishment of a Federal Department of Welfare.

On January 17, two days after the report of the Committee on Economic Security was submitted, President Roosevelt conveyed it to Congress with the following words:

In addressing you on June 8, 1934, I summarized the main objectives of our American Program. Among these was, and is, the security of the men, women and children of the Nation against certain hazards and vicissitudes of life. This purpose is an essential part of our task. In my annual message [7] to you I promised to submit a definite program of action. This I do in the form of a report to me by a Committee on Economic Security, appointed by me for the purpose of surveying the field and of recommending the basis of legislation.

I am gratified with the work of this Committee and of those who have helped it. . . . It is my best judgment that this legislation should be brought forward with a minimum of delay. Federal action is necessary to and conditioned upon the actions of States. Forty-four legislatures are meeting or will meet soon. In order that the necessary State action may be taken promptly, it is important that the Federal government proceed speedily.

Congressional Action

The Social Security Bill which was at that time introduced into Congress contained provisions for grants to states for Old Age Assistance and for Aid to Dependent Children; for Unemployment Compensation Administration; and for Maternal and Child Welfare, including Maternal and Child Health Services, Services for Crippled Children, Child Welfare Services and Vocational Rehabilitation; and for Public Health Work. It also provided for Federal Old-Age Benefits, for taxation connected with both forms of insurance, and for the creation of a new agency, the Social Security Board, under the Department of Labor.[8] The bill assigned to this Board the administrative responsibility for both forms of insurance; to the

[7] January 4, 1935. In this message, President Roosevelt discussed the proposed Federal Works Program and the responsibility of the states for the "unemployables." See Part III, Chapter 7.

[8] The bill embodies X titles, later increased to XI, with the addition of "Grants for Aid to the Blind."

United States Public Health Service the grants for Public Health Work; to the Office of Education in the Department of the Interior the grants for Vocational Rehabilitation; to the Children's Bureau in the Department of Labor the Services for Maternal and Child Health, Crippled Children and Child Welfare and to the Federal Emergency Relief Administration the grants for Old Age Assistance and Aid to Dependent Children.

In spite of the President's request for speedy action on the bill, it did not become law until August 14, 1935. The measure with its numerous and complicated provisions was given protracted hearings in committees of both houses of Congress. During this process, which lasted nearly seven months, many important changes were made in the bill, a number of which had a direct effect upon the administration of the assistance provisions and the future handling of the entire relief program. Also the scope of the bill was broadened by the addition of a title which provided for assistance "to needy individuals who are blind."

The changes made in the assistance titles affected standards of aid and of personnel, the administrative auspices, and the scope of the provision for aid to dependent children.

The bill as originally introduced into Congress provided that grants be made to states "For the purpose of enabling each State to furnish financial assistance assuring as far as practicable under the conditions in such State, a reasonable subsistence compatible with decency and health" to aged individuals and dependent children. Congress cut out the provision for "reasonable subsistence compatible with decency and health." The only indication of standards of aid in the Act as it was finally passed, lay in the maximum amounts on which Federal grants could be computed: The 50 percent Federal reimbursement to the states was not allowed on any payment to an aged person which exceeded $30 in any month and the one-third Federal reimbursement could not be paid on any monthly allowance which exceeded $18 for the first child in a given family and $12 for each additional child in the same home.[9] The expense of payments above these amounts must

[9] See Part IV, Chapter 14.

be carried by the states and localities themselves without any help from the Federal Government.

The bill as introduced provided that grants could be made only after a state had submitted and had had approved by the Federal agency administering the program a plan which provided, among other things, for such methods of administration as are found by the Federal agency "to be necessary for the efficient operation of the plan." This provision was intended to give the Federal agency ample powers to develop in the states adequate standards of administration of which the qualifications of the personnel were undoubtedly the most important. Congress, however, was unwilling that the Federal agency should be in a position to have anything to do with the selection of personnel in the states, and, accordingly, inserted a clause which provided for the approval of "methods of administration (other than those relating to selection, tenure of office, and compensation of personnel). . . ." [10]

Both of the above changes, which so seriously affected both state standards and the powers of the Federal agency, were without question evidences of a distinct reaction, reflected in the attitudes of representatives and senators in Congress, to the authoritative regime of the FERA and its efforts to raise and maintain standards of relief, and to secure sound administration in the states through the appointment of qualified personnel. [11]

The Act finally placed the administration of grants for the aged and children as well as the new provision for aid to the blind under the Social Security Board which was made an independent agency, instead of being put under the Department of Labor as the original bill had provided.

Much of the discussion regarding the future administration of aid to dependent children, especially the testimony presented in the committee hearings, revolved around the fact that the FERA and the Children's Bureau had quite different conceptions of the purpose of the title and of the way in which

[10] An amendment to the Social Security Act in August, 1939, removed the parenthetical clause and provided that each state receiving grants should employ its personnel according to an approved merit system. See Part IV, Chapter 15.

[11] See Part III, Chapters 9, 10 and 11.

it should be administered. These differences are closely related to the changes which were made by Congress in the
definition of a "dependent child" and to the shaping of Federal policy regarding relief, the liquidation of the FERA and
the future provision for the care of many of the "unemployables."

The report of the Committee on Economic Security designated the FERA "as the most appropriate existing agency for
the administration of non-contributory old-age pensions and
grants in aid to dependent children," and also recommended
that "all social welfare activities of the Federal Government
be coordinated and systematized." Whatever may have been
the thinking of the Committee, there was undoubtedly a definite intention on the part of the Federal Administration early
in 1935 to try out the attitude of Congress towards the continuation of the FERA by asking that it be given responsibility for part of the new permanent welfare program.

Since the FERA was designated in the original bill to administer aid to the aged and to dependent children, its Federal staff were asked by the Committee to prepare drafts of
the titles to be incorporated in the bill. The definition of dependent children which was proposed by the FERA at this
time reflects the policy of the Federal Administration and its
plans for the future handling of the relief problem:

As used in this title, "dependent children" shall mean children under
the age of sixteen in their own homes, in which there is no adult
person, other than one needed to care for the child or children, who
is able to work and provide the family with a reasonable subsistence
compatible with decency and health.

This definition not only provided for a "decency and health"
standard, but placed the determination of eligibility upon a
consideration of the needs of the family as a whole and not of
the individual child. It put the burden of proof upon the
actual provision of subsistence and not upon the presence or
absence of any member of the family or upon any physical
or mental disability which prevented support and which might
be difficult to define and to diagnose.

Moreover this definition, under a liberal interpretation,

would have provided aid within the limits of available funds to practically every family in need in which there was a child under sixteen, subject only to the one-year residence requirement in another section of the Act. "Able to work" might have been interpreted to mean not only persons who were incapacitated, but those who could not find employment either in private industry or on the public work program. In other words the FERA envisaged grants-in-aid under such a definition as providing for so large a majority of the "unemployables" that the remainder might without hardship be left to the states and localities. "Aid to Dependent Children" as conceived by the FERA meant general relief or assistance on a family basis to all families having children under sixteen.[12]

By the time the bill was introduced into Congress the definition had been changed by the Committee, in consultation with the FERA, but the essential features remained which permitted the broadest type of program.[13]

When the Social Security Bill became law on August 14, 1935, the definition contained the addition which is italicized in the following quotation:

The term "dependent child" means a child under the age of sixteen *who has been deprived of parental support or care by reason of the death, continued absence from the home, or physical or mental incapacity of a parent, and* who is living with his father, mother, grandfather, grandmother, brother, sister, stepfather, stepmother, stepbrother, stepsister, uncle or aunt, in a place of residence maintained by one or more of such relatives as his or their own home.

---

[12] "There are at the moment [1934] over 7,400,000 children under 16 years of age on the relief rolls." . . . "Among these children most especial attention must be given to the children deprived of a father's support usually designated as the objects of mothers' aid or mothers' pension laws, of whom there are now above 700,000 on relief lists." From the Report to the President of the Committee on Economic Security, U. S. Gov't Printing Office, 1935.

[13] The subsistence standard was put in another section and the definition merely stated the age and defined "own home" in terms of the relatives with whom a child might live in order to be eligible: "The term 'dependent child' means a child under the age of sixteen who is living with his father, mother, grandfather, grandmother, brother, sister, stepfather, stepmother, stepbrother, stepsister, uncle, or aunt, in a place of residence maintained by one or more of such relatives as his or their own home."

This addition which specified reasons of dependency in terms of the death, absence, or incapacity of a parent, definitely put the measure in the category of Mothers' Aid legislation, which in the early years of its development in the states was often appropriately called "Widows' Aid." [14] Obviously the new clause limited the scope of the title drastically and pointed to its administration as an expansion and perpetuation of the Mothers' Aid program which had begun in 1911. The change in the definition as well as a movement to give the administrative responsibility to the Children's Bureau was influenced by leaders in the child welfare field who had played an important part in the early Mothers' Aid movement in the states and saw the Federal social security program as an opportunity to strengthen and enlarge the existing state programs.[15]

The child welfare leaders argued that Mothers' Aid had succeeded in segregating for special care and assistance in their own homes a group of children who would have otherwise been left to the mercies of poor relief officials or placed in institutions. They believed that the standards of administration attained under the Mothers' Aid program should be capitalized by continuing it, on a somewhat broader basis, strengthened by Federal grants, but still within the statutory system which arbitrarily selected one group, or category, out of all the people in need, for special care. They believed that the broader administration of this title, which the FERA had planned to administer entirely outside the 45 state Mothers' Aid laws then on the statute books, would necessarily pull down the carefully built standards of the Mothers' Aid program and virtually result in giving children aid which was little better than local poor relief. They questioned the ability of the FERA to maintain local standards in view of the fact that local emergency relief units were not indigenous and had not yet been integrated with the permanent public welfare structure. In other words they were inclined to discount the

[14] See Part I, Chapter 1.
[15] See p. 38 for reference to the important part played earlier by the Federal Children's Bureau in developing Mothers' Aid programs in the states. For excerpts from the Hearings on the Act before the Committees of the Senate and House, see Appendix M.

emergency program and to see the future of Mothers' Aid against the background of local poor relief, much as it had appeared to the careful observer during the 1920's. They were not willing to recognize the widespread changes which had taken place under the FERA.

On the other hand the FERA saw an opportunity to capitalize the recent gains in standards of relief and administration [16] and to use the emergency structure to bridge over the transition period until the states could establish permanent public welfare programs to administer the public assistance titles of the Social Security Act.

These were the possibilities under the terms of the Social Security Bill as it was introduced in Congress and as President Roosevelt made the now famous announcement of January, 1935, that the Federal Government "must quit this business of relief." Relief for the able-bodied unemployed was to be given up in favor of a work program. Emergency relief for the "unemployables" was to be given up in favor of a permanent system of Federal grants-in-aid for public assistance to certain selected groups or categories on the broad basis described above. These new Federal grants would have met one-third to one-half of practically all of the states' expenditures for relief and assistance, if Congress had passed the Social Security Bill in the form in which it was introduced. The choice lay between building on the Mothers' Aid program which had changed very little since pre-depression days, and building a general public assistance program directly out of the current, realistic emergency relief experience with all its assets and liabilities. Congress decided upon Mothers' Aid and showed in unmistakable terms their adverse reaction to emergency relief. For this reason the Administration had no choice but to liquidate the FERA.

The Final Emergency Relief Grants to the States

The Emergency Relief Appropriation Act of 1935, which had been introduced in Congress in January about ten days prior to the introduction of the Social Security Act, was approved on April 8th. This measure appropriated $4,880,000,-

[16] See Part III, Chapter 10.

000, "to provide relief, work relief and to increase employment by providing for useful projects. . . ."[17] This Act, which was the authority for the initiation of the Federal Works Program, also allowed for relief purposes "such part of the appropriation made herein as the President may deem necessary for continuing relief as authorized under the Federal Emergency Relief Act of 1933, as amended. . . ."

Under the authority of this Act the President allocated to the FERA a total of $938,530,085, which was used for relief expenditures during the transfer of employable persons on the relief rolls to the Works Program and for the expenses incurred in liquidating the program. In November and December final relief grants were made to the states.[18]

Congress decided early in the year against giving to the FERA responsibility for the administration of any part of the Social Security Act. The staff of the relief administration had, therefore, approximately eight months in which to transfer their responsibilities to the Works Program or to the states and localities and to carry out an orderly liquidation of the huge emergency program.

The states needed three kinds of help: money to supplement state and local funds for relief to the "unemployables" and to the "employables" who were not assigned to project jobs on the Works Program: advice and financial assistance in saving at least a nucleus of their social work staffs, in the face of drastic administrative cuts, until their own legislatures and Federal Social Security funds could come to the rescue: help in planning and making the legislative and organizational moves which were advisable during the transition period in order to further the development of permanent state departments of public welfare under which relief, categorical assistance and child welfare functions might all be integrated at some later time.

[17] See Part III, Chapter 7.

[18] Only relatively small grants were made during the first half of 1936 to meet commitments made before the beginning of that year. After July 1, 1936, no grants of $100,000 or more were made to states by the FERA. See FERA Monthly Report, May and June, 1936, and testimony of Harry L. Hopkins in Hearings before House Committee on First Deficiency Appropriation Bill for 1937, p. 143.

During the summer and early fall of 1935, it was evident that the states and localities were providing less and less money for relief. Between June and November, 1935, state and local monthly expenditures dropped from over $42,000,-000 to $28,000,000. State funds decreased 19 percent and local funds 45 percent. At the same time estimates made by the FERA showed an increasing number of people who would probably need relief in the winter of 1936, even after the Works Program had put its maximum load of 3,500,000 to work. On the basis of estimates made in December only 7 states were expected to have adequate funds to care for their share of the relief load; 5 others were doubtful; while the remaining 36 states and the District of Columbia were listed as not having sufficient funds.

Although the FERA secured data and made plans in the summer of 1935 to make final grants to the states which would be large enough to supplement their funds for relief and administrative expenditures until July 1, 1936, the actual grants, when they were made in November and December, were much smaller than expected and in some cases represented only a fraction of the early estimates. The demands of the Works Program upon the $4,880,000,000 appropriated by Congress in April were of such magnitude that a smaller amount than had been anticipated was allocated to the FERA to be used for this purpose.

In addition to the demands of the Works Program, the sum of $20,000,000 was allocated from this appropriation to the Resettlement Administration to be used for direct relief. This fund was to be disbursed during the first half of 1936 in the form of emergency relief benefits to farmers who were to be transferred from the rolls of the local emergency relief administrations to the care of the Resettlement Administration. This action was designed to relieve the Federal Works Program and state relief funds of the necessity of caring for approximately 150,000 needy farm families.

The transfer to the Resettlement Administration began in November and by the end of December was nearly completed. It was impossible, however, for the states to begin at the same time to make transfers from the relief rolls to agencies where benefits were provided for the aged, the blind, and dependent children through the Social Security program because no funds were appropriated by Congress for the purposes of the Social Security Act until February 11, 1936, although the Act itself was approved on August 14, 1935.[19]

In spite of the gaps in the program occasioned by this delay, and in spite of the difficulties attendant upon the cessation of relief grants to the states and the pressures to transfer over 3,000,000 people to the projects of the WPA, the social workers in the Federal and state Social Service Divisions of the FERA were determined to use every means in their power to further the sound development of permanent public welfare departments in the states.[20]   This they were in a strategic position to do because of the unusually fine relationship which the FERA field staff had established with the states.[21]   The experience which they had acquired in the emergency program, their knowledge of public welfare and social work principles and practice and of community and organization problems constituted the best possible preparation for handling a task which required the utmost skill.   They had the confidence of state officials, and they had acquired much pertinent information about agencies, financial resources, relief needs, state legislation and other matters which bore directly on the difficult problems involved in helping the states through this transition period until the Social Security program could get under way.

The interest of the FERA in the development of state public welfare programs is evident from the following letter written by Mr. Hopkins to one of the State Administrators:

I have recently made available $————— to your state for relief purposes. This is to be regarded as the final Federal relief grant to

[19] Failure to appropriate funds was due to the filibuster by Senator Huey Long of Louisiana which prevented a vote on the Deficiency Appropriations Bill before the time fixed by Congress for adjournment.

[20] The Federal Social Service staff, including the Regional Social Workers (see Part III, Chapter 9) became the Division of Intake and Certification of the WPA when that agency was set up in May, 1935: they, therefore, carried a double responsibility until the liquidation of the FERA on December 31, 1935: the staffs of the state WPA Divisions of Intake and Certification were selected from the Social Service Divisions of the state ERA's.

[21] See Part III, Chapter 9.

your state and shall be expended in such a way as to permit the orderly liquidation of the relief administration.

I am asking that you immediately prepare a plan for the expenditure of this money, submitting it to the field representative and social worker for consideration and approval. In drawing up this plan you are urged to bear in mind the necessity for providing a continuing machinery for intake and certification for the work program and the advantages of integrating this function into the permanent public welfare organization of the state. Good public welfare standards are essential in both state and local administrative units and to whatever extent the Federal Emergency Relief Administration has been of assistance in establishing them, I should like to see them continue. Through careful planning, I feel confident that it will be possible to build up a permanent welfare and relief service which will insure provisions for dealing with your state and local problems. . . .

I need not remind you, I am sure, that the primary consideration in this process of liquidation is the immediate and eventual welfare of the relief clients. It is the intent of the President to discontinue relief in favor of employment for this group. It is our responsibility to bring about this transition in a way which will cause suffering to no one and contribute to the successful development of the work program and an adequate state or local program for those persons not eligible for work.

The position taken in this letter in regard to public welfare is entirely consistent with an earlier memorandum which Mr. Hopkins sent, under date of July 24, 1935, to the Field Representatives and Regional Social Workers, which said in part:

Persons unable to work and dependent upon public assistance will be the responsibility of the states and localities. This administration will be prepared to furnish advice and assistance to the states in planning and putting into effect permanent public welfare programs suited to their conditions and resources. This is in keeping with the provisions made for Federal public assistance under the Social Security bill now before Congress.[22]

This memorandum was followed by another from Mr. Aubrey Williams, Assistant Administrator, which included this statement:

We should like to see the transfer from Federal Emergency Relief to state and local responsibility of the cases not cared for by the

[22] FERA 5995, July 24, 1935.

Works Progress Administration consummated in such a manner that there shall be no unnecessary suffering. This supplements our expressed desire that efficient intake procedure be continued.

It is clear that this can only be accomplished if local units retain an adequate number of trained social workers. We look to you to impress this upon state executives and administrators. Our final appropriations to states are being made with this purpose in view, so that during the transitional period present administrative standards may be continued.

Largely because of the entire inadequacy of state and local funds and the small final Federal grants, there was a great deal of suffering during the winter of 1936. The average benefits per family showed a marked decrease, and hundreds of thousands of applications for relief were refused because of lack of funds to provide even minimum food allowances.

In the face of this great inadequacy the Regional Social Workers of the FERA adhered to the policy of recommending that the states use their final Federal grants for administrative purposes, in order to hold the best of their social workers through the transition period. Most of these grants were less than $500,000. This amount, if spent for relief, would have lasted only a short time, a week perhaps, or a month if the case load was small. The value of having somewhat more adequate relief in a state for this limited time was slight compared to the advantage of retaining the nucleus of a good social work staff which would serve as the foundation for sound standards of public welfare administration for years to come.[23]

There was an immediate value to the WPA and a number of other Federal agencies in retaining the social work staffs of the state and local relief administrations. They were needed not only to certify the eligibility of employable relief recipients to the Works Program but they performed the same service for the NYA and to some extent for the RA. They were also responsible for the selection of all of the boys who were sent to the camps of the CCC and for approving lists of families who were to receive food and other surpluses from the Federal Surplus Commodities Corporation. It would have been to the advantage of these Federal agencies if greater effort and

[23] See Part III, Chapter 12.

more money had been devoted to retaining these staffs upon whose services their programs were so dependent.

As a matter of fact several of the states [24] promptly effected a complete liquidation of their Emergency Relief Administrations with no immediate provision for another agency to administer relief or render service to the Federal agencies. The social work staffs were allowed to scatter and the public welfare departments which were set up later found it necessary to start all over again with new personnel. In at least one state where this happened the final Federal grant was held during the interim and used for the initial administrative expenses of the new permanent department.

State Agencies in Transition

Each state presented a somewhat different picture during this difficult first stage of transition from emergency relief to public welfare in the winter and spring of 1936. It is impossible, therefore, to make an exact classification of the organization changes which took place, but the states may be grouped roughly under three general headings.

In 17 states and the District of Columbia, Departments of Public Welfare assumed at least part of the responsibilities of the former Emergency Relief Administrations, using FERA funds from the final grants and employing the reduced state emergency relief staffs.[25] These agencies carried a variety of names [26] and differed somewhat in their functions, but they all were charged with either administrative or supervisory responsibility for relief and assistance to people in need and they looked forward to participation in the Federal Social Security program. Several of these states were ready to submit plans and apply for Social Security funds even before they were available in February, 1936.[27]

[24] See p. 319 below.

[25] Alabama, Arizona, Arkansas, Florida, Maryland, New Mexico, North Carolina, North Dakota, Oklahoma, Oregon, South Carolina, South Dakota, Tennessee, Utah, Washington, Wisconsin and Wyoming.

[26] For example, the Alabama Department of Public Welfare; the New Mexico Relief and Security Authority; and the Oregon State Relief Committee.

[27] In Alabama, the new Department of Public Welfare was formed by the integration of the ERA with the long established State Child Welfare

The second group comprised 14 states in which the ERA was continued as an independent agency using chiefly funds which were available within the states. In a number of these states it was later liquidated and the responsibility for general relief was then left entirely to the local communities to be administered by them according to standards and methods which varied from traditional poor relief practices in most of the rural counties to good public welfare administration in many of the urban centers. Other states in this group continued their emergency administrations until they could be integrated with the established public welfare agencies, or until the state legislatures were prepared to authorize new agencies to administer Federal and state funds under the Social Security Act.[28]

In the third group there were 17 states in each of which the ERA was liquidated promptly and no state agency continued to be responsible for the administration of general relief. In most of these states part of the final Federal grant was used to hold a carefully selected group of social workers under the supervision of the state WPA to certify the eligibility of relief recipients to the Works Program and other Federal agencies or to supervise this certification where it was done by the local relief officials. These social workers were employed later in several of the states by the agencies created or reorganized to administer the Social Security assistance program. In the

Department. In North Carolina the permanent State Department was given part of the final Federal relief grant with which to employ the best part of the social work staff of the ERA which was in the process of liquidation. The social work staff was retained by the state department in preparation for the administration of public assistance under the Social Security Act. In Maryland the ERA had throughout the emergency relief program operated as part of the State Board of Aid and Charities and that agency merely adapted its functions to the new program. In all of the other states in this group new public welfare agencies were established either by legislation or by executive order (South Carolina, Tennessee and Wisconsin).

[28] The ERA's were later liquidated in Colorado, Connecticut, Illinois (deprived of supervisory powers), Kansas, Nebraska, New Jersey: Integrated with public welfare agencies in New York, Pennsylvania: new agencies set up in Iowa, Montana, West Virginia; partial integration in Minnesota. Michigan and California also belong in this group but do not fall into any of these subclassifications.

other states of this group these emergency staffs could not be retained long enough to be useful to the new program, or for some other reason were not acceptable to the new agencies.[29]

A careful analysis of each one of these state situations would undoubtedly show that every stage of development or of retrogression was conditioned not only by the recent experience with emergency relief and by Federal plans for Social Security, but by the older and more deep-seated attitudes and traditions of which so much has already been said. These conservative influences were not only important factors in every local community but they affected the thinking and planning in state offices as well. The majority of the legislators in most of the states come from small communities and represent rural constituents, and many governors and other important state officials are small town citizens. Somewhere in the three thousand-odd counties of the country every degree of local autonomy and every variety of practice in the care of the poor was represented before the depression. The impact of the emergency and relief programs resulted in every kind of attitude toward state and Federal governments, and toward social work. The circumstances under which each state and county made and developed its first acquaintance with social work and public relief administration, and the way in which the social work job was done were vital factors in the changes which took place in state and local programs, not only during this transition but through the following years. The direct effect of strong social work leadership and of sound public welfare developments in earlier years can be seen in the progress made in many of the states during this period.[30]

The problem of the far West and the South in establishing permanent local welfare units was less serious than that of the states in the East and the Middle West. The southern and

[29] States in which a number of the ERA social workers were taken over by the new agencies: Georgia, Nevada, New Hampshire, Virginia, Kentucky, Missouri, Indiana, Louisiana. Other states in this group are: Delaware, Idaho, Maine, Massachusetts, Mississippi, Ohio, Rhode Island, Texas and Vermont.

[30] Alabama established its new department in 1935, building upon the state-wide county unit organization which was already well established in 1929. See Part I, Chapter 1.

western states had less local relief autonomy, almost no township jurisdiction, and fewer traditions regarding relief to the poor. The Elizabethan poor law had taken deep root in the East where local autonomy was strong and counties as well as townships and towns were accustomed to care for their own and make their own rules. The states in the Middle West had followed the eastern pattern with a combination of county and township responsibility for care of the poor which staunchly resisted state domination. These are a few of the reasons why states like Washington and Oregon were able to effect a fairly smooth transfer from the emergency to the permanent basis, while Pennsylvania and New York, in spite of their strong leadership and long public welfare history, had so many social and psychological obstacles to overcome in achieving the same objective. These factors also help to explain the utter confusion into which Minnesota, Wisconsin and Michigan were thrown; the almost complete reversion to local poor relief of New Jersey, Ohio and Illinois; and the little change which has taken place in local relief in New England. Most of these states had city and county social agencies of long standing. Several of them had developed state agencies with responsibilities for Mothers' Aid and general child welfare. Yet southern and western states with only a fraction of this experience set up integrated departments of public welfare within a fairly short time after the liquidation of FERA.

One of the greatest difficulties in the way of sound organization was political interference with legislation and with standards of personnel. This was to be expected in a program which was to a great extent new to government officials and which involved the expenditure of such huge sums of money. Possibly the development of public welfare during the transition period was not affected adversely by political maneuvering more than are other large government agencies at the time of their inception. The fact remains that much of the confusion and many of the backward steps taken in state and local administration were due to political pressures.

State Legislation

An unprecedented amount of state legislation on matters connected with relief, public welfare and social security was passed during 1935. Forty-four legislatures held regular sessions; sixteen convened in special sessions. The Louisiana legislature met four times and several others held three sessions apiece. Virginia was the only state which did not convene its legislature during the year.[31] Stimulated by the introduction in Congress of the Social Security Bill and by the warning that Federal relief would be discontinued and that the states would be held responsible for the care of "unemployables," legislation was drafted hurriedly in many cases, and in a number of instances premature action was taken which later had to be rescinded. These were measures which anticipated the passage of the Social Security Act by Congress and were based on specific provisions of the bill which were changed before the Act was approved. Other state laws passed at that time contained general provisions which authorized the state authorities to take advantage of the Federal Act by meeting the conditions which it established, subject to later confirmation by the state legislature.

Laws were passed providing for the creation or reorganization of state and county public welfare agencies; for state participation in old age assistance and aid to dependent children; for the handicapped and for child welfare; and for changes in poor relief and settlement laws.[32] Model laws and suggestions for amendments to state laws which would conform to the Federal Act were issued by the staff of the Committee on Economic Security, which also gave advice to state officials on specific measures. This service concerned only old age assistance and unemployment compensation. The Children's Bureau advised the states on maternal and child welfare and the American Public Welfare Association co-operated with the field staff of the FERA in consulting with state officials regarding plans for permanent public welfare programs.[33]

[31] Stevenson and Posanski, *Digest of Social Welfare Legislation, 1935.* American Public Welfare Association, Chicago.

[32] See Part I, Chapter 1. Other social welfare legislation, not directly in the field of public welfare organization, relief and categorical assistance, concerned Public Works, Employment Service, Unemployment Compensation, Conservation Work, Rural Rehabilitation and Planning Boards. See Stevenson and Posanski, *op. cit.*

[33] In February, 1935, the American Public Welfare Association issued a statement of methods and principles of public welfare organization for

Throughout the period of emergency relief the American Public Welfare Association, while working closely with the RFC and the FERA, had been constantly and consistently building, in all their contacts with Federal, state and local agencies, toward permanent public welfare administration. As their support and assistance had been invaluable in the crucial fight of 1932-33 for Federal relief, so now at another crucial period in public welfare history this Association made a distinguished contribution in its work of interpretation, advice and assistance to governors and legislatures and to state welfare commissions; by the publication of a monthly news sheet of legislative digests, and of suggested state legislation for Social Security; and the collection and circulation of data on methods, policies, procedures and other material needed by the agencies which were preparing to administer Social Security benefits. In October, 1935, two months after the Social Security Act became law, Mr. Frank Bane who had been Director of the American Public Welfare Association since the year following its organization in 1930 [34] was appointed Executive Director of the Federal Social Security Board.[35]

State and Local Responsibility in the New Program

The passage of the Federal Emergency Relief Act in 1933 had marked the first assumption of responsibility for relief by the Federal Government. The passage of the Social Security Act two years later was no less epoch-making in that it established permanent Federal responsibility for public assistance to at least a part of the population and moreover extended that responsibility to social insurance and certain forms of service, both remedial and preventive.

The Act discarded the discretionary and equalization basis for grants to the states which had been used in the emergency program, and returned to the accepted and tried Federal practice of grants-in-aid on a "matching basis," that is, in amounts

the use of the states in shaping legislation and developing their agencies. *Public Welfare Organization.* Multigraphed.

[34] See Part II, Chapter 4.

[35] On August 23, the Senate ratified the appointment of John G. Winant, Chairman; Vincent M. Miles and Arthur J. Altmeyer as the three members of the Social Security Board.

equal to a fixed percentage of expenditures made by the states. The Social Security Board was given the right to withhold Federal grants under certain conditions but its powers of direct supervision of state programs was strictly limited, particularly in regard to the selection of personnel.

The states were relieved by the Federal Works Program of the care of the majority of the able-bodied unemployed who were in need. As a result between June, 1935, and March, 1936, the direct relief load throughout the country dropped from 4,500,000 to 2,000,000 cases. Relatively few states were ready to take advantage of Social Security assistance grants when they became available in February, 1936. By June 42 states [36] and the District of Columbia were receiving grants under one or more of the assistance titles. Due largely to this fact and to seasonal employment, the general relief load was reduced to one million and a half, or approximately six million individuals, by the middle of the year. As had been predicted, the funds of the states and localities were entirely inadequate. Many state legislatures made appropriations for the new public assistance benefits in order to secure the Federal matching grants rather than spend the money on general relief which drew no Federal funds to the states.

After the authoritative, centralized administration of Federal relief, the new program of 1936 was essentially one of state and local responsibility and initiative. Not only in the realm of general relief but in that of Social Security assistance was this true. The original decision as to participation in this part of the Social Security program was left to the states which also determined the extent of the program over a wide range in matters concerning administration and eligibility not defined by the Federal Act. Every county must participate if Federal funds were to be used in the state at all, but the extent to which each county should furnish funds was a matter for state or local decision.

This return of jurisdiction over the welfare of people in need to local communities and to the representatives of local citizens who sat in state legislatures was indicative of the strength of the theory of local responsibility and of the intense regard

[36] See First Annual Report of the Social Security Board, 1936, also Part IV, Chapter 14.

for local perogatives which prevailed throughout the country. The pendulum had swung far in the direction of Federal power under the pressures of the emergency. It was not unexpected or unreasonable that, when the emergency was declared at an end, it should swing in reaction rather far towards the opposite pole. In spite of the suffering due to inadequate funds, in spite of the losses in personnel and much administrative confusion, this swing of the pendulum to local control had certain positive values.

During the two years and a half of the Federal Emergency Relief Administration it had been practically impossible to use local boards or committees and other usual devices for the encouragement of local participation and understanding. The local and state activities of the FERA might be considered a kind of demonstration of certain values on the one hand and things to be avoided on the other. But, at best, the ordinary local emergency relief administration did not become truly fixed. This is the crux of the matter, for unless a program, and particularly a public welfare program, really takes root in a local community it will not endure.

The period of transition, after the liquidation of the FERA at the end of 1935, stands out as a time of confusion and near chaos in the history of public relief. It was a time of uncertainty, insecurity and even terror for the relief client who could not get a work relief job and who had no sure niche in the developing categorical programs. Suffering was acute in too many sections of the country. Funds for general relief were inadequate or entirely lacking in state after state.

Administratively the transition period was, at best, a difficult time of testing the ability of state governments and local communities to assimilate and use whatever values they might have found in their experience with emergency relief. It was a test of the extent to which they were willing to go in providing assistance for their own people, in developing strong agencies and in adopting good standards, and as a rule, the public welfare agencies produced by this transition experience showed a strength and a quality of endurance which carried them through many temporary upheavals in the years that followed.

PUBLIC RELIEF

Summary

The year of transition ended with the primary responsibility for direct relief and categorical assistance centered in the states. The Federal Government carried the major costs of work relief for a large number of the employable people who were in need; was committed to make grants to the states for categorical assistance; and continued to give direct relief in the form of emergency benefits to farmers under the Resettlement Administration and surplus food which was distributed to the states by the Federal Surplus Commodities Corporation. The states and localities were struggling with the problems involved in providing funds for general relief and making the organizational changes and financial provisions necessary for participation in the Social Security program.

Chapter 14

Financial and Administrative Developments

∽∽∽∽∽∽∽∽∽∽∽∽∽∽∽∽∽∽∽∽∽∽∽∽∽∽∽∽∽∽∽∽∽∽∽∽

During the four years which followed the inauguration of the Social Security program and the liquidation of the Federal Emergency Relief Administration, no fundamental changes were made in the governmental system for assistance to people in need which had been established by Congress in 1935. It will be sufficient, therefore, to point out the more important developments of this period, particularly those which have to do with the financial responsibilities assumed by government; the organization of public welfare agencies for the administration of relief and categorical assistance; methods of giving aid to people in need; standards of aid and of personnel; and the relationship of governmental programs to the profession of social work and to the activities of private social agencies.

THE NUMBER OF PEOPLE AIDED AND THE COST

Categorical Assistance Under the Social Security Act

The eleven titles of the Social Security Act provided for three general types of Federal aid: insurance; assistance to persons in need; and health and welfare services. For one program, Old-Age Insurance, the Federal Government assumed sole financial and administrative responsibility. The other titles provided Federal grants to state agencies. The Act established a new independent Federal agency, the Social Security Board, to be responsible for "the Federal aspects of the five programs under which, in one way or another, cash payments are made to individuals. These are old age insurance, unemployment compensation, and public assistance to the needy aged, the needy blind, and dependent children. The remaining provisions, in which the purpose is to promote public health and welfare services, are directed by Federal agencies already operating in these fields." [1]

Public assistance was the first part of the Act to get under way, probably because it offered an opportunity to the states to expand their existing provisions for these categories and also to secure Federal funds which would replace at least partially the Federal emergency relief grants which had ceased.[2] Many states had enacted enabling legislation even before the Federal Act was approved in August, 1935. During that year 35 states passed new legislation or revised existing statutes relating to public assistance, with the intention of meeting the conditions laid down in the Federal Act.

States wishing to take advantage of the public assistance grants were required to take the initiative in appropriating funds and in submitting plans for the operation of the program in question which would meet the conditions of the Federal Act and the approval of the Social Security Board.[3] Grants from Federal funds were to equal one-half the expenditures made in the state for old age assistance and for aid to the blind, and one-third of the expenditures for aid to dependent children.[4]

In December, 1935, state plans began coming in to the Social Security Board. By February 11, 1936, when the first funds were made available by Congress, 39 plans had been approved by the Board for one or more forms of assistance in 20 different states and the District of Columbia.[5] The first

[1] Bane, Frank, "The Social Security Board and State Organizations," *Annals* of the American Academy of Political and Social Science, March, 1939, p. 137.

[2] See Part I, Chapter 1, and Part IV, Chapter 13.

[3] The Act provided that a state which was prevented by its constitution from providing funds for assistance need not meet this condition before July 1, 1937.

[4] In 1939 Congress amended the Act, effective January 1, 1940, to provide from Federal funds one-half of the expenditures for children.

[5] Old-age assistance in 17 states; blind assistance in 10 states; aid to dependent children in 9 states. Plans for all three forms of assistance were approved for Idaho, Maine, Mississippi, Nebraska, New Hampshire, Wisconsin, Wyoming and the District of Columbia.

Since three plans may be approved for each of the 48 states and the

CHART III

Payments to recipients of mothers' aid and aid to dependent children from Federal funds and from state and local funds in the continental United States, 1932-38 (see Table 4).

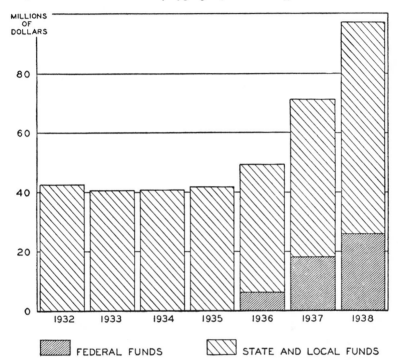

FEDERAL FUNDS   STATE AND LOCAL FUNDS

Source: Bucklin, Dorothy R., "Public Aid for the Care of Dependent Children in Their Own Homes," *Social Security Bulletin*, Vol. 2, No. 4, April, 1939.

grants were made to the states on the same day on which the Federal appropriation was made. By December 15 of that year, one hundred plans had been approved in 43 states. On June 30, 1939, 135 plans were in operation in 51 jurisdictions.[6]

District of Columbia, Alaska and Hawaii, the total number of possible plans is 153. On June 30, 1937, 115 plans had been approved.

[6] On June 30, 1939, plans were not in operation for aid to dependent children in Alaska, Connecticut, Illinois, Iowa, Kentucky, Mississippi, Nevada, South Dakota and Texas; for aid to the blind in Alaska, Dela-

TABLE 4

Mothers' Aid and Aid to Dependent Children in the Continental United States, by Years, 1932-38

Year	Number of recipients [1]		Number of children in whose behalf payments were made per 1,000 estimated population under 16 years of age [2]	Payments to recipients [3] (in thousands)			Median amount per inhabitant [4]
	Families	Children		Total	From Federal funds	From state and local funds	
1932	113,587	289,271	5	$42,573	......	$42,573	$0.27
1933	111,800	282,752	5	40,504	......	40,504	.27
1934	113,009	279,792	5	40,686	......	40,686	.26
1935	116,817	285,717	8	41,727	......	41,727	.26
1936	160,171	401,359	14	49,370	$ 6,364	43,006	.36
1937	227,869	564,536	16	71,260	18,140	53,120	.59
1938	279,657	684,282	20	97,355	25,965	71,390	.76

[1] Figures were either reported to or estimated by the Social Security Board.
[2] Median for states making payments. (See Table 1, pp. 30-31.)
[3] Exclusive of administrative expense.
[4] Median for states making payments.
[5] Not computed, because estimates of population under age 16 are not available.

Source: Bucklin, Dorothy R., "Public Aid for the Care of Dependent Children in Their Own Homes," *Social Security Bulletin*, Vol. 2, No. 4, April, 1939.

The rapid increase in the total assistance paid to beneficiaries can be plainly seen in the expenditures which were made
from month to month. Federal, state and local funds spent
in February, 1936, in states with plans approved by the Social
Security Board, amounted to slightly more than $4,600,000,
for all three forms of assistance. In May of that year this
sum had doubled and by October it had doubled again. In
July, 1939, expenditures had increased to between ten and
eleven times the amount spent in February, 1936, with the
result that ten times as much money was going to eight times
as many old-age beneficiaries; fifteen times as much money
to ten times as many dependent children; and expenditures
and recipients of aid to the blind had both multiplied by four.
In three years and eleven months, from February, 1936,
through December, 1939, the combined expenditures of all
three areas of government for these special types of public
assistance amounted to approximately $1,600,000,000.

The overwhelming preponderance of old-age assistance in
expenditures and in numbers of recipients as well as the fact
that all of the 51 jurisdictions have taken advantage of this
part of the Federal Social Security program are evidence of
the widespread interest throughout the country in problems
of old-age security. This interest, stimulated by the "Town-
send Plan" and other similar proposals, took definite form in
several states where efforts were concentrated "upon developing and expanding old-age assistance while giving relatively
little attention to dependent children, the blind, or other groups
in need of public aid." [7] As a result there have been marked
differences in the rate of development of these programs. "In
States which administered Federal Funds for these purposes
throughout the fiscal year, 1938-39, the lowest expenditures
per habitant for the three special types of public assistance
were: for old-age assistance, 62 cents per inhabitant in Alabama; for aid to dependent children, 20 cents per inhabitant
in Arkansas; and for aid to the blind, 2 cents per inhabitant in
Alabama." [8]

ware, Illinois, Kentucky, Missouri, Nevada, Pennsylvania, Rhode Island
and Texas. Plans for old-age assistance have been approved in all 51
jurisdictions since July, 1938.

[7] Third Annual Report of the Social Security Board, 1938, p. 99.

[8] Fourth Annual Report of the Social Security Board, 1939, p. 117.

TABLE 5

Special Types of Public Assistance in States with Plans Approved by the Social Security Board, February, 1936, and December, 1939 [1]

Year and month	Old-age assistance		Aid to dependent children		Aid to the blind	
	Amount of obligations	Number of recipients	Amount of obligations [2]	Number of recipients (children)	Amount of obligations [2]	Number of recipients
February, 1936	$ 3,752,000	247,000	$ 605,000	69,000	$ 287,000	12,000
December, 1939	36,973,000	1,912,000	9,708,000	728,000	1,070,000	46,000

[1] Figures from the *Social Security Bulletin*, Volume 3, No. 2 (February, 1940); include relatively small numbers of cases eligible under the state laws for which no Federal funds may be expended and payments to individuals in excess of amounts which can be matched from Federal funds. Figures are excluded for states not administering Federal funds.

[2] From Federal, state and local funds; excludes cost of administration and of hospitalization and burials.

The recommendation of the Social Security Board that Congress increase the proportion of Federal aid to dependent children from one-third to one-half of the expenditures in the states was prompted not only by the desire to put the Federal participation in all three forms of assistance on the same basis but by the hope that the increase in the percentage reimbursement might induce the states with approved plans to expand their assistance programs for children and encourage the few states not yet included to submit plans and make this form of Federal aid available to children within their borders.

TABLE 6

Special Types of Public Assistance: Amount of Obligations Incurred for Payments to Recipients in States with Plans Approved by the Social Security Board

Year and month	Total amount of obligations incurred for payments to recipients of the three special types of public assistance [1]
1936	
February	$ 4,640,000
May	10,780,000
October	21,440,000
1939	
December	47,750,000

[1] From Federal, state, and local funds; excludes cost of administration and of hospitalization and burials. For 1936, obligations incurred for assistance in kind and for payments to persons other than recipients for rendering services to recipients excluded.

This amendment [9] will increase Federal expenditures for children, and other changes in the Act, made at the same time, will increase the amounts to be expended for old age and blind assistance. As amended the Act provides that the maximum benefit in both these categories which is reimbursable by Federal funds be increased to $40 a month from the $30 of the original Act. This increase is undoubtedly a recognition of the continuing interest and concern for the future of old people who are not covered by Federal Old-Age Insurance.

[9] See Appendix N—Excerpts from Fourth Annual Report of the Social Security Board, 1939, Amendments to the Social Security Act in 1939, pp. 166-184.

Another amendment made by the 1939 Congress placed old-age assistance definitely on a needs or means test basis and distinguishes it sharply from insurance. This prevents it being turned into a benefit paid to all people over 65, regardless of their circumstances or need. Efforts to develop the latter type of program had been made in two or three states and were undoubtedly the occasion of the following amendment which becomes effective July 1, 1941: "That the State agency shall, in determining need, take under consideration any other income and resources of an individual claiming old-age assistance." A similar provision is added to the two other assistance titles of the Act.

The 1939 Congress not only provided for the increases cited above, but made changes of great importance in the provisions for Old-Age Insurance, one of which has a direct bearing on the future development of aid to dependent children. The date for the first payments of insurance was moved two years ahead, to January 1, 1940, from January 1, 1942, of the original Act. Provision was also made for increased benefits to cover the aged spouse and dependent children of an insured worker, and, most significant of all, the "survivors" of deceased beneficiaries, both widows and minor children, were designated as recipients of insurance which would have been due to their husbands and fathers.

Federal Direct Relief

In spite of the policy announced in 1935 by the Federal Relief Administration that Federal funds would be withdrawn from relief and devoted to a program of work for the unemployed, the Federal Government continued to finance and administer two distinct programs of direct relief: emergency grants to farmers in need and surplus commodities in the form of food and clothing to people who were eligible for other forms of relief.[10]

Emergency relief to farmers was begun by the Resettlement Administration in November, 1935,[11] and continued under the

[10] See Part III, Chapter 11, and Part IV, Chapter 13; also "Subsistence Payments to Farmers," Chart I (frontispiece) and Appendix O.
[11] See Part IV, Chapter 13.

Farm Security Administration [12] of the Department of Agriculture. This relief has been given mainly in the drought areas as a supplement to the loans made to farmers by the Rural Rehabilitation Division of the same agency. Expenditures and numbers of farmers aided have increased each winter and dropped decidedly each summer. The peak of the program was reached in the first four months of 1937, when monthly expenditures averaged $5,013,000, and the average number of recipient farmers was 297,000. The lowest record for summer was in July, 1936, when 42,000 farmers received $563,000. The program was almost as small as this in the summer of 1939 but increased decidedly in the fall because of drought in the Middle West. The total sums spent on this program are so small in comparison with the expenditures made by the other agencies that they are indicated by only a thin line on the chart.[13]

The Federal Surplus Commodities Corporation continued after 1935 with the same general functions which it had discharged during the Federal Emergency Relief Administration.[14] Commodities were shipped in carload lots to state departments of welfare and distributed under their sponsorship by projects financed by the WPA. In the fiscal year 1938-39, the Corporation spent approximately $66,500,000 for nearly two billion pounds of surplus farm commodities. "Purchases were made of nearly 40 different surplus agricultural commodities including dairy and poultry products, fruits and vegetables, and flour and cereals. Some 3 million families, nearly 11 million people a month in all States, the District of Columbia, Puerto Rico, and the Virgin Islands received these commodities."[15]

[12] On September 1, 1937, the Resettlement Administration became the Farm Security Administration of the Department of Agriculture.

[13] See *Social Security Bulletin,* Vol. 3, No. 2, Feb., 1940.

[14] See Part III, Chapter 5. Upon the liquidation of the Federal Emergency Relief Administration, the Corporation functioned under the Department of Agriculture. The name was changed in November, 1935, from Federal Surplus Relief Corporation. The life of the Corporation was extended by Congress in February, 1938, to June 30, 1942. (Public No. 430, Seventy-fifth Congress.)

[15] Report of Federal Surplus Commodities Corporation for the Fiscal Year 1939. Issued October 31, 1939, U. S. Government Printing Office, Washington, D. C.

State and Local General Relief

Aside from these two relatively small Federal programs, general relief to needy people who were not eligible for categorical assistance and who did not succeed in securing employment on the Federal Works Program was left entirely to the responsibility of the state and local governments after December, 1935. Conditions in the states and localities have been so uneven that statistics give a most inadequate picture of the real extent of need. The numbers of people who have actually received relief are only the numbers who could be aided by the funds which were available in any particular place. There is nothing at all to show how many local offices found their funds quite inadequate to meet the need, or how many of them had no money at all for general relief. No count has been kept on a national basis of the numbers of applicants who were turned away empty-handed.

General relief expenditures for the first six months of 1936 show vividly the shift in responsibility which had just taken place. In 1935 the Federal Government had contributed 74 percent of the total amount spent by the emergency relief administrations throughout the country. The share of the states and of localities had been 12.3 and 13.7 percent respectively. Between January and June of the following year Federal funds represented 4.6 percent,[16] the states 56.4 and the localities 39 percent. The actual amount spent from state appropriations during these first six months of primary state responsibility was slightly over $139,660,000 or nearly $20,000,000 more than they had spent from their own funds in the first six months of 1935. The actual amount spent by the local governments, however ($96,458,000), was considerably less than their expenditures for the earlier period, probably because their funds were drawn upon to supply part of the cost of projects sponsored locally under the Federal Works Program.

During the four years after the liquidation of FERA, the number of families and individuals aided in any one month from general relief funds ranged from one million and a quarter to slightly over two million, and expenditures per month varied from twenty-eight to forty-eight million dollars.

[16] Final grants of the FERA; see also p. 204.

TABLE 7

Amount of Obligations Incurred for General Relief[1] Extended to Cases by Sources of Funds,[2] July, 1935, through June 30, 1939

Continental United States

Period	Total	Federal		State and local		State		Local	
		Amount	Percent	Amount	Percent	Amount	Percent	Amount	Percent
1935									
Jan.-June ...	$1,118,148,547	$852,978,193	76.3	$265,170,354	23.7	$120,090,426	10.7	$145,079,928	13.0
July-Dec. ...	547,846,957	385,441,295	70.4	162,405,662	29.6	92,699,427	16.9	69,706,235	12.7
1936									
Jan.-June ...	247,564,618	11,443,904	4.6	226,120,714	95.4	139,663,002	56.4	96,457,712	39.0
July-Dec. ...	189,569,852	1,089,298	0.6	188,480,554	99.4	105,442,070	55.6	83,038,484	43.8
1937									
Jan.-June ...	211,522,358	471,606	(1)	211,049,752	100.0	122,873,623	58.0	88,176,129	42.0
Fiscal Year									
1937-1938 ...	451,476,000	66,000	(1)	442,410,000	100.0	254,200,000	56.3	197,210,000	43.7
1938-1939 ...	472,360,000	1,009	(1)	472,359,000	100.0	279,915,000	59.3	192,444,000	40.9

[1] From Federal, state and local funds; excludes cost of administration; of materials, equipment, and other items incident to operation of work programs; and of special programs, hospitalization, and burials. Federal funds, after December, 1935, represent balances of FERA funds available in the states.

[2] Data partially estimated for months subsequent to December, 1935.

(1) Less than five-hundredths of one percent.

Source: Figures Jan., 1935, to March 31, 1937, from Division of Statistics, Work Projects Administration, Federal Works Agency; April, 1937, to June 30, 1939, from *Social Security Bulletin*, February, 1940. Division of Research and Statistics, Social Security Board, Federal Security Agency.

In eleven states local governments furnished all of whatever funds were expended for general relief during this period, and, in a few of the others, the state appropriations were so small as to be negligible. In 1939, Idaho [17] and New Hampshire had raised to 13 the number of states appropriating no state funds for general relief, while in 4 states the total amount came from state funds and in 31 a combination of state and local funds was spent.[18]

In the winters of 1938 and 1939 the states and localities kept their average monthly expenditures for general relief payments to persons in need, up to the maximum level of their contributions for emergency relief during the FERA.[19] Their annual obligations for general relief for the four years 1936-1939 averaged $450,955,000, which is slightly higher than their average annual contributions in 1934 and 1935 under the stimulus of the Federal Emergency Relief Administration grants.[20]

[17] Legally the localities in Idaho are entirely responsible, but state funds are actually being expended in those counties unable to finance general relief.

[18] Eleven states making no appropriation in one or more of the four years in question: Georgia, Florida, Indiana, Kentucky, Mississippi, Nebraska, North Carolina, South Dakota, Tennessee, Texas, Vermont. A number of these states failed to appropriate funds during the FERA. See Part III, Chapter 2; Arkansas, Arizona, Louisiana, Pennsylvania spent state funds for all or most general relief purposes in 1939. In addition most states still make provision for aid to needy soldiers and sailors. This aid is included in the figures for general relief in some states. See Geddes, *Trends in Relief Expenditures: 1910-1935,* pp. 3, 10, 41, and Part I, Chapter 1, above.

[19] The peak of state and local contributions to emergency relief came in the first four months of 1935 with an average monthly expenditure of $44,900,000. The monthly average for general relief was $45,568,-000 for the first four months of 1938 and $44,143,000 for the corresponding months of 1939. The amounts spent in 1938 and 1939 are even more significant because they include only general relief extended to cases, while the figures for 1935 include not only emergency relief extended to cases but also the cost of administration and special programs, purchases of materials, supplies and equipment, rentals of equipment, earnings of non-relief persons and other costs of the Emergency Work Relief Program. Source of figures for 1938 and 1939, *Social Security Bulletin,* Feb., 1940; those for 1935 from Work Projects Administration, Federal Works Agency, Division of Statistics.

[20] Figures for 1934 and 1935 include cost of administration, etc. Later figures do not include such costs. See previous footnotes.

CHART IV

OBLIGATIONS INCURRED FOR GENERAL AND EMERGENCY RELIEF, BY SOURCES OF FUNDS, CONTINENTAL U.S.

January 1933 through March 1937

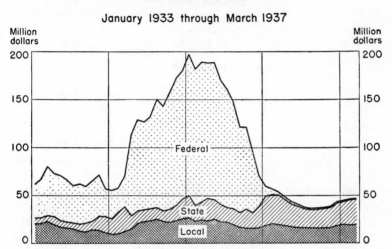

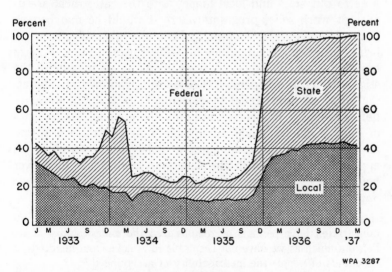

WPA 3287

Source: Division of Statistics, Work Projects Administration, Federal Works Agency, Washington, D. C., March 5, 1940.

TABLE 8

State and Local Obligations

Year	Emergency relief, including cost of administration, etc.	General relief extended to cases exclusive of cost of administration, etc.
1934	$423,310,456	....
1935	476,453,420	....
Average, 2 years	$449,881,988	....
1936	....	$439,015,000
1937	....	406,881,000
1938	....	476,201,000
1939	....	481,723,000
Average, 4 years	....	$450,955,000

This increase in general relief appropriations by the states and localities for what came to be known as the "residual relief load" is particularly significant because it was done without the stimulus of Federal grants, and in the face of the urge to put state and local money into the categorical assistance or work relief programs where it would be matched by Federal funds or, by sponsoring Federal work projects, would bring additional relief wages into the states. These general relief appropriations also continued to be made in spite of the stigma which the Federal Relief Administration itself had attached to all direct relief by rejecting it in favor of work relief. The great influence exerted by the opinions and policies of Federal officials made it much more difficult to secure state and local relief and undoubtedly had a deterrent effect on appropriations, although the need was more acute than ever before. Mr. Hopkins conceded this point in *Spending to Save:*

In our own anxiety to achieve a work program I think we as an administration have perhaps overemphasized the undesirability of relief, inasmuch as we have not been able to remove from hundreds of thousands of people the inescapability of accepting it.[21]

In 1938, however, Mr. Hopkins was as definite on this point as he had been when the FERA was liquidated:

[21] *Op. cit.*, p. 110.

On the question of a work program as against direct relief, it is my conviction, and one of the strongest convictions I hold, that the Federal Government should never return to a direct relief program. It is degrading to the individual; it destroys morale and self-respect; it results in no increase in the wealth of the community, it tends to destroy the ability of the individual to perform useful work in the future and it tends to establish a permanent body of dependents. We should do away with direct relief for the unemployed in the United States.[22]

Although the general relief appropriations by states and localities have shown some increase, the fact remains that they have been pitifully inadequate to meet the need, not only of the unemployables uncovered by categorical assistance, but of hundreds of thousands of "employables" for whom the Federal work programs have failed to provide their semi-adequate wages.

These general relief figures make a fair showing for the country as a whole but the actual amounts and benefits are, as a matter of fact, very unevenly distributed among the states. In December, 1938, eight states,[23] representing 45 percent of the population of the United States, gave 79 percent of all the general relief benefits in the country to 68 percent of the cases. The percentages were virtually the same a year later. In these eight states per capita incomes as well as relief loads are above the average for the country. The effect of this uneven distribution of expenditures upon the lives of people is, however, best shown by the wide variations in average monthly benefits per family and per person which are discussed below.[24]

Federal Work Relief

The creation of two major categories, the "employables" and the "unemployables," by the Federal Government in 1935, and the announcement of a Federal works program for the "employables" led to the expectation on the part of both state

[22] Statement of Harry L. Hopkins before Special Committee to Investigate Unemployment and Relief, April 8, 1938.

[23] California, Illinois, Massachusetts, Michigan, New Jersey, New York, Ohio, Pennsylvania.

[24] See pp. 385-87.

and local agencies and the general public that the Federal Government had committed itself to make provision for all the able-bodied unemployed who needed relief. As a matter of fact the Works Program gave work relief to the large majority of the needy unemployed, but left hundreds of thousands of the "employables" to become dependent upon state and local funds which were already taxed to the limit in providing for the "unemployables" and in matching Federal grants for categorical assistance.[25]

The employment goal of the Works Program was 3,500,000 project workers. This objective was more than attained in February, 1936, when approximately 3,850,000 were on the payroll. Of this number more than 3,000,000 were on projects of the WPA, 450,000 in camps of the CCC and about 350,000 were employed on projects by other Federal agencies.[26] As these Federal agencies increased their heavy construction projects during the spring and summer of 1936, the WPA decreased its employment to about 2,300,000. Severe drought in the Middle West necessitated putting 350,000 needy farmers on projects during the fall. These farmers were, however, transferred at the beginning of winter to the Resettlement Administration to receive from that agency direct relief in the form of "emergency grants" which averaged for each farm family about half the amount which they had been paid in wages by the Works Progress Administration.[27]

As business conditions improved in 1937 the number of projects workers on the WPA declined in September to about

[25] See Part III, Chapter 7.
[26] Department of Agriculture (excluding public roads) .. 60,000
Navy Department 17,000
Public Roads 68,000
Public Works Administration 41,000
Resettlement Administration 47,000
War Department 54,000
All other 68,000
Total 355,000
See Hearing on the First Deficiency Appropriation Bill for 1937. Statements of Harry L. Hopkins, U. S. Government Printing Office, Washington, 1937. Table 2—Works program employment by major agencies, excluding administrative employees July, 1935, to December, 1936, p. 11.
[27] See p. 314 above.

1,454,000, the low point of the four-year period. The subsequent business recession necessitated an increase which brought the total by November, 1938, to 3,239,000, slightly more than the earlier peak load of February, 1936. During 1939 the figure declined again to 1,908,000 in August, due largely to the refusal of Congress to appropriate the funds needed for a more nearly adequate program.[28]

During this four-year period, the NYA employed on projects and in the Student Aid program between 300,000 and 600,000 young people each month. The CCC continued to operate camps which provided work for an annual aggregate of 450,000 youths, 50,000 veterans and 15,000 Indians and territorials. The monthly relief payroll of the other Federal agencies included from 300,000 to 875,000 people.

The total expenditures for wages to persons employed under these Federal programs between January, 1936, and July, 1939, inclusive, amounted to $8,700,000,000. The average paid out *monthly* over the 43 months was $202,000,000, divided as follows: $129,000,000 by the WPA; $5,000,000 by the NYA; $21,000,000 by the CCC; and $47,000,000 by other Federal agencies.[29] These amounts are the measure of the extent to which the Federal Government, by providing relief for "employables," succeeded in removing responsibility from the states and localities. They must be discounted somewhat, since at least part of the contributions made by the states and localities towards the costs of operating projects would presumably have been available for general relief if the Federal work program had not existed.

Federal, State and Local Relief Expenditures

In the single month of June, 1935, Federal, state and local funds combined amounted to $204,359,000 given as work and direct relief to 6,404,000 households in which there were

[28] *Social Security Bulletin*, Vol. 3, No. 2, Feb., 1940.

[29] See Chart I (frontispiece) and Appendix O for distribution of these amounts in relation to general relief and categorical assistance payments and changes during the four years in question. From January 1, 1936, to December 31, 1939, the earnings under the different work relief programs were as follows: $6,009,015,000 in WPA; $247,496,000 in NYA; $998,-978,000 in CCC; and $2,172,642 in other Federal work and construction projects. See *Social Security Bulletin*, Vol. 3, No. 2, Feb., 1940.

22,457,000 people. Four years later approximately the same number of households in which there were 19,500,000 persons were aided in the one month of June, at a cost of $304,523,000 which was an increase of slightly less than one hundred million dollars. This means a higher average cost per household and per person aided and is reflected in higher standards of assistance. Most of the increase appears to be due to the fact that a much greater percentage of relief recipients were employed on work relief projects in June, 1939, than four years earlier, and that the security wage paid since the beginning of the Federal work program averaged somewhat over $50 a month, about twice the average work relief benefit under the FERA.[30]

ORGANIZATION AND ADMINISTRATION

The most significant administrative developments during the four years under consideration are found in the reorganization of Federal agencies in 1939; in the administration of public assistance by the Social Security Board; and in the continued development of state and local departments of public welfare to administer categorical assistance and general relief.

Reorganization of Federal Agencies

In January, 1937, the President's Committee on Administrative Management [31] submitted a broad plan for the reorganization of the Federal Government which included a recommendation that the welfare, educational and health activities be co-ordinated under a Federal Department of Public Welfare, to be constituted a major department of the govern-

---

[30] June, 1935, was the last month before the FERA relief recipients began to be transferred to the Federal Works Program. The amounts given here are approximate and represent payments to recipients of public assistance and general relief, and earnings of persons employed on the Federal work programs in the Continental United States. Figures exclude cost of administration and of materials, equipment, and other items incident to operation of work programs. Figures are partly estimated and subject to revision. See *Social Security Bulletin*, April and September, 1939. Also *FERA Monthly Report*, May, 1936.

[31] Administrative Management in the Government of the United States, January, 1937, Report of the President's Committee on Administrative Management, U. S. Government Printing Office, Washington, 1937.

ment with a secretary who would be a member of the Cabinet.[32]

In 1937 and 1938 Congress failed to enact legislation based on the report of this committee. On April 25, 1939, the President under the authority given to him by the Reorganization Act [33] which had been passed three weeks earlier, submitted to Congress his "Reorganization Plan No. 1." [34] This plan included provisions for the establishment of three general agencies in order to carry out the purposes of the Act "to group, coordinate, and consolidate agencies of the Government according to major purposes and to reduce the number of agencies by consolidating those having similar functions under a single head. . . ." [35] Two of the new agencies so established involved Federal activities in relief and categorical assistance.

The Federal Security Agency which resembled in function the previously proposed Department of Public Welfare, but lacked the status of a major department, included under its jurisdiction the Social Security Board, the United States Employment Service, transferred from the Department of Labor, the Office of Education, from the Department of the Interior, the Public Health Service, from the Treasury Department, the NYA, from the WPA, and the CCC, formerly an independent agency. The United States Employment Service was integrated with the unemployment compensation function of the Social Security Board under a new Bureau of Employment Security.

As defined in the President's Message, these were the agencies, "the major purposes of which are to promote social and economic security, educational opportunity, and the health of the citizens of the Nation." The inclusion in this group of

[32] For records of earlier attempts to secure a Federal department see Breckinridge, Sophonisba P., "Public Welfare Administration: Select Documents, A National Program and Proposals for a Federal Department of Public Welfare."

[33] Reorganization Act of 1939, Public No. 19, Seventy-sixth Congress. Approved April 3, 1939.

[34] Effective July 1, 1939, Under Public Resolution 20, Seventy-sixth Congress. Approved June 7, 1939.

[35] President's Message to Congress transmitting Reorganization Plan No. 1.

the NYA and the CCC, which had formerly been regarded as parts of the general Federal work program, clearly emphasized their educational and training functions and related them more closely to the Office of Education and to the employment service. Also the Federal Security Agency included all agencies charged with administration of programs under the Social Security Act except the Children's Bureau which continued under the Department of Labor to administer Maternal and Child Health Services, Child Welfare Services and Services to Crippled Children.

The Federal Works Agency included "those agencies of the Federal Government dealing with public works not incidental to the normal work of other departments, and which administer Federal grants or loans to State and local governments or other agencies for the purposes of construction." In this agency the WPA, named Work Projects Administration in the new plan, was grouped with the Bureau of Public Roads, from the Department of Agriculture; the Public Buildings Branch of the Procurement Division, from the Treasury Department; the Branch of Building Management of the National Park Service and the United States Housing Authority from the Department of the Interior; and the Federal Emergency Administration of Public Works, formerly an independent agency.[36]

In thus grouping the Work Projects Administration with agencies concerned chiefly or exclusively with construction, additional emphasis was given to the fact that work for the unemployed, rather than merely relief, was its major purpose.[37]

Social Security Board—Bureau of Public Assistance

The Social Security Board recognized from the beginning that the administration of public assistance is a social work function, and also realized the importance of placing in one bureau and under the direction of a single staff the administration of the three titles of the Act which provided benefits to people in need. The Bureau of Public Assistance was,

[36] President's Message to Congress, April, 1939.
[37] See Part III, Chapter 7, and Part IV, Chapter 13.

therefore, established as one of the three operating bureaus [38] directly responsible to the Executive Director of the Board, and staffed by professional social workers who were selected in accordance with the standards of the Federal Civil Service Commission.[39]

The Bureau of Public Assistance "recommends to the Board the approval of State plans for the three types of public aid which satisfy the requirements of the Act. It exercises a continuous supervision over the operation of State plans through its review prior to recommendations to the Board for the certification of grants." [40]

Field representatives of the Bureau, assigned to the twelve regional offices [41] of the Social Security Board, visit the state agencies and render a consultation service on the administration of public assistance and the development of procedures and standards; interpret the requirements of the Act and the

[38] "The operating bureaus, concerned with the three major fields of the Board's responsibility, are the Bureau of Old-Age Insurance (until September 17, 1937, this Bureau was known as the Bureau of Federal Old-Age Benefits), the Bureau of Public Assistance, and the Bureau of Unemployment Compensation. The service bureaus and offices are the Bureau of Accounts and Audits, Bureau of Business Management, Bureau of Research and Statistics, Office of the General Counsel and the Informational Service." Second Annual Report of the Social Security Board, p. 6. After July 1, 1939, the U. S. Employment Service was integrated with the Bureau of Unemployment Compensation which became the Bureau of Employment Security.

[39] At the beginning of the program, social work and other professional personnel were employed under the "expert" provision in the Act. Later all staff personnel came under the regulations of the Civil Service Commission.

[40] First Annual Report of the Social Security Board for the Fiscal Year 1935-36.

[41] The Social Security Board divided the country into twelve regions in order "to effect the utmost practicable decentralization of administration. The field organization included at the end of the [fiscal] year [1938-39] 327 field offices, which conduct local operations, primarily in connection with the Federal old-age insurance system." Fourth Annual Report, p. 5.

Each of the 12 regional offices is in charge of a Regional Director who is directly responsible to the Executive Director of the Board. To each of the regional offices are assigned field representatives of each of the three operating and five service bureaus.

policies and regulations of the Board and advise on legislation, finance and organization problems.

The Bureau has furnished, when requested by the states, special advisory services on "methods of determining need and otherwise establishing eligibility, medical care, family budgets, programs for ophthalmological examinations of the blind; on procedures for developing standards of assistance; on standards for the appointment, classification and training of State and local personnel; and on the development and use of reporting forms and auditing and accounting procedures." Administrative studies are also made when requested, in order to "provide agencies with detailed and objective information on the operation of State and local programs as an aid to planning improvements." [42]

"Under the Social Security Act the Board is responsible for seeing that a state plan provides for efficient administration and guarantees adequate supervision of the program by a single State agency." [43] This responsibility has been interpreted by the Board and its Bureau of Public Assistance in terms of advice and leadership to the states, in the development of high standards of administration, effective service to people receiving assistance and sound public welfare agencies. A measure of control was specifically provided in the Act which states that if a state fails to administer its plans in conformity with the requirements of the law, or has imposed conditions which are prohibited by the Act, no further grants may be made until the situation is remedied. The Board has hesitated to use this power just as the Federal Relief Administrator was reluctant to use his power of withholding relief funds, because such action penalized so severely the people in need. For this reason the suspension of Federal grants has been regarded by the Board "as a last resort, to be utilized only after all other methods of persuasion and negotiation have been exhausted." During four years this power has been invoked in only three states, Illinois, Ohio and Oklahoma. [44]

[42] The Bureau of Public Assistance, in discharging these responsibilities, collaborates with the service bureaus of the Board, and the offices charged with special aspects of the program such as statistical reporting, research, legal counsel, auditing, personnel administration, and public information.

[43] *Third Annual Report*, p. 91.

[44] *Third Annual Report*, p. 99; see also *Fourth Annual Report*, p. 81.

State and Local Public Welfare Agencies

1. Legislation

Notable progress has been made during the four years in the development of state and local departments of welfare to administer public assistance, general relief and child welfare services. This is in spite of serious set-backs to several promising state programs caused by political activities which have occasioned complete or partial changes in personnel, and in spite of protracted delays in the adoption of sound methods of general relief administration on the part of a number of states including three with large industrial populations, namely, Illinois, New Jersey and Ohio.

Under the stimulus of the Social Security Act the activity of state legislatures, which began in 1935, continued throughout the succeeding years.[45] The number of bills introduced and laws passed in the general fields of public welfare and social security was unprecedented in the history of the country. The laws passed in many of the states were the results of the work of legislative or executive commissions which were appointed to study the welfare needs and financial resources of their states and make recommendations to the legislatures for suitable measures to conform to the Federal Social Security Act and to provide for the general relief burden which was left in their hands by the liquidation of the FERA.

The early legislation of the period was concerned chiefly with bringing state laws into conformity with the Federal Act and in authorizing new agencies or reorganizing old ones to administer one or more of the categorical assistance and relief programs. In 1937, forty-eight state legislatures were in session, in each one of which from one to sixty-six bills on public welfare were introduced.[46] The laws enacted varied greatly in their value and effectiveness, because of the differences in the states in experience and knowledge of sound public welfare principles. On the whole, however, definite progress was made. An all-time record was set in the establishing of 18 new state public welfare agencies, and the reorganization of

[45] See pp. 321-22 above.
[46] Hoey, Jane M., "Our Common Stake in the Development of the Social Security Program," *The Family*, Jan., 1938.

four others, including the integration, in New York State, of the TERA with the long established permanent Department of Social Welfare.[47]

By the end of 1938, public assistance programs in most states had "already passed beyond the stage of primary concern with legislation and initial organization" and had begun to "center on detailed planning for the development of more adequate organization, improved procedures, and greater recognition of the service responsibilities of State and local agencies."[48] The passing of this stage also marked the beginning of further legislative activity in amending and strengthening the laws on which the public assistance plans and the general relief programs were based.

In 1939, when 44 state legislatures met in regular session, as they did in 1935 and 1937, over six hundred state welfare statutes were enacted, "covering a wide range of subjects, such as public assistance, child welfare, state and county public welfare organization and unemployment compensation." New state welfare departments were established in seven states and five others made substantial changes in the organization of existing agencies. Other states made changes of minor importance.[49]

2. Categorical Assistance

The provisions of the Social Security Act which undoubtedly have had the greatest effect upon the organization and administration of public welfare agencies in the states are the first three clauses of the section on state plans in each of the assistance titles:

(a) A State plan for old-age assistance must (1) provide that it shall be in effect in all political subdivisions of the State, and, if administered by them, be mandatory upon them; (2) provide for financial participation by the State; (3) either provide for the estab-

[47] See *Public Welfare News*, July, 1937, American Public Welfare Association.

[48] *Third Annual Report*, p. 89.

[49] The new departments were established in Idaho, Maryland, Michigan, Minnesota, Oregon, Rhode Island and Texas. All of these were essentially reorganizations. Substantial changes were made in Iowa, Kansas, Maine, Tennessee and Washington. For further discussion see Stevenson, Marietta, "Trends in Public Welfare Legislation," *Social Service Review*, September, 1939.

lishment or designation of a single State agency to administer the plan, or provide for the establishment or designation of a single State agency to supervise the administration of the plan. . . .

In other words, if Federal assistance grants are to go to a state, the benefits must be available to people living in every part of the state. The state government as distinguished from the counties, towns and cities must carry at least part of the cost of financing the program.[50] The Federal Government would not deal directly with cities and counties but only with one state agency which must be responsible for the administration or the supervision of the plan. The stipulation of "a single State agency" was in the interest of "uniformity of procedure and administration, equality of treatment, and adequate supervision of the program within the State." [51]

Much of the earlier state legislation for Mothers' Aid, Old-Age and Blind Pensions had been permissive, and often little or no state money was provided. The administrative and supervisory powers of most state agencies were not clearly defined or effective. This local option and decentralization of responsibility resulted in programs that were at best only 50 percent effective.[52] By September, 1938, three years after the Federal Act was passed, one or more of the three types of public assistance had been made available in every county in the United States.

The requirement of state financial participation has produced equally notable results. States which had never made money available for categorical assistance and had appropriated no funds for emergency relief during the FERA, and which left to their counties and cities the entire responsibility for the "unemployables" after that program stopped, responded to the terms of the Social Security Act and made available millions of dollars to match the Federal public as-

[50] The three titles of the Act also provided that financial participation was not required until July 1, 1937, of states in which the constitutions prohibited the appropriation of funds for this purpose.

[51] First Annual Report, p. 10.

[52] See Part I, Chapter 1; also Social Security in America, Publication No. 20, Social Security Board, 1937, 592 pp.; Report of the Committee on Economic Security already cited; Part IV, Chapter 13, above; Chart II and Table 1.

sistance grants.[53]   Numbers of other states which made funds available for relief during and after the FERA made their first appropriations for categorical assistance because state financial participation was required in order to meet the conditions imposed by the Social Security Act.   The need for such a requirement to stimulate the appropriation of state funds is clearly shown by the situation in 1934.   Of the 45 states with Mothers' Aid laws, only 14 appropriated state funds in that year and in 5 of these the fund was too small to be of much assistance.   In the same year, of the 28 states with Old-Age Pension laws, 16 spent state funds and state funds were spent in 11 states of the 24 having laws for Blind Pensions.[54]

The Federal Act left to the states the decision as to further division of financial and administrative responsibilities between the state agencies and their political subdivisions.   The result has been a wide variety of practice ranging from centralization of both types of responsibility in the state agency, to programs in which a substantial share of the costs is met from local funds and in which local units administer the program under state supervision.   "There has been a continuing tendency on the part of the States to use State, rather than State and local, funds for the non-Federal costs of assistance payments.   In June 1937, 47 of the 115 approved plans were financed without participation by the local governmental subdivisions; in June 1938, of 130 plans, 60 had no local financial participation.   The relatively greater ability of the State as contrasted with that of local governmental units, to utilize tax resources and to make some provision for meeting the special needs of distressed local areas seems to have been largely responsible for this development."[55]   In June, 1939, 69 out of 131[56] plans provided for financial participation by the state and Federal governments only.   Not only did Idaho, Louisiana

[53] Florida, Georgia, Nebraska, South Dakota, appropriated no emergency relief funds.   Indiana and Mississippi appropriated negligible amounts.   See Part III, Chapter 8.   All of these states have since 1935 appropriated considerable funds to match Federal grants for categorical assistance, but have appropriated little or no state funds for general relief.

[54] See Part I, Chapter 1.

[55] *Third Annual Report*, p. 101.

[56] This does not include four plans approved for Territories.

and Washington provide for state financing of the costs of all three assistance categories, making the 9 additional state plans during the fiscal year 1938-1939, but during that year "13 States have decreased the proportion of public assistance costs to be borne by local governmental subdivisions. The need for more substantial State participation in the cost of administration in the local community has also been increasingly recognized." [57]

As a rule the administrative authority has been centralized in the state agency where the state furnishes all or most of the non-Federal funds; local administration under state supervision is more likely to be found where the political subdivisions carry a considerable share of the financial responsibility. In either case the state agency is responsible to the Federal Social Security Board for seeing not only that the local units meet the minimum requirements of the state and Federal laws, but that efficient methods of administration are developed and maintained on a state-wide basis.

In discharging these responsibilities the state agency assumes a definite obligation "to establish objective standards for the selection of both State and local personnel; to establish equitable standards of need and of assistance; to exercise adequate auditing procedures and controls over local agencies; to develop whatever consultative and advisory services its local units may need; and . . . to strengthen the local agencies, to supplement their efforts, and to help train their workers for their own duties." [58]

Many state agencies have found it exceedingly difficult to achieve even a fair degree of uniformity in methods and standards within their local units, even with the aid of a centralized administrative authority. Whether or not local funds constituted a large share of the cost of the program, local autonomy and local traditions often succeeded in keeping standards of both personnel and assistance payments at low levels. [59]

[57] *Fourth Annual Report,* p. 118.

[58] Bane, Frank, "Social Security Board and State Organization," March, 1939, *Annals,* AAPSS.

[59] ". . . in certain States in which assistance programs are financed wholly from State and Federal Funds, certain local agencies have maintained assistance grants at almost as low a level as that which prevailed

State public assistance agencies have been faced with a problem of distribution of Federal and state funds to local units similar to that which had to be met by the SERA's.[60] With the opportunity for more careful planning and operation which was offered by the permanent program, and profiting to some extent at least by the experience gained with emergency relief funds, the states have made considerable progress in developing methods of equalizing the uneven resources of their local subdivisions. In a number of states, however, legislation has required the allocation of funds on a population or other fixed basis which has made it impossible to distribute them according to need.

Probably the most important factor in the relationship between the state agency and its local units has been the work of the state field staffs, the members of which have served as representatives of the state agency, interpreters of state policies, advisors and supervisors in the localities. They have proved to be essential to the state agencies' function, and have been invaluable assets in carrying out the state's objective that persons equally in need receive similar treatment under the program in all parts of the state. That the Social Security Board considers the state field staff of primary importance in the administration of the program is clear from the following statement: "Whether the offices responsible for local administration of the program are branch offices of the State agency or separate county or municipal agencies under State supervision, the State agency *must* establish a clearly defined channel—the State field staff—through which to carry on the processes of guidance and consultation which enter into the development of the State-local relationship." [61]

The announcement of this policy by the Social Security Board was particularly significant because of the practice followed in the early days of the program in a number of state departments of welfare of employing as many as three or four separate field staffs, each responsible for the functions carried

when only local tax funds were used to finance the programs." *Third Annual Report*, p. 101.

[60] See Part III, Chapter 10.

[61] *Third Annual Report*, p. 94. Italics are the writer's.

on by one of the divisions of the state office.[62] The recommended set-up, which has been put into effect in most of the states, consists of one "well-qualified field staff responsible for State-local relations in all the public-assistance programs, supplemented with consultants attached to the State office and available for specialized technical service to localities."

This type of state-local relationship involved an internal integration which has been considered by the Social Security Board to be as important as the integration of the three types of public assistance under one state agency.

Although the Social Security Board has consistently encouraged the integration of all three types of public assistance under the jurisdiction of one state agency and its local units, the responsibility for decision on this important matter has rested entirely with each state.[63]

The new provisions for categorical assistance were grafted on the existing systems of state and local organization for mothers' aid, and "pensions" for the aged and the blind. One or more of these programs already existed in almost every state. Many of the agencies were firmly established and strongly entrenched.[64] A number of states had originally set up their "pensions" under departments of welfare, but there were in 1935 many separate agencies, such as old-age pension commissions, old-age assistance boards, child welfare departments or boards, and commissions for the blind.

In spite of this complexity of older agencies, more than half of the states, when they set up their categorical assistance programs in 1936 and 1937, placed all three forms of assistance under one state agency. By June 30, 1938, of the 44 jurisdictions with more than one plan approved by the Social Security Board, 31 designated one central agency as respon-

[62] *Ibid.*

[63] "Clearly the most effective methods of integrating and utilizing various resources available for aid to persons in need must be determined by each State in line with its specific problems and the means available for meeting them. . . . In general, the Board has repeatedly affirmed its belief that an essential first step in this direction is effective integration, on both State and local levels, of the three programs for public assistance provided under the Social Security Act, and whenever possible, State or State and local provisions for general relief." *Third Annual Report.*

[64] See Part I, Chapter 1, and also Part IV, Chapter 13.

sible for all three programs and 11 put two forms of assistance under one central agency. One year later, in July, 1939, three additional states had consolidated the administration of all three programs in a single state agency.[65]

The process of integration has been further complicated by the fact that a number of states provided, in 1935 and 1936, for the establishment of new separate single state agencies to administer in each case one type of public assistance. This was in conformity with the requirement for a single state agency made in the Federal Act, which did not provide that all three types of public assistance be administered by the *same* single state agency. Subsequent legislation in a number of these states provided for reorganization and integration of functions, but, in others, the separate agencies were still operating in 1939.

On the whole the tendency to place all three types of assistance under one state agency has been particularly evident in the states where there were no strongly entrenched "pension" agencies and where there had been prior to 1930 no definite development of non-institutional public welfare activities on a state-wide basis. Integration has also been much more marked in states where the Emergency Relief Administrations were continued or transformed, virtually intact, into permanent departments of welfare, or where the emergency programs were incorporated with permanent departments.[66] In either case the resulting agencies, almost invariably, provided integrated administration in both state and local operations not only of the three types of public assistance but of general relief and child welfare services as well.

3. General Relief

After the liquidation of the FERA, satisfactory administrative provisions for general relief in the states and localities developed much more slowly than those for the special types of public assistance sponsored by the Federal Government. Integration of general relief with the assistance programs has also proceeded less rapidly than the integration within the categorical assistance program itself.

[65] *Third Annual Report,* p. 93; *Fourth Annual Report,* p. 106.
[66] See Part IV, Chapter 13.

In the fall of 1939, general relief was administered in five states through state agencies and financed either wholly or in part from the state treasuries.[67] In 19 states, local administration was supervised by a state agency; in 15 states there was local administration with no state supervision; and in each of 7 states at least two distinct systems were in use, either state responsibility for employables and local for unemployables or a division made according to state and local settlement or on some other basis.[68]

Wherever there was no provision for state administration or supervision, general relief was literally turned back to the local communities. Local option then determined the kind of agency, the personnel, the eligibility requirements and the methods and standards according to which needy people should be helped. The localities which placed the administration of their general relief funds under the same agencies and in charge of the same staffs which administered the state-supervised categorical assistance, did this as a matter of local decision. The extent to which such integration was effected throughout the country may be taken as some indication of the degree to which sound public welfare principles and practice had become established, and as the ultimate test of the extent to which they had actually taken root in the communities. Integration meant that general relief was committed to agencies and staffs which were directly under the supervision of state public welfare departments and subject to Federal and state

[67] Arizona, Delaware, Michigan, New Mexico, Pennsylvania. Most of the general relief in Arizona and all in Pennsylvania came from state funds.

[68] 11 of the 15 states with local unsupervised administration spent only local funds: Florida, Georgia, Indiana, Kentucky, Mississippi, Nebraska, New Hampshire, North Carolina, South Dakota, Tennessee, Vermont; Idaho, Ohio and New Jersey spent both state and local funds but provided no state supervision. Of the 7 states with two systems, California and Nevada have state-administered relief for employables and local unsupervised for unemployables; Connecticut and Massachusetts have state relief for the state unsettled. Maine has state relief for the unsettled and also for all the poor in certain towns not able to finance their own relief; Oklahoma and South Carolina have even more complicated systems. Three state programs were in the process of reorganization and information was not available: Michigan, Minnesota and Rhode Island.

legal and administrative provisions governing standards of personnel and benefits. Although these Federal and state regulations were limited in their technical application to the administration of categorical assistance, they necessarily influenced the general relief methods and standards. On the other hand, numerous other counties, cities and towns preferred to maintain their own separate relief agencies which more often than not reverted to early poor relief levels.[69] These localities used types of agencies and methods which are too varied for analysis.[70] The following comment on the situation in Illinois early in 1937 gives some idea of the character of this confusion:

The patchwork character of local public assistance administration is emphasized by the fact that, in the single county of the state having the largest number of townships, there are 41 different and independent authorities administering public funds for the benefit of dependent families, needy mothers with children, the blind, the veterans, and the aged. For the entire State there was a total of 1860 local administrative authorities distributing funds and services for the benefit of these closely related categories of need. Moreover, the scattered administrative responsibility inherent in the local welfare setup within the average Illinois county gives little assurance that the quality of welfare work will reach desirable standards of performance. In the average county the personnel charged with the management of the relief and welfare activities are persons elected by popular vote primarily to perform other tasks.[71]

[69] See Part I, Chapter 1. See also Dunn, Catherine M., "What Price Local Poor Relief," a study of local practice in Pennsylvania, New Hampshire, Indiana, and Alabama, published by the American Public Welfare Association, February, 1936.

[70] In 1937, local integration with the three types of public assistance in states having approved plans: Georgia, 47 counties; Maine, certain towns; Maryland, Baltimore and all but 5 counties; Minnesota, California, certain counties; Nebraska, most counties; South Carolina, 37 counties; Wisconsin, 13 counties, integrated with ADC and OAA; Florida, 2 counties with OAA; there was no relationship on a local level in Vermont, Texas, Tennessee, Rhode Island, Oklahoma, Ohio, New Jersey, Mississippi, Kentucky, Indiana. Data taken from "Administration of General Relief in the Continental United States as of December 1937," *Social Security Bulletin*, Vol. I, No. II, Nov., 1938.

[71] Reynolds, Wilfred S., "Illinois' Patchwork," *Social Service Review*, March, 1937.

4. Integration of General Relief and Categorical Assistance

In addition to local integration, decided by local option, state legislation or administrative policy have effected consolidation of programs in both states and localities. In the fall of 1938, 17 state agencies which administered or supervised aid-to-dependent children, old-age and blind assistance, also discharged the same type of responsibility for general relief. In all but one of these states the local programs were also integrated.[72]

In Michigan and Missouri, general relief was administered by the agency which was responsible for two of the public assistance programs and in Delaware the same staff in the state agency was responsible for both general relief and old-age assistance.

The primary value in the integration of these programs was described by the Social Security Board in its *First Annual Report,* in terms of the welfare of the families and individuals who are the recipients of the various public benefits. This report calls attention to the "wisdom of considering the needs of the family group in which an individual is living, even though assistance be granted to him on the basis of his specific eligibility for a particular type of aid." [73]

The *Second Annual Report* gave additional emphasis to the value of integration by citing specific problems to illustrate the point:

In States in which the only program for general relief is that of the traditional local poor law, difficulties have sometimes arisen because the relief officer, desiring to conserve local funds, regarded all households in which one of the three types of public assistance was provided as ineligible for local aid, without consideration of other persons in the household whose needs were not being met. In many States, recipients of old-age assistance, aid to the blind or aid to dependent children are prohibited by State law from receiving other types of public aid. The whole problem of the relationship between general relief and the various public assistance programs illustrates

[72] Alabama, Arizona, Arkansas, Colorado, Idaho, Kansas, Louisiana, Montana, New Mexico, New York (ADC separate in most local districts), North Dakota, Oregon, Pennsylvania, Utah, Washington, West Virginia and Wyoming.

[73] P. 32.

the need for integration of administrative organization and of policy on both the State and local levels of all the public assistance and relief activities of the State. In States in which the same State agency and the same local agencies are responsible for both public assistance and general relief, many of these difficulties have been worked out in a satisfactory manner.

Much of the difficulty recognized by this report arose from the fact that each type of categorical public assistance provided benefits to individuals as such, to an old person, to a child, or to a blind person, while general relief, whether given by a local public welfare agency which was also administering categorical assistance, or by a poor relief official from a separate office, was intended not for a member of a family but for a *family as such*. Hence the value of placing in the hands of a single agency and a single staff the responsibility for deciding upon the amounts of each type of aid which should go to individuals and to the families of which they are members.

Statistics and Research

The establishment by the Federal Emergency Relief Administration in 1933 of a Division of Research, Statistics and Finance marked the beginning of a system "which produced the first national statistics of relief approaching adequacy for any purpose." [74] The WPA continued and expanded this system and enlarged the program of administrative studies and research in the fields of relief, destitution and unemployment which had been started under the FERA. Financing of state and local research projects, particularly in connection with universities, was begun under the FERA and CWA. The WPA, during its first three years, financed the operation of nearly 4,000 local statistical research projects, many of which were concerned with relief and public welfare problems. [75]

The Social Security Board through its Bureau of Research and Statistics established, in 1936, a system for the collection of national statistics of categorical relief for administrative

[74] Hurlin, Ralph G., "Statistics in the Administration of a Public Welfare Program," *Proceedings* of the National Conference of Social Work, June, 1938. See also Part III, Chapter 7.

[75] See Index of Research Projects, Works Progress Administration, 1938, 1939 and 1940.

use. Although no Federal agency had administrative responsibility for general relief after the liquidation of the FERA, reports from the states on general relief statistics were collected jointly by both the WPA and the Social Security Board. The latter agency, in co-operation with the WPA, has developed a series of consolidated relief statistics for the country as a whole, including not only categorical and general relief but obligations incurred by the Federal work programs and by the Farm Security Administration for emergency grants (subsistence payments) to farmers. In gathering material for this comprehensive picture of the obligations incurred by governmental agencies, the Bureau of Research and Statistics collects reports from many private agencies, and compiles and issues data regularly on the operations of "more than 4,400 agencies concerned with provision of aid to persons in need." [76] The other functions of the Bureau include a wide variety of administrative studies "of particular problems of insecurity and of possible measures for their solution" and the conduct of long range research "into basic economic and social factors affecting the need for security and the adequacy of existing provisions." The data collected by the Bureau on public assistance was released monthly, beginning with February, 1936. This release was expanded into the *Social Security Bulletin*, the monthly publication of which was undertaken in March, 1938. The bulletin reports current data and the results of research, and also carries valuable signed articles on subjects relating to the activities for which the Board is responsible.[77]

The Bureau of Research and Statistics has also given an advisory service to the research and statistical units of the state departments of welfare, many of which are continuations of units built up earlier under the supervision of the FERA. There has been a gradual improvement in the standards of statistical reporting by state agencies during the past four years. This is particularly evident in relation to general relief reporting which suffered severely throughout the country and

[76] *Third Annual Report,* 1937-1938, p. 96.
[77] For information on other Federal agencies which secure statistics and conduct research in this and related fields, see Myers, Howard B., "Research and Statistics in Social Work," *Social Work Year Book,* 1939.

ceased entirely in many states for some time after Federal relief funds were withdrawn.

The collecting of statistics by the Federal agencies began as an adjunct of accounting. It has developed as an independent administrative procedure, and great progress has been made during these four years in the technique of translating the figures and other data into forms which are useful for administrative purposes. There is growing understanding of their social significance; of the need for collecting them; their interpretation after they have been secured, and their use for public information.

Government activity in the fields of statistics and research has stimulated corresponding activity in private agencies, particularly the Social Science Research Council, through its Committees on Public Administration and Social Security. Increased interest of Schools of Social Work in this field has given promise of a much needed supply in the future of professional people who will have added training in statistics and research to their social work equipment.

Chapter 15

Methods of Helping People and Standards of Aid

∽∽∽∽∽∽∽∽∽∽∽∽∽∽∽∽∽∽∽∽∽∽∽∽∽∽∽∽∽∽∽∽∽∽∽

Categorical Confusion

Local general relief agencies, whether or not they were also responsible for administering the three special types of public assistance, have been faced with the triple problem of giving relief to the "residual load" of needy people who were not cared for by any of the other programs; of supplementing work relief wages and other forms of assistance which were inadequate; and of certifying the eligibility of applicants for four or five different Federal programs. These services to the Works Progress Administration, the National Youth Administration, the Civilian Conservation Corps, the Federal Surplus Commodities Corporation, and in some places to the Farm Security Administration, have continued to present serious local problems of policy and to make inroads upon administrative funds and heavy demands upon the time of the social work staffs.[1]

Federal and state funds which were available for local administrative costs of categorical assistance could not be used for any other part of the local program. Consequently state and local general relief funds, or local funds alone have had to carry the entire expense of interviewing, investigating and certifying the prospective beneficiaries of the Federal agencies.[2] These services and the general relief programs of which they are a part, have been the only local activities concerned

[1] See Part IV, Chapter 13.
[2] Intermittent assistance in certain states and localities had been given to state and local agencies by the WPA in the form of additional personnel to do part or all of the certification to that program for certain periods.

363

with relief, work-relief or assistance for people in need which have not been at least partially supported by Federal funds.

The problems of policy involved in these certification services arise from the complications of the categorical system which has developed with great rapidity during the past five years, and from the numbers of different agencies, representing different levels of government, with varying resources, standards and methods of meeting need, which have been operating in each local community.

Applicants to the local public assistance and relief agencies might be eligible for one or more of eight different forms of government aid [3] for which a "means test" was required. In addition, as unemployment compensation payments were made in state after state, this category presented new and complex problems of relationship with other programs, and also needed frequent supplementation from general relief funds. Provision for "survivors' insurance" in the 1939 amendment to the Old-Age Insurance title of the Social Security Act adds yet another type of category which is closely related to aid to dependent children.[4] For each one of these categories the basic eligibility requirements have been defined by Federal law or by the administrative rulings of a Federal agency. State laws and state agencies have added to the definitions of certain categories. Local agencies have had little or nothing to say about these definitions, although they have necessarily carried the responsibility for putting them into effect.

General relief funds and surplus commodities, as far as they have been available, have served as a "catchall" for the individuals and families who did not fit into the inelastic categorical pattern. They have also been used to supplement inadequate benefits and to supply medical care, chiefly in the families of workers on WPA, and to children, the aged and the blind who were receiving categorical assistance.[5] The necessity for supplementary relief has been due to the inade-

---

[3] See Part IV, Chapter 13.

[4] See Part IV, Chapter 14.

[5] In December, 1937, general relief funds were being used to supplement WPA wages in 31 states and ADC in 28, OAA in 28, and AB in 24 states. *Social Security Bulletin*, Nov., 1938. (Data cleared with the states as of October, 1938.)

quacy of the WPA security wage to provide for families of more than three or four members, and to the pitifully small assistance grants given in several states. It has also been due to the fact that most of the categorical programs provide assistance or wages to individuals, while general relief has been given on the basis of family needs. In a family of seven members, one of the children, perhaps a blind boy, and the grandfather, over 65, might have been eligible for categorical assistance; in another family of similar size one boy might have gone to a CCC camp and his brother be employed on an NYA project, or only one member of the family might have been working and receiving wages from WPA. Usually the government benefits accruing to these individuals have fallen far short of supporting, even on the barest minimum standard, the families of which the beneficiaries were members. Moreover it has been contrary to the policy of the public assistance agencies that grants to their individual beneficiaries should be counted toward the support of other members of their families. It has therefore remained for the agencies administering general relief to deal with the question of need from the standpoint of the whole family, giving due credit to each type of government aid coming into the household as part of the family income.[6]

While the Social Security Board had been recommending the integration of categorical assistance and general relief, and the states and localities had made considerable progress in that direction, the other categories, which were entirely under the control of Federal agencies, showed less uniformity at the end of the four-year period than they did at the beginning, in eligibility requirements and the methods used in receiving applications and determining need.

[6] "While payments for all three types of assistance are intended primarily to meet the specific needs of individual recipients, the assistance check is often regarded as part of the general household income. It is important, therefore, to know the amount of the budget needed for the entire household and the amount of the total family resources so that the payment made to the recipient of public assistance may be adjusted, within the limits set by State law and funds, to constitute his appropriate contribution to household expenses." Social Security Board, *Third Annual Report*, p. 102.

Decentralization of Intake

In 1936, one agency in each locality received applications and certified eligible people to WPA, NYA, Federal Surplus Commodities Corporation, CCC; served as a central application bureau in many counties for the subsistence grants of the Resettlement Administration, and, in about half the states, administered categorical assistance as well as general relief. In other words intake was fairly well centralized in the first year after the FERA; applications for all or almost all benefits were made to one office which applied the same local standard of eligibility to all alike. In 1939 the Federal Surplus Commodities Corporation [7] was the only one of these Federal agencies which continued to delegate to the local agency the same type of responsibility in respect to determination of need and standards of eligibility. Applications for WPA and CCC were still made to the local relief office. The CCC had liberalized its standard of eligibility to include, in addition to boys who were from families eligible for local relief, boys who were "unemployed and in need of employment" and who, being otherwise suitable enrollees, "need the employment, the job training, the educational and other opportunities offered by the CCC; and who themselves, or whose families, due to financial limitations, are not in a position to secure or provide comparable experience and training." [8] The WPA set its own standards which were graduated to conform to the differences in cost of living in various sections of the country, in order to give to unemployed people everywhere a more uniform opportunity to be certified to the Federal work relief program. These standards, in the form of family budgets planned to provide a reasonable subsistence compatible with decency and health, were given by the WPA to the state and local agencies in the spring of

[7] During 1939 the Federal Surplus Commodities Corporation instituted its "stamp plan" on an experimental basis, in a few cities, selling stamps through the local post offices. Sale of stamps which can be exchanged for surplus commodities to so-called "marginal" families is being tried. See bulletins and reports of the Federal Surplus Commodities Corporation.

[8] Civilian Conservation Corps, Standards of Eligibility and Selection for Junior Enrollees. Office of the Director, Government Printing Office, Washington, D. C.

1939 to be used as guides in determining need. Employable persons found to be in need according to these standards were not to be certified but referred by local agencies to the WPA Employment Division. The WPA reserved to itself the right to decide which of the people referred were then eligible for final certification and assignment to projects instead of leaving that responsibility to the local agencies as had been done previously.

The NYA assumed responsibility for its own "intake" in July, 1939; that is, the local relief agencies no longer received applications, except in certain communities where the NYA office was not conveniently located. This administration did not plan to reinvestigate the need of young people whose families had already been found eligible for relief by another public agency but considered them eligible and also accepted others who belong in a "marginal" group which is rather vaguely defined but which is definitely above the relief level.

The Farm Security Administration, which took over the responsibilities of the Resettlement Administration, has, during this period, used the local relief agencies less and less as "application bureaus" in their program of emergency grants to farmers. In 1939, practically all of the intake for this form of relief was handled in the county offices of the Farm Security Administration, according to their own methods and standards of need.

Each locality therefore had in 1939 three or four different and largely unco-ordinated agencies to which applications for various government benefits might be made, with different definitions of need and of eligibility which might be dictated by local or state or Federal policy or by a combination of policies originating from two of these levels of government or from all three sources.

Methods of Determining Eligibility and Giving Aid

Information regarding the actual practice of local agencies throughout the country in dealing with people in need, the attitudes shown and the methods used in determining eligibility and giving aid, is available on a national basis only for the categorical assistance programs. These are the only local programs directly concerned with people in need which have been, throughout this four-year period, under the supervision of social work staffs in state and Federal agencies. Social work staffs in the state and Federal Employment Divisions of the WPA, and in the regional and Federal offices of the Farm Management Division of the Farm Security Administration, have had highly specialized functions and have not been concerned with the general area of administration of relief or assistance. The social workers in the Farm Security Administration have been responsible for the selection of families for resettlement, separately, or in communities built by the agency, and have had no relation to the administration of emergency grants (subsistence payments) to farmers by the Farm Security Administration.

The reports and evaluations of the supervising staffs in the categorical assistance programs show certain significant trends in the methods used locally in the administration of the three types of public assistance. The extent to which these trends also apply to the administration of general relief depends to some extent upon whether or not the two programs are integrated in a particular locality and consequently administered by the same personnel. Because the extent of integration of the programs is so limited and uneven in different sections of the country, and because no Federal agency is responsible for supervising or evaluating the administration of general relief,[9] no conclusions can be drawn regarding recent trends in general relief practices. On the other hand, material regarding the administration of categorical assistance has been available to the Bureau of Public Assistance of the Social Security Board through their reviews of state plans and current changes in state policies and procedures, as well as through the contacts of the field representatives and their reports on local conditions and practices.

The policies of the Bureau of Public Assistance and their recommendations to the states have been entirely in keeping with the democratic principles and practice established in many localities during the administration of unemployment

[9] Statistical information is regularly secured by the Bureau of Research and Statistics of the Social Security Board and information assembled at intervals regarding legislation and administrative responsibilities of the states and localities. See *Social Security Bulletin*, especially Nov., 1938.

relief. This practice constituted a recognition, in the realm
of governmental relief, of the dignity and worth of the individual and of his rights as a member of the commonwealth to a
means of livelihood which would furnish him with a reasonable
subsistence compatible with decency and health.[10]

The annual reports of the Social Security Board show, however, that local traditions, timeworn attitudes toward the
needy, and practices which were inherited from the "pension"
systems upon which the categorical assistance programs were
grafted, all contributed to retard the full acceptance of the
democratic principles and their application in practice.

The position of the Board in regard to the concealment of
income by recipients of assistance and their right to spend
their money without dictation by the welfare agency which
bestows it, is significant as indicating respect for the rights of
people in need and understanding of their difficulties.

Recipients of old-age assistance, aid to the blind, and aid to dependent children usually require aid over an extended period, and their
needs must be met on something more than an emergency basis. In
certain States which have not made allowance for medical care,
clothing or other essential items, recipients are compelled to use por-
tions of the assistance grant intended for rent or food to meet these
items. In other instances, the failure of the State to recognize the
inevitability of expenditures for such items as clothing may have led
to the concealment of income or resources by the recipient, in order
that these expenditures might be met. The amounts concealed have
usually been small, and the needs to be met have usually been pressing, but the fact that official policy would not permit the recipient
to meet these obvious needs has impeded the establishment of a
frank and honest relationship between the recipient and the agency.

The utility of a budgetary system is not confined solely to the determination of need and the amount of assistance to be awarded.
Since the budget represents a careful determination of the amounts
to be expended for various living costs it may serve as a substantial
aid to recipients who must manage on very small incomes. Obviously, since recipients of assistance have had responsibility for managing their own incomes before they came on the assistance rolls,
the budget is not intended as a restriction on their specific expendi-

[10] See Part III, Chapter 10.

tures. It does furnish a useful tool to aid them in planning their expenditures on the most economical and efficient basis.[11]

Equally constructive has been the Board's policy regarding the responsibility of relatives for the support of persons who might be otherwise eligible for public assistance. Many state laws deny assistance to those whose legally responsible relatives can assist them. This is a usual and accepted condition of poor relief administration. The Federal Social Security Act left to the states decisions on this matter, as on other factors affecting the determination of need. However, when the states have requested advice regarding the difficult questions which arise in judging the ability of relatives to assume support, especially when they are unwilling to do so, the Board has "declared its belief that decisions of this kind should be made, within the latitude permissible by state law, on the ground of the best interests of both the recipient and the legally responsible relative," and that a "rigid or merely legalistic requirement that relatives assume these responsibilities may produce problems more serious than those it solves, especially in borderline cases when, at most, only small amounts of support are involved." At the same time, the Board has called attention to the care that should be taken to see that the administration of "these aspects of State public assistance programs should not be such as to weaken the sense of family integrity on which children and the aged have always relied." [12]

Because the earlier Mothers' Aid laws had placed their emphasis upon assistance to children of widowed mothers, many of the states were slow to take advantage of the broader provisions in the Federal Act which included children deprived of parental support because of physical or mental incapacity, and also children who are living in the home of any one of a comprehensive list of relatives. This delay on the part of a number of states, obviously arising from the traditions of the former system, has been a contributing factor in the great discrepancy which has existed, since the beginning of the program, between the number of children and the number of old persons aided under the Social Security Act.

[11] Third Annual Report, pp. 103-104.
[12] Third Annual Report, p. 105; see also Fourth Annual Report, p. 106.

Many of the early Mothers' Aid laws limited benefits to children whose mothers or guardians were "fit, and proper, morally, physically and mentally" to care for them. This requirement was a perpetuation of the traditional regard for community prejudices and the community's alleged but always uncertain right to pass judgment upon the poor and penalize them for behavior, actual or reputed, which did not have the approval of the community.[13] In modifying these laws the states were, to a notable extent, influenced by the absence of any such limitations in the Federal Act and by the substitute provision suggested by the American Public Welfare Association that the children should live "in a suitable family home meeting the standards of care and health, fixed by the laws of this State and the rules and regulations of the State Department thereunder."[14] While almost half [15] of the states had on October 1, 1939, incorporated the suggested provision in their laws, practically verbatim, 4 states and the District of Columbia retained a requirement that the home or the parent or both be "fit" or "proper." Three states included the words "morally, physically and mentally." The remaining state laws failed to characterize the relatives or stipulate the standards to be required in the home.[16]

The position of the Social Security Board on this fundamental question is consistent with its other constructive policies:

In some places it has been the traditional practice to give mothers' aid only to selected applicants and to leave to the overseer of the poor or other local official the families in which serious social problems existed. Modern practice in the States recognizes that the

13 See Part I, Chapter 1, and Part III, Chapter 10.

14 *Suggested State Legislation for Social Security,* American Public Welfare Association, Chicago, 1935.

15 19 states out of 40 with plans approved on that date. On January 1, 1934, 39 states required that mothers or other guardians must be "fit and proper" or "mentally, morally and physically fit," according to a Tabular Summary of state laws relating to Public Aid to Children in their own homes, issued by the Children's Bureau of the Department of Labor, 1934.

16 *Characteristics of State Plans for Aid to Dependent Children,* Revised October 1, 1939. Bureau of Public Assistance, Social Security Board, U. S. Government Printing Office, Washington, 1940, 25 pp.

major consideration must be *the welfare of the children rather than the conduct of the parents* and that the existence of social problems in a family group usually indicates the need for more intensive service rather than for curtailment of aid.[17]

An equally serious problem has been presented by the ancient, deeply intrenched and invidious practice of publishing the names of people who were on the poor lists and the related custom of considering that if they receive public funds, the details of their personal affairs are public property. In keeping with the definite stand which had been taken by the FERA in regard to the names and records of the people on the emergency relief rolls, the Social Security Board included in its third annual report the following statement:

In some states the public-assistance rolls are public documents and, as such, are open to candidates for office. To obviate any chance for political or other use of these lists to exploit recipients, it is believed that the public assistance rolls should be considered confidential and should be used only for administrative purposes.

This is a recognition on the part of the Board that the problem exists and is serious, but without some provision in the Federal Act the statement of policy has been merely a recommendation. The decision to follow or not follow the recommendation for confidential records has therefore rested with the states and localities where the policies followed have been influenced in varying degrees by local tradition.

During the state legislative sessions of 1938-1939 "legislation authorizing or strengthening the authority of the state agency to safeguard the confidential character of records for all three public assistance programs" was enacted by nine states. Three other states took similar action in regard to one type of assistance, one state "authorized county welfare boards to publish all expenditures." [18]

In 1939, Congress gave the Social Security Board authority to deal with this problem after July 1, 1941, by amending the

[17] *Third Annual Report,* p. 100; the italics are the writer's.
[18] *Fourth Annual Report,* p. 108. The nine states were Alabama, Idaho, Louisiana, Maine, Michigan, Montana, Oklahoma, Oregon, Tennessee: Delaware for ADC only; North Carolina and Vermont for OAA only. Minnesota made a general provision to safeguard records.

Act to state that a state plan must "provide safeguards which restrict the use or disclosure of information concerning applicants and recipients to purposes directly connected with the administration of" the three types of public assistance provided for in the Act.

A particularly significant provision of the Social Security Act, which has had a decided influence upon local practice, is one which recognizes the rights of the individual by requiring that a state plan for assistance provide for a "fair hearing" by the state or other central agency of any applicant whose claim to public assistance is denied. Prior to the passage of this Act practically no formal machinery had been set up in the states for hearings of this nature, although informal precedents were undoubtedly established by the widespread practice of hearing complaints and petitions of organized and unorganized groups of relief clients and project workers in the offices of the Federal Emergency Relief and Works Programs. The recognition of the principle of "fair hearing" by the Federal Government in the Social Security Act was an official confirmation of the policy adopted by the emergency Federal agencies. It meant the establishment, as part of the permanent program, of an appeal procedure which assured just treatment to individuals, and also made possible the exercise of certain controls by state agencies over local procedure and policy in the administration of the law.[19]

1. Settlement

The settlement provisions of the state poor laws have been superseded by the residence requirements of the public assistance laws for all recipients of categorical aid. The influence of local tradition is seen, however, in the exacting nature of the requirements made by the Federal Act and necessarily followed by the state laws for old-age assistance and aid to the blind. The Act provides that the Social Security Board shall not approve any plan which imposes as a condition of eligibility for old-age assistance or for aid to the blind, "any residence requirement which excludes any resident of the state

[19] "A similar provision for a fair hearing is required before a State can qualify for an administrative grant for unemployment compensation," *First Annual Report,* p. 10.

who has resided therein the five years during the nine years immediately preceding the application for old-age assistance (aid-to-the-blind) and has resided therein continuously for one year immediately preceding the application." A state plan for aid to dependent children shall not be approved if it imposes a residence requirement which denies aid to a child "who has resided in the State for one year immediately preceding application for such aid or who was born within the State within one year immediately preceding application if its mother has resided in the State for one year immediately preceding the birth."

The requirement that the person concerned must *be* actually in the state for one year prior to the application has meant a new interpretation of settlement which now, for all dependents receiving categorical assistance, can be retained during certain specified periods of absence from the state. The restriction of residence for a period before application to actual physical presence in the state has presented serious complications in the attempt to develop interstate services to recipients, particularly persons receiving old-age assistance. It may prevent a recipient from going "to another State to relatives who can offer him a home or a share of his support, even when such an arrangement will result in a saving of public funds as well as the greater happiness of the individuals concerned." The Social Security Board calls attention to the seriousness of this type of situation and adds that a recipient of assistance, if obliged to change his state residence, may "have to seek general relief or poor relief or private philanthropy in the new locality," and that "when these forms of aid are obtainable, they must be borne by the community to which he has moved, without benefit of Federal funds such as are available for the special types of public assistance." The Board recommends "carefully worked out reciprocal agreements" between states in order to provide for such situations. The crux of the problem is, however, in the rigid residence requirements in the new state assistance laws which add to the conditions of settlement the factor of continuous physical presence within a geographical area.[20]

---

[20] *Third Annual Report,* p. 108. See Lansdale, Long, Leisy, Hipple, *The Administration of Old-Age Assistance,* Public Administration Service, Chicago, pp. 80-81. 1939.

All applicants for local or state relief who do not fall within the three types of categorical assistance are subject to the settlement provisions of the state poor laws.[21] The increase in migration and transiency since the beginning of the depression has caused a number of states to lengthen their periods required to gain settlement within their borders. The movement to tighten up on residence requirements was further aggravated by the difficulties encountered in attempting to care for unsettled persons after the liquidation of the FERA Transient Bureaus in 1935 and 1936.[22]

In an attempt to deal with this situation, the Committee on Interstate Problems [23] of the American Public Welfare Association secured the assistance of the National Conference of Commissioners on Uniform State Laws in drafting a "Uniform Transfer of Dependents Act." This Act was approved by the American Bar Association, and recommended to the states. If adopted in any state, it would authorize the state department of welfare to enter into reciprocal agreements with corresponding agencies in other states regarding interstate transportation of "poor and indigent persons." The Act was indorsed in January, 1937, by the Inter-State Commission on Social Security of the Council of State Governments.[24]

[21] See Part I, Chapter 1.

[22] Between 1930 and 1937 nineteen states increased their requirements for gaining state settlement by periods ranging from six months to 3 years, while only two states decreased their requirements. Between 1937 and 1939 two other states decreased their requirements, while six increased by periods ranging from 6 months to four years. In 1930, 7 states had no requirement for state settlement; in 1939 there were only two states, Arkansas and Maryland, which specified no definite period. See *Compilation of Settlement Laws*, Revised as of September, 1939, American Public Welfare Association, Chicago, 1939; also references in Bibliography.

[23] Committee on Uniform Settlement Laws and the Transfer of Dependents, later called the Committee on Interstate Problems. Chairman 1931-1937, Frank W. Goodhue, Director of the Division of Aid and Relief of the Mass. State Dept. of Welfare; Chairman 1937-39, William J. Ellis, Commissioner N. J. Department of Institutions and Agencies.

[24] Largely as a result of the early discussions of the APWA committee, laws authorizing reciprocal agreements were passed by New Hampshire and Connecticut in 1933 and by Massachusetts in 1934; see *Interstate Problems in the Field of Public Welfare Administration*, May, 1937, com-

An interstate conference on Transients and Settlement Laws was held in March, 1936, in Trenton,[25] attended by representatives from 21 states, and a year later a second conference in St. Paul, Minnesota, brought together 210 representatives from 12 states in the Middle West.[26] These groups have agreed with the principles set forth by the American Public Welfare Association committee and their discussions have furthered the understanding and interest of the states in the Uniform Transfer of Dependents Act and the proposal for reciprocal state agreements.

In 1939, the Committee on Interstate Problems of the American Public Welfare Association recommended a series of regional conferences "with a view of achieving more uniformity in reciprocal services among the states and in state policies relating to non-residence." [27]   The committee co-operated with the Public Assistance Bureau of the Social Security Board and the Council of State Governments in holding conferences in the Central States, in the Eastern States, and in New England.   Other regional meetings were planned for 1940.

These conferences have developed a much better understanding between states in addition to some definite interstate agreements which have been undertaken.   There is also a new awakening to the importance of the problem and a greater concern on the part of welfare officials generally for the welfare of transient people.

2. Cash and Kind

The past four years have seen a marked increase in the use of cash payments to recipients of public aid, in place of groceries, clothing and other relief in "kind" which predominated,

piled by Louis E. Hosch, APWA, Chicago.   Mimeographed.   Contains reports on conferences and meetings on interstate problems, also a bibliography.   30 pp.

[25] Interstate Conference on Transients and Settlement Laws, Trenton, N. J., March, 1936, under the auspices of the New Jersey, New York and Pennsylvania Commissions on Interstate Co-operation.   For report of conference see The Transient, March, 1937.   New York.

[26] Midwest Conference on Transiency and Uniform Settlement Laws. St. Paul, Minn.   March 11-12, 1937, called by APWA.

[27] Public Welfare News, Sept., 1939, APWA, Chicago.

prior to and during the administration of emergency relief.[28] The precedent established under most of the early "pension" laws of the states of paying benefits by check or in cash was continued by the requirement for "money payments" to beneficiaries which was written into the Social Security Act. All categorical assistance under approved plans has, therefore, since the Act, been paid in the states in money, usually by check.

The practice followed in the administration of general relief has undoubtedly been affected by the Federal-state policy in public assistance payments as well as by the increase in the use of cash which was marked during the last year of the FERA. In September, 1938, 9 states and the District of Columbia used cash only in the Administration of general relief, 20 states gave relief in both cash and "kind" and 19 still limited their aid to "kind" alone.[29]

One of the two Federal relief programs, the Federal Surplus Commodities Corporation, supplies the states with surplus food and cotton and distributes clothing from the WPA sewing rooms. This is the only relief in "kind" to be distributed in those states which have adopted cash as the method which they prefer for relief to the people who are in need within their borders. On the other hand, the emergency relief grants of the Farm Security Administration are mailed by check from that agency's regional disbursing offices to the farmer recipients. Other Federal benefits are paid in the form of cash wages by the WPA, NYA and CCC. Not only has cash become the predominate form of public relief, but work relief has to an increasing extent overshadowed all forms of direct aid taken together.[30]

3. Work Relief

Work relief continued as a major Federal program, operated on the principles which were established in 1935,[31] including the payment of a monthly security wage, related to the type of work performed and not to the "budget-deficiency"

[28] Part III, Chapter 10.
[29] *Social Security Bulletin*, Vol. I, No. 11, Nov., 1938.
[30] See Chart I.
[31] See Part III, Chapters 7 and 10.

of the worker. The number of hours in the working week depended upon the relation between the security wage and the prevailing rate of wages per hour for the type of work performed. This system of computing hours was changed by Congress in the Emergency Relief Appropriation Act of 1939 to a requirement of 130 hours per month, with an exception provided for workers with no dependents who might be allowed to work fewer hours and also be paid less money.

The Federal work relief agencies have continued to put their emphasis on the work aspects rather than on the relief aspects of their programs. They have emphasized the employment opportunities offered, the assignment of workers on the basis of qualifications for the jobs to be done, and the operation of socially useful projects. On the other hand they have made the relief aspects as insignificant as was consistent with the fact that almost all of their workers have come from the relief rolls and that it was therefore necessary to plan projects which were suited to the skills, in all varying degrees, of relief labor and to locate projects where the relief labor was to be had.

In spite of administrative efforts to the contrary, the relief aspect of the WPA was strongly emphasized by the 1939 Congress which required that preference in employment should "be determined, as far as practicable, on the basis of relative needs . . ." and provided that "the Commissioner shall cause a periodic investigation to be made of the rolls of relief employees on work projects, and shall eliminate from the rolls those not in actual need, such investigation to be made so that each case is investigated not less frequently than once every six months."

Work relief has not been limited to the Federal program. 1938 and 1939 have seen a rapid development of work relief under local auspices, in at least one-third and probably in one-half of the states. In the fall of 1939 between 80,000 and 100,000 persons were employed on these programs which had been set up by local governments for one or more of the following reasons:

1. The conviction that the needy unemployed should have work, instead of direct relief. This position has been strongly influenced

by the poor relief tradition that able-bodied relief recipients should be expected to work in return for their "doles." [32]

2. The Federal work program failed to employ hundreds of thousands of needy unemployed who were left to receive relief in some form at the hands of local public officials. Their numbers have been increased by drastic cuts in WPA appropriations and employment, and by the enforced lay-off of all workers who have been continuously employed for 18 months.[33] Local officials have said to these destitute people, "if the Federal government won't give you jobs, we will."

3. Sponsors have found it more and more difficult to raise the 25 percent contribution required for Federal work projects.

4. In some instances municipalities have found it difficult to meet the maintenance cost of many of the buildings, parks and airports constructed by Federal works agencies, and therefore have been reluctant to sponsor additional Federal projects of the same type.

In these local work relief programs the majority of the workers have been engaged in unskilled maintenance jobs. Often they have displaced regular city or county employees. They have cut grass and weeds, trimmed bushes and cleaned buildings, and done minor road repair work. In some places they have been carrying out essential functions such as collecting garbage and cleaning sewage disposal plants. In one county where the majority of municipal facilities were maintained by relief labor, over 5,000 individuals have been employed at one time on the local work relief program. In the towns of this county even firemen and policemen were relief workers!

This type of "work-for-relief" is a return to the low standard program [34] of 1932 and the early months of 1933 before the initiation of the CWA. Wages have dropped to a starvation level,[35] and are paid on the old "budget deficiency basis." [36] There is no test of "employability" and little at-

[32] See Part I, Chapter 1.
[33] Provision of the Emergency Relief Appropriation Act of 1939, see p. 391.
[34] See p. 157. See also Gill, Corrington, "Local Non-WPA Work Relief," *American Federationist,* April, 1940, and *Survey Midmonthly,* May, 1940.
[35] See pp. 390-91.
[36] See pp. 237-40.

tempt to fit the skill or experience of the worker to the demands of the job.

The system has taken on many characteristics of the poor relief work-test in which the needy person is required to prove his "worthiness" to receive relief.

4. Almshouse Care

There are no nation-wide figures on which to base a comparison between almshouse care and out-door relief during these four years. It is undoubtedly true, however, that the almshouse which in the eighteenth and nineteenth centuries was the predominant form of local public poor relief, and which decreased in relative importance during the first thirty years of the twentieth century,[37] remained a definite factor in the local relief picture during the period of the FERA. Since 1935 the administration of old-age assistance and the requirement of the Social Security Act that benefits may not be paid to persons in public institutions, has had some effect upon the number of people in almshouses throughout the country and upon the number of almshouses in several of the states. While no marked decrease has taken place in the country as a whole there are trends, particularly in the South, toward the closing of small local almshouses and the establishment of one institution to serve a district comprising a number of counties. There is also a trend toward the replacement of almshouses by infirmaries where old people who are chronically ill may be cared for. The almshouse is still primarily a local function, and a local responsibility over which state departments of welfare have little or no jurisdiction.[38]

5. Medical Care

Medical care of needy persons has had no Federal support since the liquidation of the FERA and the cessation of the

[37] The last survey of the number of almshouses and their population made by the Bureau of Labor Statistics in 1923 showed some 2,046 almshouses with 85,889 inmates during the fiscal year. See Tyson, "Homes and Almshouses," *Social Work Year Book*, 1939.

[38] See *First Annual Report*, Social Security Board, p. 30; Austin, Nancy L., "Old Folks Without Homes," *Survey Midmonthly*, Jan., 1939; Tyson, Helen Glenn, "The Poorhouse Persists," *Survey Midmonthly*, March, 1938; "The Vanishing Almshouse," editorial, and Dunn, Loula, "Status of County Almshouses in Alabama," *Public Welfare News*, March, 1938.

few state medical relief programs which continued to be financed in 1936 from final Federal relief grants. The Social Security Board recognized the great need for public medical care throughout the country and the inadequacy of existing resources to meet them. The Board's *Third Annual Report* states that the "amounts granted to recipients of old-age assistance, aid to dependent children and aid to the blind rarely include allowance for medical services, although some states have made some provision for special diets and for expensive medicines." Public provisions for medical care in urban centers have usually been inadequate and "in rural areas, as well as in some of the cities, such medical care as is available to needy individuals has usually been furnished by private physicians who receive little or no remuneration." Although this situation is very similar to that which existed at the beginning of the depression, there are evidences that the FERA medical care program stimulated concern for health needs and enlarged "a previously more limited public responsibility for the medical care of persons without incomes."[39] Studies made by the American Public Welfare Association show that the period from 1936-1939 has witnessed "some extension of local systems of home medical care, as compared with the pre-depression period; new legislation in several states placing upon public welfare departments responsibility for the medical care of their beneficiaries; and a greatly increased consciousness, among social workers and welfare administrators, of the importance and complexity of this problem."[40]

The Federal Interdepartmental Committee to Co-ordinate Health and Welfare Activities, appointed by the President on August 15, 1935, through its Technical Committee on Medical Care, made recommendations regarding the need for a national health program and the nature and scope of such a program. In 1938 the committee sponsored a National Health Conference at which reports were presented incorporating the findings of the National Health Survey made in 1935-1936 by the United States Public Health Service, with the aid of WPA funds.[41] The result of these reports and recommendations

[39] Davis, "Medical Care," *Social Work Year Book*, 1939.
[40] *Ibid.*
[41] The survey was made by means of a house to house canvass of 740,000 families in urban communities in 19 states and 36,000 families in

was the introduction into Congress of the National Health Act of 1939, "to provide for the general welfare by enabling the several States to make more adequate provision for public health, prevention and control of disease, maternal and child health services, construction and maintenance of needed hospitals and health centers, care of the sick, disability insurance, and training of personnel; to amend the Social Security Act and for other purposes." The bill was introduced on February 28, and referred to the Committee on Education and Labor. It was not reported out of Committee during 1939.

A number of states have arranged for medical and surgical care for blind recipients of public assistance and have also planned programs for the prevention of blindness. In cooperation with commissions for the blind, state health departments and other agencies interested in the welfare of the handicapped, substantial progress has been made "toward the provision of more adequate facilities for education, vocational training, placement, medical care, and other services for the blind, as well as in the improved utilization of existing facilities." [42]

This progress in the provision of medical care for recipients of assistance has continued to increase during the fiscal year 1938-1939. It has been "reflected in many legislative proposals and enactments, as well as by administrative action of agencies on the basis of the general provisions in the State poor laws. The trend . . . is to broaden the definition of services which may be provided and to make specific the responsibility for medical care of the indigent. But . . . there is little evidence that during the past year States have had sufficient funds to effect any substantial improvement in the scope, adequacy, or quality of general medical services provided to public assistance recipients." [43]

selected rural areas in 3 states. "The National Health Survey: Significance, Scope and Method," *Bulletin,* USPHS, Washington, 1939.

[42] *Third Annual Report,* Social Security Board, p. 110.

[43] *Fourth Annual Report,* p. 112. See also *Organization and Administration of Tax-Supported Medical Care,* Committee on Medical Care, American Public Welfare Association, Chicago, Dec., 1939. Multigraphed, 8 pp.

6. Standards of Aid

The average amounts of work relief wages and of categorical assistance paid to individuals and families have been considerably higher during the past four years than during the administration of emergency relief, while the average general relief benefits have been somewhat less. The averages have varied between the states for many of the same reasons which were given for their variations under the FERA,[44] and there are also the same difficulties in using averages as a measure of the standards employed in any state or locality. They are useful only as giving some indication of the extent to which standards of aid have varied between different parts of the country, as well as between different governmental programs, and the changes which may indicate trends from year to year.

a. Categorical Assistance

While benefits have varied considerably as between the major programs during the four-year period, the standards which were established in each program early in 1936 have changed very little. The variations between states have been striking in all three types of assistance throughout the four years and there has been little change in their relative standards as indicated by comparisons of the average grants. Some idea of the extreme variations which exist is shown by the figures of December, 1939, when Arkansas stood at the bottom of the list in all three types of assistance with averages of $8.10 for families with dependent children; $6.01 for recipients of old age assistance; and $6.48 for blind persons; while Massachusetts topped the dependent children list with $61.07 per family; and California had the highest averages in both old age assistance and aid to the blind: $32.97 and $48.17, respectively.[45] The median average payment was $18.90 for old age assistance; $30.42 per family for aid to dependent children and $20.89 for aid to the blind.[46]

[44] See Part III, Chapter 10.
[45] *Social Security Bulletin*, Vol. 3, No. 2, Feb., 1940.
[46] The average monthly payments in one half of the states with approved plans in each type of assistance, are above the median figure, and one half are below.

The wide variations between the states are evidence that no approach to uniformity has been achieved by the Federal Act and that state standards are largely determined by local factors, traditional attitudes toward the poor, economic conditions, financial resources, the number of people who are eligible for assistance, and general standards of living. On the whole, the average grants for categorical assistance under the Federal Social Security Act have shown somewhat wider variations between states than the average benefits under the FERA.

The original Social Security Bill required that the states maintain standards "compatible with decency and health." Congress substituted for this provision fixed amounts for individual monthly grants; $30 for old-age assistance and aid to the blind, and $18 for the first dependent child in a family and $12 for each of the others.[47] Grants to recipients above these amounts in any one month could not be counted in computing the Federal reimbursement of fifty percent for old-age and blind assistance and one third for aid to dependent children. In 1939, the maximum for the aged and the blind was increased to $40,[48] effective January 1, 1940. Payments to individuals in excess of these amounts were to be made entirely from state or local funds. The maximums set in the Federal Act therefore tended to discourage the states from paying larger amounts. Many state laws repeated the fixed maximum amounts of the Social Security Act, but several others maintained standards in the statutes and in practice which were considerably higher. On the other hand, the exceedingly low standards in the large majority of states indicate that the offer of the Federal Government to reimburse one-half or one-third of the total expenditures for much larger grants than have been actually given has done relatively little to insure more adequate assistance for the beneficiaries. It remains to be seen to what extent the increase to $40 will affect the amounts actually given to the aged and blind in 1940.

The Social Security Board recommended to Congress in 1939 that the provision for dependent children be liberalized

---

[47] The practice of setting fixed amounts in the law had been followed in the earlier state "pension" legislation.
[48] See p. 333 above.

also "since in most cases the mother must also be supported." This change was not included in the amendments to the Act, and Congress also failed to accept another recommendation made by the Board which was intended to equalize to some extent at least the great variations in assistance grants between states.

The Chairman of the Board told the Senate Finance Committee that the grants

are made to all States on the same percentage basis, regardless of the varying capacity among the States to bear their portion of this cost. The result has been wide difference between the States, both in number of persons aided and average payments to individuals. . . . While these variations may be explained in part on other grounds, there is no question that they are due in very large measure to the varying economic capacities of the States. The Board believes that it is essential to change from the present system of uniform percentage grants to a system whereby the percentage of the total cost in each State met through a Federal grant would vary in accordance with the relative economic capacity of the State. There should, however, be a minimum and maximum limitation to the percentage of the total cost in a State which will be met through Federal grants. The present system of uniform percentage grants results at best in an unnecessarily large amount of money flowing in and out of the Federal Treasury, and at worst in increasing the inequalities which now exist in the relative economic capacities of the States.[49]

This proposal is particularly interesting because it contemplates an equalization basis for grants-in-aid which would attempt to reduce to a formula the relationship between state needs and resources which proved so baffling a problem in the administration of FERA discretionary grants.

b. General Relief

When the liquidation of the FERA was announced, many social workers predicted that the return of responsibility for the "unemployables" to the states and localities would result in a sudden, deep and permanent slump in standards to the

[49] Statement of Arthur J. Altmeyer, Chairman of the Social Security Board, before the Senate Finance Committee on Amendments to the Social Security Act. June 12, 1939.

low levels of early poor relief.[50]   The figures for 1936-1939 show that this prediction was not entirely fulfilled.   Although general relief after 1936 was inadequate and showed great variations between states, the general average during the four years in question was not far below the average amounts given under the FERA.   This is more readily seen if the comparison takes into account the fact that the general relief averages are brought down to a lower level by a considerable number of supplementary grants which are made to families receiving benefits from other programs, including the three types of categorical assistance.[51]

In April, 1935, before the beginning of the Federal Works Program had affected the FERA rolls, the average monthly relief benefit was $28.96.   In April, 1939, the average general relief benefit was $23.86.[52]   In general the states which gave the low categorical assistance grants also stood at the bottom of the general relief list.   On the whole, the general relief average has shown a general trend upward since the middle of 1936 when Federal funds from the final grants to the states no longer affected the standards.   In June of that year, the average monthly benefit had dropped to $21.42.   One year later it was $22.10, and in June, 1938, it was $22.27, having held and added to its fifty cent gain.   Another increase occurred in 1939, putting the average at $23.55 in June and at $25.27 in December.[53]

These averages conceal rather less extreme variations between states than are found in the categorical assistance figures.[54]   In December, 1939, the monthly average general relief benefit was below $10 in eleven states, between $10 and $20 in 16 states and between $20 and $30 in 12 states, with 7 states not reporting.

As a rule the states with high per capita income and large relief loads spend the largest sums of money and provide the

[50] Abbott, Edith, "Abolish the Pauper Laws," *Social Service Review*, March, 1934, also *This Business of Relief, Proceedings* of Delegate Conference, American Association of Social Workers, New York, Feb., 1936. 179 pp.
[51] See pp. 364-65 above.
[52] *Social Security Bulletin*, Vol. 2, No. 8, Aug., 1939.
[53] *Social Security Bulletin*, Aug., 1939 and Feb., 1940.
[54] See p. 384 above.

high average benefits, while the poorer states with smaller relief case loads in proportion to population, appropriate less money and provide much smaller average benefits. Some idea of the extremes represented can be secured from the following table:

TABLE 9

General Relief, December, 1939 [1]

State	Number of cases receiving relief	Amount of obligations incurred for relief [2]	Average amount per case
California	149,103	$4,605,605	$30.89
Illinois	161,930	3,988,358	24.63
Massachusetts	68,018	1,971,597	28.99
New York	266,028	9,692,040	36.43
Pennsylvania	224,626	6,443,074	28.68
Alabama	2,284	20,820	9.12
Arkansas	3,800	18,468	4.86
Florida	10,140	65,996	6.51
Georgia	6,551	32,872	5.02
Mississippi	1,551	4,511	2.91
Nebraska	10,032	124,999	12.46
North Carolina	6,404	39,553	6.18

[1] Social Security Bulletin, Feb., 1940.
[2] From state and local funds. Excludes cost of administration; of materials, equipment, and other items incident to operation of work programs; and of special programs, hospitalization and burials.

The number of relief cases included in the statistical reports do not begin to represent the extent of need, especially in the poorer states where the relief standards have been very low. The Division of Social Research of the WPA estimated that in January, 1938, there were at least one million needy cases with a number awaiting assignment to Works Program employment. A little over half of this number were currently receiving general relief; the remainder were either receiving no relief, or assistance limited to small amounts of surplus commodities. The report states that in some localities, "as Cleveland and Chicago, where need is particularly acute, WPA rolls would be nearly doubled if all needy cases were given assignments. In other localities, such as St. Louis, the number receiving no aid is comparatively small, but the entire relief load is receiving grants which are much below recognized standards of adequacy. The situation is especially bad in cotton areas, where there are 200,000 rural cases now in need of aid. Coal, lumber and textile areas are also severely depressed." [55]

In the spring of 1939, the American Association of Social Workers asked its representatives in 35 states to answer this question: "What is happening to people dependent on general relief?" The answers were summarized in a press release dated May 31, from which the following statements are quoted:

Today, the millions dependent on relief are refugees just as truly as the victims of Old World oppression. They are American refugees with no place to go. And they are entitled to adequate and decent public aid if our democratic system is to fulfill the ideas of its founders. . . .

In some states, administrative machinery devised to meet the need for public aid 50 or even 100 years ago, is still being "patched up" in an effort to make it work in 1939. On the other hand, some localities have set up so much machinery that duplication of effort is inevitable. One county reports no less than 65 public agencies administering some form of general relief.

Many legislatures are still trying to control relief case loads by law, requiring such "proof" of the applicant's eligibility that his need for immediate help is overshadowed. Since January 1931 the Ohio legislature has passed 82 bills dealing with relief.

One state reports that food grants are approximately one-fifth of a minimum standard food budget such as that prescribed by the U. S. Department of Agriculture. In widespread areas general relief grants for food are far below the subsistence level.

Many states have no state-wide program of general relief. Aside from WPA the only assistance available in most of the 254 counties of Texas is Federal surplus commodities. In Vermont, general relief is administered by the Town Overseers of the Poor. Funds are local. "A wide range of policies exists as between towns from tolerably good to a beggarly dole system."

Reports from every part of the country tell of the tragic needs of transients and non-resident individuals and families. In South Carolina, for example, no public assistance is available to them. In some

[55] Typed memorandum for staff use based on field studies of "Unemployment and Relief Needs in Nine Cities, January 1938," Division of Social Research, Works Progress Administration.

of the southern counties of Florida a "hobo express" is run. This plan consists of transporting vagrants to the county line and dumping them.

An Atlanta family of four, for whom a minimum food budget would total $31.61 a month, was found to be receiving a food grant of $6.70 a month.

In New Mexico, the estimated minimum budget for food is $7 per individual per month. In Taos County the amount actually granted averages $2.50 per month.

In an Indiana township a family of four receives $2.85 a week for groceries, plus a quart of milk for the baby, from the Township Trustee. This is the regular amount of food allotted to a family of this size. It allows them to eat two meals a day, mostly bread, potatoes, cereal and beans. They cannot afford fresh vegetables, fruit or meat. The baby gets milk but there is none for the six-year-old child.

Harassed parents have come to the offices of voluntary relief agencies in Chicago seeking to arrange for the adoption of their children because they could not be cared for properly on relief budgets.

The Social Service Review, March, 1940, gave the following graphic report of the suffering in Omaha, Nebraska during the winter of 1939-1940:

One of the most severe winters within the memory of the present generation has brought added cruelties to the bitter situation faced by very large numbers of unemployed men and their families. The situation in Omaha, Nebraska is unfortunately typical of widespread suffering that has been meagerly and grudgingly relieved by our state and local governments since federal aid for home relief through the Federal Emergency Relief Administration came to an end. This long and exhausting period of hardship and deprivation has been endured with great courage by the relief clients. In Omaha, with the thermometer at 18 below zero, the indifference of the county commissioners about providing fuel has continued. The suffering among the destitute has been almost indescribable. The federal government has seen this tragedy but has done nothing. The state government will do nothing. Children are too hungry to go to school, and stay huddled in bed because there are no fires to heat their miserable homes. With rents not paid, these unhappy people live where and as they can. . . .[56]

[56] P. 133, Vol. XIV, No. 1.

c. Work Relief

Work-relief wages under the FERA were usually somewhat higher than the amounts allowed for direct relief.[57]   The averages given in the discussion of FERA standards include both relief and direct relief. The Federal Works Program, however, inaugurated a new standard for relief wages, in the "security wage." [58]   The average monthly wage actually earned during the first four years of the WPA was approximately $52.50 per worker for all types of jobs and all parts of the country. The rates varied from $21 for unskilled labor in certain rural areas to $90 and over for professional and technical services in the largest industrial centers.   On September 1, 1939, changes were made in accordance with the Emergency Relief Appropriation Act of 1939 which provided that the monthly earning schedule "shall not be varied for workers of the same type in different geographical areas to any greater extent than may be justified by differences in the cost of living."   As a result of this provision, wages have been cut in certain brackets and increased in others, in order to meet another requirement of the Act that the changes might not "substantially affect the current national average labor cost per person."

Even the higher wage standards of the work program have proved inadequate for all but the barest necessities of life for families of average size. The widespread practice of supplementation which has already been mentioned is evidence of the complete inadequacy of these wages for the needs of large families.

Wages on local work-relief or "work-for-relief" projects [59] have been much lower than those paid by the WPA. They are based on the budget deficiency of the worker and not on a monthly security wage. The use of the budget-deficiency as the measure of total wages, brings the earning capacity of this relief labor down to the level of the low general relief grants and far below the already inadequate Federal security wage. The resulting low hourly rates tend to depress the prevailing wage rates. Many cities have had two different wage scales

[57] Part III, Chapter 10.
[58] See Part III, Chapter 7.
[59] See pp. 378-379.

for the same type of work. One large city pays 50 cents an hour to relief workers and from 68 to 75 cents to regular employees for exactly the same kind of common labor. Another city pays relief labor only 25 cents an hour. Outside the large cities relief wage rates more nearly approximate prevailing wages, principally because the latter are already so low. Rural relief workers get as little as 20 cents an hour in some areas and many rural communities make their payments in kind rather than in cash.

In promoting this type of work program municipal and county officials have reverted to the repressive principles of local poor relief. In this they have followed the example of Congress which during the last four years has consistently favored the poor relief policy of "less eligibility."

Federal work-relief wages have been deliberately kept on a lower level than earnings in comparable private employment, in order, supposedly, to stimulate the relief workers to seek jobs in private industry, and lest they yield to the temptation to stay indefinitely on the payroll of the Federal Government.[60] The Appropriation Acts of 1939 and 1940 contained a provision which was intended to force more relief workers to seek private jobs and at the same time to distribute more fairly the benefits of the program. This provision required that relief workers, except veterans, should be removed from the program after eighteen months' continuous employment and not be eligible for reinstatement before the expiration of thirty days, and only then after their eligibility for relief had been established once more.

In January, 1940, the Division of Research of the Work Projects Administration made the following report:

In July and August more than 775,000 WPA project workers were dropped from their jobs in accordance with the 18-months provision of the 1939 Relief Act. A survey covering more than 138,000 of these workers, in 23 large and representative cities, disclosed that 3 to 4 weeks after their lay-off 7.6 percent were employed in private jobs. In November, a second interview with the same group showed that 2 to 3 months after dismissal 12.7 percent, or fewer than 100,000 of the 775,000 workers, were employed in private industry. In industrial centers like Buffalo, Cleveland, Cincinnati, Detroit and

[60] Part I, Chapter 1, and Part III, Chapter 10.

Birmingham, the proportion with jobs was about one in six, in eight of the 23 cities it was about one in ten.[61]

d. Children Under the Categorical System

The White House Conference on Children in a Democracy, the fourth decennial conference on the welfare of the children of the nation since 1909,[62] reported to its final session on January 18-20, 1940, its conclusions and recommendations regarding "Economic Aid to Families." The following statements taken from this report constitute a significant commentary upon the present system of categorical aid in relation to child welfare.

Children in America whose families need economic assistance do not fare alike. Nor is the treatment they get determined by what is best for them, but by accidents of residence and family composition. Numbers of children are distributed somewhat as follows: [63]

In families receiving	March 1939	August 1939
WPA wages	4,500,000	3,000,000
General relief	2,400,000	2,000,000
Aid to dependent children	721,000	751,000
FSA subsistence grants	250,000	150,000
Surplus commodities only	?	?
Aid from private agencies	A few	A few
No assistance	Many	Many

They may be in a family whose father last winter was lucky enough to have work on WPA at a "security wage" and whose mother was a good enough manager to make the wage "do." The father may have been laid off in June, and unable to find work. He may live in a place where no public relief is given to families with an employable member, and where there are no private agencies. His church may have no means of helping. His relatives may be as hard up as he is. By this time he may have figured that his family will be better off without him. Suppose he eliminates himself. It may be

[61] Workers dropped from WPA in accordance with the 18-months provision in the 1939 Relief Act. Division of Research, Work Projects Administration, Federal Works Agency, Jan. 24, 1940.

[62] See Chapter 2.

[63] There are many children in families receiving grants for the aged and the blind, but it is not possible to estimate their number nor to what extent they share in such grants.

months before "aid to dependent children" can be secured and then it may not be enough to meet the needs of the whole family.

Or suppose he lives in a place where general relief is available, even to families with an able-bodied man, and stays with his family. According to where it is, they may get grocery orders; or $5 or $10 occasionally; or a small monthly allowance sufficient to buy enough food to keep them alive and possibly to pay rent in the poorest quarters; or they may get a regular allowance calculated to meet the cost of all the essentials of normal living and supplemented by medical care and sympathetic consideration of other than economic needs.

Or suppose, again, he hears there is a chance of work in some other town, and decides to take his family and go after it. If he is disappointed, as he is likely to be, the probability is that they are now worse off than ever, and are on the way to becoming a tragic migrant family.

The greatest need of the children of America in 1940 is work for the 8 million or 9 million unemployed adults—"real work at real wages," whether in private employment or on a Federal work program—and a prospect that there will be work for the children themselves as they reach working age. . . .

At present the weakest spots are the failure of the Federal work program to employ all the employables in need; the inadequate provision of other kinds of assistance for the children of employables who cannot get on WPA, particularly the children of aliens; the relatively slow development of the program of aid to dependent children, as compared with the program for the blind and the aged; the lack of adequate general assistance for a large part of the population of the country who are not eligible for, or are not cared for by, any of the special programs, particularly families who live in rural areas and families who cannot meet the residence requirements in the places where they live.

Enlargement of the Federal work program to provide work for all the employables in need, and adoption of a stabilized, flexible program to this end, is the first essential in filling in the gaps in our present provisions. For families on farms where WPA work is not feasible or advisable, extension of the rural-rehabilitation program of the Farm Security Administration is desirable.[64]

The pattern on which our program of public assistance has been started is a pattern of categories. Four years have demonstrated not only that the special program for children has lagged behind the

[64] It is estimated that the rural-rehabilitation program now reaches little more than half the families who are eligible for its loans.

other two, but that preoccupation with the needs of these three categories tends to distract attention from the needs of persons outside the categories, and to delay in most States the development of a comprehensive program of public assistance for all.[65]

[65] "Economic Aid to Families," White House Conference on Children in a Democracy. United States Children's Bureau, Washington, D. C. Jan., 1940.

Chapter 16

Social Work in Government and the Role of the Private Agencies

Relief Investigators

The great expansion of social work under public auspices which took place in 1932 and 1933, when state and Federal governments undertook the administration of emergency relief to the unemployed, was closely associated in the minds of government officials and in public opinion alike with the need for "investigators" who would protect the tax-payers' interests and see to it that the money which was available for relief went to the people who needed it most. The Rules and Regulations of the FERA had called for "trained and experienced investigators." In his report to Congress in 1935 the Federal Emergency Relief Administrator stated that the administrative costs reported by the states included "the large number of trained social workers who determine the eligibility of persons applying for relief, and who save literally millions of relief dollars for needy persons by preventing persons who have other resources from receiving relief." One of the major differences between the work program which began in 1935 and the work relief program of the FERA was considered to be the fact that, under the WPA, the man who got a job on a project was "paid wages and the social worker drops out of the picture," whereas on work relief "his need is still determined by a social worker, and he feels himself to be something of a public ward, with small freedom of choice." [1] And the difference between the work program and relief is pointed up by the following graphic description of the role of the investigator:

[1] Hopkins, Harry L., *Spending to Save*, p. 114.

395

Then there is the humiliation of relief, a humiliation that we cannot help inflicting, for the "means test" is our one way of keeping panhandlers off the rolls. It calls for the most detailed prying into the lives and habits of every applicant for relief. We butt into their homes, digging around to find out if they have any hidden resources, or some relative who is able to aid.[2]

1. Social Work in Work Relief

In spite of the change in program, however, investigation of the relief needs of most of the WPA project workers has continued to be necessary.[3] The major responsibility for these investigations was placed upon local public agencies. The WPA, however, has employed a staff of social workers in Federal, state and district or area offices, numbering, the country over, between 500 and 1,000 at different periods. This social work staff was originally employed in 1935 to see that the employable people who were on the relief rolls of the FERA were properly transferred to the jobs on the WPA. They also acted in a liaison capacity between the WPA, the relief agencies which investigated and certified the need, and the public employment offices where all applicants for WPA jobs were required to register. The social work Division of Intake and Certification, therefore, was responsible for the intake of the work program. Social workers stood at the door of this program which was entered by way of a "means test," as they had stood at the door of the FERA.

Since January, 1937, the Division of Intake and Certification has been part of the Employment Division which was organized to include intake, assignment and labor relations.[4]

[2] "They'd Rather Work," by Harry L. Hopkins, *Collier's*, November 16, 1935.

[3] See Part III, Chapter 7. Part IV, Chapters 14 and 15.

[4] *Functions of Intake and Certification Section.* The State Director or Assistant State Director of the Division of Employment shall be a social worker. Such social worker shall be approved by the Regional Director and the Assistant Commissioner in charge of the Division of Employment. There shall also be employed in the Division of Employment a sufficient number of qualified social workers to perform the functions of the Intake and Certification Section. The duties of this staff shall be coordinated with other functions of the Division of Employment and shall be under the supervision of a social worker in the State Division of Employment. *Operating Procedure Memorandum,* Work Projects Administration, July 31, 1939. Part II, Section 4.

The social workers have continued to be responsible for the validity of certifications or referrals made by relief agencies and it has also been their duty to make periodic reviews of the circumstances of project workers to discover those who are not in need of relief so that they may be dropped from the program.[5]

In general, the function of the social worker in the WPA has been one of interpretation, liaison, and adjustment, all of which are effective in three directions, with the workers on projects, with the other divisions of the WPA, and with the community, including other agencies, private and public, Federal, state and local. The Employment Division and social work as a part of that division, is primarily concerned with what is happening to people and with the safeguarding of human values in a program which deals so largely in engineering problems and the materials used in construction.[6]

2. In Categorical Assistance

Among the permanent agencies established by Federal and state governments since 1935, social work personnel has been used most extensively in the programs in which the giving of benefits has been based upon the determination of need: that is, in the Federal, state and local agencies which administer categorical assistance [7] and in those responsible for state and local general relief as well as for the certification or referral of employable persons in need to the Federal work relief programs.

a. Personnel

The Social Security Board not only recognized from the beginning that the administration of public assistance was a social work function, but adopted definite policies in regard to the value of qualified personnel, the importance of professional

[5] See Part IV, Chapter 15. The Emergency Relief Appropriation Act of 1939 provided that such a review be made every six months. The 1940 Act changed this provision to every twelve months.

[6] Brown, J. C., *Social Work in the Works Progress Administration,* Works Progress Administration, May, 1936, multigraphed, 9223.

[7] In 1939 approximately 60,000 persons, including clerical workers, were employed in administering categorical assistance in state and local Divisions of Public Assistance throughout the country. Many of these divisions also administered general relief.

education, the selection of staff in accordance with a merit system, and the dangers of political bias and activity in relation to staff appointments.

At the beginning of the Federal program, social work and other professional personnel were employed under the "expert" provision of the Act. Later all staff personnel were put under the regulations of the Federal Civil Service Commission. In September, 1938, the Commission held its first open competitive examination for social work positions in the Bureaus of Public Assistance and Research and Statistics of the Social Security Board. 2,050 persons applied for the four positions covered by the examination. These positions ranged from Senior Consultant in Public Assistance at $4,600 a year to Assistant Consultant in Public Assistance at $2,600. 802 persons were given ratings as a result of the examination. More than half of the successful applicants received ratings for the lowest of the four positions and only 28 were found to be eligible for the position of Senior Consultant.

The Social Security Act specifically excepted from the scope of the Board's approval of state plans those methods of administration "relating to selection, tenure of office, and compensation of personnel." [8] This clause was interpreted by the Board to refer to the designation of individuals for specified jobs and not to the methods which might be used in selecting qualified employees. The Board therefore ruled that "since effective administration is dependent largely upon qualified personnel," a state plan be required to "contain provisions relative to minimum qualifications to be used as a basis for staff selection in State and local agencies." [9]

The basic objective is the establishment, in all participating jurisdictions, of personnel standards which will ensure sound and continuing development of the social security program. It has been necessary also to consider occasional problems which have arisen in a few jurisdictions, where, at times, partisan conduct of administration has been inconsistent with the purposes of the State law and the Federal Act. The Board believes that it is sound public policy to place the entire administrative responsibility with a State agency as regards the selection, tenure of office, and compensation of in-

[8] See Part IV, Chapter 13.
[9] *Third Annual Report*, p. 91.

dividual employees. It believes, further, that effective administration requires establishment and maintenance of objective standards for personnel engaged in the State public-assistance and unemployment compensation programs and, to this end, has consistently advocated that States adopt an effective merit system.

. . . an approved State plan must contain provisions relative to minimum objective standards of education, training, and experience for State and local personnel. A career service, which is founded on unbiased selection of the best qualified persons available, job classification based upon analysis of duties and responsibilities, an equitable plan of compensation, and promotion or dismissal on the basis of merit and performance, offers the public—whether as taxpayers or recipients of public assistance—a quality of service in keeping with the objectives of the Social Security Act and of State laws, and some assurance of reasonable administrative costs.[10]

The Board has further emphasized the necessity of employing "the best qualified persons available" because upon these people rests the responsibility of making decisions, in the course of their day-to-day work, "which affect the lives of persons who are living on the margin of subsistence," and which "require capacity to observe, evaluate and, to the greatest possible extent, to harmonize the often tangled and apparently conflicting interests of public policy and personal relationships. They underscore the need for permanent, experienced personnel in the staffs of State and local public assistance agencies and for a level of education and training which will ensure that these staffs have both a mastery of the necessary professional skills and a broad and unbiased understanding of the purpose of the program and of the individuals with whom they are dealing." [11]

Under the stimulus of this strong position taken by the Social Security Board, the states as a whole made considerable progress in establishing merit systems in some form for the selection of their public assistance personnel. In June, 1939, the Chairman of the Board reported to the Senate Finance Committee that 22 state public assistance agencies were already operating under merit systems and that "in varying degrees all the States have set up objective standards of some

[10] *Ibid.*, pp. 13 and 91.
[11] *Third Annual Report*, pp. 105-6.

sort."[12]   This progress had been achieved in spite of many handicaps, such as the increasing limitations imposed by residence requirements, low salary scales, and rigid restrictions placed upon expenditures for administrative purposes.[13]

One of the greatest hindrances to the development of satisfactory social work staffs in state and county departments of public welfare has been the failure of public officials in many states to appreciate the value of qualified personnel. This failure has seemed to be due in part at least to the unfortunate conceptions of the nature and function of social work and of social workers which grew up in certain parts of the country during the administration of emergency unemployment relief.[14]

Although adverse reactions to social work under the FERA were evident in many communities, most of the states capitalized the major gains in social work personnel and in experience which were made in the administration of emergency relief. The culling of staffs which was necessary in the fall and winter of 1935-1936 furnished an opportunity, in the states which did not have to demobilize completely, to conserve the best of their personnel. Added to this, they were able to draw on the nucleus of workers who had had a beginning of professional education under the training program of the FERA.[15] Even in the states where it was not possible to use these newly "trained" workers, the very fact that the Federal Government had invested money to send state residents to study at schools of social work created a predisposition within official state circles in favor of professional social work personnel. It was possible for the representatives of the Federal Bureau of Public Assistance to point to the fact that there were state residents who had had the type of education which they were recommending. It was easier for state officials to accept good

[12] "To date, seventeen states have civil service laws in effect, those of Alabama, Minnesota, New Mexico, and Rhode Island being new additions this year." Stevenson, Marietta, "Recent Trends in Public Welfare Legislation," *Social Service Review*, Sept., 1939. The 22 merit systems mentioned in the text include the Civil Service laws in these 17 states.

[13] See *Third Annual Report* for discussion of these limitations.

[14] See Part III, Chapters 10 and 12.

[15] See Part III, Chapter 12. For example, in 1939, North Dakota had 19 of its 32 FERA students in administrative or supervisory public welfare positions.

personnel standards because they were not merely theoretical qualifications but were exemplified in people who actually belonged in the state.

Nevertheless, political patronage and other types of political interference have worked havoc with carefully built-up staffs in a few of the states and have partly demolished them in several others. A program which gave to a branch of government responsibility for spending such large sums of money was bound to be considered the legitimate prey of unscrupulous public officials. The wonder is that politics has, in the past four years, affected adversely relatively small percentages of both the total personnel and the total public expenditures for categorical assistance throughout the country.

The Social Security Board recommended to the 1939 regular session of Congress that in addition to the clause which withheld from the Board's jurisdiction the methods of state administration relating to selection, tenure of office and compensation of personnel, there be inserted the requirement that the states establish approved merit systems for the selection and maintenance of personnel. The Board maintained that such a change in the Act would "strengthen State administration, safeguard taxpayers and beneficiaries, and place Federal-State relations on a more stable and automatic basis." [16]

The same report recommended that the 5 percent allowed for administration in addition to the grants for old-age and blind assistance be amended to provide for Federal grants which would reimburse the states for 50 percent of the necessary cost of proper administration on the ground that this would establish a Federal precedent for more adequate provision of administrative funds in the states and facilitate the operation of satisfactory merit systems.

In August, 1939, Congress amended the Social Security Act, to provide that, beginning January 1, 1940, the Federal Government would pay one-half of administrative costs "as found necessary by the Board for the proper and efficient administra-

[16] Statement of Arthur J. Altmeyer, Chairman of the Social Security Board, before the Senate Finance Committee on Amendments to the Social Security Act, June, 1939. The same recommendation was made regarding personnel in the administration of State Unemployment Compensation Laws.

tion" of aid to dependent children and to the blind; although the original provision for the payment to the states of 5 percent of the old-age assistance grants, for administration, was retained in the Act. It further gave the Board authority to require that state plans for the three types of public assistance and for unemployment compensation "provide such methods of administration (including after Jan. 1, 1940, methods relating to the establishment and maintenance of personnel standards on a merit basis . . .) as are found by the Board to be necessary for the proper and efficient operation of the plan."

This action was particularly significant as evidence of acceptance by the states and their representatives in Congress of the stand already taken and the methods used by the Social Security Board in handling this difficult problem. It was also an evidence that the pendulum was swinging back from the extreme reaction of 1935 against the authoritative regime of the FERA to an acceptance by the states of this type of Federal requirement in regard to state personnel.

Under the Social Security Act as amended, the Board issued on November 1, 1939, "Standards for a Merit System of Personnel Administration in State Employment Security and State Public Assistance Agencies," with the following instructions:

Rules and regulations to effectuate a merit system in accordance with these minimum standards shall be adopted by the State agencies and submitted as a part of the public-assistance plan, of the State unemployment compensation law, and of the plan for the operation of State public-employment offices, to be reviewed by the Board under the Social Security Act or the Wagner-Peyser Act.

b. Training

Largely because of the restrictive personnel clause in the Act, The Social Security Board made no pronouncement regarding the use of funds by the states for the training of social work staff during the first two years of the program. This delay may have been due also to regard for the general reaction against the highly centralized Federal Relief Administration and a reluctance to give to the states a Federal policy on social work training so soon after the FERA program had come to an end.[17]

[17] See Part III, Chapter 12.

In December, 1937, the Board "established a policy that its auditors will not take exception to the use of Federal administrative funds by States for paying salaries of staff members on educational leave in schools of social work." [18] The announcement of this policy was accompanied by recommendations to the states from the Bureau of Public Assistance that workers who were granted such "educational leave" should attend only those schools of social work which met the standards of the American Association of Schools of Social Work; that they should spend at least an academic year at school if they had had no previous professional education; and that they should plan to return for service to the state public assistance program for a reasonable period following their educational leave. In other words, the fundamental principles which were tried out in the earlier emergency training program of the FERA were incorporated two years later in the permanent Federal-state public assistance program. [19]

In 1936-1937, when state departments were still in a transition stage and before the Social Security Board had announced its approval of "educational leaves," a few state agencies sent staff members away to schools of social work, using for this purpose in two or three states at least, money left over from the final grants of the Federal Emergency Relief Administration. After the policy of the Board was announced in the winter of 1937, several more states granted educational leaves. During the following year agencies in nine states gave some financial assistance to approximately fifty-four staff members in order that they might attend accredited schools of social work. Also 155 workers went from 22 states entirely at their own expense. During 1939 three states—Washington, South Carolina and Ohio—wrote into their public assistance plans definite provisions for educational leave. At least one state appropriated funds specifically for educational leave of social work staff members. Workers have continued to secure leave of absence for study at their own expense or with financial help from the public welfare agencies. As late as 1939 small rem-

[18] Mimeographed statement issued by the Bureau of Public Assistance.
[19] Title VI—Public Health Work, of the Social Security Act, provides funds for "the training of personnel for State and local health work," as well as for "establishing and maintaining adequate public-health services."

nants of Federal Emergency Relief funds were being used in a few states for this purpose.

3. In General Relief

The personnel standards and provisions for social work training which have developed in state and local categorical assistance programs under the leadership of the Social Security Board apply to the administration of general relief insofar as these functions are integrated in the same agencies and discharged by the same staffs.

Also, 17 of the state public welfare departments which have been charged with the administration or supervision of general relief, have been given specific legal responsibility of some kind in regard to the qualifications, approval, or actual appointment of general relief personnel.[20]

4. In Child Welfare

The Children's Bureau of the Department of Labor has followed the precedent, already established in its own practice and in that of other permanent agencies, of employing experienced and qualified professional people from the fields of health and of social work as they were needed to administer the new programs under the Social Security Act.[21]

The Children's Bureau has from the beginning of these programs taken a position comparable to that taken later by the Social Security Board in regard to the desirable qualifications of state and local personnel and the use of administrative funds for training. The Bureau was in a position to set defi-

[20] As of September, 1939, Alabama, Arizona, Arkansas, Colorado, Kansas, Maryland, New Mexico, New York, North Dakota, Oklahoma, Oregon, South Carolina, Utah, Virginia (except in specified localities), Washington, West Virginia and Wyoming.

[21] The Children's Bureau has employed professional social workers and other professional services required by its program since its establishment in 1912. Social workers have also been employed by other Federal agencies, including the Veterans Administration, the Office of Indian Affairs, and the Department of Justice, and to a limited extent by the United States Housing Authority and by local agencies concerned with housing, to assist in the selection of tenants. In 1939 the permanent housing program had, however, barely made a beginning in the definition of staff functions.

nite standards because the grants made to the states, under all three of its programs, were to be used for administrative purposes only, and many of the social workers and other professional personnel employed by the states to administer the child welfare and health programs, were paid entirely or in part from these Federal funds. Largely because of this use of Federal money for salaries, a considerable number of child welfare workers were released by state departments of welfare on "educational leave" to go to schools of social work before most of the states were prepared to use their own administrative funds for the training of social workers either for child welfare or public assistance; and before the Social Security Board had authorized the use of Federal public assistance funds for this purpose. The standards and conditions governing the use of Federal funds for the training of child welfare workers, as set forth by the Children's Bureau, followed closely the principles of the FERA training program.[22]

On January 1, 1939, there were, in 47 states, Hawaii, Alaska and the District of Columbia, 706 persons, paid in whole or in part by Federal funds, performing professional social services for children, under the supervision of the Children's Bureau. From February 1, 1936, to January 1, 1939, "educational leave" for study at schools of social work had been granted by 35 states and Hawaii, to a total of 256 persons.

5. In the Selection of Families for Resettlement

The Resettlement Administration, which became the Farm Security Administration in 1937, has maintained a small staff of social workers in its Federal and regional offices to select the low income families to occupy the rural and suburban communities constructed by that agency, and to assist in the resettlement of the families living on the sub-marginal land which had been purchased by its Land Use Division. The one relief function of the Farm Security Administration, assistance to needy farm families in the form of "subsistence payments," or "emergency grants,"[23] has not been discharged by social

[22] Atkinson, Mary Irene, "Children's Bureau Policies on Training," *The Compass*, May, 1938.
[23] See Part IV, Chapter 13.

workers but integrated with the other rural rehabilitation activities carried on by the county farm and home supervisors.

Social Work a Permanent Function of Government

The experience with the permanent public assistance and relief programs during the past four years has shown beyond a doubt that social work has become an accepted and established function of government, Federal, state and local, in every section of the United States. The degree to which this function has developed varies greatly from state to state and often from county to county. It is frequently limited in practice if not in theory to the determination of need, but the foundation has been laid in the permanent program of public welfare upon which to build a quality of service in keeping with the best which the profession has to offer. The following editorial comment from *Public Management* in the issue of March, 1938, is an example of the way in which social work has been accepted as a regular government service by an increasing number of public officials.

"Anybody Can Hand Out Relief"

. . . such utterance shows a lack of understanding of a vast and complicated social phenomenon. During the past seven years every municipality has been faced with new responsibilities in social welfare. To many public officials social work, a few years ago, meant dispensing relief through the local private charity; and in the minds of some officials the larger task of providing shelter, food, and other essentials for thousands of law-abiding citizens is still confused with this earlier experience.

But consider the complicated problems of the confused families and individuals who are the victims of this phenomenon. Are these problems so simple that anybody can do the job? Isn't it time that those with training and experience in good social welfare techniques be put on this job and that well-wishers or political charity mongers be sent to the benches? We need those who have had training in the human side of government and in meeting the social problems of a community.

Impartial studies of relief and welfare administration prove how false economy in administrative costs increases the cost of relief. For example a committee which recently investigated relief administration in a large city reported that:

"Successful operation is dependent upon the allocation of sufficient funds for administrative purposes. The maximum of 8 percent now allocated by law for administrative expense is inadequate. . . . Insufficient administrative funds have resulted in a reduction in the number of case workers to a point where it is physically impossible for them to perform their duties. The survey shows that a majority of the relief clients had not been visited by case workers for over four months. Adequate supervision of relief cases would reduce fraud and uncover resources which would remove many people from the relief rolls. This is impossible with the present reduced staff. Each case worker is now required to carry a load of approximately 500 cases."

The chief executives of many municipalities have recognized the need for placing welfare administration on a sound long-term basis under the direction of carefully selected and trained personnel. In such cities and counties it has been found that a few extra dollars for administration not only result in better care of those in need of assistance but also save thousands of dollars of relief expenditures.[24]

The American Public Welfare Association

The American Public Welfare Association, although supported since the year following its organization in 1930 by membership dues and grants from private Foundations, has worked so closely with governmental agencies and officials that it has come to be regarded as more in the category of a public than of a private agency.[25] Its interests have continued to be exclusively in the public field, and its influence has been an important factor in shaping the policies and practice of Federal and state governments during the past four years, particularly in the administration of the public assistance titles of the Social Security Act.

During 1935, the year of transition from the emergency to the permanent program, when 44 legislatures were in session, the Association threw the weight of its influence and most of the time of its staff into advisory service to governors, legis-

[24] Vol. XX, No. 3. pp. 65 and 66.
[25] This Association has been the only one among the many national agencies supported by private funds which has had a constituency made up entirely of governmental agencies, public officials and persons who are members because of their interest in the field of public welfare. See Part II, Chapter 4.

latures and welfare officials on problems of legislation, organization and administration. Draft bills were prepared, forms suggested, and procedures worked out to help the states in setting up the new programs. This service continued through the subsequent stages of organization, reorganization, readjustment, and amendment of earlier legislation.[26]

Assistance to the states in the recruiting and placement of personnel has been a major part of the Association program. In this area the non-governmental agency was in a position to make a direct approach to state personnel problems when the Social Security Board, for reasons of strategy and expediency, could not do so.

The office of the Association has become a clearing house of information on public welfare, second in importance only to that of the Social Security Board, and covering a wider range of subject matter than comes within the scope of the Federal agency. Material has been assembled in the files and library comprising an invaluable collection of laws, bulletins, procedures, regulations and other official documents. The *Public Welfare News*, a monthly bulletin, which first appeared in the spring of 1933 at the beginning of the FERA, constitutes an invaluable running record of important developments in public welfare since that time.

Surveys and studies of state and local public welfare services and needs, often made jointly with other national organizations such as the Public Administration Service, have led to important changes and the acceptance of higher standards of administration and assistance in a number of agencies. The Association has devoted much attention also to the relationship between public assistance and unemployment compensation; to the integration of the latter program with the employment service; to the problem of general relief faced by the states and localities; and to the development of better facilities for medical and hospital care for persons in need.

A significant contribution to the development of better facilities for medical care by state departments of health and welfare has been made in co-operation with the American Medical Association and the American Hospital Association, and

[26] The APWA reported that during 1936 more than 40 states used the recommended draft bills prepared by their staff members.

through the close connection established with the Federal Interdepartmental Committee on Health and Welfare. These activities had a direct bearing upon the program recommended by the National Health Conference, already mentioned, and upon the framing of the National Health Act of 1939.

A distinctive contribution to public welfare development has been made by the Association in the annual Round Table Conferences which have been held regularly in Washington, D. C. beginning in December, 1936, the first year of the Social Security program. These conferences have given public welfare officials an opportunity to confer with each other and with the staff members of Federal agencies and have served as a forum for the discussion of current problems. Practically every state and territorial jurisdiction receiving Social Security grants from Federal agencies has been represented at each of the conferences. The printed proceedings contain invaluable material on current practice and opinion in the field and constitute an important part of the permanent record of the development of public welfare in the United States.

At the Conference held in December, 1939, the "National Council of State Public Assistance and Welfare Administrators" was formed within the structure of the American Public Welfare Association. This Council planned to hold regional conferences in seven areas during 1940, in order to provide an opportunity for the various states to discuss problems peculiar to each region.[27] Its general purpose is to afford State Administrators a means of discussing their common problems and gathering and exchanging information relative to their particular responsibilities in maintaining high standards of leadership in their state programs.

The Community Chests

The rapid development of permanent public welfare programs and the extensive responsibility assumed by government for relief and categorical assistance, have profoundly affected the privately supported social agencies, especially the community chests and the family welfare societies.

---

[27] See *Public Welfare News*, Feb., 1940, American Public Welfare Association.

Prior to and during the early years of the depression, the community chests based their appeals for funds almost entirely upon the need for material relief. When the responsibility for meeting this need was virtually taken over by government, the chests were forced to find ways of showing why the services rendered by their member agencies were sufficiently important to the welfare of the respective communities to justify the generous contributions which they still expected and asked from private citizens and business concerns. Their money raising was, of course, also handicapped by the fact that private incomes had suffered severely from the same depression which increased the need for relief and social services. Appeals for contributions were often met by the excuse that since the government was taking care of relief and taxes were increasing, private social services were needed less or perhaps not at all. Simultaneous payments of taxes and chest contributions were said to involve unreasonable demands upon the same pocketbook.

Finding an answer to these arguments, and giving an adequate interpretation of the place of the private social agencies in the community program of the late 1930's, has been the absorbing and unfinished task of the local chests, their constituent agencies and their national association. There has been an effort to define more clearly or to redefine the whole field of private social endeavor. "Social welfare planning" has gradually replaced the term "community organization," the primary function of councils of social agencies.

The community today is not as independent a unit for the statesmanlike planning of social work activities as it used to be. Far-flung programs and an increasingly comprehensive network of social welfare administration under the federal and state governments cover much of the social work area that previously had been left to the localities. . . . It is now a question not merely of recognizing that tax-supported social work is far more extensive than private activities, but rather of adjusting and accommodating local social work plans to the extensive and growing programs under state and Federal leadership.[28]

[28] Klein, Philip, "Social Welfare Planning," *Social Work Year Book*, 1939.

Public officials from the President down have consistently maintained by radio and press that the work of private agencies is not only valuable but necessary. Most of the supporters of government responsibility for social services agree that private endeavor will always be needed regardless of the extent to which public services are developed. However, it is not clear that private social work has made much progress during the past four to six years to meet the challenge implied in this statement.[29] It is also impossible to say how far the future of private social work is reflected in the fact that the incomes of community chests have been generally less than they were for some years before the beginning of the depression. The peak income in 1932 was, of course, due to efforts to meet the needs of the unemployed. After that year the total amount raised by chests throughout the country decreased markedly until 1936. Since then the total income has steadily increased, and in 1938 the average chest came within ten percent of amounts raised in 1929. However, the increase in total income is accounted for in part by the fact that during the ten years ending in 1938, the number of chests increased by more than one hundred and fifty. Because of this fact, instead of the increase indicated by a comparison of totals from 1936 to 1938, there was an actual decline in the results of the various individual campaigns. This decline is relative, since trends in chest income reflect trends in the national income, and the period in question has been too full of complicating factors to justify definite conclusions as to the significance of successive chest failures to meet their full quotas. However, it is probable that the decline of the last few years will become absolute rather than relative unless the private social work field succeeds in meeting the challenge of the new public program by redefining its objectives and reformulating its program "in logical relation to governmental welfare activities."[30]

[29] Jeter and Beckelman, "Future of the Private Field—II," *Social Work Today*, May, 1939.

[30] Jeter and Beckelman, *op. cit.* See also Fisher, Jacob, "Future of the Private Field—I," in the April, 1939, issue. For figures on the chest campaigns and description of the movement, see Blanchard, Ralph, "Community Chests," *Social Work Year Book*, 1939. Mr. Blanchard says that in "1928 there were 314 [chests], raising about $68,500,000. . . . By

The decline, however, appeared to become absolute in 1939, in which 518 chests raised a total of $82,808,000 as against $83,789,000 raised by 480 chests the preceding year.

TABLE 10

Total Amounts Raised by the Same 171 Chests 1925-1939
(By Years)

1925	$52,574,000	1933	$60,961,000
1926	55,456,000	1934	52,195,000
1927	56,948,000	1935	50,927,000
1928	58,934,000	1936	52,588,000
1929	60,678,000	1937	54,587,000
1930	62,104,000	1938	54,745,000
1931	67,567,000	1939	52,669,000
1932	78,542,000		

In the effort to increase contributions, the national publicity methods initiated under the pressures of the unemployment emergency have been used during the past four years to their fullest extent. The Committee on the Mobilization of Relief Resources [31] which in 1931 conducted a national drive to stimulate contributions in order to meet the needs of the unemployed, has been continued and has annually called a Conference on the Community Mobilization of Human Needs, preceding the fall and winter campaigns.

Although the local chests and their national association, Community Chests, Inc., have been chiefly occupied since the early years of the depression in building up a new basis for community support, there has also been a definite effort to influence the relief policy of the Federal Government by pressure from the important industrial leaders who held positions on national and local chest directorates. Aroused over the increases in the national debt, the tax situation, and the huge sums being spent for relief, particularly work relief after 1935, these leaders in the chest movement have advocated consistently a return to Federal direct relief.

1938 the number of chests had increased to 475, with a sum of nearly $84,000,000 raised."
[31] See Part II, Chapter 4.

Early in 1938, they presented a plan for Federal relief to the Senate Committee to Investigate Unemployment and Relief. The plan recommended the abandonment of the Federal work relief program in favor of a less expensive form of relief and claimed to be "the most practicable way to care for human needs in view of all governmental resources which are available." The proposal involved substituting for the Federal work program a system of Federal grants to states on a matching basis for "a general relief program, including work relief." States and localities were to be responsible for deciding "the amount and character of work relief" and the conditions of eligibility for relief. The plan also provided for special grants to care for inter-state transients.

Other private national agencies were asked to co-operate in bringing pressure upon Congress through their national and local board members in behalf of this proposal, on the ground that "the new relief crisis" contained a "threat to private social work under the pressure of necessary national economy," and that "if this situation is not met in some such way, private social work will be left holding the bag of emergency relief and our programs of service will be badly disrupted." [32]

This plan is chiefly interesting because of the point of view which it indicates and the position taken by the community chest group in relation to the existing work relief program of the Federal Government. Although a strong minority in Congress continued to support similar proposals, the Senate Committee to Investigate Unemployment and Relief did not include the plan in its report to Congress. The Federal work relief program has continued to operate in spite of the pressures for economy which have thus far succeeded only in affecting some decreases in the amounts of Federal funds appropriated.

Family Welfare Agencies

During this period of expansion of public relief expenditures, the family welfare agencies have continued to be the

[32] Letter to "Presidents and Executives of Cooperating National Agencies" from Charles P. Taft, Chairman, Community Mobilization for Human Needs, December 28, 1937.

largest relief givers in the private welfare field.[33] Having been forced to recognize, in 1932 and 1933, that private agencies could not carry the load of unemployment relief, they relinquished the responsibility to public agencies and entered upon a period of readjustment, seeking to redefine their function and their relationship with the public welfare field.[34] A number of the smaller agencies became inactive, others were absorbed into public relief administrations. Most of the agencies which had been receiving public relief subsidies were forced to reorganize when those funds were withdrawn in accordance with the FERA ruling in 1933.[35] Generally speaking the family agencies, large and small, have placed the emphasis more and more upon the non-material aspects of their services. This has not involved denying relief to applicants but "rather the use of relief funds for special needs in a constructive program to prevent breakdown and to promote the stability of individuals and families."[36] Theoretically many of them have disavowed responsibility for meeting the major economic needs of families in distress, leaving this to the public welfare departments. Practically most of them have given substantial amounts in relief to supplement the inadequacies of the governmental programs as well as to meet the special

[33] Writing on "Family Social Work" in the *Social Work Year Book*, 1939, Harold H. Lund says: "Of 232 agencies reporting in 1936, 123 use the word 'family' in the name of the agency, 110 use 'welfare,' and 77 use 'service.' Only 18 use 'charity' and 4 'relief.' Changes were made during the year by 17 agencies and 65 different names were in use. This concern with names is in accord with the whole development of family social work from an expression of benevolence and superior wisdom in behalf of inferior groups to a professional service potentially useful to persons in all walks of life." This comment, however, does not apply to Catholic diocesan agencies of which there were 139 in the country in 1938 engaged in family welfare and relief work. The majority of these agencies retain the word "charities" in their names as expressing the essential nature of their responsibility for service. "The Catholic Church . . . has regarded charity as one of the strong bonds of brotherhood binding together its members." See "Catholic Social Work," *ibid.*, p. 58.

[34] See Part I, Chapter 2, and Part II, Chapters 3, 4 and 5.

[35] See Part III, Chapter 8. In spite of the general practice instituted by the ruling of FERA that public funds must be spent by public agencies, a few family welfare societies still received small local public subsidies in 1938.

[36] *Ibid.*, p. 138.

needs of the families for whom they were supplying other services. This partly explains the fact that, in 1936, considerably more than half of the total expenditures of 197 private family agencies went for relief. The remainder was spent for administration and the costs of social case work services which they have emphasized as their primary function.[37]

Relief expenditures from private funds in 116 urban areas comprising, according to the 1930 census, 37 percent of the total population of the United States, dropped from approximately 24 percent of total relief expenditures in 1929, to 1.3 percent in 1935; and from the beginning of 1937 until the end of 1939, they constituted about 1 percent of the total.[38] These proportions are particularly significant as showing the relative importance of the expenditures of family welfare agencies which are distinctly urban organizations, only a small fraction of them being countywide or in cities of less than 25,000 population.

The change made by the Federal Government, at the end of 1935, from a general relief program to work relief for the unemployed, caused great consternation in the family welfare field. The confusion resulting from the announcement that Federal grants to the states would be discontinued and that responsibility for the "unemployables" would be left to the states and localities was increased by the liquidation of the Federal transient program, and by the limitations of the new Works Program which meant that thousands of needy "employables" could not be assigned to project jobs, and were therefore left to be cared for by some state or local agency.

Anticipating a great increase in local relief burdens, the Family Welfare Association of America conferred with its

[37] 197 agencies reporting to the Family Welfare Association of America spent in 1936 $7,700,000 for relief, $4,600,000 for case work services to clients, and $1,100,000 for administration. The median percentage of total expenditures going for relief was 45.4, with agencies in larger cities spending proportionately more for this purpose than those in smaller cities. Only three private agencies made no relief expenditures. Total budgets ranged from less than $2,000 to more than $1,000,000 annually, with 82 percent spending less than $150,000. *Ibid.*, p. 139.

[38] Source: Social Security Bulletin, April, 1940. Figures upon which percentages are based include special types of public assistance and Federal work program earnings as well as general relief.

membership of some 220 agencies, all but 11 of which were private organizations. In many respects the situation appeared similar to that of 1930-1932 with considerable public opinion assuming that local voluntary resources could meet the need. There was also much distrust of the capacity or willingness of state and local governments to rise to the challenge of the "unemployables." Old attitudes of suspicion colored the thinking of many private agency staffs and board members who questioned the intent and the ability of the states to develop sound public welfare programs out of the anticipated wreck of the emergency relief administrations.

Answers to the inquiries made by the Family Welfare Association of America showed that, in spite of their fears regarding future relief demands and extensive suffering, the private family agencies had profited by the lesson of the early 1930's and resolved to leave the major responsibility for relief at the doors of governmental agencies. In other words, they agreed that "it would be folly for private agencies in general to attempt to meet any appreciable part of the relief burden being abandoned by the Federal Government, or to raise money on that basis," especially in view of the fact that only a small percentage of total relief needs was being met at that time from voluntary contributions. They also decided that any attempt to assume such an overwhelming relief burden would "almost inevitably wreck the programs of constructive and preventive service which many such [family] agencies have been better able to develop since they were free from previous community relief burdens . . . and would serve not only to retard promising developments in local public agencies, but would also serve as an easy excuse for inertia on the part of higher State and local public authorities."

Many of these agencies, moreover, announced that they would use their influence in bringing pressure to bear upon governmental bodies to further the development of sound public welfare agencies and secure adequate funds for relief.[39] They also outlined what they considered to be a desirable re-

[39] "The Crisis in Community Programs," A Summary of Discussion in Association Board of Directors Meeting, October 19-20, 1935. Family Welfare Association of America, New York, Multigraphed.

lationship with public agencies.   Their position has not
changed appreciably and is, therefore, worth recording:

Private and public family agencies, when properly set up, supplement each other, differing not in the quality of their work, but rather
in the kinds of problems with which they deal. The public agency
devotes itself in general to material relief of persons in need. The
private agency uses relief only when it is essential in dealing with
problems which are other than economic. . . .

Family agencies oppose supplementation of public work relief or private wages as a general policy. About 50 percent [of the 93 agencies replying to the FWAA questionnaire] will supplement either
public work relief or private wages in cases of emergency. About
30 percent will supplement only private wages, and 20 percent will
supplement neither public nor private. . . .

About one third of the agencies have taken active steps to rally public support for adequate standards and personnel in the public field.
One-third are interested but relatively inactive and one-third are in-
different.[40]

In the fall of 1937, the Association issued a statement to the
effect that "some local governments are abandoning their relief
activities in the absence of leadership and participation from
their state governments and the Federal Government, and that
great pressures are being brought on the private family welfare agencies in these communities to assume a general public
relief burden which is not only far greater than any possible
increase in their resources, but would wreck their present programs. . . . Private agencies are also having pressed upon
them grants or subsidies from tax funds, as a partial or complete substitute for the organization or continuance of a genuine public relief program." The Board of Directors of the
Association, in the light of this situation, reaffirmed the stand
taken two years earlier, and added their disapproval of the
acceptance of subsidies by private agencies, reiterating their
belief in the principle that "tax funds should be expended only
by governmental agencies." [41]

[40] "The Crisis in Community Programs," A Report on Responses of
Local Family Agency Boards to Questions Submitted by the National
Board in December, 1935: FWAA, February, 1936.
[41] Multigraphed letter "To the Association Membership," Nov. 18,
1937, FWAA, New York. The FWAA being a voluntary association of

During 1937 the Association also raised fundamental questions regarding the future relief function of the family welfare field. These questions are significant not only because they indicate the acuteness of many of the problems in public relief but state them from the point of view of the private agency.

The time will come, we hope, when all items essential for decent living will be allowed in family budgets by public agencies, a more individual consideration of needs will permit supplementing earnings when necessary, residence laws will be relaxed, public agencies . . . will see relief less in terms of eligibility under a certain category and more in terms of the whole need of the individual.

What will be the relief service of the private agency when it no longer conveniently fills in these crevices left by our present categorical patchwork? Will it not be to continue to put the weight of its relief funds as it puts the weight of its case work service where it can help to maintain values in families—in short, where it can prevent breakdown? Will there not always be certain relief needs where flexibility and immediate response are as essential as the amounts themselves? Will freedom to meet such needs remain the basic relief function of the private agency? [42]

As permanent governmental programs have expanded and improved in quality, it has been more than ever apparent that essential differences exist between the public and private fields. Both fields have been developing along lines which are fairly independent of each other. Since the beginning of the permanent public program national and local private agencies

member agencies included in the letter the following: "It should also be clear that the foregoing statement from the Association Board does not constitute a dictum or authoritative action, but merely an expression of the sort of opinion growing out of experience in the field, which the Association membership has a right to expect in the way of leadership through a national Board composed of its own representatives."

[42] Wead, Margaret, "The Function of Family Case Work Agencies," FWAA, New York, May, 1937. Multigraphed. The eleven local public welfare agencies, which have been interested in belonging to the Family Welfare Association of America as the national standard setting association in the family case work field and have been able to meet its membership requirements, probably represent the vanguard of public welfare development in the area of specialized social case work services. The total number of these agencies as well as their identity has changed very little during the expansion of public welfare programs.

have had little contact with Federal and state agencies, such as they had during the concerted drive for unemployment relief funds from 1931 to 1933. The private field has remained fundamentally a local movement, concerned largely with the problems of individuals and families. The public welfare field has become more and more a state and Federal movement, dealing with problems common to whole sections of the population and concerned with the individual in relation to those problems. Public welfare has become governmental social action, concerned with the economic and social security of the people of the United States.

Chapter 17

Conclusion and Trends

∽∽∽∽∽∽∽∽∽∽∽∽∽∽∽∽∽∽∽∽∽∽∽∽∽∽∽∽∽∽∽∽∽∽∽

The changes which have taken place in the field of public relief during the past decade should be sufficiently obvious from the preceding account to make further review unnecessary. Many of these changes, however, hold such significance for the future that it will be worth while to comment briefly on their relative value for the permanent public welfare program.

It is axiomatic that governmental functions increase during periods of depression. The recent increases in Federal and state welfare functions, have been proportionate to the seriousness of the industrial crisis. Federal responsibility for unemployment relief was assumed as an emergency measure and in recognition of the national aspects of the economic disaster. It resulted in Federal commitment to permanent responsibility for social and economic security. This Federal action recognized all persons in need of security as members of the national commonwealth, for whose welfare the Federal government has a constitutional responsibility. The resulting program, while admittedly as yet incomplete and inadequate, includes, among other measures, insurance for old-age, grants-in-aid to the states for special types of public assistance to persons in need and administrative costs of state unemployment compensation.

Large sections of the working population plus approximately two million persons now on local relief rolls are not yet covered by the Federal provisions. Broader coverage for the insurance titles of the Social Security Act and the provision of grants-in-aid for General Public Assistance will be necessary if the Federal Government is to eliminate the present arbitrary discrimination against millions of people who are in need of insurance protection or of assistance benefits.

An essential part of this social security program is the provision of work projects and the "security wage" for the unemployed who are not eligible for unemployment compensation or who have exhausted their benefits. The WPA is still an emergency agency. Its value in the permanent program would be considerably increased if it were closely aligned with the public employment offices and unemployment compensation instead of with the public relief agencies as at present. This would co-ordinate the three governmental agencies which are now concerned with unemployment, and would put them in a more strategic position to effect a dynamic relationship between the skills and capacities of the unemployed, the training possibilities of the work program and the employment opportunities in private industry.

State governments have extended their responsibilities widely during the decade, first in emergency relief, and since 1935, in the assumption of permanent financial and administrative functions, following the lead of the Federal Government. There is still, however, great unevenness in the extent to which the states have taken advantage of the Federal grants, and there is wide variation in their operation, both as to quality of administration and standards of assistance. These differences are due in part to economic conditions and other local factors, but also to the failure of the Federal Government to provide grants-in-aid to cover all types of need, and to distribute the grants according to an equalization system which would take into account economic and cost-of-living differences and the fiscal capacity of each of the states.

The present trend in local, state and Federal relations appears to be in the direction of a more clearly marked Federal leadership than has existed since the end of the centralized administration of Federal emergency relief. Just as that emergency program represented a violent swing of the pendulum from the pre-depression local autonomy in public relief, so the reaction against Federal authority, in 1935, was a definite assertion of states' rights. The Social Security Act, in providing grants for unemployment compensation and public assistance, left all initiative to the states. The states, however, in order to obtain the Federal grants, were bound in their turn to make assistance available to eligible persons in every one of their political subdivisions. This meant in the permanent program, as was the case in emergency relief, that some Federal funds are administered in every county in the United States and has involved a reckoning with the ancient and deepseated principle of local autonomy. Hence the dangers arising from the superimposition of state programs on the localities are serious. The traditions of local autonomy in public relief are based on the fundamental concepts that the members of a community should have some responsibility for, and some part in planning and carrying out, measures which vitally affect their lives and their welfare. An emergency, temporary program might ignore these basic principles with impunity. This is not true of permanent *public* welfare administration.

The permanent public welfare agencies created during this past decade are still in the pioneer stage of their development. Changes which have already taken place in the relative responsibilities of the three phases of government indicate that the next few years may witness a better balance in Federal, state and local planning, financing and operation.

An important factor in attaining this balance has been the renewed recognition of Federal leadership which has been evident in the amendments to the Social Security Act made by Congress in 1939. Much of this recognition, coming so soon after the adverse reactions to Federal control in 1935, is largely due to the skill and wisdom shown by the Social Security Board and staff in their dealings with the states. In fact one of the outstanding contributions of the decade is the description of the program given in the Board's *Third Annual Report*, issued in 1938. This report, which has been quoted repeatedly in the preceding pages, describes, in simple, untechnical terms, the way in which the Board has discharged its responsibility, in accordance with the social philosophy implicit in the Act. The Board not only recognizes the administration of public assistance to be a social work function, but sets forth definite principles and policies regarding standards of personnel, adequacy of benefits, and attitudes toward people in need which recognize their right to public aid and which respect the dignity and worth of the individual. That a permanent Federal agency should make such a report to the Congress of the United States is an epoch-making event in social work history.

It has particular significance because ten years earlier the Federal Government recognized no responsibility in this field, and because the Act which embodied the basic social philosophy of the report, was passed by Congress only three years after the Federal Government had rejected all responsibility for unemployment relief.

The 1939 amendment to the Social Security Act which required the Board to approve state merit systems for the selection of personnel, marks another milestone in social work history. Professional standards and professional recognition, which have been a matter of extra-legal determination and agreement within the profession, now may be on their way to statutory regulation and state or even Federal registry.

Social workers have been learning throughout this decade, first in the administration of emergency relief and later in the pioneer stages of the permanent program, to adjust their professional techniques to the essential processes of democracy; to take political upheavals as all in the day's work and as part of the price that must be paid for the sake of larger issues and fundamental objectives. A new social work role has developed which demands broader knowledge of public affairs, the acquisition of skill in public relations and an understanding of the basic principles of democracy. Evidence of ability to meet the challenge of the governmental programs in which social work is already engaged, promises to open up other opportunities for public service in the insurance programs and in the employment services.

The erection, in the midst of the unemployment emergency, of this permanent structure for social security, with its millions of beneficiaries and huge expenditures, was possible because of a new public awareness of human need created by the industrial crisis. Relief became front page news. Whereas formerly it had been the concern of social workers and a small number of socially-minded citizens, it suddenly proved to be a major concern of economists, of big business, of state legislatures, of Congress and of the President of the United States. The nation became public-welfare-minded for the first time in its history, and relief became a major item in Federal financing and Federal planning.

Also for the first time in our history nation-wide statistics were collected and studies made of sub-standard living conditions and the distribution of income. At least one-third of our population were found to have incomes below a decent subsistence level.

Approximately one-sixth of the total population have been and are now receiving some form of public aid, and an undetermined number are in need and not able to get relief. Undoubtedly a large percentage, probably from two-thirds to three-quarters, of the present relief load can be considered a permanent dependency problem, regardless of business recovery.

Governmental relief rather than private relief has become a matter of course. In 1929, private relief loomed large in the consciousness of the socially-minded citizen, in spite of the fact that public expenditures were at least three times as great as those of private agencies. At present all but one percent of the huge total comes from public treasuries. Equally axiomatic is the practice of making public agencies responsible for the administration of public funds. This principle which was, in 1933, first applied to relief agencies on a nation-wide basis, has been extended into the permanent program as a matter of course.

A new "philosophy of adequacy" has come to prevail in the majority of governmental programs. Standards of relief and assistance in many parts of the country are two or three times as high at the end of the decade as they were at the beginning. The "security wage" has introduced, for the first time on a nation-wide basis, a type of guaranteed wage for employed people. Security wages, while lower than payments for comparable work in private industry, have yet averaged at least twice the average amounts of grants for general relief and categorical assistance. Even this progress has failed to bring either the benefits or the wages within any reasonable distance of the subsistence standards of living which are generally considered the minimum decency level for American people.

Outside of the inadequacies and inequalities of relief benefits, the most serious problem in public welfare today is found in the multiplicity of agencies, of categories, of standards, of methods of intake and of definitions of eligibility. The local confusion resulting from this complexity has serious implications for agency staffs and for the recipients or would-be recipients of the various types of aid. Next in importance to supplying Federal grants for general relief, and an equalization system for all of the Federal grants to the states, is the provision of a planned, co-ordinated and integrated program, Federal, state and local, which will make possible a fair amount of uniformity, and some approach to equality of treatment of all persons in need who apply for public aid.

APPENDIX

~~~~~~

Appendix A

(See Chapter 1, p. 36, and Chapter 4, p. 89 f.)

FEDERAL RELIEF LEGISLATION
PRIOR TO 1932

The following table includes all the appropriations made by Congress between 1803 and 1931 for direct relief to persons in need. It is taken from "a statement showing appropriations and relief legislation provided by Congress for the relief of sufferers caused by earthquakes, floods, fires, and other disasters during the fiscal years 1803 to 1931, inclusive," inserted in the record of Hearings on S. 5125, Seventy-third Congress, 1st Session, February 3, 1933, Part II.

In addition to these 31 appropriations Congress also enacted in the same period approximately seventy statutes in the interest of disaster sufferers, including extension of time on bonds for customs duties, waiving of duties on imports, suspension of taxes and rentals; authorization of food, clothing, and medical supplies from army stores or other Federal sources with no additional appropriation; feed and seed loan and farm loan appropriations and other legislation for the relief of agriculture; appropriations for so-called flood relief in the form of bridge building and other construction work. One appropriation was made for studies of rural sanitation by the United States Public Health Service.

TABLE 11

Federal Relief

Year

1827	Sufferers from fire at Alexandria, Virginia ...... $	20,000
1874	Food: (Mississippi River flood)	190,000
	Food: Mississippi and Tennessee Rivers—flood relief	400,000
1875	Sufferers from grasshopper ravages	
	Seeds	30,000
	Food and clothing	150,000
1882	Seeds—Mississippi flood	20,000
	Rations—Mississippi flood	100,000
	Rations—Mississippi flood	150,000
	Rations—Mississippi flood	100,000
1882	Relief—Mississippi flood	15,000
1884	Relief—Ohio River flood	300,000
	Relief—Ohio River flood	200,000
1890	Tents, flood sufferers	
	Arkansas, Mississippi, Louisiana	25,000
	Relief—Mississippi flood	150,000
1897	Tents—Mississippi flood	8,000
	Relief—Mississippi flood	200,000
1897	Relief—mining regions of Alaska	200,000
1903	Distress in the Philippine Islands	3,000,000
1906	Relief—San Francisco earthquake and fire	1,000,000
	Relief—San Francisco earthquake and fire	1,500,000
1908	Sufferers from cyclone in certain southern states	250,000
1912	Relief—Mississippi and Ohio floods	1,239,000
	Relief—Mississippi and Ohio floods	4,500
	Sufferers from Allegheny River flood in 1907 ...	17,500
	Sufferers from volcano, Alaska	30,000
1913	Sufferers from flood, Middle West	5,000
	Sufferers from floods, tornadoes and conflagrations in Mississippi and Ohio Valleys, etc. ...	654,000
	Sufferers from flood in Ohio and Indiana	131,000
1914	Sufferers from fire, Salem, Massachusetts	200,000
1916	Destitute Americans in Mexico	300,000
	Flood sufferers in certain southern states	540,000
	Total	$11,178,000

Appendix B

(See Chapter 2, p. 57)

TABLE 12

Expenditures for Relief from Public and Private Funds in 120
Urban Areas, 1929-1935

Year	Grand total	Public funds Total	Public funds General	Special allowances	Private funds
		AMOUNTS IN THOUSANDS			
Total, 7 years	$2,553,045	$2,365,350	$2,104,509	$260,841	$187,695
1929	43,745	33,449	14,853	18,596	10,296
1930	71,425	54,754	33,510	21,244	16,671
1931	172,749	123,320	88,594	34,726	49,429
1932	308,185	251,104	208,694	42,410	57,081
1933	[1] 448,921	[1] 421,032	[1] 379,722	41,310	27,889
1934	[1] 667,153	[1] 652,467	[1] 608,880	43,587	14,686
1935	[2] 840,867	[2] 829,224	[2] 770,256	58,968	11,643
		PERCENT DISTRIBUTION [3]			
Total, 7 years	100.0	92.6	82.4	10.2	7.4
1929	100.0	76.5	34.0	42.5	23.5
1930	100.0	76.7	46.9	29.8	23.3
1931	100.0	71.4	51.3	20.1	28.6
1932	100.0	81.5	67.7	13.8	18.5
1933	[1] 100.0	[1] 93.8	[1] 84.6	9.2	6.2
1934	[1] 100.0	[1] 97.8	[1] 91.3	6.5	2.2
1935	[2] 100.0	[2] 98.6	[2] 91.6	7.0	1.4

1 Excludes expenditures under the Civil Works Administration.
2 Excludes expenditures under the Works Program.
3 Computed from unrounded data.
Source: Winslow, Emma A., *Trends in Different Types of Public and Private Relief in Urban Areas, 1929-35,* Publication 237, U. S. Department of Labor, Children's Bureau, 1937. Cited by Geddes in *Trends in Relief Expenditures, 1910-1935.*
"Special allowances" in the above table are expenditures for mothers' aid, old-age pensions and aid to the blind (author's note).

Appendix C

(See Chapter 3, p. 83)

PRESS RELEASE OF THE PRESIDENT'S EMERGENCY COMMITTEE ON EMPLOYMENT

On June 20, 1931, the following statement was released to the press by the President's Emergency Committee on Employment. It reiterated the principle of local responsibility for unemployment relief and announced its program for the months ahead, which would be carried out in close co-operation with private national organizations having extensive local contacts. The news release is an excellent bit of documentary evidence of the philosophy and methods which were characteristic of the Hoover Administration in dealing with the increasing unemployment and destitution in the country.

PROGRAM FOR ORGANIZATION OF LOCAL RELIEF RESOURCES

Washington, D. C., June, 1931.—The forces of two national welfare associations have been added to the expanded program initiated by the President's Emergency Committee for Employment to strengthen the country's capacity to meet relief needs locally through organized community resources, it was announced today by Fred C. Croxton, acting chairman of the committee.

The associations are the American Association of Public Welfare Officials and the Family Welfare Association of America.

The program in which they will cooperate with the President's Committee in dealing with problems of relief comprises numerous projects to be carried out by several national agencies. The various phases have been undertaken by the agencies especially experienced in the several fields.

Mr. Croxton pointed out that in its activities relating to relief the committee is placing emphasis on assistance to communities in organizing their own resources to meet local needs.

"The committee's contacts with states and hundreds of local communities last fall, winter, and spring," he said, "verify the sound and tested principle that the best and most effective relief of unemployment distress is accomplished through locally-provided funds, locally administered.

"It is on this basis that the President's Committee has requested and received the cooperation of several national organizations with experienced staffs and extensive local contacts.

"The President's Emergency Committee for Employment realizes whatever the trend of business during the balance of the year, the demand for relief will be unusually heavy next fall and winter. It is evident that there has been no emergency since the war which has demanded the thoughtful help of public-spirited organizations more than that of the present unemployment situation and the problems which are growing out of it."

The Association of Community Chests and Councils has accepted the responsibility of carrying out four tasks. They are set forth in a letter from Mr. Croxton to J. Herbert Case, president of the association, quoted as follows:

"1. Getting information as to the present status of relief needs and funds to meet the same in cities of 25,000 and over. This information should cover both public and private charitable funds.

"2. Using all possible resources of leadership, both of your own organization and of the local community, to secure maximum results in the way of needed relief both from charitable campaigns and public appropriations in those cities which have Community Chests.

"3. Promoting adequate organization for these same purposes in non-chest cities of 25,000 and over, wherever practicable, and also in smaller cities where unusually acute needs become evident to the President's Emergency Committee for Employment.

"4. Developing, through national channels, widespread understanding of the necessity for using all available local resources, public and private, for absolutely essential relief."

The American Association of Public Welfare Officials, which includes in its membership state and local public welfare officials, will give its attention to promoting the organization of local social and economic resources and to the best methods of administration of relief, especially in the less populous localities.

Discussing the work of the regional representatives with regard to relief, Mr. Croxton pointed out that through them the President's Committee will continue to work closely with state and local employment and relief committees and state departments of public welfare.

"If it develops that with local resources organized, there are less-favored localities which will require outside aid," Mr. Croxton said, "a way must be found to relieve human distress in such communities, and this will no doubt require assistance from more fortunate localities. The extent of these areas and the size of the problem can be more accurately determined if organization of local resources goes forward rapidly."

In a letter addressed to Linton B. Swift, executive secretary, the Family Welfare Association, which has contacts in approximately 400 cities, Mr. Croxton stated:

"The demands upon relief funds in many communities have been so heavy that greatly increased efforts will be necessary to discover and develop additional local resources. If communities are to administer their relief activities to the best advantage it is essential that they have, as a basis for such work, the practical experience gained by many communities during the past year.

"Regarding your association as one of our principal channels of cooperation in the social work field, and recognizing its special fitness for gathering information on unemployment and relief, and advising with reference to the administration of relief, we should greatly appreciate your undertaking certain work as soon as possible."

The work to be carried by the association includes the promotion of reasonable standards of administration of relief, particularly in the less populous communities, the furnishing of current information concerning changing conditions, and the preparation of guidance reports on especially difficult relief problems.

In addition to these projects, several studies are under way to provide local relief-administering agencies with suggestions based on sound procedures for handling various phases of the problem. At the request of the President's Committee, the Research Department of the Russell Sage Foundation is preparing an analysis of successful methods of carrying out "made work" programs in connection with relief.

The Family Welfare Association is working on a report of methods used in caring for the homeless unemployed with a view to furnishing guidance to communities. Both reports are scheduled for completion by early fall.

The President's Emergency Committee for Employment will continue to have the cooperation of numerous other fact-finding agencies, as well as its own staff. Information on public and private relief expenditures of cities is collected for it by the Children's Bureau, U. S. Department of Labor, and the Russell Sage Foundation.

Appendix D

(See Chapter 4, p. 88)

EMERGENCY PROGRAM OF AMERICAN ASSOCIATION OF PUBLIC WELFARE OFFICIALS[1]

General Purpose: To strengthen public welfare departments, state and local, in preparing them to take an effective part in meeting the relief problem connected with the present emergency.

[1] Adopted Aug., 1931.

The methods to be used in carrying out this purpose include the following:

1. Assistance in assembling and interpreting nationwide material on relief expenditures, resources and needs in the United States, with special reference to public relief and to the smaller communities, through

  a. Stimulation of and assistance to state welfare departments in developing state programs of study and conference, with a view to ascertaining areas of greatest need and resources available in these areas.

  b. Study and analysis supplemented by field visits, of available information on financial condition, tax systems and resources for relief purposes in states, counties, municipalities and towns.

  c. Study and analysis of available relief statistics.

2. Examination of proposals for state and Federal relief and rehabilitation in the light of the probable extent of the need, estimated cost, character and location of especially depressed areas, possibilities of state cooperation, and resources for administration of funds in accordance with sound principles of relief and welfare service.

3. Stimulation of appropriations for relief purposes through consultation service in the preparation of relief budgets and conferences with those participating in the determination of financial policies of the states and local subdivisions.

4. Encouragement of the administration of relief by competent personnel, through publicity regarding standards of relief administration and participation in statewide and local conferences.

5. Assistance in the coordination of the services of state departments of labor, education and welfare in developing programs of re-education or retraining of those who have been engaged in an industry in which reemployment of the whole group is not to be expected.

Appendix E

(See Chapter 4, p. 89)

NEWS RELEASE OF PRESIDENT'S ORGANIZATION ON UNEMPLOYMENT RELIEF, SEPTEMBER, 1931

The following news release is particularly interesting because it shows the beginning recognition of public funds and state responsibility as necessary sources of aid for the unemployed. The objectives and methods of the emergency program of the American Association of Public Welfare Officials are here given official Federal sanction.

Walter S. Gifford today expressed his gratification over the selection of Frank Bane, Virginia Commissioner of Public Welfare, as Executive Director of the recently organized American Association of Public Welfare Officials. "Since it is local public relief that bore the major share of the relief burden in the cities of this country last winter," said Mr. Gifford, "it is especially fortunate that the President's Organization on Unemployment Relief is to have the active cooperation of the organized public welfare officials of the country, state and local, under the executive direction of a man of such broad practical experience as Frank Bane. Through his state work in Virginia, his administration of the welfare work of Knoxville, Tennessee, and the studies of welfare organization in various states which he has made," Mr. Gifford continued, "Mr. Bane has accumulated broad practical experience in state and local welfare and relief administration and will be able to exercise great influence in developing state and local efforts for meeting relief needs."

The Association of Public Welfare Officials was organized in Boston in 1930 and held its first annual meeting in Minneapolis last June. William J. Ellis, Commissioner of Institutions and Agencies of the State of New Jersey, is president of the Association. Its objects are to promote and maintain effective standards of public welfare work. While an independent national organization, it has been one of the national voluntary agencies which have been called upon to cooperate with that organization in working out a relief program.

The following statement was issued today by President Ellis and Director Bane through the President's Organization, to the Public Welfare Officials of the country:

"The American Association of Public Welfare Officials calls upon all state and local welfare officials throughout the country to redouble the great efforts which they made last year to extend relief to those in distress because of lack of employment. Figures for 75 cities, including such large communities as Detroit, Buffalo, Cleveland, and Newark, show that in the aggregate, while private agencies increased their relief budgets 48 per cent in 1930, public departments expended nearly two and one-half times the amount spent for relief purposes in 1929. The records of the first six months of 1931 show that public officials are assuming a still heavier burden than in 1930. Many families which received only food and perhaps fuel last year, because of the further exhaustion of their resources, will need help in supplying rent, clothing and other items. Other families which have not hitherto asked for relief are at the end of their resources. Relief policies should be based as much as possible upon the principle that work is the only satisfactory method of providing for the unemployed. Welfare officials have a special responsibility for initiating and cooperating in the development of plans for giving employment, especially on public projects, instead of relief. While you, as public welfare officials, do not control appropriations, we hope you will acquaint the general public and the taxing and appropriating authorities with the extent of the need which comes to your attention, the best measures for meeting it, and the requirements of your offices for overhead expenditures adequate to provide wise administration.

"If needs are to be met in both larger and smaller communities coordinated statewide planning will be necessary. The Association of Public Welfare Officials through its Director and field assistants will shortly be prepared to give assistance to state welfare departments in developing state programs of study and conference, similar to the comprehensive program recently initiated in Virginia and efforts carried on in New York, New Jersey, Pennsylvania, Ohio and other states. The Association will also be available for consultation service in the preparation of relief budgets and consideration of relief policies of the states and local subdivisions.

"It is our hope that the public will increasingly realize the importance of the administration of relief by competent personnel, in accordance with generally accepted standards of relief administration.

"The Association pledges its whole-hearted cooperation to organizations engaged in stimulating relief from private sources. United effort on the part of both public and private agencies will be necessary in the performance of the common task which lies before us, of mitigating so far as relief measures can do so, the suffering and distress which unemployment brings.

"The work of the Association as it relates to the relief of unemployment will be under the direction of a special committee on public relief and welfare service. The members of the committee are as follows:

William J. Ellis, Commissioner, State Department of Institutions and Agencies, Trenton, N. J.—President American Ass'n of Public Welfare Officials.
Grace Abbott, Chief, Children's Bureau, U. S. Department of Labor.

Mary Irene Atkinson, Superintendent, Division of Charities of the Department of Public Welfare, Columbus, Ohio.

Frank Bane, Executive Director, American Association of Public Welfare Officials.

Richard K. Conant, Commissioner, State Department of Public Welfare, Boston, Massachusetts.

L. A. Halbert, Director of State Institutions, State Public Welfare Commission, Providence, R. I.

Fred K. Hoehler, Director of Public Welfare of Hamilton County and Cincinnati, Ohio.

Charles H. Johnson, Commissioner, Department of Social Welfare, Albany, New York."

Appendix F

(See Chapter 6, pp. 114 and 129)

MEMORANDUM ON WISCONSIN APPLI-CATION FOR FUNDS TO RFC

This recommendation from the director of the Emergency Relief Division to the Directors of the RFC, that $3,000,000 be made available to the state of Wisconsin, is illustrative of the procedure followed in regard to applications for advances under the Emergency Relief and Construction Act of 1932; and of the type of information assembled regarding the availability of state and local funds, the existing need and the administrative provisions for allocating and disbursing the funds to the unemployed.

Memorandum

August 19, 1932.

To: THE DIRECTORS
FROM: MR. FRED CROXTON

Recommendations

In view of the application of the Governor of Wisconsin with its supporting data and the further evidence presented by representatives of the Governor, it is hereby recommended that a total of $3,000,000.00 be made available to the State of Wisconsin at this time to meet current emergency relief needs beginning September 1,

1932, under Title I, Section 1, subsection (c) of the Emergency Relief and Construction Act of 1932. This recommendation made upon the basis of the supporting data should not be understood as establishing a precedent in considering later applications.

Application

The total supplementary relief needs for the period from September 1, 1932, to December 31, 1932, is certified by the Governor to be $6,414,865.28. This total amount sought, it is stated, would provide supplementary relief funds for 57 of the 71 counties of the State and would be administered through the State Industrial Commission which has been in charge of relief work in the State of Wisconsin for the past two years. The supporting data and conference with representatives of the Governor clearly show that approximately ⅔ of these 57 counties are well organized and have been making every effort to meet their relief needs in a manner satisfactory to the State of Wisconsin. Approximately ⅓ of these 57 counties, however, to date have set up no adequate relief organizations and have apparently made but little effort to meet their own needs in a way that is satisfactory to the State. Because of such lack of organization it can not be established at this time that these particular localities know the extent of their need or have exhausted their own ability to meet the need.

(Exhibit A filed with the Governor's Application lists the counties and shows the estimated needs of each county.)

Statement of Facts

During the past two years the State of Wisconsin through its State Industrial Commission, its Unemployment Commission, and other agencies has exerted far reaching efforts to improve the standards and methods of local poor relief administration. The supporting data reveal that in a number of cases, neighboring political subdivisions join together and set up a centralized relief agency with trained case workers in charge. In several cities the State Industrial Commission has been instrumental in organizing local committees on unemployment who engaged full time workers to set up work-relief programs and take charge of all unemployment relief. Poor relief set-ups have been reorganized in many localities.

The State of Wisconsin under Chapter 22, Laws of 1931, approved by the Governor, added two cents additional to its gasoline tax "to provide emergency relief for unemployment by carrying out a program of railroad grade crossing elimination. Such program contemplates carrying out the amount of work that normally would be accomplished in three years, not to exceed 91 projects." Up to July 1, 1932, a total of 11,076 men had worked directly on 72 grade crossings under authority of this Act and had received wages totaling approximately $2,000,000. Most towns and cities have used their share of the extra gasoline tax money for road maintenance or unemployment relief work.

The State also empowered its Unemployment Commission to take over other State public works in order that such labor provisions might be incorporated in the contracts as would tend to relieve unemployment.

In February 1932, the Wisconsin Legislature passed a bill approximately doubling the State income tax for one year and levied a two-year license tax on chain stores. These extra taxes provide about $6,000,000 which has been used for distribution to local communities to help them with their unemployment relief.

It has been through the use of certain of these State funds "that the Industrial Commission has been able to insist that local communities improve their standards of relief administration in order to get necessary State aid."

The above named amount of $3,000,000 recommended to be made available to the Governor of Wisconsin, would supplement the emergency relief funds in those counties and political subdivisions where the State recognized that the burden of relief has been heaviest and where all reasonable efforts have been made to meet the needs.

Although Wisconsin traditionally has recognized relief to be a public responsibility, private relief agencies have rendered substantial aid both in the way of funds and by providing services of trained personnel. Such private efforts and contributions should, of course, be maintained and it must be fully understood that any Federal funds which are made available under the intent of the Act, are not in lieu of but merely supplementary, not only to all local and State funds but to private contributions as well.

The question has been raised as to why the counties for which relief is requested have not exhausted their borrowing power up to the legal debt limit. Only eleven of the counties for which relief is requested are, by reason of being on the so-called county system of relief, legally authorized to issue bonds for relief purposes. The briefs filed covering this question show that Milwaukee County, the largest of the eleven counties, has incurred indebtedness up to approximately one-half of its legal limit. The legal limitations on the annual tax levy are such as to make it impossible at the present time for this county to avail itself of its remaining borrowing power.

The briefs also show that the situation with respect to the borrowing power and limitations thereon in the other ten counties for which relief is requested, is similar to that of Milwaukee County.

Appendix G

(See Chapter 7, p. 162)

I. FACTUAL DATA BEARING ON THE SUBJECT OF FORBIDDING THE USE OF FEDERAL FUNDS FOR NON-UN-EMPLOYMENT RELIEF CASES

The Research Section of the FERA, Division of Research and Statistics, issued a confidential bulletin for the use of the administrative staff on July 23, 1934, entitled: *Financial Data Bearing on the Subject of Forbidding the Use of Federal Funds for Non-Unemployment Relief Cases.*

The *Summary* and *Conclusion* of this Bulletin are given below, as they present a careful evaluation and critical analysis of the problem of financing relief for the "unemployables."

Summary

(1) As a result of the depression, the number and financial burden of relief cases other than strictly unemployment relief cases is much greater than in pre-depression years.

(2) If the Federal Emergency Relief Administration should forbid the use of Federal funds for non-unemployment relief cases, localities and states would divert funds now contributed for general relief insofar as available and necessary to finance non-unemployment cases.

(3) Local funds if so diverted would probably not be sufficient to care for the non-unemployment cases in the majority of counties.

(4) State funds would be available to supplement local funds in many states, and combined State and local funds if diverted to non-unemployment cases would be sufficient to care for such cases in most of the states.

(5) The states in which the smallest amounts are available for the diversion are for the most part southern states and are, in general, the poorest states.

(6) In general, private agencies would not find it possible to finance the non-unemployment relief load.

(7) Localities, in general, would not be able to increase materially their funds for relief during the present fiscal year.

(8) Many localities and states would not be able to increase their contributions for relief substantially for the coming fiscal year.

(9) In some localities and states, especially in the sections where most needed, the lack of a sense of social responsibility would be an obstacle to the raising of funds to care for non-unemployment relief cases even where ability was present.

(10) If the purpose of such a move is to secure additional state and local funds, accounting and statistical segregation of non-unemployment cases for specific bargaining purposes would be an equally productive method.

Conclusion

Local and State funds for unemployment relief are sufficient in amount in most states to care for non-unemployment cases, if diverted to that purpose. With few exceptions, they legally can be and probably would be so diverted. In many counties and states, however, additional funds would have to be raised if these cases were to be cared for. The greatest need for additional funds would be in southern states where the ability is smallest and the sense of responsibility for relief the least well developed. As a result, it may be forecast that a substantial number of people would starve or suffer very low standards of relief. There is little likelihood that forbidding the use of Federal funds for non-employment relief cases would greatly increase total State and local contributions for relief. The use in financial negotiations of an accounting segregation of such cases appears to be an equally productive and more reasonable procedure from the financial point of view.

II. MEMORANDA SHOWING PROCEDURE FOR DROPPING UNEMPLOYABLES

The following memoranda show the actual procedure through which the order to drop unemployables in Alabama, Arkansas, Louisiana, Mississippi, Oklahoma and Texas, was transmitted from the Federal Relief Administration, through the Field Representative to the State Administrators. The memorandum from the Regional Social Worker shows the role which the Social Service Division played in the analysis of the relief load and in an attempt to secure provision for the "unemployables" through some other program.

907 Canal Bank Bldg.
New Orleans, La.
December 14, 1934

Memorandum

To: Mr. Harry L. Hopkins, Administrator
FROM: M. J. Miller, Field Representative
SUBJECT: Removal of Unemployables from Relief Rolls in States of Region 6.

In telephone conversation with Mr. Aubrey Williams, Assistant Administrator, at 11:30 AM, CST, December 12, 1934, Mr. Williams agreed to my recommendation that I be authorized to announce that all unemployables on the relief rolls in these six states would be removed from the relief rolls on a given date. After full discussion and consultation with the Relief Administrators of these six states it was agreed that the effective date should be February 1, 1935, and official announcement was made to that effect.

Attached hereto please find copy of the official announcement authorizing this action.

This order is effective in all of the states in this territory with the exception of Louisiana in which State the unemployables were removed from the relief rolls by Administrator Early as of July 31, 1934.

I think this action will have a most wholesome effect on the entire relief program and I am most happy that I have been permitted to authorize it, as I have recommended it in numerous reports previously filed.

Attached hereto find newspaper clipping showing how this was handled by the local papers. It was also handled by the Associated Press.

M. J. Miller
Field Representative

907 Canal Bank Building
New Orleans, Louisiana
December 14, 1934

Memorandum

To: ALL STATE ADMINISTRATORS
FROM: M. J. Miller, Field Representative

Attached hereto please find statement issued after telephone conversation with Mr. Aubrey Williams, Assistant Administrator, on December 12. This statement authorizes the removal of all unemployables from the relief rolls as of February 1, 1935.

I think that wide publicity should be given to this statement of policy and it is suggested that you make this rule known to the responsible officials in your state.

If the Regional Staff can aid you in convincing the State and local authorities that this rule is going to be put into effect, as announced, please do not hesitate to call on us.

Your Social Service Division should immediately analyze your relief rolls and ascertain the total number of unemployable persons on the relief rolls by location, in order that we may supply this information to the State and local authorities by January 15, 1935.

M. J. Miller
Field Representative

(Enclosure to State Administrators)

At the Regional Conference held in New Orleans of the Emergency Relief Administration officials for the states of Alabama, Mississippi, Louisiana, Arkansas, Oklahoma and Texas, comprising Region 6, lengthy discussion and full consideration has been given to the removal of unemployables from the relief rolls. As a representative of the Federal Emergency Relief Administration, I am authorized to announce that the removal of the unemployables from the relief rolls in these six states will be effective as of February 1, 1935. On and after that date funds made available to the states by the Federal Emergency Relief Administration cannot be used for the care and maintenance of those unemployables. The responsibility for the care of this group rests on the local city, county and state officials.

In fixing the effective date of this order due consideration was given to the fact that in five of the six states regular sessions of the Legislative bodies will be held during the month of January enabling the State Legislatures to take proper action to provide for the care of these dependents, where such provision is not now in existence.

The Relief Administrations of these states will work in close cooperation with the State and local authorities in seeing that this transfer is properly made with the least possible inconvenience to those affected.

It may be stated that an unemployable person is one that is incapable of performing a day's work on account of age or physical disability, or where home and family duties will render it impossible for the individual to work.

M. J. Miller
Field Representative
Federal Emergency Relief Administration

New Orleans, Louisiana
December 16, 1934

To: THE DIRECTORS OF SOCIAL SERVICE
FROM: LOULA DUNN, REGIONAL SOCIAL WORKER

Attached hereto you will find copy of memorandum which Mr. Miller has just released to State Administrators in which it is indicated the State Emergency Relief Administrators will be expected to discontinue service to unemployables by February 1, 1935. Will you please confer with your Administrator and work out plan for an analysis of your present relief load which will indicate the approximate number of unemployables now on relief and send this information to us by January 15, 1935.

We should also like to have a report from each state which will indicate the plan you expect to follow in transferring unemployables to local governmental units. In some states there are statutes by which provision for care can be made for unemployables. There are also partially functioning public units of service to which some of this load can be transferred. In some other states it may be necessary to offer the services of one of your best local workers in the relief agency to service these families as local units assume financial responsibility for this group of people. You will recall that Miss Barrett outlined at our recent meeting the plan which Louisiana is using and which is proving a sound one.

We are anxious to hear what your analysis shows and what plan you are able to develop as soon as possible.

CY: ALABAMA
    ARKANSAS
    LOUISIANA
    MISSISSIPPI
    OKLAHOMA
    TEXAS

444   APPENDIX

Ala-180

ALABAMA RELIEF ADMINISTRATION
Montgomery, Alabama
Office of the Director
January 8, 1935

TO ALL LOCAL RELIEF ADMINISTRATIONS:
Effective February 1st, unemployables will no longer be eligible
for relief from Federal relief funds in Alabama.

For the time being, these unemployables to be removed will include only those who are mentally or physically incapacitated for
work.

It is hoped that the cost of relief for these unemployables will be
developed from resources other than local governmental tax funds
but as a last resort such tax funds must be made available.

Full instructions for transfer of unemployables are attached
hereto. You may continue to service them with your present relief
organization.

Plans for transfer of these unemployables must be made immediately with your local relief board.

                    Yours truly,
                        ALABAMA RELIEF ADMINISTRATION
                        By Thad Holt
                            Director.

H/el
cc-Chairman Local Board
   County Commissioners
   Mayors

Appendix H

(See Chapter 7, p. 167)

ALLOCATION OF FUNDS UNDER THE
EMERGENCY RELIEF APPROPRIA-
TION ACT OF 1935

Report of the President of the United States to the Congress
showing the Status of Funds and Operations under the Emergency Relief Appropriation Acts of 1935, 1936, 1937 and
1938, as of December 31, 1938. United States Government
Printing Office, January 10, 1939.

TABLE 13

	1935 Act *April 8, 1935* Amount	*Percent of total allocations*
Description		
Net funds made available	$4,545,900,170.38	
Unallocated	346,056.20	
Allocated	4,545,554,114.18	

Allocated to

Agriculture:

Exclusive of Public Roads and Farm Security Adm.	73,253,635.96	1.6
Bureau of Public Roads	497,248,461.21	10.9
Farm Security Administration.	219,800,013.76	4.8
Civilian Conservation Corps	593,619,080.26	13.1
Commerce	8,904,830.41	.2
Employees' Compensation Commission	22,800,000.00	.5
Farm Credit Administration	16,884,200.31	.4
Federal Emergency Relief Administration	934,592,359.00	20.6
General Accounting Office	5,000,000.00	.1
Interior:		
Puerto Rico Reconstruction Administration	35,098,988.04	.8
Exclusive of Puerto Rico Reconstruction Adm.	102,501,013.90	2.3
Justice	1,705,309.00	. . .
Labor	12,106,536.44	.3
Library of Congress	249,371.19	. . .
National Emergency Council . . .	2,666,041.63	.1
National Resources Committee .	1,798,241.81	. . .
Navy	17,347,780.14	.4
Public Works Administration . .	396,194,391.22	8.7
Rural Electrification Administration	15,420,938.50	.3
State	. . . .	. . .
Treasury	39,494,585.21	.9
Veterans' Administration	1,226,854.94	. . .
War:		
Corps of Engineers (rivers and harbors, etc.)	130,486,710.84	2.9

Description	1935 Act April 8, 1935 Amount	Percent of total allocations
Exclusive of Corps of Engineers	$ 18,953,688.19	.4
Water conservation and utility projects	....	...
Works Progress Administration .	1,396,939,691.25	30.7
All Other Organizations	1,261,390.97	...
Total allocations	$4,545,554,114.18	100.0

Appendix I

(See Chapter 8, p. 181)

FORMS OF PUBLIC, QUASI-PUBLIC AND PRIVATE AGENCIES ADMINISTERING PUBLIC RELIEF FUNDS IN THE EARLY MONTHS OF 1933[2]

1. A public agency is created by or under specific authority of law, responsible in all of its operations to the legally constituted public authorities, and financed by tax funds or by other funds administered under direct governmental supervision.

2. A temporary agency, such as an emergency relief commission, not yet authorized by law but created by and responsible to public officials, sometimes as a preliminary to legal authorization.

3. An independent agency legally designated under contract as an agency of government for specific purposes, but continuing to be governed by a board of directors which is neither appointed by nor responsible to the public authorities.

4. An agency whose executive only is officially appointed an agent of government, but whose staff is used in the expenditure of public funds while still under the control of a private board.

5. An independent agency the *major portion* of whose budget consists of grants (whether outright or conditional) from tax funds, where such grants are given as a means of discharging a public responsibility.

[2] Adapted from a paper read by Linton B. Swift at the annual meeting of the American Public Welfare Association in June, 1933. Proceedings, *Social Service Review*, Sept., 1933, Vol. VII, No. 3, pp. 454-5, University of Chicago Press.

6. A so-called private agency, having no direct relationship with government, but seeking its support from a majority of the public and considering itself responsible to that majority in meeting a general community need.

Appendix J

(See Chapter 9, p. 196)

A SUMMARY OF THE ADMINISTRATIVE SET-UPS OF UNEMPLOYMENT COMMISSIONS

The following analysis of the policies, functions and procedures of State Emergency Relief Administrations which were organized in 1931 and 1932 reveal the extent to which these early programs set the pace and "wrote the ticket" for the Federal and State Emergency Relief Administrations of 1933-1935 and thereby influenced the later permanent state and local public welfare programs.

The material is taken from a multigraphed bulletin of the Family Welfare Association of America.

A Summary of the Administrative Set-ups of Unemployment Commissions

April, 1933

Includes the following states: Illinois, New Jersey, New York, Pennsylvania, West Virginia, Wisconsin.

Includes such items as creation of the commission, purposes and powers, administrative units, standards and forms of relief, source of funds, conditions upon which state aid is granted, personnel and administration, publications.

Prepared by Stockton Raymond from pamphlets issued by state commissions, and other material, and later checked by each commission.

Illinois: Illinois Emergency Relief Commission
10 South LaSalle Street, Chicago
Wilfred S. Reynolds, Executive Secretary
and
Illinois Emergency Relief Commission (Federal)

(First organization handles state funds; second Federal from R.F.C. Membership, policies, etc. identical.)

(Federal Commission appointed by Governor and organized August 5, 1932)

Creation

February 6, 1932—Commission of seven members to be appointed by the Governor—created by act of the State Legislature; 3 state officials since added as ex-officio members: State Treasurer, Director Dept. of Finance, and State Auditor.

Purpose

To provide relief for residents of Illinois who by reason of unemployment or *otherwise* are destitute and in necessitous circumstances.

Type of Relief

Cash, supplies or any other means deemed desirable by the commission. (Cash rarely given except as work relief wages—less than 8% of total.)

Administrative Units—County

The Commission may make use of and cooperate with counties, townships and other municipal corporations charged by law with the duty of poor relief and with other local relief agencies. In making allocations of state funds the county is the unit and is responsible for administration.

Forms of Relief

Work relief is given instead of direct relief in a limited number of units where there are employable persons. Wages in work relief are based upon the same standard as direct relief.[3] The rate of pay is the regular rate prevailing in the community for the particular kind of work. Work projects must be approved in advance by the State Commission.

[3] Actually the standards are somewhat higher.

General Policy

1. To insure prompt relief.

2. To extend relief only where needed and after resources both public and private have been utilized to the fullest financial ability of local communities.

3. To insure satisfactory standards of relief administration.

Conditions upon Which State Aid Is Given

Applications by official action of the county board of supervisors or county board of commissioners except where county board does not act and need is apparent when application may be made by municipal officer, qualified relief agency or citizen of the community.

Need for state funds in any county must be verified by field representative of the commission and presented by representative of the local community.

Following the initial allocation of funds further contacts with the local units are maintained by field representatives of the commission.

Standards

Adequate relief—The policy of the Commission is to provide adequate relief to citizens of Illinois who are in need *because of unemployment*. Adequate relief is defined as "sufficient to maintain a standard of living which will prevent suffering."

Investigation is required to determine:

1. Legal residence in Illinois

2. Financial need

3. Financial resources

Home Visits

Follow up visits are required at least once a month. Limited personnel sometimes prevents such frequent visits in practice.

Personnel

Funds provided through state and Federal aid are to be administered by trained and experienced workers. Workers are employed locally and not directly by the Commission. On March 1, 1932, the Commission ruled that only workers resident in the state would be paid from funds allocated by it.

Case Load

The Commission recommends a maximum case load of 150 per worker. (Actual case loads sometimes heavier.)

Equipment

Office space sufficient in size and so arranged as to secure privacy in interviewing applicants as well as proper heating, lighting, ventilation and other facilities are recommended by the Commission.

Clerical Assistance and Transportation

The Commission recommends that clerical assistance and adequate transportation facilities be provided for worker.

Set-up of Emergency Relief Commission

Executive Secretary

Associate executive secretary.

Statistics—chief of division of statistics of the Department of Labor.

Auditing and accounting staff.

Counsel—attorney general and assistant attorney.

Loan of Workers

Department of Public Welfare and Public Welfare Commission.

Field Staff

Five district representatives work with local communities receiving allocations from the Commission.

Three special representatives visit counties at request of district representatives for social service organization and administrative service. Also a director of work relief and a director of gardens for down-state counties.

Types of Relief Funds Available for Local Communities

October 17, 1932—diversion of motor fuel tax by counties for relief purposes after payment of their share of principle and interest on relief bonds. (This is purely optional with county.)

November 29, 1932—any county until January 1, 1934, by vote of two-thirds county board and without popular vote authorized to issue bonds for relief purposes not to exceed six times motor fuel tax allocated to the county in the preceding calendar year. (Sale temporarily, at least, held up by litigation.)

November 29, 1932—Cook County authorized by resolution of the county board and without popular vote to sell bonds for poor relief in amount not exceeding in the aggregate 17 million dollars. (These bonds unsalable but accepted in part by R.F.C. as security for loan.)

December 5, 1932—Any county in Illinois authorized until July

1, 1933, to impose tax not to exceed 1 per cent on certain retail sales within its boundaries. (Inoperative.)

March 22, 1933—State tax of 3% on retail sales—proceeds to be distributed to counties on basis of population for relief or other purposes. Compulsory administration of such relief funds by Illinois Emergency Relief Commission only in Cook County.

Result of New Legislation

Policy of relief commission to make allotments from state funds only to counties which are unable to meet their own relief needs from local funds resulted in prompt utilization of the authority granted to the counties by the legislation.

State Relief Funds

February 1932—20 million dollars appropriated by the Legislature.

25 million dollar state-wide property tax imposed and at the same time authority granted to issue tax anticipation notes up to 75 per cent of levy and immediate sale of notes to secure funds for use of commission. The tax was not to be extended if bonds to pay the notes were voted at the election in November 1932. These bonds were voted and are being paid by diversion for that purpose of the part of the motor vehicle tax allocated to the counties.

Federal Funds

$36,211,621 (to February 11, 1933) have been allocated to Illinois from federal funds under Title I, Section C, of the act establishing the RFC. In addition, $12,252,000 has been allocated from federal funds to Cook County under Title I, Section E, of the Act. The granting of federal aid to Cook County had the effect of changing the relationship of the Emergency Relief Commission toward the relief work in that county.

Total relief through April 15, 1933, from R.F.C. $52,088,621. This is the largest amount granted to any state.

Publications: *Relief Guidance and Control,* Nov. 25, 1932. 93-page pamphlet. *Relief Standards and Procedures in Dealing with Families of the Unemployed, December 1932.*—115-page pamphlet.

New Jersey: Emergency Relief Administration
        540 Broad Street, Newark
            Colonel Joseph D. Sears, Assistant Director

Creation

October 13, 1931, modified by relief acts of 1932. Consists of State Director of Emergency Relief appointed by the Governor—

Single unpaid executive officer. State administrative council composed of state officials serving ex-officio is responsible to the Director.

Purposes and Powers

1. To control allotment and payment of state aid funds and with certain authority of investigation and coordination of both public and private relief work.

2. To make study of extent of unemployment in the state, relief being provided, adequacy of relief and public work which might be undertaken by state and political subdivisions and public and private resources available.

3. To prescribe duties of advisory councils or committees and all employees.

4. To establish policies and prescribe programs of state and local relief and make rules for County Directors, advisory groups and employees.

Administrative Unit

1. Municipalities—state aid to counties was discontinued under act of July 1, 1932.

Forms of Relief

1. Method of distribution is discretionary with State Director.

2. Home relief.

3. Work relief—only on the basis of Home relief but given in return for services or labor.

Persons Qualified to Receive Relief

Actual need.

Conditions Under Which State Aid Is Given

1. Schedule applying under normal conditions.

Population of city	Municipal initial share	State share	Additional state share	Additional municipal share	Maximum state share
Under 10,000	10¢ per mo. per person	Up to 10¢ per.	50% add. exp. up to 10¢ per.	Balance of exp.	20¢ per person per month
10,000-50,000	15¢	Up to 15¢	50% add. up to 10¢ per.	Balance of exp.	25¢ per person per month
Over 50,000	15¢	Up to 15¢	50% add. up to 15¢ per.	Balance of exp.	30¢ per person per month

2. Special "A" grants:

Where municipality is able to finance only part of the relief work or where burden of relief is so heavy as to justify claim of exceptional conditions as basis for more than normal state aid, special "A" grant may be made after careful inquiry.

3. Special "B" grants:

When municipality or its citizens upon investigation are found to be temporarily unable to finance relief expenditures without crippling other essential services and it is not possible to finance normal part of municipal participation by private contributions special "B" grants may be made pending development of normal municipal responsibility.

Time for Which Grants Are Made

1. Normal grants are continuous until revoked but payments are made by the State on the basis of monthly municipal expenditures. Special "A" and "B" Grants are made on a monthly basis.

Local Responsibility

1. The primary responsibility for the giving of relief and its financing, rests upon local government. State funds are supplied to supplement inadequate local resources. The extent of State supervision depends upon the type of grant. Supervision is nominal in the case of normal grants although periodic reports are required and the municipalities must agree to accept recommendations of the State Administration which will improve local methods. Under a "B" grant, full responsibility for the administration of relief rests directly upon the State Administration although in most instances local personnel is used. Under an "A" grant the placing of the responsibility upon the State or the municipality depends upon what seems to the best interest of the Administration at the time the grant is made. In most instances, the municipalities are asked to assume responsibility for the administration of relief.

Standards

The standards of relief and relief administration used by the New Jersey Administration are those outlined in the State Laws for the Relief and Settlement of the Poor as interpreted by the Rules and Regulations of the Administration.

State Set-up

State Director—serves without pay.

Administrative Council—passes upon allotments. Otherwise State Director has complete authority except that he must utilize state, county and municipal employees when suitable and available and was prohibited from paying salaries to County Directors.

State Director appoints unpaid county director of emergency relief in each county, also such advisory councils and committees as he deems best.

General Council of sixty-six persons—not yet formally discontinued. Advisory Council and Leisure Time Activities have largely been drawn from this group.

Headquarters organization to handle investigation, research consultation, and financial allotment, disbursement and audit;

> Deputy state director
> Department of administration and personnel
> Department of finance and accounting
> Department of relief appropriations
> Relief service department
> Department of work relief
> Department of publicity
> Department of research and statistics

State funds may be used for personnel and administration. County directors may appoint, with approval of State Director, temporary assistants and employees from present public employees, if possible, in which case they receive no additional pay but if necessary others, to be paid for their services, may be appointed. County directors appoint deputy county directors, district or municipal directors and members of county or municipal councils. Municipal directors keep in touch with local conditions and local officials and have charge of relief work when it is conducted directly by the Emergency Relief Administration.

Source of Funds—State

Original appropriation—$1,500,000.

Bond issue—$8,000,000—interest and principal to be paid from proceeds of motor vehicle fuel tax in eight years—if insufficient tax on real and personal property is authorized.

Diversion from teachers pensions' annuity fund to be repaid from sale of bonds.

Proceeds received from Delaware River Joint Commission.

Source of Funds—Local

Authority to refinance abnormal relief expenditures during 1931 instead of including in 1932 budget.

Authority to finance relief expenditures under program approved by the state director over a ten year period up to $3/4$ of 1% of the average property valuation notwithstanding any debt limitation.

Authority subject to approval of state director to undertake major construction by contract under the Bond Acts without regard to or limitation by debt statement with the privilege of having amortization begin at the beginning of the third instead of the second year.

Municipalities may receive voluntary contributions of money which may be used in the same way as funds appropriated by them.

Special Features of New Jersey Program

Survey of unemployment.

Advisory Section on social welfare problems.

Committee on Emergency Leisure Time Activities.

Publication: *The Five Reports of the Advisory Section re Social Welfare Problems,* Jan. 21, 1932.

New York: Temporary Emergency Relief Administration
              124 East 28th Street, New York City
                    Frederick I. Daniels, Executive Director

Creation

Law establishing the Temporary Emergency Relief Administration became effective November 1, 1931. It was entitled "An act to relieve the people of the State from the hardships and suffering caused by unemployment."

Purpose

The purpose of the Act was to provide State aid to cities and counties in meeting relief needs.

Administrative Units

Incorporated cities and county territory outside city limits were defined as public welfare units. In counties where relief is administered on a town basis, town relief officials are required to cooperate through County Commissioners of Public Welfare. (Nine counties of the 57 outside New York City are on a County unit basis.)

Conditions for Participation

All cities and counties may participate. In April 1933 all but one of the 115 welfare districts cooperated with the TERA.

Forms of Relief

Home relief—administered through local commissioners of public welfare. Includes food, shelter, clothing, light, fuel, household supplies, medicines, medical supplies and medical attendance. Home relief cannot be given in cash.[4]

Work relief—administered by Emergency Work Bureau administered by Committee appointed by chief administrative officer of

---

[4] Unless Legislature changes this provision—now being discussed.

city or governing board of county—is defined as wages paid by a municipal corporation to persons who are unemployed or whose employment is inadequate to provide the necessities of life for themselves and their dependents. Wages must be paid in cash or by check for work done in accordance with wage rate in the locality for the particular type of work. Discrimination because of race, color, etc., is prohibited.

Persons Qualified to Receive Work Relief or Home Relief

Residents of the State for two years prior to date of application are eligible for either home or work relief.

Conditions Under Which State Aid Is Given

State may reimburse 40% of expenditures by city and county units for either home or work relief. State may provide additional funds where otherwise adequate relief is not possible. Reimbursement subject to conditions prescribed in law and rules made by TERA.

Standards Prescribed by the TERA

"Needy persons shall receive sufficient relief to prevent physical suffering and to maintain minimum standards of living."

Relief must be based upon budget estimate of weekly needs and resources of each applicant.

Investigation of each applicant is required, including visit to home and inquiry as to property and other resources.

Registration of all applicants in central index. Where none exists it must be established by the Public Welfare Commissioner.

Visit to each family at least once a month; reapplication at office by family for individual orders should be avoided.

Personnel

Each municipal corporation "should have at least one trained and experienced investigator on its staff; if additional investigators are to be employed to meet this emergency, the first one employed should have had training and experience." Supervisor with training and experience required in larger offices. Similarly, work bureaus are required to have at least one trained and experienced worker or supervisor.

Coordination of Home Relief and Emergency Work Relief with activities of private relief agencies is the joint responsibility of the chairman of the Emergency Work Bureau and the commissioner of public welfare.

Facilities required for both Home Relief and Work Relief include sufficient office space to insure privacy in interviewing applicants and satisfactory waiting room, including proper heating, lighting and ventilation.

Records are prescribed for case recording and for financial accounting. Other suggested forms for case records are also furnished free. Accountants and field auditors employed by the TERA assist local offices which ask help in bringing their records up to required standards.

Reimbursement to Cities and Counties for Salaries of Certain Types of Employees

In the case of home relief, State may reimburse local units in whole or in part for salaries of investigators and supervisors with social service experience whose employment has been approved by the Administration. Reimbursement to work relief bureaus may be made up to 50% for salaries of workers of this kind and of certain administrative and technical employees.

The TERA in meeting requests for social workers from local units gives preference to workers who are residents of the particular city or county, whenever they have had requisite training and experience. When qualified local workers are not available locally, others are recommended with the assistance of the Joint Vocational Service or the field staff.

Use of private funds as basis of reimbursement by State. Local private relief funds cannot be counted in the total used as the basis for reimbursement from the State unless such private funds have been turned into the public treasury.

Relationship Between Public and Private Agencies

No basis for division of responsibility between public and private agencies has been worked out for up-State districts. A study is being made of this subject. In New York City the Welfare Council has worked on this question and certain general decisions were made when public relief began.

Turning over records of private agency to public agency

The TERA does not approve of turning over private records. In one city in the State the records of the private agency were turned over to the public agency when the families were transferred. Questions arose as to how the future of the family agency might be affected by this procedure. The Executive Director of the TERA agreed that the records should be "unscrambled."

Administrative Set-up of TERA as of April 1933

Administration: Executive chairman and four other members appointed by the Governor.

Counsel (Solicitor General of the State—part time).

Executive Director.

Accounting Department—including staff of accountants, office and field auditors, clerical and stenographic, and staff of auditors for the State Comptroller's Office.

Research and Statistics department.

Information service (publicity).

Personnel service (Joint Vocational Service—part time).

Office administration—office manager and staff of stenographers, etc.

Medical service (Doctor from the State Health Department and temporary field service of nurses from State Health Department).

Engineer (field) and two special assistants (office) on work projects.

Field Service Department:

Two regional directors (each in charge of nine or ten field representatives).

Nineteen field representatives (each assigned from six to ten districts).

Field service also by field auditors and two or more "case investigators" for special check-up of relief methods.

"Liaison worker" cooperating with all departments of the Administration.

Nutrition consultants.

Financial Resources

State

Original appropriation $20,000,000

March 31, 1932, additional 5,000,000

November 1932 bond issue 30,000,000 authorized by referendum vote

1933 Request from R.F.C.. 19,800,000 through April

Local

Appropriations for relief work by municipal corporations.

Authority granted for local units to create obligations to secure funds for relief provided.

a. paid in 3 to 10 years.

b. not in excess of debt limitations.

Municipalities authorized to do public work other than that
done by contract through Emergency Relief Bureau.

Local Responsibility

1. Local administration of relief.
2. TERA functions only in cooperation with local units.
3. TERA has broad powers in setting up rules and conditions
   under which state funds will be used to assist local units.

Economy in Supplying Adequate Relief

a. *Food.* The Administration has emphasized the necessity for
reducing food costs in order that funds so saved may make it possible to provide adequate food allowances to needy families. Experiments in the reduction of food costs in a number of welfare districts have demonstrated the possibility of making substantial savings through careful selection of stores and checking of prices. Savings averaging about 10 per cent have been effected through price
agreements with retail and wholesale merchants. Welfare districts
that have leaned toward the commissary or public food store plan
have been urged to try out other methods of cutting costs, with the
result that only one food store plan has been initiated (in two heavy
relief centers in one county); two food stores were in operation before the TERA period, one of them in a small city. The Administration recommends the appointment of a small committee in each
city or large town or county area to concern itself with the question
of reducing food costs to the end that relief funds may be conserved
for families in need of assistance. (New material on this subject is
now being prepared.)

b. *Shelter.* (It is assumed that no local unit will be able to provide all the costs of shelter for all dependent families and that on
this account wise use of limited funds is essential.) In some districts agreements are made with landlords on the basis of taxes and
up-keep charges. Committees in some cities advise distressed property owners.

c. *Fuel:*

1. In some county units, wood rather than coal is provided.
2. Wood from tree-trimming and wood cutting projects is utilized.
3. Trade agreements with dealers have been tried in some units.

d. *Clothing:*

1. TERA has assisted local committees in purchase of new clothing at wholesale prices. Clothing bureaus in most of the welfare
districts. 100% reimbursement allowed by TERA for women employed in making or remaking garments last winter.
2. Reconditioning old clothing and making new garments by volunteers or as work bureau projects for unemployed women.

3. Purchase of shoes and other government clothing at low price.

e. *Subsistence Gardens or Farms:*

1. Subsistence gardens promoted by TERA with assistance of advisors from Cornell University.

2. TERA reimbursed emergency work bureaus 40% cost of fitting land for gardens and relief units, 40% of cost of seeds, fertilizer and limited number of garden tools.

3. TERA assisted in financing limited number of farm placements recommended by local relief units. Agricultural advisor assisted local units in locating land suitable for placement.

Publication:

1. Rules Concerning Home Relief, Nov., 1931.

2. Explanations Governing Rules on Home Relief Relating to Records, Nov., 1931.

3. Rules Governing Work Relief, Nov., 1931.

4. Report of the T.E.R.A., Jan., 1932.

5. Explanations Governing Rules on Home Relief Relating to Records, May, 1932.

6. Explanations Governing Rules on Work Relief Relating to Records, May, 1932.

7. Rules Governing Home Relief and Work Relief, June, 1932. Monthly Statistical Bulletin Concerning Relief Expenditures.

8. Food Allowances, Aug., 1932.

9. Report of the New York State T.E.R.A., Oct., 1932.

Pennsylvania: State Emergency Relief Board
                Harrisburg
                    W. B. Rodgers, Executive Director

Creation

August 1932—superseding relief act of December 1931. Board is composed of five state officials.

Powers and Duties

1. Make equitable allotment from state funds among counties on basis of relief needs and resources.

    (a) State funds are allocated by law on the basis of the number of unemployed in each county in proportion to the total number of unemployed in the State.

    (b) Federal funds are allocated to the counties to supplement state funds giving consideration to the need by figures presented by the county boards.

2. Determine what part, if any, of state funds allotted to counties shall be used for state highways and bridges.

3. Prescribe method and manner of distributing relief.

4. Designate public or private agencies through which relief will be administered and the way in which *private* agencies shall be organized in communities where this is necessary.

5. Plan and adopt program for expenditure of Federal funds.

Administrative Unit—County, usually divided into districts for administrative purposes

County Emergency Relief Boards, consisting of seven unpaid members, appointed by the State E.R.B. in each county, have responsibility for administering state and federal funds either directly or through existing public or private agencies or both, subject to the approval of the S.E.R.B.

Forms of Relief

Food orders, work relief or other forms of actual relief. At first only food orders given except cash for work on highways. In the latter case men are paid directly by the highway department from funds transferred to this department from the monies allocated to the county boards. Later fuel was authorized and shoes, and in a few instances funds for the care of the homeless and shelters.

Persons Entitled to Receive Relief

1. Residents of Pennsylvania for one year on basis of actual need.

2. Work relief, in some counties all relief, is given on this basis. In other counties work relief is granted to a certain portion of the unemployed selected in various ways.

3. Direct relief—A few larger counties operate entirely through direct relief. In counties where it is not possible to provide work for all, direct relief and work relief are coordinated in various ways.

Administrative Expenses

At first state funds could not be used for salaries or other administrative expenses. Later experience showed need for qualified staff subject to the County and State Boards and funds were allowed for this purpose.

Conditions Under Which State Aid Is Given

State Emergency Relief Board allocates funds to counties in such sums and in such proportions as in its judgment may seem equitable, based upon monthly applications from county boards indicating current relief loads and estimated needs for the next month.

Local Responsibility

Principle of almost complete local responsibility originally adopted is giving way to increased central control as a means of insuring a sound program. The State Board reserves the right to approve all appointments of Executive Directors and Comptrollers in the various counties although the County Boards may make provisional appointments.

Standards

The State Board recognizes that unemployment relief must be administered on something like a disaster basis but has attempted to establish minimum standards including determination of need, adjustment of relief to size of family and its needs and revisitation to determine whether or not needs have changed. Emphasis is placed on intelligent service at the point of receiving applications and reasonable limitation of case load per worker.

The appointment of qualified personnel in the various counties as well as the coordination of relief resources both public and private is being fostered by the State Board.

Set-up of Emergency Relief Board

Commission of five state officials including Governor appointed by act of Legislature.

Executive Director.
Assistant Director.
Comptroller.
Field Director and Administrative Assistant.
Seven field representatives.
Nutritionist.
Publicity Director.
Personnel Director.
Purchasing agent and an assistant on clothing.
Director of community markets and two assistants.
Twenty-two clerical workers.
Advisory committees have been appointed: on grants, nutrition, shoes and gardens.

Set-up of County Boards

County Board of from 5 to 7 members.
County Executive Director.
Comptroller.
Such other employees as are necessary, which may include
Supervisor.
Assistant Supervisor.

Visitors.

Interviewers.

Clerks and typists.

Appropriation

From state funds $12,000,000 with special limitations as to amounts of expenditures by months.

From Federal funds—$29,929,875, of which $26,955,446 has been received to March 22, 1933.

Source of State Funds

State tax of 1% on gross income derived from the sale of tangible property.

RFC grants—$34,929,874 through May 1933.

Publication: Handbook in preparation.

West Virginia: Unemployment Relief Administration

State Capitol, Charleston,

Major Francis Turner, Director

Creation

August 19, 1932. West Virginia Unemployment Relief Administration, to be appointed by the Governor with a bi-partisan Board of four members. The Commission chose the West Virginia Department of Public Welfare as its administrative agent and selected the Director of that Department as Executive officer. There is a state staff of 4 field directors, each supervising about 11 counties.

Purposes and Powers

1. To assist the Governor in analyzing applications from political sub-divisions of the state for Federal funds.

2. To promulgate rules.

3. Establish and sanction policies and procedure governing the use of Federal funds.

Administrative Unit—County

Local Responsibility

Unemployment Relief Administration creates County organization.

Powers and duties of County organization to include

1. Survey of County to determine relief needs and resources.

2. Preparation of applications for grants.

3. Organize County Welfare Board.

4. Supervise and administer relief program in the County.

Forms of Relief

Work relief—When individual is able to render service for relief given, he is required to render such useful service as may be designated by the county organization.

Federal Funds

$9,655,218 made available by RFC (through May 1933).

Publication: Organization and Activities, State of West Virginia Department of Public Welfare and Unemployment Relief Administration, Aug., 1932, Jan., 1933.

Appendix K

(See Chapter 9, p. 204)

Total Federal Emergency Relief Administration grants for the period May 23, 1933-Mar. 31, 1935, total population, percent of total grants, and percent of total population, by States [5]

States	Total Federal Emergency Relief Administration grants for period May 23, 1933- Mar. 31, 1935	Population [1]	Percentage of total grants	Percentage of total population
Alabama	$40,332,022	2,646,248	1.9	2.2
Arizona	11,783,782	435,573	.6	.4
Arkansas	33,464,050	1,854,482	1.6	1.5
California	97,401,707	5,677,251	4.7	4.6
Colorado	26,973,492	1,035,791	1.3	.8
Connecticut	16,860,682	1,606,903	.8	1.3
Delaware	1,988,706	238,380	.1	.2
District of Columbia	11,162,500	486,869	.5	.4
Florida	37,874,999	1,468,211	1.8	1.2
Georgia	39,360,816	2,908,506	1.9	2.4
Idaho	10,461,314	445,032	.5	.4
Illinois	141,994,146	7,630,654	6.8	6.2
Indiana	38,245,559	3,238,503	1.8	2.6
Iowa	20,403,615	2,470,939	1.0	2.0
Kansas	30,113,076	1,880,999	1.5	1.5

[5] From Expenditure of Funds, Federal Emergency Relief Administration, Report to the Senate Committee on Appropriations. Exhibit Q, p. 637.

States	Total Federal Emergency Relief Administration grants for period May 23, 1933- Mar. 31, 1935	Population [1]	Percentage of total grants	Percentage of total population
Kentucky	$24,843,878	2,614,589	1.2	2.1
Louisiana	36,958,982	2,101,593	1.8	1.7
Maine	9,339,544	797,423	.5	.6
Maryland	27,866,063	1,631,526	1.3	1.3
Massachusetts	73,318,302	4,249,614	3.5	3.5
Michigan	85,534,398	4,842,325	4.1	3.9
Minnesota	54,838,588	2,563,953	2.6	2.1
Mississippi	26,205,297	2,009,821	1.3	1.6
Missouri	50,359,443	3,629,367	2.4	3.0
Montana	19,662,470	537,606	.9	.4
Nebraska	20,528,997	1,377,963	1.0	1.1
Nevada	4,199,804	91,058	.2	.1
New Hampshire	5,081,105	465,293	.2	.4
New Jersey	65,189,171	4,041,334	3.1	3.3
New Mexico	13,109,147	423,317	.6	.3
New York	266,563,334	12,588,066	12.8	10.3
North Carolina	28,976,358	3,170,276	1.4	2.6
North Dakota	27,288,850	680,845	1.3	.6
Ohio	115,794,156	6,646,697	5.6	5.4
Oklahoma	34,164,368	2,396,040	1.6	2.0
Oregon	14,917,260	953,786	.7	.8
Pennsylvania	196,241,114	9,631,350	9.4	7.8
Rhode Island	5,505,712	687,497	.3	.6
South Carolina	28,621,045	1,738,765	1.4	1.4
South Dakota	36,382,980	692,849	1.8	.6
Tennessee	26,754,867	2,616,556	1.3	2.1
Texas	69,997,371	5,824,715	3.4	4.7
Utah	15,367,082	507,847	.7	.4
Vermont	2,823,226	359,611	.1	.3
Virginia	17,256,881	2,421,851	.8	2.0
Washington	24,777,230	1,563,396	1.2	1.3
West Virginia	33,675,986	1,729,205	1.6	1.4
Wisconsin	55,675,294	2,939,006	2.7	2.4
Wyoming	7,283,643	225,565	.4	.2
Total, Continental United States	$2,083,522,412	122,775,046	100.0	100.0

[1] Based on 1930 Census of Population.

Appendix L

(See Chapter 10, pp. 234 and 249)

AVERAGE MONTHLY RELIEF BENEFITS
PER FAMILY[6]
MAY 1933 THROUGH MAY 1935

	Amount of benefits				Amount of benefits		
	Total United States	Prin- cipal cities	Remain- der of the country		Total United States	Prin- cipal cities	Remain- der of the country
1933				*1934—Cont'd*			
May	$15.59	$21.23	$11.48	July	$24.05	$31.51	$18.59
July	15.07	19.86	10.83	August ...	25.83	34.20	19.96
September	17.17	21.93	12.64	September	24.10	31.42	18.93
October ..	19.18	24.60	14.27	October ..	26.24	33.67	20.78
November	18.31	23.74	13.54	November	28.31	35.74	22.94
December .	16.88	21.46	12.42	December .	28.37	35.95	22.94
1934				*1935*			
January ..	16.71	21.46	12.95	January ..	30.43	38.97	24.39
February .	16.57	24.22	11.84	February .	28.08	35.76	22.64
March ...	17.93	24.83	13.14	March ...	28.73	36.91	23.06
April	20.98	26.68	16.28	April	28.96	36.91	23.06
May	23.90	30.80	18.53	May	29.34	36.76	23.64
June	23.28	29.92	18.14				

Source: *FERA Monthly Report*, June, 1935, p. 31.

[6] Average monthly relief benefits are computed by dividing the total amount of relief (both direct relief and Emergency Work Relief Program earnings) extended to all relief families under the general relief program by the total number of such families who received aid at any time in the course of the month. Since this family total includes those who received relief during only a part of the month, as well as those who received only supplementary aid, the resulting averages always understate to some extent the amounts actually paid to families who were entirely dependent on public agencies for subsistence throughout the month.

Appendix M

(See Chapter 13, p. 311)

HEARINGS ON ECONOMIC SECURITY ACT

Hearings on the Economic Security Act before the Committee on Ways and Means of the House of Representatives, January and February, 1935. H.R. 4120. Seventy-fourth Congress, 1st Session.

Mrs. A. M. Tunstall, Director of Alabama Child Welfare Department: "I should like to see both sections [Aid to Dependent Children and Child Welfare Services] put under the Children's Bureau, and I am speaking now in terms of aid to children in their own homes as involving so many other problems than that of just relief." p. 449.

J. Prentice Murphy, Children's Bureau of Philadelphia: "Also, in regard to the administration of the proposed mothers' assistance Federal-State program, that might very properly be left to the Children's Bureau of the Department of Labor." p. 532.

Jacob Kepecs, representing the Child Welfare League of America: ". . . the administration of mothers' aid should be placed in the Federal Children's Bureau rather than in the Emergency Relief Administration, which is a temporary organization. The Children's Bureau, as you know, has had considerable experience with mothers' aid through studies over a long period of time in that field. It has established very excellent working relationships with State departments of public welfare which administer mothers' aid." p. 501.

Miss Sophonisba Breckinridge, School of Social Service Administration, University of Chicago; letter to a member of the House of Representatives: ". . . to urge that if the President's program for relief, including the plan for mothers' pensions and old-age pensions should come under your consideration you give favorable thought to the possibility of placing the administration of those two projects in the Department of Labor rather than under the Relief Administration." p. 1069.

Miss Grace Abbott, Member of the Advisory Council on Economic Security: "I am sorry that the administration of this grant-in-aid program is not given to the Children's Bureau. I think it belongs in a permanent Bureau instead of in an emergency Bureau, and the Children's Bureau has worked for 21 or 22 years on this problem with the States." p. 496.

Hearings on the Economic Security Act before the Committee on Finance of the United States Senate, February, 1935. S. 1130.

Miss Grace Abbott: "Now, I am sorry to say I do not agree with the lodging of the administration of the mothers' aid in the Federal Emergency Relief Administration, or, as the Act provides, such other Government Bureau as the President may designate . . . I think it belongs in the Children's Bureau . . . and I think you would find that State departments of public welfare would generally prefer administration by the Children's Bureau to administration by the Emergency Relief Administration which is, after all, in another category entirely, as a temporary emergency administration." pp. 1080-81.

The following testimony was opposed to categorical assistance:

Miss Dorothy Kahn, representing the American Association of Social Workers: "We believe that the social hazards referred to in this bill, aggravated by the depression, affect families in a variety of ways, and that unified programs of general assistance are required to provide for the needs of great numbers of families who do not fall in the particular classifications or categories like those mentioned in titles I and II of the bill. These family situations, however, represent individual problems and are in constant change. Measures for dealing with them must, therefore, be unified and must be general enough so each person is not shifted from one jurisdiction to another when a change of category occurs." p. 649.

Appendix N

(See Chapter 14, p. 333)

Excerpts from the *Fourth Annual Report* of the Social Security Board, Supplementary Data, July 1-October 31, 1939, pp. 166-184.

Amendments to the Social Security Act in 1939

. . . . .

The changes effected by the Social Security Act Amendments of 1939 are substantial and comprehensive in that they modify all titles of the original act. The most important changes are those dealing with the Federal old-age insurance program, which was revised and expanded to form a program for Federal old-age and survivors insurance. Other amendments related to the Federal-State systems of unemployment insurance and public assistance.

The amendments also increased the amounts authorized for Federal grants to States for maternal and child health, crippled children, child welfare, vocational rehabilitation, and public health, under programs of the Social Security Act directed by Federal agencies other than the Social Security Board.

Federal Old-Age and Survivors Insurance

In amending the Social Security Act, the old-age insurance program was revised in six important respects:

1. The payment of monthly benefits is advanced to January 1, 1940;

2. Eligibility requirements in the early years are liberalized to permit those who have attained age 65 to qualify for benefits in 1940 or shortly thereafter;

3. The average benefits payable in the early years are increased;

4. Protection is extended to the aged wife and dependent children of beneficiaries and to certain survivors of insured workers;

5. A Federal old-age and survivors insurance trust fund is created, to be supervised by a Board of Trustees; and

6. The old-age insurance tax on workers and employers is continued at 1 percent of taxable wages and 1 percent of pay rolls for the 3 calendar years 1940-42.

· · · · ·

Public Assistance

The amendments relating to public assistance are designed chiefly to liberalize and clarify existing Federal provisions and to simplify the administration of the State plans. No fundamental change in the Federal-State basis was made.

Federal participation in the program for aid to dependent children is increased from one-third to one-half of the costs incurred for administration and assistance under approved State plans, not including amounts by which monthly payments exceed $18 for one dependent child and $12 for each additional child aided in the same home. The age limit for children toward whose payments Federal funds are used is raised from 16 to 18 years if the State agency finds that the child is regularly attending school. It is estimated that these changes will enable the State to provide monthly payments for many additional children and to grant more adequate funds to many of the very needy cases now on State rolls. Furthermore, these amendments should encourage the nine jurisdictions (eight States and Alaska) which are not participating in this program to adopt a State plan which will entitle them to Federal aid and so provide more adequate aid to dependent children.

Changes in financial arrangements were made with respect to Federal participation in assistance to needy aged persons and needy blind persons. Under the 1935 law the Federal Government matched half the assistance costs incurred under an approved State plan, not including amounts by which individual payments exceeded $30 a month. The amended law increases that maximum from $30 to $40 as of January 1, 1940, so that the maximum amount of Federal funds used for the monthly payment to an aged or a blind recipient of assistance is increased from $15 to $20. The extent of liberalization under these amendments will depend entirely upon the degree to which the States take advantage of the more liberal amount which the Federal Government will match.

Several amendments relate to administration of public assistance. The States are required, beginning July 1, 1941, to provide safeguards which restrict the use or disclosure of information concerning applicants and recipients to purposes directly connected with the administration of the plan. All three assistance titles are amended in this manner to ensure efficient administration and to protect recipients from humiliation and exploitation. To promote more efficient administration of State plans, the provisions for aid to the blind were amended so that the Federal Government, as in the amended provisions for aid to dependent children, will pay half the necessary costs involved in administration of an approved plan. The purpose of the public-assistance programs was clarified by the insertion of the word "needy" in the definitions of those who may receive old-age assistance, aid to dependent children, and aid to the blind. A closely related clarifying amendment provides that the States, beginning July 1, 1941, in determining need must consider any other income and other resources of applicants for any of these types of assistance.

· · · · ·

State Personnel

After January 1, 1940, the amended Federal law provides for the establishment of objective standards for merit systems for both State and local personnel as one of the conditions the States must meet in order to receive Federal grants. This requirement applies to all three public-assistance programs and also to unemployment compensation and to the services for maternal and child health and for crippled children. The amended law provides that the States, to receive Federal funds, must include, in addition to other standards of efficient administration, methods relating to the establishment and maintenance of personnel standards on a merit basis. Specific provision is made to prevent the exercise of Federal authority with respect to the selection, tenure of office, and compensation of any individual employed in accordance with such methods.

Other Federal-State Programs

Additional Federal funds have been authorized for the health and welfare programs administered by other Federal agencies under the Social Security Act. The addition of $7,612,000 brings to $25,700,-000 the total Federal authorization for these services. The changes in annual authorizations for these programs are as follows:

Program	1935 provisions	1939 provisions
Maternal and child health	$3,800,000	$ 5,820,000
Services for crippled children	2,850,000	3,870,000
Child-welfare services	1,500,000	1,510,000
Vocational rehabilitation	1,938,000	3,500,000
Public Health	8,000,000	11,000,000

Effective January 1, 1940, Puerto Rico may participate under the Social Security Act in all these health and welfare programs.

Appendix O

(See Chart I, page x)

TABLE 14

Public Assistance and Federal Work Programs: Amount of Public Assistance and Earnings of Persons Employed Under Federal Work Programs in the Continental United States, by Programs and by 6-Month Periods, July, 1935-June, 1939 [1]

Program	Fiscal year 1935-36		Fiscal year 1936-37		Fiscal year 1937-38		Fiscal year 1938-39		
	July-December 1935	*January-June 1936*	*July-December 1936*	*January-June 1937*	*July-December 1937*	*January-June 1938*	*July-December 1938*	*January-June 1939*	*July-December 1939*
	AMOUNT (IN THOUSANDS)								
All public assistance and earnings of persons employed under Federal work programs	$1,315,030	$1,606,981	$1,651,373	$1,534,470	$1,334,898	$1,597,895	$1,887,866	$1,866,074	$1,627,115
I. Public assistance:									
A. Special types [2]	61,080	82,019	135,496	181,196	216,671	247,004	262,105	278,149	288,689
1. Old-age assistance	35,861	52,762	102,477	141,305	169,137	191,037	201,483	211,926	218,981
2. Aid to dependent children	21,139	23,237	26,226	32,323	38,931	46,556	50,882	56,144	58,769
3. Aid to the blind	4,080	6,020	6,793	7,568	8,603	9,411	9,740	10,079	10,339
B. General relief [3]	580,302	248,780	190,235	211,684	195,184	256,124	219,938	252,095	228,865
C. Special programs of the Federal Emergency Relief Administration [4]	29,702	2,688	1,185	467	......	......	......	......	......
D. Subsistence payments certified by the Farm Security Administration [5]	2,541	12,802	7,563	26,959	8,935	13,502	9,098	12,421	6,621
II. Earnings of persons employed under Federal work programs [6]	641,404	1,260,692	1,316,864	1,114,164	914,108	1,081,265	1,396,725	1,323,409	1,103,540

Amounts:

	1	2	3	4	5	6	7	8	9
A. Civilian Conservation Corps [7]	112,036	118,477	119,082	111,084	114,252	131,504	139,112	153,279	193,360
B. Works Progress Administration: [8]									
1. Projects operated by the Works Progress Administration	624,476	883,960	991,029	731,248	506,092	680,174	775,139	816,900	238,018
2. Projects operated by other Federal agencies	21,043	34,929	28,554	......	......	......	......	......	......
C. National Youth Administration: [9]									
1. Student aid	8,578	14,093	7,022	12,576	5,796	18,491	9,120	16,781	6,364
2. Work projects	25,638	25,847	24,155	17,405	13,889	18,775	16,634	12,249	......
D. Other Federal work and construction projects [10]	311,769	246,103	226,883	208,952	274,079	265,220	376,889	261,483	203,662

All public assistance and earnings of persons employed under Federal work programs

PERCENTAGE DISTRIBUTION

	1	2	3	4	5	6	7	8	9
All public assistance and earnings of persons employed under Federal work programs	100.0	100.0	100.0	100.0	100.0	100.0	100.0	100.0	100.0
I. Public assistance:									
A. Special types: [2]									
1. Old-age assistance	13.4	11.4	10.7	12.0	12.7	9.2	6.2	3.3	2.7
2. Aid to dependent children	3.6	3.0	2.7	2.9	2.9	2.1	1.6	1.4	1.6
3. Aid to the blind	.6	.5	.6	.6	.7	.5	.4	.4	.3
B. General relief [3]	14.1	13.5	11.6	16.0	14.6	13.8	11.5	15.5	44.1
C. Special programs of the Federal Emergency Relief Administration [4]	......	......	......	......	......	(11)	.1	.2	2.3
D. Subsistence payments certified by the Farm Security Administration [5]	.4	.7	.5	.8	.7	1.8	.5	.8	.2
II. Earnings of persons employed under Federal work programs: [6]									
A. Civilian Conservation Corps [7]	6.9	6.3	6.3	6.9	8.6	8.6	8.4	9.5	14.7
B. Works Progress Administration: [8]									
1. Projects operated by the Works Progress Administration	38.4	47.4	52.5	45.8	37.9	44.3	46.9	50.8	18.1
2. Projects operated by other Federal agencies	1.3	1.9	1.5	......	......	......	......	......	......
C. National Youth Administration: [9]									
1. Student aid	.5	.7	.4	.8	.4	1.2	.6	1.0	.5
2. Work projects	1.6	1.4	1.3	1.1	1.0	1.2	1.0	.8	......
D. Other Federal work and construction projects [10]	19.2	13.2	12.0	13.1	20.5	17.3	22.8	16.3	15.5

[Continued on next page]

TABLE 14 (Cont.)

Program	Fiscal year 1935-36		Fiscal year 1936-37		Fiscal year 1937-38		Fiscal year 1938-39		
	July-December 1935	January-June 1936	July-December 1936	January-June 1937	July-December 1937	January-June 1938	July-December 1938	January-June 1939	July-December 1939
All public assistance and earnings of persons employed under Federal work programs	$10.31	$12.52	$12.86	$11.87	$10.33	$12.36	$14.61	$14.44	$12.59
AMOUNT PER INHABITANT [12]									
I. Public assistance:									
A. Special types: [2]									
1. Old-age assistance	.28	.41	.80	1.09	1.31	1.48	1.56	1.64	1.69
2. Aid to dependent children	.17	.18	.20	.25	.30	.36	.39	.43	.45
3. Aid to the blind	.03	.05	.05	.06	.07	.07	.08	.08	.08
B. General relief [3]	4.55	1.94	1.48	1.64	1.51	1.98	1.70	1.95	1.77
C. Special programs of the Federal Emergency Relief Administration [4]	.23	.02	.01	(13)	......	......	......	......	......
D. Subsistence payments certified by the Farm Security Administration [5]	.02	.10	.06	.21	.07	.10	.07	.10	.05
II. Earnings of persons employed under Federal work programs: [6]									
A. Civilian Conservation Corps [7]	1.52	1.19	1.08	1.02	.88	.86	.92	.92	.87
B. Works Progress Administration: [8]									
1. Projects operated by the Works Progress Administration	1.87	6.36	6.04	5.26	3.92	5.66	7.67	6.84	4.83
2. Projects operated by other Federal agencies	......	......	......	......	......	......	......	......	......
C. National Youth Administration: [9]									
1. Student aid	.05	.13	.07	.14	.04	.10	.05	.11	.16
2. Work projects	......	.10	.13	.15	.11	.13	.10	.20	.07
D. Other Federal work and construction projects [10]	1.60	2.04	2.93	2.05	2.12	1.62	1.76	1.90	2.41

1 Figures exclude cost of administration and of materials, equipment, and other items incident to operation of work programs. Figures are partly estimated and subject to revision. For information by months for January, 1933-June, 1939, see *Social Security Bulletin*, Vol. 2, No. 8 (August, 1939).

2 Figures for July, 1935-January, 1936, represent payments from state and local funds only. Figures for subsequent months represent payments to recipients from Federal, state, and local funds in states administering the 3 special types of public assistance under the Social Security Act, and from state and local funds only in states not participating under the Act.

3 Figures for July, 1935-March, 1937, from the WPA, Division of Statistics. Figures for 1935 include obligations incurred for direct relief, earnings of relief and nonrelief persons (other than of administrative employees) employed under the general relief program of the FERA, and the estimated amount of obligations incurred for relief extended to cases by local authorities from public funds under the poor laws.

4 Figures from the WPA, Division of Statistics, include obligations incurred for relief extended to cases under the emergency education, student aid, rural rehabilitation, and transient programs of the emergency relief administrations largely financed from FERA funds.

5 Figures from the FSA represent net amount of emergency grant vouchers certified to cases during each month of period.

6 Figures include earnings of persons certified as in need of relief and earnings of all other persons employed on work and construction projects financed in whole or in part from Federal funds. Figures for the CCC include earnings of enrolled persons only.

7 Figures estimated by the CCC by multiplying average monthly number of persons enrolled by an average of $70 per month. This average amount is based on amount of obligations incurred for cash allowances and for clothing, shelter, subsistence, and medical care of persons enrolled, and for certain other items.

8 Figures from the WPA, Division of Statistics, represent earnings of persons employed on projects financed from WPA funds and cover all pay-roll periods ended during each month of period.

9 Figures from the WPA, Division of Statistics, represent earnings during all pay-roll periods ended during each month of period.

10 Figures from the Bureau of Labor Statistics, Division of Construction and Public Employment, represent earnings on other work and construction projects financed in whole or in part from Federal funds and cover all pay-roll periods ended during monthly period ended on 15th of specified month.

11 Less than 0.1 per cent.

12 Based on population estimated by the U. S. Bureau of the Census as of July 1 of each year except 1938 and 1939, which are based on estimated population as of July 1, 1937.

13 Less than 1 cent.

Source of table: Fourth Annual Report, Social Security Board, 1939, Appendix D, pp. 273-5, and Bureau of Research and Statistics, Social Security Board.

BIBLIOGRAPHY

Selected Bibliography

BY PERIODS AND PROGRAMS

GENERAL

Abbott, Edith, *Public Assistance, American Principles and Policies.* In Five Parts with Select Documents, The University of Chicago Press, Chicago, 1940.

Breckinridge, Sophonisba P., *Public Welfare Administration in the United States,* Select Documents. The University of Chicago Press, Chicago, 1938. 1229 pp., Bibliography.

Abbott, Grace, *The Child and the State.* Select Documents with Introductory Notes, University of Chicago Press, Chicago, 1938. 2 Vols. 1402 pp.

Feder, Leah Hannah, *Unemployment Relief in Periods of Depression, A Study of Measures Adopted in Certain American Cities.* Russell Sage Foundation, New York, 1936. 384 pp.

Watson, Frank Dekker, *The Charity Organization Movement in the United States,* Macmillan, New York, 1922. 560 pp.

Recent Social Trends in the United States, President's Research Commission on Social Trends. McGraw-Hill, 1934. 1568 pp.

Schneider, David, *The History of Public Welfare in New York State, 1609-1866,* University of Chicago Press, 1938, 381 pp.

Schneider, David M., *The Road Upward, Three Hundred Years of Public Welfare in New York State,* Department of Public Welfare, Albany, New York, 1939. Pamphlet.

Cahn and Bary, *Welfare Activities of Federal, State and Local Governments in California, 1850-1934,* University of California Press, Berkeley, California, 1936. 422 pp.

"Social Welfare in the National Recovery Program," *Annals* of the American Academy of Political and Social Science, Nov., 1934.

Social Work Year Book, Published biennially, 1929-1939, Russell Sage Foundation, New York.

White, Leonard D., *Introduction to the Study of Public Administration,* Macmillan, New York, 1939. 611 pp.

MacDonald, Austin, *Federal Aid,* Thomas Crowell, New York, 1928. 285 pp.

Key, V. O., Jr., *The Administration of Federal Grants to States.* Published for the Committee on Public Administration of the Social Science Research Council by Public Administration Service, Chicago, 1937. 388 pp.

Millspaugh, Arthur C., *Public Welfare Organization.* Brookings Institution, Washington, D. C., 1935. 700 pp.

Stevenson, Marietta, *Public Welfare Administration.* Macmillan, New York, 1938. 352 pp.

White House Conference on the Care of Dependent Children, January 25, 26, 1909; Special Message of the President of the United States Recommending Legislation Desired by the Conference and Transmitting the Proceedings of the Conference: Senate Doc. No. 712, 1909. Reprinted in U. S. Children's Bureau Publication No. 136, *Foster Home Care for Dependent Children.*

Report of Children's Bureau Conferences, May and June, 1919: *Standards of Child Welfare, Minimum Standards for the Protection of Children in Need of Special Care,* Publication No. 60, 1919.

White House Conference on Child Care and Protection. Section IV-A. Organization for the Care of Handicapped Children, 1932, 365 pp.

White House Conference on Children in a Democracy, 1940, Children's Bureau, Department of Labor. General Conference Report, also Report on Economic Aid to Families.

The Children's Bureau: Yesterday, Today, and Tomorrow, 1937. Gov't Printing Office.

Winslow, Emma A., *Trends in Different Types of Public and Private Relief in Urban Areas, 1929-35.* Publication No. 237. U. S. Department of Labor, Children's Bureau, 1937.

Geddes, Anne E., *Trends in Relief Expenditures, 1910-1935,* WPA, 1937. 117 pp.

Activities of the Federal Emergency Agencies, 1933-1938, prepared by the National Emergency Council, October, 1938, Report No. 7, 87 pp.

Chronology of Federal Relief Legislation, 1932-1939. Prepared by the Legislative Reference Service of the WPA Library, Work Projects Administration, Federal Works Agency, July, 1938. Revised December, 1939. 15 pp., multigraphed.

BIBLIOGRAPHY

POOR RELIEF BEFORE THE TWENTIETH CENTURY

Webb, Sidney and Beatrice, *English Poor Law Policy*, Longmans, Green, London, 1910. 379 pp.

Jernegan, Marcus Wilson, "The Development of Poor Relief in Colonial Virginia," *Social Service Review*, March, 1929. "Poor Relief in Colonial New England," *ibid.*, June, 1931.

Kelso, Robert W., *The History of Public Poor Relief in Massachusetts, 1620-1920*, Houghton Mifflin, 1922. 195 pp.

Schneider, David, *The History of Public Welfare in New York State, 1609-1866*, University of Chicago Press, Chicago, 1938.

Massachusetts General Court, Committee on Pauper Laws, Report of Committee to Whom Was Referred the Consideration of the Pauper Laws of the Commonwealth, 1821. (Josiah Quincy Report, in Breckinridge, *Public Welfare Administration*, Select Documents.)

Report and Other Papers on Subject of Laws for Relief and Settlement of Poor, to New York State Legislature, 1824. Reprinted in thirty-fourth Annual Report of the State Board of Charities of the State of New York, 1900. (Yates Report, in Breckinridge, *Public Welfare Administration*, Select Documents.)

Folks, Homer, *The Care of Destitute, Neglected and Delinquent Children*, Macmillan, New York, 1902.

Parkhurst, "Poor Relief in a Massachusetts Village in the Eighteenth Century," *Social Service Review*, Sept., 1939.

Abbott, Edith, *Some American Pioneers in Social Welfare*, University of Chicago Press, 1937, 189 pp.

Marshall, Helen E., Dorothea Dix, *Forgotten Samaritan*, University of North Carolina Press, Chapel Hill, North Carolina, 1937. 298 pp., Bibliography.

Low, Seth, "Outdoor Relief in the United States," *Proceedings* of the National Conference of Charities and Correction, 1881.

Lowell, Josephine Shaw, *Public Relief and Private Charity*, Putnam's, 1884, New York, 111 pp.

Ayres, Dr., "Experiment in Relief and Work," *Proceedings* of the National Conference of Charities and Correction. University of Chicago Press, 1892.

Wright, Isaac P., "Arguments in Favor of Public Outdoor Relief," *Proceedings* of the National Conference of Charities and Correction, 1891.

Warner, Amos G., *American Charities.* A Study in Philanthropy and Economics, Thomas Crowell. (First published 1894, revised edition, 1919.)

Henderson, C. R., "Public Outdoor Relief," *Proceedings* of the National Conference of Charities and Correction, 1891; also "Poor Laws of the United States," *Proceedings*, 1897.

Wilson, G. S., "Outdoor Relief in Relation to Charity Organization," *Proceedings* of the National Conference of Charities and Correction, 1900.

Relief Legislation, 1803-1931; in Hearings before a Subcommittee of the Committee on Manufactures, United States Senate, on S. 5125. Gov't Printing Office, Washington, 1933.

1 9 0 0 - 1 9 2 9

Relief, A primer for the Family Rehabilitation Work of the Buffalo Charity Organization Society, prepared by its Secretary, Frederic Almy. Reprinted by The Charity Organization Department of the Russell Sage Foundation, New York, 1910. 34 pp.

"Reports from States: Outdoor Relief," *Proceedings* National Conference of Charities and Correction, 1909.

Ratcliffe, S. C., "Some Illinois County Poor Relief Records," *Social Service Review*, III, 1929. pp. 460-75.

Butler, Amos W., "Official Outdoor Relief and the State," *Proceedings* of the National Conference of Charities and Correction, 1915. Also *Indiana Bulletin of Charities and Corrections*, March, 1906.

Vaile, Gertrude, "Principles and Methods of Outdoor Relief," *Proceedings* of the National Conference of Charities and Correction, 1915.

Estabrook, "Poor Relief in Kentucky," *Social Service Review*, June, 1929.

Hurlin, Ralph G., "The Mounting Bill for Relief," *The Survey*, November 15, 1926.

Brown, Lucy W., *Poor Relief Laws. A Digest,* American Public Welfare Association, Chicago, Pamphlet, 1934.

Abbott, Edith, "Abolish the Pauper Laws," *Social Service Review*, March, 1934, and "Poor Law Provision for Family Responsibility," *ibid.*, Dec., 1938.

Report of the Commission to Study Pauper Laws, State of Connecticut, 1937, 225 pp.

Lundberg, Emma O., *Child Dependency in the United States.* Methods of Statistical Reporting and a Census of Dependent

Children in 31 States, Child Welfare League of America, New York, 1933, 149 pp.
Summary of State Laws Relating to the Dependent Classes, 1913. Bureau of the Census, U. S. Department of Commerce, 1914. 346 pp. Gov't Printing Office, Washington.
Paupers in Almshouses. Reports published in 1904, 1910 and 1923. Bureau of the Census, U. S. Department of Commerce and Labor, Government Printing Office, Washington, 1906.
Johnson, Alexander, "Almshouses," in the *Encyclopedia of Social Sciences,* II, 8-10, 1930.
Johnson, Alexander, *The Almshouse,* Russell Sage Foundation, New York, 1911.
Devine, Edward T., *Principles of Relief,* Macmillan, New York, 1904.
Richmond, Mary, *The Long View.* Russell Sage Foundation, New York, 1930. 648 pp.
McLean, Francis H., *The Formation of Charity Organization Societies in Smaller Cities,* Russell Sage Foundation, New York, 1910. 51 pp. *The Organization of Family Social Work Societies in Smaller Cities,* 1923. 140 pp. *Organizing Family Social Work in Smaller Cities,* 32 pp. 1932. Family Welfare Association of America, New York.
Johnson, Arlien, *Public Policy and Private Charities,* University of Chicago Press, Chicago, 1931. 230 pp.
McMillen, A. W., "Some Statistical Comparisons of Public and Private Family Social Work," *Proceedings* of the National Conference of Social Work, 1929. Also "Taxes and Private Relief Funds," *Midmonthly Survey,* New York, Nov., 1930.
Rubinow, I. M., "Can Private Philanthropy Do It?" *Social Service Review,* Sept., 1929.

Porter, Kirk Harold, *County and Township Government in the United States,* Macmillan, New York, 1902. 362 pp.
Publications of Children's Bureau, U. S. Department of Labor: Lundberg, Emma O., *The County as a Unit for an Organization Program of Child Caring and Protective Work,* 1926; No. 107. *County Organization and Child Care and Protection,* 1922; No. 169. Curry, H. I., *Public Child Caring Work in Certain Counties of Minnesota, North Carolina and New York,* 1927; No. 224. Colby, Mary R., *The County as an Administrative Unit for Social Work,* 1933.
Annals of the American Academy of Political and Social Science, Public Welfare in the United States, January, 1923.

Smith, Mary Phlegar, "Public Welfare and Social Work, Trends in Municipal Administration of Public Welfare: 1900-1930," *Social Forces*, Vol. X, No. 3, March, 1932.

Odum, Howard W., "County Unit as a Basis of Social Work and Public Welfare in North Carolina," *Proceedings* of the National Conference of Social Work, 1926.

Steiner, Jesse Frederick, *Community Organization*, Appleton-Century, New York, 1930. 453 pp.

Carstens, C. C., "State Programs for Child Welfare," *Proceedings* of the National Conference of Social Work, 1917. University of Chicago Press.

Reeves, Margaret, "The Indirect Responsibility of a State Department for Children," *The Family*, July, 1927.

Breckinridge, S. P., "Frontiers of Control in Public Welfare Administration," *Social Service Review*, I, pp. 84-99, 1927.

Bond, Elsie M., "New York's New Public Welfare Law," *Social Service Review*, Sept., 1929.

Heisterman, Carl A., "Constitutional Limitations Affecting State and Local Relief Funds," *Social Service Review*, March, 1932, and "Further Poor Law Notes," *ibid.*, March, 1934.

Fogarty, Rev. James, *State Aid in Several Forms of Public Relief*, A Dissertation, Catholic University of America, Washington, D. C. 1932.

Corwin, Edward S., "The Spending Power of Congress—Apropos the Maternity Act," *Harvard Law Review*, vol. 36, no. 5 (March, 1923), pp. 548-582.

Carstens, C. C., *Public Pensions to Widows with Children: A Study of Their Administration in Several American Cities.* Russell Sage Foundation, New York, 1913.

Bogue, Mary F., *Administration of Mothers' Aid in Ten Localities*, U. S. Children's Bureau, Publication No. 184, 1928.

Lundberg, Emma O., *Public Aid to Mothers with Dependent Children, Extent and Fundamental Principles*, U. S. Children's Bureau, Publication No. 162, 1928.

Report of the President's Conference on Unemployment, September 27 to October 13, 1921, Washington, D. C.

Lundberg, Emma O., *Unemployment and Child Welfare, A Study Made in a Middle Western and an Eastern City During the Industrial Depression of 1921 and 1922*, U. S. Children's Bureau, Publication No. 125, 1923, 173 pp. (Racine, Wisconsin, and Springfield, Massachusetts.)

LOCAL POOR RELIEF SINCE 1910

Studies and Reports

Connecticut: Commission to Study the Pauper Laws, State of Connecticut, 1937.

Florida: Lundberg, Emma O., *Social Welfare in Florida*, State Board of Public Welfare, Tallahassee, Florida, 1935.

Georgia: Barker, Ada M., *Social Security in Georgia*, State Department of Public Welfare, Atlanta, 1937, 128 pp.

Indiana: Shaffer, Keefer and Breckinridge, *The Indiana Poor Law*, University of Chicago Press, 1936, 378 pp.

Iowa: Brookings Institution, Report on a Survey of Administration in Iowa, 1933. Section on Public Welfare, pp. 219-247.

Kansas: *Handbook of Kansas Social Resources, Health, Education and Social Welfare.* Edited by a Special Committee of the Kansas Conference of Social Work, Topeka, Kansas, 1932, 302 pp.

Louisiana: Wisner, Elizabeth, *Public Welfare Administration in Louisiana*, University of Chicago Press, Chicago, 1930.

Browning, Grace A., *The Development of Poor Relief Legislation in Kansas*, University of Chicago Press, 1935.

Maine: National Institute of Public Administration, State Administrative Consolidation in Maine, Section on Public Welfare, New York, 1930.

Maryland: Bogue, Mary F., Report of a Study of Needs and Resources for Unemployment Relief in Maryland Under the Auspices of the Maryland State Conference of Social Work, Baltimore, 1932, 83 pp.

Bellman, Earl S., *A Study of the Care of the Needy Aged in Maryland Counties*, Baltimore, 1933.

Massachusetts: Kelso, Robert W., *History of Public Poor Relief in Massachusetts, 1620-1920*, Houghton Mifflin, Boston, 1922, 200 pp.

Michigan: Matson, Opal V., *Local Relief to Dependents.* A Report to the Michigan Commission of Inquiry into County, Township and School District Government, Detroit, 1933, 70 pp.

Bruce and Eickhoff, *The Michigan Poor Law*, University of Chicago Press, 1936. 287 pp.

Mississippi: Brookings Institution, Report on a Survey of the Organization and Administration of State and County Governments in Mississippi, 1932. Section on Public Welfare, pp. 555-562.

Missouri: Warfield, George A., *Outdoor Relief in Missouri,* A Study of Its Administration by County Officials. Survey Associates, New York, 1915, 140 pp.

Montana: Veeder, Fredric R., *The Development of the Montana Poor Laws,* University of Chicago Press, 1938, 131 pp.

Nebraska: *Survey of Social Resources,* 2 Vols., Nebraska Emergency Relief Administration, Lincoln, Nebraska, 1936.

Stott, Leland H., A Study of Relief Activities in Seven Nebraska Counties, 1927-1934, Research Bulletin No. 89. Agricultural Experiment Station, College of Agriculture, University of Nebraska, Lincoln, Nebraska, 1937.

New Hampshire: Brookings Institution, Report on a Survey of the Organization and Administration of the State, County and Town Governments of New Hampshire, 1932, Section on Public Welfare, pp. 225-243.

New Jersey: McLean, Francis H., *The Poor and Alms Department and the Almshouse of Newark, New Jersey,* The Russell Sage Foundation, New York, 1919.

U. S. Children's Bureau, Publication No. 180, *Child Welfare in New Jersey,* Part 4. Local Provision for Dependent and Delinquent Children in Relation to the State's Program. 1927, 76 pp.

State of New Jersey Pension Survey Commission, Report No. 2, State, County and Municipal Expenditures for Dependency Relief, 1929-31, Report No. 5, State Care of Dependent Children in New Jersey, 1932.

Stanton, Rev. Martin W., *History of Public Poor Relief in New Jersey, 1609-1934,* Dissertation, Fordham University, New York, 1934. 126 pp.

North Carolina: Brown, Roy M., *Public Poor Relief in North Carolina,* University of North Carolina Press, Chapel Hill, North Carolina, 1928. 184 pp.

Brookings Institution, Report on a Survey of the Organization and Administration of the State Government of North Carolina, 1930. Section on Public Welfare, pp. 247-297.

Ohio: Report of the Ohio Commission on Unemployment Insurance, Part II. Ohio's Statutory Provisions for Poor Relief, State House, Columbus, Ohio, Jan., 1933.

Kennedy, Aileen Elizabeth, *The Ohio Poor Law and Its Administration,* University of Chicago Press, Chicago, 1934. 233 pp.

Pennsylvania: Report and Recommendations of the Commission to Codify and Revise the Laws Relating to Poor Districts and the Care of the Poor to the General Assembly of Pennsylvania, Harrisburg, 1925, 42 pp.

Frankel, Emil, *Poor Relief in Pennsylvania,* State Department of Welfare, Harrisburg, 1925.

Deardorff, Neva R., *The Extent of Child Dependency and Delinquency in Seven Pennsylvania Counties,* U. S. Children's Bureau, 1927.

The Philadelphia Relief Study, A Study of the Family Relief Needs and Resources of Philadelphia, 1926, published by the Committee on the Philadelphia Relief Study, 311 S. Juniper St., Philadelphia.

Child Welfare Conditions and Resources in Seven Pennsylvania Counties, U. S. Children's Bureau, Publication No. 172, 1927.

Poor Relief Administration in Pennsylvania, State Department of Welfare Bulletin No. 61, Harrisburg, 1934, 308 pp.

Bruner, David Kenneth, *The Township and Borough System of Poor Relief in Pennsylvania,* Philadelphia, 1937. Thesis, University of Pennsylvania, Photoprinted, 172 pp.

Rhode Island: Creech, *Three Centuries of Poor Law Administration,* A Study of Legislation in Rhode Island. University of Chicago Press, 1936, 331 pp.

Vermont: *Rural Vermont,* Vermont Country Life Commission, Burlington, 1931, 385 pp.

Vietheer, George C., *Relief Administration in the Urban Communities in Vermont.* A Norwich University Study, made under the joint auspices of the Department of Social Sciences at Norwich University, Northfield, Vermont, and the School of Citizenship and Public Affairs, Syracuse University, Syracuse, New York, 1937.

Virginia: Hoffer, Frank William, *Counties in Transition,* A Study of County Public and Private Welfare Administration in Virginia. The Institute for Research in the Social Sciences, University of Virginia, 1929.

A Study of Welfare Activities in a Group of Virginia Communities, Bureau of County and City Organization, Virginia Department of Public Welfare, Richmond, 1933.

Washington: Hathaway and Rodemaker, *Public Relief in Washington, 1853-1933,* Washington Emergency Relief Administration, Olympia, Washington, 1934, 111 pp.

Buck, Mildred E., *Public Welfare in Washington,* Washington State Planning Council, Olympia, 1934, 138 pp.

1929-1932

U. S. Department of Commerce, Bureau of the Census, Special report, Relief Expenditures by Governmental and Private Organizations, 1929 and 1931.

Haynes, Rowland, *State Legislation for Unemployment Relief from January 1, 1931, to May 31, 1932.* President's Organization on Unemployment Relief, U. S. Government Printing Office, Washington, 1932.

Hayes, E. P., *Activities of the President's Emergency Committee for Employment, 1930-1931,* Rumford Press, Concord, New Hampshire, 1936, 157 pp.

"Relief Needs and Conditions in Pennsylvania, August, 1931," Report of Governor's Planning Committee on Unemployment Relief. *Social Service Review,* Dec., 1931.

Abbott, Grace, "Improvement in Rural Public Relief: The Lesson of the Coal-Mining Communities," *Social Service Review,* June, 1932.

Hodson, William, "An Open Letter to the President on Federal Relief Appropriations," *Survey Graphic,* New York, Nov., 1931.

Pinchot, Gifford, and Hoover, Herbert, "The Case for and Against Federal Relief," *Survey Graphic,* Jan., 1932, New York.

A Social Work Study of Federal Aid for Unemployment Relief, Report of Steering Committee, Social Work Conference on Federal Action on Unemployment, Jan., 1932.

Walker, Wilma, "Distress in a Southern Illinois County," *Social Service Review,* V, 1931, pp. 558-81.

Hearings before a Subcommittee of the Committee on Manufactures, U. S. Senate on S. 174 and S. 262. Seventy-second Congress, First Session. Government Printing Office, 1932.

Governmental Relief, The Report of a Pathfinding Study, Family Welfare Association of America, New York, May, 1932, 104 pp.

Public Relief—Where Are We Going? Family Welfare Association of America, New York, 1932. Leaflet.

Pinchot, Gifford, "The Opportunity of Social Work in View of the Trend from Private to Public Relief," *Proceedings* of the National Conference of Social Work, 1932.

Feder, Leah H., "The Relation of Private Case Working Agencies to Programs of Public Welfare," *Social Forces,* Vol. IX, No. 4, June, 1931.

Lurie, Harry L., "The Drift to Public Relief," *Proceedings* of the National Conference of Social Work, 1931; "The Place of Federal Aid in Unemployment Relief," *Social Service Review*, Vol. 5, 1931.

Swift, Linton B., "The Future of Public Social Work in America: From the Point of View of the Private Agency," *Proceedings* of the National Conference of Social Work, 1931.

Springer, Gertrude, "Funds for Another Bleak Winter," *Survey Midmonthly*, June, 1931; "The Challenge of Hard Times," *ibid.*, July, 1931.

Organization and Administration of Unemployment Relief, American Association of Public Welfare Officials, Nov., 1931. Pamphlet.

Procedures in Giving Relief to Families of the Unemployed, Family Welfare Association of America, 1931, New York. Pamphlet.

Suggestions for Dealing with Unemployment Emergencies in Smaller Communities, November, 1931, American Public Welfare Association, Chicago. Pamphlet, 9 pp.

Unemployment Relief Methods, A Monthly Summary of Changes in Relief Situations in the Family Welfare Field. Monthly, December, 1931, to May, 1932. Margaret Wead, Editor, Family Welfare Association of America, New York.

Porter, Rose, *The Organization and Administration of Public Relief Agencies*, Family Welfare Association of America, New York, 1931, 63 pp.

Colcord, Joanna C., *Setting up a Program of Work Relief*, Russell Sage Foundation, New York, 1931. Pamphlet.

The Family: Family Welfare Association of America, New York.

Hollis, "Function of a Family Society," Oct., 1931.

Queen, "What Is Unemployment Doing to Social Case Work?" Feb., 1932.

Wead, Margaret, "Unemployment Relief," Nov., 1932.

News Letter: Family Welfare Association of America, New York.

"Unemployment, October and December, 1931," Jan., 1932.

"Acceptance of Unemployment Cases," December, 1931 (Supplement).

Colcord, Joanna C., "Facing the Coming Winter," *Survey Midmonthly*, Nov., 1930.

Community Planning in Unemployment Emergencies, Russell Sage Foundation, New York, 1930.

Rich, Margaret E., *The Administration of Relief in Unemployment Emergencies*, Family Welfare Association of America, New York, 1930. Pamphlet.

Anderson and Rich, *Care of the Homeless in Unemployment Emergencies*, Family Welfare Association of America, New York, 1930. Pamphlet.

1932-1933

Emergency Relief and Construction Act of 1932. Public No. 302, Seventy-second Congress, 47 Stat., 709 Ch. 520.

Statement regarding Expenditure of Funds under the Relief and Reconstruction Act of 1932. Report to Congress on Expenditure of Funds. FERA, May, 1935. Government Printing Office, Washington, D. C.

Hearings before a Subcommittee of the Committee on Manufactures, on S. 5125, Parts I and II, Seventy-third Congress, 1933.

Conference on the Maintenance of Welfare Standards, Nov. 18-20, 1932, Report, American Public Welfare Association, Chicago. Pamphlet, 1933.

City Problems of 1933, Annual Proceedings of the United States Conference of Mayors, Paul V. Betters, Editor, Chicago, 1933.

Kurtz, Russell R., "American Relief Caravan," Survey Midmonthly, Jan., 1933.

Baker, Newton D., "The State Key to Relief, A Challenge to Forty Legislatures to Meet the Winter's Needs," Survey, Jan., 1933.

Standards of Relief in Selected Cities of the United States, 1933, Compiled under the direction of the Heller Committee for Research in Social Economics of the University of California, University of California, Berkeley, June, 1934. 18 pp., pamphlet.

Reynolds, W. S., "Organizing Governmental Agencies for Unemployment Relief," Proceedings of the National Conference of Social Work, 1933.

Colcord, Koplovitz and Kurtz, Emergency Work Relief, Russell Sage Foundation, New York, 1932, 286 pp.

Hill, Frances L., "Disaster Philosophy and Technique in Unemployment Work," The Family, Feb., 1932, New York.

No Money for Rent, A Study of the Rental Problems of Unemployment Relief Families and Their Landlords. Publication No. 6, Oct., 1933. Joint Committee on Research of the Community Council of Philadelphia and the Pennsylvania School of Social Work, 80 pp.

Personal Loans in Unemployment Relief, Community Council of Philadelphia, June, 1933, 74 pp.

Williams, J. M., Human Aspects of Unemployment and Relief, With Special Reference to the Effects of the Depression on Children, 1933. University of North Carolina Press, Chapel Hill, North Carolina, 235 pp.

Articles in Social Work Year Book, 1933. Russell Sage Foundation, New York: "Federal Agencies in Social Work"; "Public Family Welfare Work"; "Public Social Work."

1933-1935

General

Messages of the President of the United States to Congress, regarding unemployment and relief: March 21, 1933—H. Doc. 6, 73rd Congress; May 17, 1933—H. Doc. 37, 73rd Congress; May 15, 1934—H. Doc. 372, 73rd Congress.

National Industrial Recovery Act, Public No. 67, Seventy-third Congress, 48 Stat. 195 Ch. 90. Approved June 16, 1933.

Emergency Relief Appropriation Act of 1935, Pub. Res. No. 11, 74th Congress, 49 Stat. 115 Ch. 48. Approved April 8, 1935.

Welfare, Relief and Recovery Legislation, 1933-34, A digest of Federal and State legislation affecting relief, welfare and recovery, Prepared by American Public Welfare Association, 1935, 34 pp.

Financing Relief and Recovery, edited by L. Laszlo Ecker-R. Reprinted from the *Municipal Year Book*, April, 1937. Published by International City Managers' Association, Chicago.

Hopkins, Harry L., *Spending to Save*, Norton, New York. 197 pp.

Taylor, Ruth, "Problems the Public Welfare Field Presents to the Social Worker," *Bulletin*, New York School of Social Work, July, 1934.

Bane, Frank, "Public Welfare in 1934," *Social Service Review*, VIII, 1934, pp. 408-14.

Adie, David C., "The Organization of a National Welfare Program," *ibid.*, pp. 423-33.

Dunham, Arthur, "Pennsylvania and Unemployment Relief, 1929-34." *Social Service Review*, VIII, 1934, pp. 246-88.

Glick, Frank Z., "The Illinois Emergency Relief Commission," *Social Service Review*, VII, 1933, pp. 23-48.

Lundberg, Emma O., "County Welfare Boards and Emergency Relief," *Social Service Review*, VIII, 1934, pp. 238-45.

Johnson, Fred R., "The Integration of Emergency Relief with State and Local Departments of Public Welfare," *Proceedings* of the National Conference of Social Work, 1935. University of Chicago Press.

Swift, Linton, *New Alignments Between Public and Private Agencies*, Family Welfare Association of America, 1934, 72 pp.

Federal Emergency Relief Administration

Hearings, April, 1933, on H.R. 4606. A Bill to Provide for Cooperation by the Federal Government with the Several States and Territories and the District of Columbia in Relieving the Hardship and Suffering Caused by Unemployment and for Other Purposes. Seventy-third Congress, 1st Session, 1933.

Federal Emergency Relief Act of 1933, approved May 12. Public No. 15, Seventy-third Congress, 48 Stat. 55 Ch. 30.

Hopkins, Harry L., "The Developing National Program of Relief," *Proceedings* of the National Conference of Social Work, 1933.

FERA Monthly Reports, Government Printing Office, Washington, May, 1933-June, 1936.

Chronology of the FERA, May 12, 1933, to December 31, 1935. WPA, Division of Social Research, Research Monograph VI, 1937. 276 pp.

Expenditure of Funds, FERA. Letter from the Administrator of the FERA transmitting to the Chairman of the Committee on Appropriations in Response to Senate Resolution No. 115, a report on Expenditures of Certain Funds. Government Printing Office, May 1, 1935. Document No. 56.

McCormick, M. Riggs, "FERA Grants," *FERA Monthly Report*, Dec., 1935.

Wells, Anita, "The Allocation of Relief Funds by the States Among Their Political Subdivisions," *FERA Monthly Report*, June, 1936.

Unemployment Relief Census, October, 1933, Federal Emergency Relief Administration. Government Printing Office, Washington, 115 pp.

Lundberg, Emma O., "Social Service Personnel in Local Public Relief Administration," *Research Bulletin*, TERA, Division of Research and Statistics, New York, Feb., 1935.

Report of Mayor La Guardia's Committee on Unemployment Relief, New York City, 1935, 60 pp.

Williams, Edward A., *Federal Aid for Relief*, Columbia University Press, New York, 1939, 269 pp.

Wilcox, Jerome K., *Unemployment Relief Documents;* guide to the official publications and releases of FERA and 48 State relief agencies. The H. W. Wilson Company, New York, 1936. 95 pp.

Methods of Giving Relief

"Cash Relief and Relief 'In Kind,'" *FERA Monthly Report*, Jan., 1935.

A Study of Cash Relief in Ohio, FERA in Ohio, March, 1935, Columbus, Ohio, multigraphed, 68 pp.

Colcord, Joanna C., *Cash Relief*. Russell Sage Foundation, 1936.

Burns, Arthur E., "Work Relief Wage Policies, 1930-1936," *FERA Monthly Report*, June, 1936.

Work Relief in the State of New York, Report of Governor's Com-

mission on Unemployment Relief. Albany, New York, 1936.
113 pp.

Medical Care for Relief Clients, American Association of Medical Social Workers, Chicago, 1935.

"The Federal Surplus Relief Corporation," *FERA Monthly Report,* Nov., 1933, July, 1935, Feb., 1936.

Nicol, Mary A., "Family Relief Budgets," *FERA Monthly Report,* June, 1936.

Smith, Alfred Edgar, "The Negro and Relief," *FERA Monthly Report,* March, 1936.

Seymour, Helen, *When Clients Organize,* American Public Welfare Association, 1937.

Self-Help Cooperative Associations, Exhibit J. Extract from Hearings before the Sub-Committee of the Committee on Appropriations, House of Representatives, First Deficiency Appropriation Bill, 1937, Seventy-fifth Congress, First Session, Statements of Harry L. Hopkins, Government Printing Office, Washington, 1937.

"Supplementation of Private Earnings by Relief," *FERA Monthly Report,* June, 1935.

Webster, Edward J., "Relief Households Among Tobacco Workers in the Virginia and North Carolina Region," *FERA Monthly Report,* Sept., 1935.

"Alleged Refusal of Employment by Relief Clients," *FERA Monthly Report,* June, 1935.

Arthur, Henry B., "Summary Study of Alleged Job Refusals by Relief Persons," *FERA Monthly Report,* Nov., 1935.

Hopkins, Harry L., "They'd Rather Work," *Collier's,* Nov. 16, 1935.

The Family: Family Welfare Association of America, New York.

Cannon, M. Antoinette, "Recent Changes in the Philosophy of Social Workers," October, 1933.

Hamilton, Gordon, "Case Work Responsibility in an Unemployment Relief Agency," July, 1934.

Paige, Clara Paul, "Casework Objectives Achieved in Volume," July, 1934.

Wallerstein, "New Trends in Case Work as Developed by the Depression," Nov., 1934.

McCord, Van Dusseldorp, and Pease, *Social Work Practice in Three Rural Counties,* Social Service Division of the FERA, August 31, 1936, multigraphed, 161 pp.

Organization and Procedures of the Maryland Board of State Aid and Charities. *Research Bulletin,* Prepared by Elizabeth Mc-

Cord under the supervision of T. J. Woofter, Jr., Co-ordinator of Rural Research, Division of Social Research, WPA, July, 1936.

The Alabama Department of Public Welfare. *Research Bulletin*, Prepared by Wilma Van Dusseldorp, under the supervision of T. J. Woofter, Jr., Co-ordinator of Research, Division of Social Research, WPA, July, 1936.

Reynolds, Bertha C., *Re-Thinking Social Case Work*, Published by Social Work Today, New York, 1938. Pamphlet, 32 pp.

Study of the Background, Development and Use of Standards of Eligibility in the Philadelphia County Relief Board, under the direction of Elizabeth H. Collins, monograph, multigraphed, 1937. Committee on Social Security, Social Science Research Council.

Glassberg, Benjamin, "Rent Policies Under Emergency Relief—Milwaukee's Experience," *Social Service Review*, Sept., 1937.

Springer, Gertrude, "Miss Bailey Says," Practical Talks in Which an Experienced Supervisor Discusses with Her Workers Their Day-by-Day Problems in Unemployment Relief—From the *Midmonthly Survey*, March-October, 1933; November, 1933-June, 1934; August, 1934-April, 1935; May, 1935-January, 1936. Four pamphlets, *The Survey*, New York.

Personnel and Training

FERA Training Program

"An Inquiry into the Results of the Social Work Training Given to FERA Students," *FERA Research Bulletin*, Series 11, No. 7, Oct., 1935, multigraphed.

"An Inquiry into the Results of the Social Work Training Given to the Second Group of FERA Students," WPA, 1936, multigraphed.

"Learning with Our FERA's, by Mary Lois Pyles," *The Family*, Jan., 1935.

Brown, Josephine C., "What We Have Learned About Emergency Training for Public Relief Administration," *Proceedings* of the National Conference of Social Work, 1935.

Breckinridge, S. P., *ibid.*, 1935.

Blackey, Eileen, "Training the Rural Relief Worker on the Job," *Proceedings* of the National Conference of Social Work, 1935.

Cannon, M. Antoinette, "An Experiment in Providing Instruction for Relief Workers," *Bulletin*, New York School of Social Work, New York, Oct., 1935.

Lundberg, Emma O., "Classification and Salary Scales for Social Service Staff," *Temporary Emergency Relief Bulletin 27*, Feb., 1934. New York TERA, 1934.
"Social Service Personnel in Local Public Relief Administration," *Research Bulletin*, Feb., 1935, New York TERA, 1935.
"Social Workers in Rural Problem Areas, Summer of 1934," *Research Bulletin C-17*, Feb. 15, 1935. Division of Research, Statistics and Finance, FERA, Washington, 1935.
Lundberg, Emma O., "A State Plans Social Welfare Reconstruction," *The Family*, April, 1934.
Acker, Marjorie Morrill, "Social Service Division Staffs of the State Emergency Relief Administrations, 1935 and 1936," *Research Bulletin*, WPA, Oct., 1937.
Fisher, Jacob, "Trade Unionism in Social Work," *Social Work Year Book*, 1939.
"The Rank and File Movement in Social Work, 1931-1936," *Bulletin*, New York School of Social Work, 1936.

Categorical Assistance

Tabular Summary of State Laws Relating to Public Aid to Children in Their Own Homes. In effect January 1, 1934 (Chart No. 3, 1934), Children's Bureau of the Department of Labor, 1934.
Abbott, Grace, "Recent Trends in Mothers' Aid," *Social Service Review*, June, 1934.
Public Old-Age Pensions and Insurance in the United States and in Foreign Countries, U. S. Bureau of Labor Statistics, Department of Labor, Bulletin 561, 1932, U. S. Government Printing Office, 367 pp.
Public Provision for Pensions for the Blind in 1934. U. S. Department of Labor, 1935, 19 pp.
Social Security in America, The Factual Background of the Social Security Act. Publication No. 20, Social Security Board, 1937. For the Committee on Economic Security. 592 pp., Government Printing Office, Washington.

EMERGENCY RELIEF ADMINISTRATION IN CERTAIN STATES

New York State

An Impressionistic View of the Winter of 1930-31 in New York City, Based on Statements from Some 900 Social Workers and Public Health Nurses, published by the Welfare Council of New York City, Feb., 1932, 91 pp.

New York Legislative Documents, 154th Session, 1931, Vol. 21, Nos. 86-114, inclusive. Containing Message of the Governor Recommending Legislation Relative to Unemployment—Leg. Doc. (1931)—No. 108. Also Report of the Joint Legislative Committee on Unemployment—No. 112. Albany, 1931.

Prospects for Unemployment Relief in 1931-32 in 45 Cities of New York State, An Evaluation of the Experience in Unemployment Relief During the Winter of 1930-31 and of the Adequacy of Existing Facilities to Meet the Need for Unemployment Relief in the Winter of 1931-32. Report of the Joint Committee on Unemployment Relief of the State Board of Social Welfare and the State Charities Aid Association, Elsie M. Bond, Executive Secretary, August, 1931. 26 pp.

Relief Activities of City and County Welfare Districts, in co-operation with the State TERA, Nov. 1, 1931-June 30, 1937, New York.

Report of TERA, Jan. 11, 1932. New York.

Relief Today in New York State, a summary of the activities of the TERA of New York State pertaining to the period, Nov. 1, 1931, to Sept. 1, 1933.

Three Years of Public Unemployment Relief in New York State, The Need and How It Has Been Met, 1931-1934. New York TERA, State Office Building, Albany, New York, Oct. 15, 1934.

Research Bulletin, Dec., 1934. *Home Relief Standards,* Comparative Study of Home Relief and Work Relief in Nine Districts. 25 pp. Division of Research and Statistics, Emma O. Lundberg, Director.

Five Million People One Billion Dollars. Final Report of the TERA, Nov. 1, 1931-June 30, 1937.

Matthews, W. H., *The Story of the Emergency Work Bureau,* New York City, Oct. 1, 1930-Aug. 31, 1933, 54 pp.

New Jersey

Emergency Relief Administration First Annual Report to the Governor and to the Senate and General Assembly, Oct. 13, 1932, 159 pp.

Unemployment and Relief Conditions in New Jersey, An Interim Report to the Governor and the Legislature, Jan., 1932. 119 pp.

Second Annual Report to the Governor and to the Senate and General Assembly, Oct. 13, 1933, 155 pp.

Third Annual Report to the Governor and to the Senate and General Assembly, Oct. 13, 1934. 101 pp.

Observations Concerning the Future Organization and Policies of Administration of Relief in New Jersey, submitted to the Joint Committee on Relief of the Senate and General Assembly of the State of New Jersey by John Colt, Chairman of the Administrative Council. Dec. 18, 1934. 21 pp.

Emergency Relief in New Jersey, October 13, 1931-April 15, 1936, Final Report to the Governor and to the Senate and General Assembly. July 31, 1936. 174 pp.

Supplementary Relief in New Jersey, study conducted by Research Division, New Jersey ERA, May, 1936. Service Project S-F-110. 51 pp.

Family Resources Under Normal Relief and WPA Economies, April, 1936, 33 pp. Confidential Report, New Jersey ERA.

Survey of New Jersey Relief Situation, prepared by the American Association of Social Workers, New York, June 23, 1936, 22 pp.

MacNeil, Douglas H., *Seven Years of Unemployment Relief in New Jersey, 1930-1936,* a report prepared for the Committee on Social Security, Social Science Research Council, 1938. 307 pp.

Pennsylvania

Dunham, Arthur, *Emergency Relief in Pennsylvania,* Public Charities Association of Pennsylvania, 30 pp.

Dunham, Arthur, *Pennsylvania and Unemployment Relief, 1929-1934,* Public Charities Association of Pennsylvania, Philadelphia.

Unemployment Relief in Pennsylvania, September 1, 1932-October 31, 1933, First Annual Report of the Executive Director of the State Emergency Relief Board of Pennsylvania, State Emergency Relief Board, Harrisburg, Pa., Dec., 1933, 152 pp.

Unemployment Relief in Pennsylvania, Second Annual Report of the Executive Director of the State Emergency Relief Board, Harrisburg, Pennsylvania, 1934.

Unemployment Relief in Pennsylvania, Third Annual Report of the Executive Director, Harrisburg, Pennsylvania, Jan., 1936.

Unemployment Relief in Pennsylvania, Fourth Annual Report of the Executive Director. Harrisburg, Pennsylvania, June, 1937

Pennsylvania Emergency Relief Handbook, State Emergency Relief Board, Harrisburg, Pennsylvania, Aug., 1933.

Carter, Isabel Gordon, *Pennsylvania Children and the Depression,* Community Council of Philadelphia and the Pennsylvania School of Social Work, Publication No. 11, Philadelphia, 1935, 37 pp.

Hamilton, Gordon A., and Pettit, Walter W., *Report of a Study of the Philadelphia County Relief Board,* New York School of Social Work, Dec. 1, 1935.

Philadelphia County Relief Board, "How Self-Supporting Are the Ineligibles?" A Study of 502 Rejected Applications for Relief. Feb. 15, 1937, 10 pp.

Illinois

First Annual Report of the Illinois Emergency Relief Commission, for the year ending February 5, 1933, issued jointly with a Report of the Illinois Emergency Relief Commission (Federal) covering the period July 27, 1932, through February 5, 1933, 145 pp.

First Interim Report of the Illinois Emergency Relief Commission, April 15, 1932, 48 pp.

Second Interim Report, Illinois Emergency Relief Commission, First Interim Report (Federal), Aug. 31, 1932, 14 pp.

Third Interim Report, Illinois Emergency Relief Commission. Second Interim Report, Illinois Emergency Relief Commission (Federal), Nov. 15, 1932, 20 pp.

Illinois Governor's Message, 1933, Inaugural Address of Henry Horner, Governor of Illinois, January 9, 1933. Delivered before a Joint Session of the General Assembly of Illinois in Springfield, 40 pp.

Fourth Interim Report, Illinois Emergency Relief Commission, Third Interim Report, Illinois Emergency Relief Commission (Federal), Jan. 20, 1933, 23 pp.

Fifth Interim Report, Illinois Emergency Relief Commission, Sept. 30, 1933, 23 pp.

Second Annual Report of the Illinois Emergency Relief Commission, covering the period February 6, 1933, through the fiscal year ending June 30, 1934, 209 pp.

Biennial Report of the Illinois Emergency Relief Commission, including a Report on Activities through November 30, 1934, Chicago, Illinois, Nov. 30, 1934. 21 pp.

Relief Guidance and Control, A Manual for County Emergency Relief Committees in Administration of Relief Funds, prepared by Illinois Emergency Relief Commission, Nov. 25, 1932. 93 pp.

Relief Standards and Procedures in Dealing with Families of the Unemployed, Illinois Emergency Relief Commission, 10 South La Salle Street, Chicago, Illinois, Dec., 1932, 115 pp.

Reynolds, Wilfred S., "The Status of Relief," *Illinois Journal of Commerce,* Sept., 1935.

1935-1939—THE PERMANENT PROGRAM

General

Clark, Jane Perry, *The Rise of a New Federalism*, Columbia University Press, New York, 1938, 347 pp.

Abbott, Edith, "Public Assistance, Whither Bound?" *Proceedings* of the National Conference of Social Work, 1937. University of Chicago Press, Chicago.

Carr, Charlotte E., "Public Relief—Its Relation to Higher Labor Standards and Social Security," *Proceedings* of the National Conference of Social Work, 1937.

"This Business of Relief," *Proceedings* of the Delegate Conference, American Association of Social Workers, New York, Feb., 1936. 269 pp.

Colcord, Joanna C., "Relief, Style 1936," *Proceedings* of the National Conference of Social Work, 1936.

Fisher, Jacob, "The Present Status of Public Relief in the United States," *Proceedings* of the National Conference of Social Work, 1936.

West, Walter, "The Present Relief Situation," *Proceedings* of the National Conference of Social Work, 1936.

Brown, Josephine C., "Present Relief Situation in the United States," *Proceedings* of the National Conference of Social Work, 1936.

Matthews, William H., "The Relief Issue: An Inside View," *New York Times*, Jan. 15, 1939.

"The Relief Problem," *National Municipal Review*, Jan., 1938.

Hodson, William, *Integration of Unemployment Compensation, Unemployment Relief and Works Programs*, Proceedings of National Conference of Social Work, 1939, Columbia University Press, New York, 655 pp.

Klein, Philip, "Social Welfare Planning," *Social Work Year Book*, 1939, Russell Sage Foundation.

The National Health Survey, Public Health Service, 1939, Government Printing Office, Washington, D. C.

Interdepartmental Committee to Coordinate Health and Welfare Activities, *The Nation's Health*, U. S. Government Printing Office, 1939, 116 pp.

"The Dispossessed: For Nearly One-Fourth of the Population There Is No Economic System—and from the Rest There is No Answer," *Fortune Magazine*, Vol. 21, No. 2, Feb., 1940.

U. S. Congress, Senate, Special committee to investigate unemployment and relief. Hearings, U. S. Senate, Seventy-fifth Congress, 3rd Session, pursuant to S. Res. 36, U. S. Government Printing Office, 1938.

Michigan, State Emergency Welfare Relief Commission. *Unemployment Relief and Economic Security,* Lansing, Michigan, 1936, 329 pp.

New York Governor's Commission on Unemployment Relief, State and Local Welfare Organization in the State of New York, *A Summary Report on the Administration of Public Relief Services, with Recommendations,* Legislative Document No. 56, 1936.

A Modern Public Assistance Program for Pennsylvania, First General Report and Recommendations of the Pennsylvania Committee on Public Assistance and Relief, submitted to Governor H. Earle. Philadelphia, Pa., Dec. 15, 1936, 115 pp.

Stevenson and Posanski, *Digest of Social Welfare Legislation, 1935,* American Public Welfare Association, Chicago, 1935, 31 pp.

Stevenson, Marietta, "Trends in Public Welfare Legislation," *Social Service Review,* Sept., 1939.

Haber, William, "Relief, A Permanent Program," *Survey Graphic,* Dec., 1938.

Chickering, Martha A., "States Look at Public Welfare," *Survey Midmonthly,* May, 1937.

Goldsmith, Samuel A., "Human Aspects of the Relief Problem," *The Compass,* May, 1938.

Final Report on Total and Partial Unemployment, 1937, Volume IV. The Enumerative Check Census, Census of Partial Employment, Unemployment and Occupations, John D. Biggers, Administrator, U. S. Government Printing Office, Washington, 1938, 187 pp.

Informational Handbook, prepared by the National Emergency Council, Washington, D. C., Oct., 1938. 39 pp.

Methods

Kahn, Dorothy D., "Democratic Principles in Public Assistance," *Proceedings* of the National Conference of Social Work, 1939.

Wessel, Rose, "Method and Skill in Public Assistance," *Journal of Social Work Process,* Vol. II, No. 1, Dec., 1938, 100 pp.

Adie, David C., "Establishment and Maintenance of Standards of Social Work in Public Service," *Proceedings* of the National Conference of Social Work, 1938, University of Chicago Press, Chicago.

Kurtz, Russell H., *The Public Assistance Worker,* Russell Sage Foundation, New York, 1938, 224 pp.

Schwartz, Saya S., *Grants-in-Aid-of-Wages*, A Study of the Problems of Supplementary Relief, Philadelphia County Relief Board, Philadelphia, Pennsylvania, June, 1937, multigraphed, 55 pp.

Brown, Josephine C., *Field Work with Public Welfare Agencies I and II*, 1936 and 1938. American Public Welfare Association, Chicago. Pamphlets.

Mental Hygiene in Old-Age (six papers), Family Welfare Association of America, 1937, 52 pp.

Hamilton, Gordon, *Case Work in Old-Age Assistance*, Family Welfare Association of America, reprint.

Hill, Ruth, *Understanding the Problems of Older People*, Family Welfare Association of America, reprint.

Belinkoff, Cornelia, "Case Work Principles in the Supplementation of Public Relief," *The Family*, Feb., 1940.

Van Dusseldorp, Wilma, *Who Builds Pine Mountain Valley?* Georgia ERA, Atlanta, Georgia, 1936, mimeographed.

Personnel and Training

Cosgrove, Elizabeth, "Selecting Social Workers for Federal Service," *Social Service Review*, Sept., 1938.

Meriam, Lewis, "Civil Service Testing for Social Work Positions," *Proceedings* of the National Conference of Social Work, 1937.

Booth, Florence, *Civil Service Procedures for Social Work Positions*, American Public Welfare Association, Chicago, 1939, 78 pp.

Personnel Administration and Procedure, personnel system for public welfare, unemployment compensation and employment service in Indiana, Public Administration Service, Chicago, 1938, 90 pp.

Clarke, George, "Recruiting of Personnel in Public Welfare Administration," *Proceedings* of the National Conference of Social Work, 1938.

Public Welfare Job Study, American Public Welfare Association, Chicago, June, 1938, 75 pp.

Breckinridge, Sophonisba P., "New Horizons of Professional Education for Social Work," *Proceedings* of the National Conference of Social Work, 1936.

Van Driel, Agnes, *In Service Training, Proceedings*, National Conference of Social Work.

Chickering, Martha A., *What a Visitor in a Public Agency Should Know. Proceedings*, National Conference of Social Work, 1938.

Robinson, Virginia, "Is Unionization Compatible with Social Work?" *The Compass*, May, 1937.

Brown, Josephine C., "In-Service Training for Public Welfare, I. The Whys, II. The Hows," *Survey Midmonthly,* Oct. and Nov., 1938.

Hendricks, Hazel A., "Training for Rural Social Work," *Survey Midmonthly,* Nov., 1939.

Organization and Administration

Stevenson and MacDonald, *State and Local Public Welfare Agencies.* An organizational and functional analysis of state and local agencies administering public welfare functions. American Public Welfare Association, Dec., 1939. 109 pp.

Lenroot, Katherine F., "The Federal Government and Desirable Standards of State and Local Administration," *Proceedings* of the National Conference of Social Work, 1937.

Haber, William, "Problems of State Administration," *Proceedings* of the National Conference of Social Work, 1937.

Ernst, Charles F., "The Job of State Administration," *Proceedings* of the National Conference of Social Work, 1938.

Greenstein, Harry, "Problems Confronting State Welfare Administrations in Accepting Grants-in-Aid," *Proceedings* of the National Conference of Social Work, 1936.

Johnson, Arlien, "The County as a Unit for Co-ordinate Planning and Service in Public and Private Social Work," *Proceedings* of the National Conference of Social Work, 1937.

Gerig, Daniel S., Jr., "The Financial Participation of the Federal Government in State Welfare Programs," *Social Security Bulletin,* Vol. 3, No. 1, Jan., 1940.

Hurlin, Ralph G., "Statistics in the Administration of a Public Welfare Program," *Proceedings* of the National Conference of Social Work, 1938.

Directory of City and County Public Welfare Administrations in Cities of over 100,000 Population. Programs noted for each agency—according to the following list:
Aid to the Blind
Aid to Dependent Children
Admission Service for Institutions
Crippled Children's Services
Court Service
Child Welfare Services
General Relief (Home relief, direct relief)
Hospital Care
Institutional Care for Delinquents
Institutional Care for Dependents

Inspection Service
Medical Care
Old-Age Assistance
Supervision of Parolees
Veterans' Relief
Published by American Public Welfare Association, Chicago,
Sept. 1, 1939, 15 pp.
Public Welfare Directory, 1940, A Listing of State and Local
Public Assistance and Welfare Agencies, including local
communities of 30,000 population and over, American Pub-
lic Welfare Association, 1940.

Public and Private Agencies

Lund, Harold H., "Family Social Work," *Social Work Year Book*,
1939. Russell Sage Foundation.
The Crisis in Community Programs, Family Welfare Association of
America, New York, 1936. Multigraphed.
Wead, Margaret, *The Function of Family Case Work Agencies*,
Family Welfare Association of America, New York, May, 1937.
Multigraphed.
Blanchard, Ralph, "Community Chests," *Social Work Year Book*,
1939. Russell Sage Foundation, New York.
Fisher, Jeter and Beckelman, "Future of the Private Welfare Field
I and II," *Social Work Today*, April and May, 1939, New
York.

FEDERAL REORGANIZATION

*Administrative Management in the Government of the United
States*, Report of the President's Committee on Administrative
Management. U. S. Government Printing Office, Washington,
D. C., 1937.
Investigation of Executive Agencies of the Government, Report to
the Selected Committee to Investigate the Executive Agencies of
the Government, No. 8. Report on the Government Activities
in the Field of Public Welfare, prepared by the Brookings Institution. U. S. Government Printing Office, Washington, 1937,
131 pp.
Reorganization Act of 1939, Public No. 19, Seventy-sixth Congress,
approved April 3, 1939.
Messages of the President of the United States to Congress, Reorganization Plan No. 1, April 25, 1939. H. Doc. 262. Reorganization Plan No. 2, May 9, 1939. H. Doc. 288. Seventy-
sixth Congress, First Session.

SOCIAL SECURITY

Message from the President of the United States to the Congress
on social and economic security, June 8, 1934, Social Security—
H. Doc. 397, Seventy-third Congress.

Report to the President of the Committee on Economic Security,
January, 1935. Government Printing Office, Washington, D. C.

Message from the President of the United States to the Congress
on social and economic security, January 17, 1935, Recommending Legislation on Economic Security—H. Doc. 81, Seventy-fourth Congress.

Hearings: Seventy-fourth Congress, First Session, House of Representatives, *Economic Security Act: Hearings Before the Committee on Ways and Means* on H. R. 4120. U. S. Government
Printing Office, Washington, D. C., 1935, 1141 pp.

Hearings: Seventy-fourth Congress, First Session, *Economic Security Act: Hearings Before the Committee on Finance,* U. S.
Senate on S. 1130. U. S. Government Printing Office, Washington, D. C., 1935, 1354 pp.

Social Security Act, Public No. 271, Seventy-fourth Congress. Approved August 14, 1935. 32 pp., U. S. Government Printing
Office.

Suggested State Legislation for Social Security, American Public
Welfare Association, November 15, 1935. 32 pp., pamphlet.

Advisory Council on Social Security . . . Final Report, Senate
Document No. 4. U. S. Government Printing Office, Washington, D. C., 1939. 29 pp.

Message from the President of the United States to the Congress
on social and economic security, January 16, 1939, Social Security—H. Doc. 120, Seventy-sixth Congress.

Hearings: Seventy-sixth Congress, First Session, *House of Representatives. Hearings Relative to the Social Security Act Amendments of 1939 Before the Committee on Ways and Means.*
U. S. Government Printing Office, Washington, D. C., 1939,
3 vols.

Hearings: Seventy-sixth Congress, First Session, U. S. Senate. *Social Security Act Amendments: Hearings Before the Committee on Finance.* U. S. Government Printing Office, Washington, D. C., 1939, 554 pp.

Statement of Arthur J. Altmeyer, Chairman of the Social Security
Board, before the Senate Finance Committee on Amendments
to the Social Security Act, June 12, 1939, Social Security Board.
Multigraphed.

Proposed Changes in the Social Security Act, a report of the Social Security Board to the President and to the Congress of the United States. U. S. Government Printing Office, 1939.

Social Security Act as Amended, 1939, with explanations and charts of new provisions. Commerce Clearing House, Inc., New York, Chicago and Washington, D. C., 1939, 131 pp.

Compilations of the Social Security Laws, Social Security Board, Federal Security Agency. Government Printing Office, 1939, 92 pp.

Social Security Board, Annual Reports, 1936, 1937, 1938, 1939. U. S. Government Printing Office, Washington, D. C.

Social Security Bulletin, Bureau of Research and Statistics, Social Security Board, issued monthly. Government Printing Office, Washington, D. C.

Employment Security Review, prior to Jan., 1940, Employment Service News published by Bureau of Employment Security, Social Security Board, Federal Security Agency. U. S. Government Printing Office, Washington, D. C.

Characteristics of State Plans for Aid to Dependent Children, Old-Age Assistance and Aid to the Blind, June 30, 1937, 1938 and October 1, 1939. Prepared by the Bureau of Public Assistance, Social Security Board. U. S. Government Printing Office, Washington, D. C.

Witte, Edwin E., "Social Security—1940 Model," *The American Labor Legislation Review,* Vol. 29, No. 3, Sept., 1939.

Perkins, Frances, "The Outlook for Economic and Social Security in America," *Proceedings* of National Conference of Social Work, 1935, University of Chicago Press.

Wayatt and Wandel, *The Social Security Act in Operation,* Graphic Arts Press, Washington, D. C., 1937, 382 pp.

"Social Security in the United States, an Evaluation," *Annals* of the American Academy of Political and Social Science, Vol. 202, March, 1939.

Lansdale, Long, Leisy, Hipple, *The Administration of Old-Age Assistance,* Public Administration Service, Chicago, 1939, 345 pp.

The Administration of Old-Age Assistance in Three States, Public Service Administration, Chicago, 1936, 78 pp. *Ibid.*

Bucklin, Dorothy R., "Public Aid for the Care of Dependent Children in Their Own Homes," *Social Security Bulletin,* Vol. 2, No. 4, April, 1939.

Grant, Margaret, *Old Age Security, Social and Financial Trends.* Committee on Social Security, Social Science Research Council, Washington, D. C., 1939. 261 pp.

Hoey, Jane M., "Our Common Stake in the Development of the Social Security Program," *The Family*, Jan., 1938.   Family Welfare Association of America, New York.

Dewhurst and Schneider, "Objectives and Social Effects of the Public Assistance and Old-Age Provisions of the Social Security
Act," *Proceedings* of the National Conference of Social Work,
1936.

Bruno, Frank J., "Social Security and Social Work," *Proceedings*
of the National Conference of Social Work, 1936.

Altmeyer, Arthur J., "The Outlook for Social Security," *Proceedings*
of the National Conference of Social Work, 1937.

Gordon and Israeli, "Distribution of Public Assistance Funds Within
States," *Social Security Bulletin*, Vol. 2, No. 12, Dec., 1939.

Johnson, Arlien, "Social Work and the Insurances," *The Compass*,
Dec., 1937.

Clague, Ewan, "The Insurances and Social Work," *Survey Midmonthly*, May, 1938.

Van Driel, Agnes, "Personnel in Social Security," *Social Service Review*, Sept., 1937.

Lansdale, Robert T., "Some Observations on the Federal Audit,"
Social Service Review, Sept., 1937.

Haber and Somers, "The Administration of Public Assistance in
Massachusetts," *Social Service Review*, Sept., 1937.

WORK RELIEF

Message from the President of the United States to Congress, January 3, 1935, recommendation for "new program of emergency
public employment," H. Doc. 1, Seventy-fourth Congress.

Message from the President of the United States to Congress, January 7, 1935, Budget Message with recommendation for work
relief appropriation of $4,000,000,000, Seventy-fourth Congress.

Emergency Relief Appropriation Act of 1935, Pub. Res. No. 11,
Seventy-fourth Congress.   Approved April 8, 1935.

President's Message regarding relief, March 18, 1936, H. Doc. 427,
Seventy-fourth Congress.

Emergency Relief Appropriation Act of 1936, Public No. 739, Seventy-fourth Congress, approved June 22, 1936.

President's Message regarding relief, April 20, 1937, H. Doc. 234,
Seventy-fifth Congress.

Emergency Relief Appropriation Act of 1937, Pub. Res. No. 47,
Seventy-fifth Congress, approved June 29, 1937.

President's Message regarding relief, April 14, 1938, H. Doc. 594, Seventy-fifth Congress.

Emergency Relief Appropriation Act of 1938, Pub. Res. No. 122, Seventy-fifth Congress, approved June 21, 1938.

President's Message regarding relief, January 5, 1939, H. Doc. 87, Seventy-sixth Congress.

President's Message regarding relief, February 7 and March 14, 1939, H. Doc. 152 and 205, Seventy-sixth Congress.

President's Message regarding relief, April 27, 1939, H. Doc. 270, Seventy-sixth Congress.

Emergency Relief Appropriation Act of 1939, Pub. Res. No. 24, Seventy-sixth Congress, approved June 30, 1939.

President's Message regarding relief, January 29, 1940, Administration Expenses of the Work Projects Administration, H. Doc. 605, Seventy-sixth Congress.

Emergency Relief Appropriation Act, fiscal year 1941, Pub. Res. No. 88, Seventy-sixth Congress, Third Session, approved June 26, 1940.

Annual and Progress Reports of the Works Progress Administration, 1935-1939, Work Projects Administration, 1940.

Williams, Aubrey C., "The Progress and Policy of the Works Progress Administration," *Proceedings* of the National Conference of Social Work, 1936.

Williams, Aubrey C., "The Federal Unemployment Program," *Proceedings* of the National Conference of Social Work, 1938.

Gill, Corrington, *Wasted Man Power: The Challenge of Unemployment*, Norton, New York, 1939. 312 pp.

O'Grady, Right Rev. Monsignor John, "Social Welfare Marches On," *The Catholic Charities Review*, Feb., 1938.

Bristol, Margaret C., "W.P.A. in Chicago, Summer, 1936," *Social Service Review*, Sept., 1937.

Bookman, C. M., "A Community Program for Reducing Unemployment and Relief," *Social Service Review*, Sept., 1937.

Lane and Steegmuller, *America on Relief*, Harcourt, Brace, New York, 1938. 180 pp.

Work Accomplishment Report—1933-1938, contains project enumerations by classes and agency, but no financial statistics. Available for each state. Prepared by the National Emergency Council, 6 pp.

GENERAL RELIEF

"General Relief and Subsistence Payments to Farmers, Statistics for the United States, by Months and Years, and by States," *So-*

cial Security Bulletin, Division of Research and Statistics, Social Security Board. Published monthly.

"Administration of General Relief in the Continental United States as of December, 1937," *Social Security Bulletin,* Vol. 1, No. 11, Nov., 1938.

Reports and Other Publications of Rural Rehabilitation Division, Farm Security Administration, Department of Agriculture.

Reports of Federal Surplus Commodities Corporation, Department of Agriculture.

✓Dunn, Catherine, *What Price Local Poor Relief,* American Public Welfare Association, Chicago, 1937. Pamphlet.

Reynolds, Wilfred S., "Illinois Patchwork," *Social Service Review,* March, 1937.

General Relief in the Fall of 1937, information furnished by state and local welfare officials to the American Public Welfare Association, Jan. 15, 1938, multigraphed. American Public Welfare Association, Chicago.

Perkins, Milo, The Challenge of Under-Consumption, Address at the Fourth Annual National Farm Institute, Des Moines, Iowa. Press release by Federal Surplus Commodities Corporation, Department of Agriculture, February 24, 1940.

"The Poorhouse Persists," *Survey Midmonthly,* March, 1938.

Austin, Nancy L., "Old Folks Without Homes," *Survey Midmonthly,* Jan., 1939.

Tyson, Helen Glenn, "Homes and Almshouses," *Social Work Year Book,* 1939, Russell Sage Foundation, New York.

Dunn, Loula, "Status of County Almshouses in Alabama," *Public Welfare News,* March, 1938. American Public Welfare Association, Chicago.

Davis, "Medical Care," *Social Work Year Book,* 1939.

Organization and Administration of Tax-Supported Medical Care. Committee on Medical Care. American Public Welfare Association, Dec., 1939, 8 pp., multigraphed.

Medical Care for Farm Security Borrowers. Farm Security Administration, U. S. Department of Agriculture, 4 pp., multigraphed. June 15, 1939.

The Rural Relief Problem, statement by Secretary of Agriculture, Henry A. Wallace, before the Hearings of the Special Senate Committee to Investigate Unemployment and Relief, March 11, 1938, release by U. S. Department of Agriculture, 9 pp., multigraphed.

Facts about the Food Stamp Plan to be Tried Out in Rochester Upon an Experimental Basis, Federal Surplus Commodities

Food Corporation, U. S. Department of Agriculture, April 18, 1939, 5 pp., multigraphed.

Cotton Stamp Plan Program, announced by Secretary Wallace, release, Feb. 6, 1940, U. S. Department of Agriculture, 7 pp., multigraphed.

"The Food Stamp Plan," *Survey Midmonthly*, May, 1939.

Colcord, Joanna C., "The Food Stamp Way," *Survey Midmonthly*, Oct., 1939.

"Food Stamps," *The Compass*, Oct., 1939. American Association of Social Workers, New York.

General Relief, pamphlet issued by American Public Welfare Association, May, 1939. Chicago.

American Association of Social Workers, New York.

A Survey of the Immediate Relief Situation in Twenty-five States. February, 1936, 15 pp.

A Survey of the Current Relief Situation in 43 Representative Areas in 28 States of the U. S., Winter of 1938.

A Summary on Some Aspects of the Relief Situation in Representative Areas in the U. S., May 31, 1939.

SETTLEMENT

Donnell, Charlotte C., "Laws Regarding Settlement in Connection with the Problem of Interstate Relationships Under a Federal System," *Social Service Review*, Sept., 1930.

Goodhue, Frank W., "Report of the Committee on Uniform Settlement Laws and the Transfer of Dependents," *Social Service Review*, Sept., 1931.

Brackett, *The Transportation Problem in American Social Work*, 1936.

Hirsch, Harry, *Our Settlement Laws, Their Origin: Their Lack of Uniformity, Proposed Measures of Reform, 1933*. Bibliography. New York State Department of Social Welfare. Pamphlet.

Heisterman, Carl A., "Removal of Non-Resident State Poor by State and Local Authorities," *Social Service Review*, June, 1934, and "Statutory Provisions Relating to Legal Settlement for Purposes of Poor Relief," *ibid.*, March, 1935.

Williams, E. A., "Legal Settlement in the United States," *FERA Monthly Report*, Aug., 1935.

Potter, "Transient and Homeless Persons," *Social Work Year Book*, 1935, p. 496.

Webb, John N., "The Transient Unemployed," *FERA Monthly Report*, Jan., 1936.

508 BIBLIOGRAPHY

"Transient Survey," *FERA Monthly Report*, January, 1936.

Wickenden, Elizabeth, "Transiency-Mobility in Trouble," *Survey Midmonthly*, Oct., 1937.

Webb and Bryan, "Migrant Families," *FERA Monthly Report*, Feb., 1936.

Hirsch, Harry, *Compilation of Settlement Laws of All States in the U. S.*, Revised as of January, 1938.

Hosch, Louis E., *Interstate Problems in the Field of Public Welfare Administration, May, 1937*. American Public Welfare Association, Chicago. Multigraphed, 30 pp.

Wilson, Robert S., "Current Relief Problems in the Care of Resident Homeless and Unattached Persons," *Proceedings*, National Conference of Social Work, 1937. University of Chicago Press, Chicago.

Potter, Ellen C., "Transiency, Migration and Non-Residence," *Social Work Year Book, 1939*. Russell Sage Foundation, New York, 1939.

Hirsch, Harry M., *Compilation of Settlement Laws*, Revised as of September, 1939, American Public Welfare Association, Chicago, 1939.

Rural Migration in the United States, Division of Research, Works Progress Administration, 1939, 92 pp.

Webb, John N., "Internal Migration," *Proceedings*, National Conference of Social Work, 1939, Columbia University Press, New York.

Blakleslee, Ruth O., "Laws and Administrative Practices as Barriers to Mobility," *Proceedings*, National Conference of Social Work, 1939, Columbia University Press, New York.

Ryan, Philip E., *Migration and Social Welfare*, Russell Sage Foundation, 1940, 128 pp.

Migrant Farm Labor: The Problem and Ways of Meeting It. Division of Information, Region IX, Farm Security Administration, United States Department of Agriculture, 1939. Multigraphed, 15 pp.

Migratory Labor, A Report to the President by The Interdepartmental Committee to Coordinate Health and Welfare Activities, Washington, D. C., July, 1940, multigraphed, 21 pp.

GENERAL REFERENCES

Periodicals

Social Service Review, University of Chicago Press, Chicago. Quarterly.

Social Security Bulletin, Social Security Board. Monthly. Gov't Printing Office.

The Child, Monthly News Summary. Children's Bureau, United States Department of Labor. Gov't Printing Office.

The Family, published by the Family Welfare Association of America, New York. Monthly, except July and August.

The Survey Midmonthly and *Survey Graphic,* published by Survey Associates, New York.

Social Forces, published by the University of North Carolina Press, Chapel Hill, North Carolina.

The Compass, official monthly publication of the American Association of Social Workers, New York.

Public Welfare News, American Public Welfare Association, Chicago. Monthly since March, 1933.

The Transient, published bi-monthly by the National Association for Travelers Aid and Transient Service, New York. March, 1934, through March, 1938.

Catholic Charities Review, published monthly except July and August by the National Conference of Catholic Charities and the Society of St. Vincent de Paul, Washington, D. C.

Social Security in the United States, published by the American Association for Social Security, Inc., New York. Annual.

Social Work Today, published monthly except July, August and September by Social Work Today, Inc., New York, beginning December, 1934.

Annals of the American Academy of Political and Social Science, Philadelphia. Quarterly.

Conference Proceedings

National Conference of Social Work, *Proceedings.* University of Chicago Press; since 1939, Columbia University Press.

American Public Welfare Association, Annual Meetings, *Proceedings, Social Service Review,* September, 1931; September, 1932; September, 1933; September, 1934; September, 1935.

American Association for Social Security, New York.

Bibliographies

Unemployment Relief, A Selected Bibliography. 1931. 4 pp. Bulletin No. 109. Russell Sage Foundation, New York.

Unemployment Relief in the United States and Canada, 1932, 12 pp. Bulletin No. 116. Russell Sage Foundation, New York.

Reference Lists for 1931-33 and for 1933-34 on Unemployment Relief, *FERA Monthly Report,* Jan., 1934.
Unemployment and Relief Documents. Bibliography of Federal, State and Local official publications and research reports. Compiled by Document Section, University of Chicago Libraries, 1934, 20 pp.
Index of Research Projects, WPA, Vols. I, II and III.
Works Progress Administration. Subject Index of Research Bulletins and Monographs issued by the FERA and WPA, Division of Social Research, Sept., 1937.
Catalogue of Research Bulletins issued by Research Section, Division of Research, Statistics and Finance, FERA; and Division of Social Research, WPA, Sept., 1937, 16 pp.
Catalogue of Publications 1933-37, Division of Research, Statistics and Records, WPA, Oct., 1937, multigraphed, 16 pp.
Selected List of Research and Statistical Publications, Work Projects Administration, Federal Works Agency, 1939, 7 pp., multigraphed.
Unemployment Compensation and Its Relation to Relief, List of References Compiled by the Research Library, WPA, revised Nov. 15, 1938. Mimeographed, 6 pp.
Bibliography of Research Projects Reports, WPA Technical Series, February 2, 1940. Division of Professional & Service Projects, Washington, D. C., 31 pp.
Social Security Board, Bureau of Public Assistance, Technical Training Division. Selective Book List on *Public Welfare and Social Work Topics,* March, 1937. (Revised June, 1938, paper, 25 pp.)
Personnel, Bibliography No. 3, June, 1938, American Public Welfare Association, Chicago, 6 pp.
Social Security, Bibliography revised as of January, 1940, American Public Welfare Association, Chicago, 8 pp.
Public Medical Service, Bibliography Prepared by Committee on Medical Care of America, American Public Welfare Association, Chicago, Oct., 1939.
State Public Welfare Surveys, compiled January, 1940, by American Public Welfare Association, Chicago, multigraphed, 4 pp.
Social Work Year Book, issued biennially beginning in 1929. List of references with each article. Russell Sage Foundation, New York.
Some Basic Readings in Social Security, Publication No. 28, April, 1939. A reading list of material on social security, including

a list of books in English dealing with social insurance in foreign countries. Social Security Board, Federal Security Agency, U. S. Government Printing Office, Washington, D. C., 64 pp.

A Selected Bibliography Relating to Suggestions for Research on Problems of Relief, Committee on Social Security, Social Science Research Council, Washington, D. C., 32 pp.

INDEX

Private agencies, *Cont.*
Released workers to emergency relief agencies, 228, 277
Subsidized by public funds, 183, 186-189
Private relief (*see also* Community Chests; FWAA; National private agencies; Private agencies), 12, 132 [39
Nineteenth century, philosophy of,
Percent increase, 121
Percent of total relief, 415
Versus public relief, 39-59
Public Administration Clearing House, 135
Public Administration Service, 408
Public agencies, FERA funds spent by, 185-190
Public agency, functions of, 48-49
Public assistance, *see* Categorical assistance; General relief
Public management, editorial quoted, 406-407
Public relief (*see also* General relief; FERA; Local relief), 424
Abuses of, 39-43
Arguments for, 45, 58-59
Criticism of, 9
Drift toward, 82
FERA funds spent by public agencies, 185-190
Increased expenditures, 1910-1935, 57
Improvement of, 42
Local resources depleted, 71
Percentage of total relief, 55-56, 74
Right to, 51
Versus private relief, 39-59
Public welfare (*see also* Administration; Categorical assistance; FERA; Legislation; State agencies):
Factors in development of, 320-321
Federal Department of, 344-345
Recommendations of Advisory Committee on Public Employment and Relief, 305
Local departments of, 49-54
In large cities, 55
Social case work in, 50
Permanent programs, 422
Role of social work in, 423
State departments, development of, 52

Public works, 167
Desirable for unemployed, 159
Federal Emergency Administration of, 157
For unemployed, 150, 156
PWA, *see* Public works

Quincy, Josiah, 8 n.

Rank and File, *see* Social workers
Reconstruction Finance Corporation, 125
Assisted by national private agencies, 131 ff.
Emergency Relief Division, 128
Relations with States, 128
Functions and activities, 129-130
Subsidies to private agencies, 184
Registration of Social Statistics, 55-56
Relief, *see* Average relief benefits; Cash relief; Direct relief; Disaster relief; Dole; Federal relief; General relief; Local relief; Medical relief; Outdoor relief; Poor relief; Private relief; Public relief; Relief in kind; Standards of relief; State relief; Strike relief; Supplementary relief; Veterans' relief
Relief in kind (*see also* FERA; Surplus Commodities Corporation, Federal), 138, 224, 376-377
Commissaries, 138
Direct relief, New York TERA, 240
FERA, 242-244
Rural work relief wages, 391
Surplus commodities, 244
Wages under FERA, 237-238
Reorganization Act of 1939, 345
Reorganization Plan No. 1, 345
Resettlement Administration (*see also* Farm Security Administration; Rural Rehabilitation), 167, 324, 342
Transfer from FERA, 314
Responsibility of relatives, 370
Reynolds, Bertha C., 224 n., 226 n.
Reynolds, Wilfred S., 358 n.
Rich, Margaret E., 70 n.
Richberg, Donald R., Testimony before Senate Committee, 107
Richmond, Mary, 46, 47, 47 n., 48, 52, 70 n., 188 n., 222 n.
Riggs, McCormick M., 251 n.